MW01148153

Thinking with Shakespeare

Thinking with Shakespeare

Essays on Politics and Life

JULIA REINHARD LUPTON

The University of Chicago Press
Chicago and London

Julia Reinhard Lupton is professor of English and comparative literature at the University of California, Irvine. She is the author, most recently, of *Design Your Life: The Pleasures and Perils of Everyday Things*, and of *Citizen-Saints: Shakespeare and Political Theology*, the latter published by the University of Chicago Press.

The University of Chicago Press, Chicago 60637
The University of Chicago Press, Ltd., London
© 2011 by The University of Chicago
All rights reserved. Published 2011
Printed in the United States of America

20 19 18 17 16 15 14 13 12 11   1 2 3 4 5

ISBN-13: 978-0-226-49671-9 (cloth)
ISBN-10: 0-226-49671-6 (cloth)

Library of Congress Cataloging-in-Publication Data

Lupton, Julia Reinhard, 1963–
    Thinking with Shakespeare : essays on politics and life / Julia Reinhard Lupton.
        p. cm.
    Includes bibliographical references and index.
    ISBN-13: 978-0-226-49671-9 (cloth : alk. paper)
    ISBN-10: 0-226-49671-6 (cloth : alk. paper) 1. Shakespeare, William,
1564–1616—Criticism and interpretation.   I. Title.
    PR2976.L826 2011
    822.3'3—dc22   2010041009

♾ The paper used in this publication meets the minimum requirements of the American National Standard for Information Sciences—Permanence of Paper for Printed Library Materials, ANSI Z39.48-1992.

For Hannah

CONTENTS

ACKNOWLEDGMENTS

A repeated theme in this book is the involuntary revelation of who someone is by dint of her accidental entry into the world of action out of other, more sequestered routines. Criticism, too, is an act, and much of what is revealed here are the ties that bind me to factical life, including my entanglements in matrimony and motherhood and my fatal attraction to the virtues of objects. Although acknowledgments usually begin with colleagues and end with family, I want to say up front that without Ken Reinhard, I would find little worth thinking, making, or doing. Not only did he read every chapter and test every idea, but he has contributed immeasurably to the world-building back stories that illuminate this book. Our children, Hannah, Isabel, Lucy, and Eliot, provide their own occasions for thought, action, and care (see under *natality*, *creature*, and *be quiet*). My parents, Bill and Mary Jane Lupton, and my step-parents, Shirley Landon Lupton and Kenneth Baldwin, have always supported the work that I do. I am deeply sorry that Shirley Lupton is no longer with us. My twin sister Ellen Lupton has led me into design research; all references to trestle tables, joint stools, and office cubbies are her doing.

Every sentence in this book reflects the presence and support of many friends, colleagues, and students. Graham Hammill has helped me understand the biopolitical and political-theological stakes of this book, while Paul Kottman has kept me focused on the Arendtian ones. Richard Halpern keeps raising the bar for thinking with Shakespeare, both in the example of his own work and in his acute responses to mine. Michael Witmore provided an intensive and illuminating reading of a late stage of the manuscript. John S. Coolidge generously corresponded with me about the legacies of the Pauline Renaissance. I was fortunate indeed to get to talk with Quentin Skinner, Gordon Schochet, and Stephen Greenblatt about consent.

Eric Santner has been a friend, reader, and continued source of inspiration. Victoria Kahn and Drew Daniel responded to versions of chapter 1. My final revisions benefited from late-blooming correspondences with Bonnie Honig and Margreta de Grazia. For more than two decades at the University of California, Irvine, Jane O. Newman, John Smith, and Bob and Vivian Folkenflik have been stellar colleagues as well as true family friends. C. J. Gordon gave the whole manuscript a thorough reading at the eleventh hour. At the University of Chicago Press, Alan Thomas kept me on task, called my attention to stylistic tics, and engaged me in collateral projects while believing in this one. As I have come to expect, Nicholas Murray provided superb copyediting.

Other fellow travelers include Elizabeth Allen, Julka Almquist, Samuel Arkin, Sos Bagramyan, Etienne Balibar, Saul Bassi, Matthew Biberman, Daniel Boyarin, Richard Burt, Linda Charnes, Jerome Christensen, Kevin Curran, Paul Dahlgren, Lars Engle, Steve Franklin, Lowell Gallagher, Kenneth Gross, Jonathan Gil Harris, Anselm Haverkamp, Rebeca Helfer, Ken Jackson, Sean Keilen, James Kearney, Lloyd Kermode, James Knapp, Anna Kornbluh, Viola Kolarov, Aaron Kunin, James Kuzner, Debra Ligorsky, Elizabeth Losh, Lynn Mally, Steve Mailloux, Tracy McNulty, Nichole Miller, Robert Moeller, Ian Munro, Scott Newstok, David Pan, Patricia Parker, Brayton Polka, James Porter, Christopher Pye, Jennifer Rust, Gilberto Sacerdoti, Martin Schwab, Laurie Shannon, Donovan Sherman, Victoria Silver, Adam Sitze, Robin Stewart, Ulrike Strasser, Brook Thomas, Shaina Trapedo, Henry Turner, Tim Turner, Ann Van Sant, Jennifer Waldron, Sara Wheaton, Christopher Wild, Richard Wilson, Catherine Winiarksi, and Timothy Wong.

Although I wrote this book at home, in the fiercely cloistered modes of dwelling and hibernation, I have had the privilege of sharing many of its pages abroad, at venues that include the University of Texas at Austin, the State University of New York at Buffalo, the University of Southern California, California State University at Long Beach, George Washington University, the Johns Hopkins University, Wayne State University, Temple University, the University of Minnesota at Duluth, Princeton University, the University of Oregon, Dartmouth College, the Wissenschaftskolleg zu Berlin, and Cornell University. I'd like to thank my hosts and audiences at each of these institutions for their responsiveness. The women and men of University Hills, Tarbut V'Torah Community Day School, and Congregation B'Nai Israel furnished those acts of neighbor-love that allowed me to raise four children while writing this book. (Nintendo and cable helped, too.)

An early version of chapter 2 appeared as "Hamlet, Prince: Tragedy, Citizenship, Political Theology," in *Alternative Shakespeares III* (London:

Routledge, 2007), edited by Diana Henderson, who provided fine responses to the draft. A version of chapter 6 appeared in *REAL* 22 (2006), under the able and perceptive editorship of Brook Thomas. Chapter 7 is reprinted by permission of the publishers from my essay "Paul Shakespeare: Exegetical Exercises," in *Religion and Drama in Early Modern England: The Performance of Religion on the Renaissance Stage*, edited by Jane Hwang Degenhardt and Elizabeth Williamson (Farnham: Ashgate, 2011). I have published two pieces on Job and Shakespeare, written in tandem with chapter 4; my thanks to Arthur Marotti, Ken Jackson, Laura Tossi, and Saul Bassi for their editorial input. I have developed some of the ideas in chapter 1 in an essay forthcoming in a special issue of *Law, Culture and the Humanities,* edited by Adam Sitze.

I wrote a first draft of this manuscript with the help of a fellowship from the American Council of Learned Societies. A UCI Chancellor's Fellowship allowed me to travel, convene meetings, procure images, and support my book problem.

A NOTE ON TEXTS

Citations from *The Taming of the Shrew* are taken from Dympna Callaghan's Norton critical edition. Citations from *Hamlet* are taken from Harold Jenkins's Arden edition. Citations from *All's Well That Ends Well* are taken from G. K. Hunter's Arden edition. Citations from *Timon of Athens* are taken from H. J. Oliver's Arden edition. Citations from *The Winter's Tale* and from *The Tempest* are taken from Stephen Orgel's Oxford editions. Citations from all other plays by Shakespeare are from David Bevington, ed., *The Complete Works of Shakespeare*. Unless otherwise noted (e.g., "KJV" for the King James Version), citations from the Bible are from *The Geneva Bible: A Facsimile of the 1560 Edition*, introduction by Lloyd E. Berry (Madison: University of Wisconsin Press, 1969).

Politics and Life

If you prick us, do we not bleed? Shylock's rhetorical question declares his
humanity by summoning bodily being onto the scene of personhood. The
blood that flows from the pricking of the skin both describes an automatic
reaction and pushes shock and pain into cry and question. A prick is not a
wound so much as a provocation, a call to speech, and the blood that it lets
is more sign and stain than gush and flow, like the "jot" or iota of the law
to which Portia will later hold Shylock accountable (4.1.302). Like Lear's
"plague-sore or embossed carbuncle" (2.4.222), Shylock's pricked flesh
conjures an exacerbation and articulation of the bodily envelope, a form of
writing that stirs the subject into protest and the demand for acknowledgment. (It is no accident that both Lear and Shylock recall the sores of Job,
king of kvetch.) Shylock's question is *political*, since it broaches the conditions of personhood, civic belonging, and human rights. His question also
bears on *life*, flaring up here as the pierced casing of creaturely existence.
And he staples politics and life together with a certain brute simplicity, the
stream of monosyllables unmediated by juridical or philosophical terminology. On its way to becoming concept, Shylock's question coagulates into
a livid emblem, at once badge and scab of social humiliation, yet it remains
fundamentally an act of speech, pointedly posed to his Christian neighbors
on the busy streets of Venice.

This book reads Shakespeare's plays for scenes and moments in which
the signifying capacities of somatic existence are excited into speech and
drawn onto the stage of public life. In the Greek and Roman traditions,
politics is the form of human living par excellence, distinguished in its public character from the work of artisans; the labor of women, slaves, and domestic animals; or the inconsequential play of children. In civic humanism,

politics functions as both the singular office that actualizes human being and as one of several conducts of living whose variety continually dissolves and reconstitutes man in a series of life worlds, both epochally and across a day, a year, a career, or a floor plan. The Hebrew Bible introduces the further horizon of a common creation both shared with and dominated by human beings who rise above the landscape of swarming things while remaining a part of it. Such distinctions among forms of life do not name a priori divisions; rather, they are subject to continual redistricting in response to changes in the organization of labor, the capacities of technology, and the disposition of social bodies.

Drama, moreover, is the medium that most insistently stages this contest between the one and the many: between the one life worth living and the many lives that circle, support, and subtend it. For in drama, the living being of the actor, all blood, sweat, and tears, becomes the vehicle for the presentation of a *persona* (a mask or character) that in turn resignifies the body that bears it without in any way erasing or diminishing its modes of physical appearing. Indeed, the great fiction of dramatic character feeds off and amplifies the equally great feint of bodily gesture and movement, and their *pas de deux* emblematizes personhood as the subjectivizing bridge that produces a persona out of embodiment. When we say that a play "comes alive in performance," we indicate the passage of the words into the transient life of the performance itself, as well as the dependence of that phenomenalization on the speaking, moving bodies of the actors. Shylock's pricked and bleeding member (finger? phallus? punctured palm of the outstretched hand?) is an image flashed in speech, not a wound displayed on stage. His question issues from a vocal, gesturing body theatrically marked as Jewish according to a spectrum of available tools, from the false nose of the Renaissance theater to the coy Yiddishisms of the modern. The startling prick of Shylock's question stitches the conditions of theater to the human condition, insofar as both bear witness to the birth of persons in acts of protest, testimony, and recognition.

Shylock's image of pricked and bleeding skin pierces together in a single bright stigma the intimacy of flesh and verbalization, as if the fold in the sentence were also a fold in existence itself: the crease between body and language repeatedly reworked in drama as event. In Shylock's discourse, the prick is neighbor to the tickle, each provoking somatic reaction into dramatic action in the region where comedy and tragedy border each other. The entwining of body and speech peculiar to Shylock derives its ingrown shape from both the internal regulation of the nation of Israel via law and kinship and the external hosting of that body by the larger Republic of Venice. If the pricked flesh testifies to the creatureliness that Shylock shares with his tormenters, it also refers him back to covenant, via the suppressed allusion to circumcision as the physical sign and seal of membership in Israel. Shylock's question pricks together not only politics and life in their constitutive relation to each other, but also *two distinct orderings of politics and life*, the Jewish and the Christian, commingled in their daily dealings and shared histories and brought face to face with each other on the streets of the republic. Shylock's question spirals outward to include all of creaturely life while circling inward to describe his citizenship in Israel. Shylock's question inflames the lining between orders of existence—Christian and Jew, human and not-human—in order to redraw their jurisdictions within the common realm of the creaturely. Creaturely life in turn does not describe a seamless order of natural life, but rather bears evidence of the void or *nihil* around which the world was created, the divisive cut, that is, made by speech as act.

Modern readers might speak here of *biopower*, a term associated with the later Foucault and his reception in Italian critical philosophy, above all in the writings of Giorgio Agamben as well as Paolo Virno and Roberto Esposito.[1] Agamben, following Aristotle, articulates the channels that connect *zoē* and *bios*, biological life in its repetitive rhythms of consumption, growth, and decay, and political life as the practice of public virtue. For Aristotle, and also for Agamben, the human polity emerges from a world of living things and material objects more broadly ensouled and more widely endowed with virtue than later Christian mappings of the cosmos would allow. Hence the *bios politikos* is itself caught up in a range of relationships—whether interdependent or agonistic, parasitic or symbiotic, exploitative or custodial—with the "mere life" or "bare life" that subtends its symbolic, legal, and ethical projects. So too, "bare life" itself is never truly naked, but harbors all manner of self-organizing properties and signifying capacities that enmesh it in the forms of governance and eloquence posited as other from it, a point made not only by critics of the new writings on biopower, but also by those writers themselves, who are as interested in the teeming marshlands between forms of life as they are in their real or conceptual partition.[2] Ongoing transformations in what counts as human

1. Key texts include works by Agamben, *Homo Sacer*, and *The Open*; Virno, *Grammar of the Multitude*; and Esposito, *Bíos*.

2. For example, Roberto Esposito writes, "Does there exist a simple life—a bare life—or does it emerge from the beginning as formed, as put into form by something that pushes it beyond itself? From this perspective as well, the category of biopolitics seems to demand a new horizon of meaning, a different interpretive key that is capable of linking the two polarities together in a way that is at the same time more limited and more complex" (*Bíos*, 44).

indicate, again and again, the lack of a single template, whether religious, philosophical, or political, that might reconcile and order the claims of nature on what counts as human, and it is these impasses that engage writers on biopower.

It was neither Agamben nor Foucault, however, but Hannah Arendt who first delimited for modernity Aristotle's disengagement of *bios* from *zoē* within an integrated account of living beings. In either forgetting that genealogy or reducing her to it, we miss out on the very different texture of Arendt's writing: her concern with the conditions of human action and its intimate relationship with both storytelling and drama; her unsentimental analyses of the cares of the *oikos* and the invention of privacy out of privation; and her respect for the world-making capacity of art as well as the limits of its powers of duration. In her lectures on Arendt and narrative, Julia Kristeva places the problem of life and life writing at the center of Arendt's project. Other contemporary writers on Arendt, including Adriana Cavarero, Paul Kottman, and Miguel Vatter, share the conviction that Arendt never simply separates the *vita activa* of the polis from the other forms of activity that sustain it.[3] In the section of *The Human Condition* devoted to the cyclic efforts of the *animal laborans*, Arendt distinguishes the activity of labor from human action in the political sense; citing Aristotle, she writes that the life of action "is itself always full of events which ultimately can be told as a story, establish a biography; it is of this life, *bios* as distinguished from mere *zoē*, that Aristotle said that it 'somehow is a kind of praxis.'"[4] Labor corresponds to *zoē*, the demands of biological living, its needs at once met and kept at bay by the world-building work of artisans. Action corresponds to plurality; *bios* is life as lived among men, whose *res gestae* can be caught up in the great narrative nets of epic, history, drama, and biography, but also in the little life stories of confrontation, revelation, disappointment, and discovery that count for action on smaller stages. The mobile membrane between *bios* and *zoē* is universal, not in the sense of being the same everywhere, but in the sense of appearing anew in arena after arena, precisely as that which fails to yield a single solution to the problem of my relation to

3. Julia Kristeva writes, "Caught up from the outset by this passion in which *life* and *thought* are one and the same, her varied yet profoundly coherent intellectual odyssey never ceased to place *life*—in and of itself, and as a concept to be elucidated—at the centre." See Kristeva, *Hannah Arendt*, 3. On Arendt and the theater of life, see Kottman, *Politics of the Scene*, and *Tragic Conditions in Shakespeare*. On Arendt and biopolitics, see Vatter, "Natality and Biopolitics in Hannah Arendt." See also Cavarero, *Relating Narratives*.

4. Arendt, *Human Condition* (1958; repr., with new intro. by Margaret Canovan, Chicago: University of Chicago Press, 1998), 97.

other beings. "The human" is not an answer to that question, but rather the iterative reembodiment and transvaluation of the shifting frontiers among forms of life.

In the famous phrase *zoon politikon*, Aristotle marks the convergence and conflict between the forms of life that human beings inhabit, reflexively body forth, and continually rezone. At stake is the relation between animal existence as interdependent systems of sense, appetite, movement, and primitive sociality, and the transformative reconstitution and reflective reprocessing of animal life, including its sociable and semantic capacities, in the self-legislating and self-documenting bodies politic composed by human actors. *Bios* is "a kind of practice" because its virtues only exist through their exercise, as their own end, in the arena of specifically human appearing that Arendt calls politics. In phenomenological terms, *bios* and *zoē* are not separate things or orders of being, but aspects or moments of vitality that make their appearance under different conditions or circumstances. *Zoē* is "mere" because of what she calls "the strict and even cruel privacy" with which "life processes manifest themselves"; here and elsewhere in Arendt, *privacy* carries the negative sense of *deprived* or *privative*, subtracted from the public realm by the sheer intensity and shame of bodily function.[5] For Arendt, privacy signals a loss first, and a right second. Yet *zoē* remains part of human being, ticking in the background as the biological support of consciousness, cognition, and action, and suddenly, sometimes awfully, in the foreground when we labor, bleed, feed, laugh, or climax. (If you prick us, do we not *become political*, bursting out of the routines of living onto the public stage of recognition, response, or their disavowal?)

Agamben's analyses of *zoē*, *bios*, and their vicissitudes in modern politics and economy have begun to enter Renaissance studies; what remains largely unremarked, however, is the extent to which Agamben's thinking is enabled by Arendt's. In the chapter of *Homo Sacer* entitled "Biopolitics and the Rights of Man," for example, Agamben credits Arendt with identifying the birth of the modern refugee with a crisis in the discourse of human rights, conceived as both the natural ground and the extra-juridical residue of the national citizen, the same stratum of life-become-political pricked into speech and visibility by Shylock's probing question. Agamben goes on to rephrase the central arguments of *The Human Condition*:

> Declarations of rights represent the originary figure of the inscription of natural life in the juridico-political order of the nation-state. The same bare life

5. Ibid., 117.

that in the *ancien régime* was politically neutral and belonged to God as creaturely life and in the classical world was (at least apparently) clearly distinguished as *zoē* from political life (*bios*) now fully enters into the structure of the state and even becomes the earthly foundation of the state's legitimacy and sovereignty.[6]

Here and elsewhere, Agamben culls the *zoē / bios* distinction from Arendt's Aristotle, passing it through the social science and genocidal architecture of Nazism in order to declare, in an oft-quoted formulation, that "the camp is the *nomos* of the modern."[7] Following Arendt as much as Foucault, Agamben argues that "the work of man" in modernity is no longer the exercise of virtue in the public sphere, but the administration of species-life, composed of actuarial risks assiduously calculated, managed, and manipulated by the bureaucratic state.[8] Agamben shares with Arendt a concern that the offices of housekeeping, understood as the maintenance of *zoē*, have overgrown and absorbed a classical politics founded on the distinction between the *oikos* and the polis. In the age of biopower, the personal is always political, and health is always "public health," since matters of life and lifestyle are not only the lightning rods for new forms of identity and solidarity, but also the enabling objects of a far-reaching administrative eye to which absolutely everything is of interest. Agamben and Arendt share the intuition that this fusion of the *oikos* and the polis is responsible for modern catastrophes great and small, from the Holocaust to the Hummer. They are also committed to thinking the positive ways in which different forms of life animate each other, in thought and in daily practice. Their difference lies, however, in Arendt's classical orientation around the autonomy of *bios*, of life as the practice of living well; and Agamben's enduring attraction to *zoē*, that is, to life as what subsists as pure potentiality, beyond all actualizations in the exercise of public virtue.

If Foucault is the acknowledged father of biopolitical discourse, Carl Schmitt is its evil uncle, the figure whose theorization of the state of emergency helped pave the way for the rise of Hitler and whose critiques of liberalism have fed a variety of positions on the left as well as the right. Schmitt wrote on both *Hamlet* and Hobbes, and his late book *Nomos of the Earth* studies the transition from medieval to modern spatial orders. Like

---

6. Agamben, *Homo Sacer*, 126, 127.

7. Agamben notes Foucault and Arendt as twin points of departure for his thought in *Homo Sacer*, 121–22.

8. Agamben develops the phrase "the work of man" in his essay of that title; see "The Work of Man."

Walter Benjamin, with whom he shared several exchanges, Schmitt's fierce analysis of the ends of modernity unfolds against the backdrop of the Renaissance and Baroque periods, which set into motion the forms of modern statehood whose birth, mutation, and collapse Schmitt diagnosed.[9] Not unlike Arendt, Schmitt was concerned to distinguish the political from ethics, economics, and culture—all regions that he associates with liberalism and the neutralization of politics in its existential dimension, as a matter of life and death that cannot be decided by reference to norms alone. The phrase *political theology* was originally associated with medieval iconographies of sacred kingship in the political, dramatic, and artistic forms of European civilization, along with the critique of traditional sovereignty mounted by Hobbes, Spinoza, Locke, and others in the seventeenth century. Schmitt's renovation of the phrase "political theology" to describe the religious kernel of sovereignty and the impasses of secularization has come to name a particular set of interests within contemporary critical theory, including states of emergency, the legal architecture of the camp, and the persistence of religious categories in modernity.[10] Reading Schmitt in relationship to Jewish Messianism, Foucauldian biopolitics, and Italian political theory, Agamben has done much to recast political theology in a framework oriented toward the historical scenes of early modernity and attentive to the afterlife of Renaissance and Baroque motifs in later literary and political formations.

Although I turn throughout this book to the Italian discourse of biopolitics, I have chosen to take my orientation from Arendt rather than Agamben. Arendt prefers a Greek discourse of citizenship based on virtue to the Roman tradition of citizenship based on law. Both traditions certainly nourish Shakespearean conceptions of character and action, but the former may yield more multidimensional portraits of human actors, especially those of women, minors, foreigners, and servants, as well as men in their semipublic

9. Major texts by Carl Schmitt include *Political Theology*; *The Concept of the Political*; *The Nomos of the Earth in the International Law of the Jus Publicum Europaeum*; and *Hamlet or Hecuba*.

10. For Renaissance scholars, political theology is associated as much with Schmitt's contemporary, Ernst Kantorowicz, as it is with Schmitt. The subtitle of Ernst Kantorowicz's classic work, *The King's Two Bodies*, is *A Study in Medieval Political Theology*, prompting scholars in recent years to query the possible connections between Schmitt and Kantorowicz. See Kahn, "Political Theology and Fiction in *The King's Two Bodies*." Marie Axton has explored the significance of the concept of the ruler's two bodies during the reign of Elizabeth in *The Queen's Two Bodies*. Other readings of Kantorowicz and Shakespeare include Haverkamp, "*Richard II*, Bracton, and the End of Political Theology"; Wilson, "'Blood Will Have Blood'"; and Halpern, "The King's Two Buckets." On the negative side, David Norbrook, Richard Hardin, and Lorna Hutson critique Kantorowicz: see Hutson, "Not the King's Two Bodies"; Norbrook, "The Emperor's New Body?"; and Hardin, *Civil Idolatry*.

capacities as friends, husbands, and hosts. Arendt's analysis, unlike Agamben's or Foucault's, is fundamentally dramatic, insofar as plurality, the presence of other people in their contingent singularity, is the "condition *sine qua non* for that space of appearance which is the public realm." Whereas later writers on biopower focus on the violence created by the exclusion of life from the polis, Arendt insists on the fragility of such spaces of human appearing, urging us against loving life not wisely but too well. In *The Human Condition*, *zoē* and *bios* never become programmatic categories, in part because, for Arendt, labor always belongs to the *oikos* and thus to a domestic economy and an object world of some complexity and duration.

The subtitle of this book is "Essays on Politics and Life," which flags my efforts, executed in partial homage to Arendt, to capture a set of moments in Shakespeare in which certain political questions come up against problems of life and living, ranging from the politics of hospitality in *Timon of Athens* and *The Winter's Tale* to forms of consent in *All's Well* and *Hamlet* and varieties of personhood in *The Taming of the Shrew* and *The Tempest*. When I speak here of *life*, I take the word as a definitional conundrum, internally caught up among creaturely and human as well as religious and political formulations. I also take *life* as that which names the existential and phenomenological interests of the plays; I am interested, that is, in the extent to which Shakespeare's plays examine through their presentational medium as well as their plots and themes the ways in which humans appear as human to themselves and others, in tandem with other life forms. With the exception of *Timon of Athens* and moments in *Hamlet*, the plays could hardly be called philosophical.[11] Yet in the chapters that follow, I pursue biopolitical and theopolitical themes in Shakespeare, not in order to prove specific attachments or discover ideological blind spots, but to apprehend Shakespeare's mise-en-scène of politics in response to life, living, and forms of life, with some sense, I hope, of their significance for the way we live now.[12] Although Arendt does not use the phrase *political theology*,

11. On *Timon* and philosophy, see Nuttall, *Shakespeare the Thinker*, 315–16. On *Hamlet* and philosophy, see especially Guillory, "'To please the wiser sort.'"

12. Recent work on religion and Renaissance literature that addresses or engages political theology includes Shuger, *The Renaissance Bible*; Kahn, "Hamlet or Hecuba," and "Political Theology and Reason of State"; Knapp, *Shakespeare's Tribe*; Greenblatt, *Hamlet in Purgatory*; Freinkel, *Shakespeare's Will*; Lampert, *Gender and Jewish Difference*; Biberman, *Masculinity, Anti-Semitism and Early Modern English Literature*; Cefalu, *English Renaissance Literature*. Essays and position papers by Ken Jackson, Philip Lorenz, Jacques Lezra, Graham Hammill, Jennifer Rust, Lowell Gallagher, and Catherine Winiarksi are available in Holsinger, ed., "The Religious Turn in Literary Criticism." See also the review essay by Marotti and Jackson, "The Religious Turn"; and the collection of essays edited by Fernie, *Spiritual Shakespeares*.

she joins Benjamin, Freud, and Rosenzweig in her deep considerations of the subjective and collective destinies of monotheism under secularization, from her own distinctive position as an ambivalent legatee of German-Jewish thought in postwar America.

Much of my work with Arendt limns the variable threshold between the *oikos* and the polis. Arendt is frequently criticized for drawing too sharply the distinction between private and public realms, and for throwing her lot in the public places of the second rather than the kitchens and factories of the first. Although she certainly prefers action to housekeeping, Arendt remains uniquely attuned to the being of things: their special forms of duration and disappearance; their fervent clinging like leaves or moths to seasonal and bodily cycles; the kinds of thinking they enable and inhibit; and their world-building and conversation-supporting capacities. Things may not be alive in a biological sense, but they mimic cycles of birth, death, and decay while extending human vitality in both time and space. Arendt may disparage the *oikos*, but she also understands it, and her willingness to give voice to its tempos and its tyrannies distinguishes her from most other political thinkers. The *oikos* is not abstract to Arendt. She has been there. It concerns her enough to draw its secrets into the open assembled by the act of writing. But she refuses to dwell in the *oikos* alone, and her books constitute testaments to these other capacities and the freedoms they manifest. Arendt knew the demands of the *oikos*, having headed a household from the precarious roosts of caregiver, breadwinner, and refugee; nonetheless, she was able to wrest a life of the mind as well as a life of action from these extraordinary demands, thanks in part to the courage that she and her husband Heinrich Blücher exercised in establishing living arrangements that allowed her to write, teach, and think.

In her own pursuit of the primal scenes of the *vita activa*, Arendt emphasizes deliberative acts of public speech before an audience of free men released from the drudgery of household labor by the efforts of others. The conjunction of "politics and life" announced in my subtitle is designed to isolate the service entrances connecting the life of the city to the life of the household in Shakespearean drama; my aim is not to distinguish politics and life, but to dramatize their essential interrelation. This means using Shakespeare to read Arendt against her own civic superego, in order to disclose instead the many places in both her writing and Shakespeare's plays in which divergent forms of life—the lives of men in their political plurality, of humans in their domestic multiplicity, of animals in their biodiversity, and of objects in both their durability and their decay—enter into world-building and future-founding relationships with each other. This book, somewhat to my surprise, has ended up being about virtue, as both the excellences practiced in civic humanism and as those capacities that subsist in things, whether animal, vegetable, or mineral. Thus political theorist Jane Bennett speaks of "thing-power" as "an active, earthy, not-quite-human capaciousness" whose self-organizing energies are not accommodated by a mechanistic account of matter.[13] Such thingly virtues are ever ready to flower into use, yet themselves participate in a dormancy that keeps its own measure in the order of being, the "blossoming time / That from the seedness the bare fallow brings / To teeming foison" (*Measure for Measure*, 1.4.41–43). Political virtues are fundamentally active, existing only in their practice, while vital virtues subsist as latencies and tendencies with the power to burst into flower, or die stillborn.[14] Human beings mobilize both aspects of virtue for different ends. In *All's Well That Ends Well*, Helena brings together the traditional attributes of feminine virtue with the pharmacist's knowledge of the virtues of things in order to identify the practice of virtue more broadly with the self-realizing interests of the new professional classes. This book returns again and again to the moments of self-enclosure, stasis, silence, and pregnancy where potentiality erects its flag, and to the way that active and passive virtues, as well as human and nonhuman ones, variously feed, check, and shadow each other in Shakespeare. Shakespearean drama shows virtue her own image, whether in scenes of action, in the byways of metaphor and concept, or in the distinctive capacity of play texts to be renewed over time.

In this book, I often have recourse to the word *zone*, as both noun and verb, to describe the functional lability of the space for action in Shakespearean drama. A zone is not a fixed location; in a city, the same street can be rezoned for commercial or residential use depending on the real or perceived needs of different interest groups. Moreover, such rezonings can result from shifts in usage on the ground as well as from policy changes imposed from above. In drama, a domestic space can be rezoned as a political one by the fact of a new action occurring within its precincts. Thus Hermione's fateful address to Polixenes in the first act of *The Winter's Tale* recasts the banqueting house of formal hospitality, organized by the semipublic exercise of semiprivate virtues, into a political scene of suspicion, accusation, and trial. In *Hamlet*, the prince's address to his fellows rezones the ramparts of spectral sovereignty into a platform for political friendship,

13. Bennett, *Vibrant Matter*, 2.
14. On latency in Shakespeare, see Haverkamp, *Shakespearean Genealogies of Power*.

election, and consent. I am drawing here on Christopher Alexander's *Pattern Language*, which emphasizes the ad hoc character of human place-making, and which tends to envision spatial orders more as software than as hardscape.[15] I am also following those strong phenomenological elements in Arendt's thought that emphasize the polis as a recurrent possibility for human action rather than the name of a particular moment in the history of democracy. Paul Kottman cites Arendt: "'Wherever you go, you will be a *polis*.'"[16] What we see in the exchanges between Petruchio and Katherine in *Shrew*, or Helena and the King in *All's Well*, or Timon and his unwelcome guests is the makeshift convocation of a political scene out of domestic and civil ones, thrown together like a pup tent or a campfire in the clearing made by action in the interminable bio-forest of routine. In the judgment of Bonnie Honig, Arendt "theorizes a democratic politics built not on already existing identities or shared experiences but on contingent sites of principled coalescence."[17] Such an impromptu polis bears no direct relation to a larger institution, state, or community, and yet it opens lines of action and testimony to those gathered in its circle of citizenship.[18]

"Wherever you go, you will be a *polis*": Arendt's formula for a portable politics resembles the ethics of psychoanalysis declared by Freud in the phrase, *Wo Es war, soll Ich werden*. Ego psychology decoded this as, "What was Id shall become Ego," while Lacan chose to remain closer to the vernacular minimalism of the original German. There, where It—the object that causes my desire—is, I shall come to be: not by translating the unconscious into consciousness but rather by acknowledging the unconscious as what produces my subjective freedom, by staking my existence as a subject there where the unconscious lies.[19] We might similarly imagine the relations between politics and life in Arendt: wherever you find the *Es* of the *oikos*—its manifold objects, bodily functions, and the labors they require—let the *We* of the polis come to be, not in order to subsume the mute order of things

15. Alexander, *A Pattern Language*.

16. Kottman, *Politics of the Scene*, 114, citing Arendt, *Human Condition*, 198.

17. Honig, "Introduction," in *Feminist Interpretations of Hannah Arendt*, ed. Honig, 3.

18. On circles of citizenship as both provisional and permanent, see Lupton, *Citizen-Saints*. On the temporary architecture of tents, see Hailey, *Camps*.

19. See the gloss by Slavoj Žižek: "The analysis achieves its end when the patient is able to recognize, in the Real of his symptom, the only support of his being. That is how we must read Freud's *wo es war, soll ich werden*: you, the subject, must identify yourself with the place where your symptom already was; in its 'pathological' particularity you must recognize the element which gives consistency to your being" (Žižek, *Sublime Object of Ideology*, 75).

into the higher loquacity of reason, but to summon chances for action in every corner opened up in the *oikos* by human acts of call and response.[20]

In "The Political Economy of Playing," Richard Halpern tracks the return of *poiesis* within the purified boundaries of *praxis* in Arendt's account of politics: "*Praxis*, having carefully distinguished itself from *poiesis*, finds itself obliged to turn back to and rely upon the durability of made things in order to sustain itself through time."[21] Halpern intuits the return of the repressed, in which what Arendt excludes (the *oikos* from the polis, making from doing, life from politics) necessarily comes back in symptomatic form. Clearly there are interdependences and cross-fertilizations between thinking, *praxis*, *poiesis*, and *techne*; Arendt might even agree that accounting for such crossings may be the most productive task for criticism. Confronted with the social formations produced by action's foreclosure in Arendt's analysis (biopolitics, consumerism, statelessness, and the ubiquity of ear buds), I find myself unwilling, however, to give up on the integrity of these human modes, choosing to remain, with Halpern, at the interfaces of thinking, making, and doing in both Shakespeare and Arendt, but in a mode of apprehension more creative-receptive than critical-cautionary.

Arendt delivers an astounding little *Tischreden* in *The Human Condition*:

> To live together in the world means essentially that a world of things is between those who have it in common, as a table is located between those who sit around it; the world, like every in-between, relates and separates men at the same time. The public realm, as the common world, gathers us together yet prevents our falling over each other, so to speak. What makes mass society so difficult to bear is not the number of people involved, or at least not primarily, but the fact that the world between them has lost its power to gather them together, to relate and to separate them. The weirdness of this situation resembles a spiritualistic séance where a number of people gathered around a table might suddenly, through some magic trick, see the table vanish from their midst, so that two persons sitting opposite each other were no longer separated but also would be entirely unrelated to each other by anything tangible.[22]

The table, an archetype of the made thing at least since Plato, contributes to the human world by fashioning a space that invites conversation and

---

20. Compare as well Alain Badiou, at once a Lacanian, a playwright, and a philosopher, who writes that "politics *takes place*, from time to time. . . . Representation *takes place*. It is a circumscribed event. There can be no permanent theater"; see his "Rhapsody," 191.

21. Halpern, "'Eclipse of Action,': *Hamlet* and the Political Economy of Playing," 457.

22. Arendt, *Human Condition*, 53.

deliberation as well as the sharing of meals and the paying of bills.[23] The table, unlike the couch, distributes distance while also creating the possibility of the face-to-face; it is quite literally the support not only of plates, notebooks, and Sabbath candles, but also of the very spacing that sustains human relationship. Contemporary design theorists would speak here of affordances and constraints: the table *affords* conversation among equal partners across its surface, as well as the bearing of cups, pens, laptops, and junk mail; the same table also *constrains* one party from strangling the other without getting out of his chair. Yet a world in which tables have become disposable consumables, flat-boxed in China and then assigned to the landfill a few years later, is not a world in which the table can easily maintain its action-promoting functions in the same way. The fact that human deliberation finds material and psychological support in the tables, or campfires, or prayer rugs, around which such interaction frequently occurs—in other words, the fact that *praxis* must be supported and fortified by *poiesis*—does not deprive *praxis* of either its integrity or its precariousness. Action, Arendt would insist, and I would concur, continues to show a different, sharper edge, radically exposed to the hazards of human response, than making, whose rounded corners concern the durability of worlds. When Arendt writes that the polis is composed of people, not walls, she is articulating the existential dimensions of action: premised on plurality, wedded to speech, transient in its appearance, and easily effaced by administrative forms of government that take economy as their end.[24]

In the essays that follow, I have chosen to set the Shakespearean table with Hannah Arendt, inviting other interlocutors—from Renaissance and early modern householders such as Gervase Markham and John Locke to modern commentators such as Schmitt, Agamben, and Virno—to join the conversation.[25] In the chapters that follow, the scenes of plurality instantiated by crises in emancipation, election, consent, friendship, minority,

---

23. Proxemics—the study of human distances initiated by Arendt's contemporary Edward Hall—has determined that tables are superior to couches for non-intimate forms of human interaction such as decision making. See Hall, "Proxemics and Design," 24–25. I use the word *afford* here in the sense that it carries in design: "The term *affordance* refers to the perceived and actual properties of the thing, primarily those fundamental properties that determine just how the thing could be possibly be used. A chair affords ('is for') support and, therefore, affords sitting. A chair can also be carried" (Norman, *Design of Everyday Thing*, 9). I return to affordance theory in chapter 1.

24. Arendt, *Human Condition*, 198.

25. Other critics who have read Arendt in relation to Shakespeare include Kottman, *Politics of the Scene*; Halpern, "Eclipse of Action"; and Gross, *Shylock Is Shakespeare*. See also Lupton, ed., "Hannah Arendt's Renaissance."

and hospitality not only delimit a set of themes capable of exposition in dramatic form, but also touch the very structure of drama as the genre *par excellence* of plurality and its profane epiphanies. In *The Taming of the Shrew*, for example, Shakespeare uses the motif of taming in order to force into manifestation the factors that link humans to animals in a common creaturely existence, while still calling attention to politics as the mode in which humans appear to each other. In *All's Well That Ends Well*, Shakespeare's painstaking anatomy of Bertram's consent to marriage draws the audience into the consensual work of maintaining Helena's fictions, which are also Shakespeare's. In *The Winter's Tale*, Leontes uses the script of hospitality in order to impel Hermione out of the dormancy of pregnancy and into the bare-bulb publicity of his paranoia. In each case, the plays invite us to audit the special appointments between politics and life convened by theater.

In this book, I tend to read Arendt as an existentialist and a phenomenologist. By *existentialism* I mean a philosophy oriented around human being in the trembling vulnerability of our multiple dependencies on each other and our permanent exposure to the scars, mutations, and new births delivered by the slings and arrows of our own signifying practices. The prematurity of the human infant deposits it instantly into a cradle of material, linguistic, and mammary prostheses. Human dependency entails not only the hunger we share with animals but also our constitutive reliance on speech, housing, clothing, and the attention of others for both physical survival and social recognition. This dependency means that bodily care is always also care for and by the social body, as well as alienation within it.[26] The politics that interest me in this book are those that arise in response to these multiple exposures to multiple dependencies. For Arendt, moreover, the existential is closely linked to the creaturely, and hence touches on theology as well as politics; though Arendt herself was concertedly secular, her early training in theology, including her dissertation on Augustine, keep reminders of monotheism and habits of exegesis at the edges of her this-worldly work.[27] Although Agamben writes of "bare life" when translating *zoē*, I will usually speak of *creaturely life*, in order to grasp the scriptural parameters of Shakespeare's sojourning among life worlds. *Creature* indicates a made or fashioned thing, given its existential urgency by the sense of continued or potential process, action, or emergence in relation to a sublime maker, be

26. Adriana Cavarero writes as follows of Aristotle's *zoon politikon*: "Man, by nature, 'cannot be without others.' Unlike the modern individual, Aristotle's man is neither self-sufficient nor autonomous." See Cavarero, *For More Than One Voice*, 183.

27. On Arendt's secularism, see Kottman, *"Novus Ordo Saecularum"*; Gordon, "Concept of the Apolitical." For a strong reading of Arendt and theology, see Vatter, "Natality and Biopolitics."

he architect, potter, logician, or a mere mixer of mud pies. Taken in a more profane sense, creactedness indicates the contingency and enigma of our existence in the world at the behest of events, desires, and relationships that precede us, at once determining us in advance and providing the peculiar set of coordinates around which we might exercise some form of freedom.[28] For Santner, creatureliness signifies "less a dimension that traverses the boundaries of human and nonhuman forms of life than a specifically human way of finding oneself caught in the midst of antagonisms in and of the political field."[29] Arendt calls this condition "natality," which describes the way in which each birth throws a human subject into the world as the chance for a fundamentally new beginning, while also requiring a world-conserving effort on the part of the guardians of public life.[30]

By *phenomenology* I mean inquiry into the conditions of human appearing; phenomenology concerns not "things in themselves" (*noumena*) but rather how things take shape in consciousness (*phenomena*). Phenomenology always concerns the subject as a point of reference, but often within an arena constituted by the attentive presence of other people as well as the draw of things. Arendt's phenomenology addresses what Dermot Moran identifies as "'*die Öffentlichkeit*' (publicity, publicness), that is, the 'public space' (*der öffentliche Raum*), the public realm, *res publica*, the 'space of appearances.'"[31] Unlike its English equivalents, *Öffentlichkeit* captures the spatial dimension—the "open" created by the fact of human assembly—that helps bring persons into view as subjects to be seen, witnessed, judged, and engaged. Drama and phenomenology are thus closely linked, since each makes the company of others into a condition of action. In Michael Witmore's assessment, Shakespeare "used the specific resources of the theater— that is, its physical limitations; its reliance on sound, speech and gesture; its indebtedness in performance to the passage of chronological time—to say equally specific things about the relatedness of beings in the world and their mutual participation in some larger, constantly changing whole."[32] As Paul Kottman demonstrates, the Renaissance motif of the *theatrum mundi* invokes the ephemeral or "phenomenal" character of human appearing,

28. See Santner, *On Creaturely Life*.

29. Ibid., xix.

30. As Arendt writes in her dissertation on Augustine, "Everything that is created exists in the mode of becoming: 'The heavens and the earth proclaim that they have become, for they change and alter'" (*Love and St. Augustine*, ed. Joanna Vecciarelli Scott and Judith Chelius Stark [Chicago: University of Chicago Press, 1996], 52).

31. Moran, *Introduction to Phenomenology*, 287–88.

32. Witmore, *Shakespearean Metaphysics*, 7.

establishes the existential stakes in taking up residence precisely in that spectral transience, and calls actors and audience alike to participate in the maintenance of a scene shared by politics, theater, and life.[33] What Arendt said of Benjamin is also true of Shakespeare: "What profoundly fascinated [him] from the beginning was never an idea, it was a phenomenon."[34]

Following the existential and phenomenological redistricting projects modeled by Arendt, I develop certain strains in political and social theory that tend to be neglected or undervalued in postcolonial, materialist, and neo-Marxist approaches to literature and culture. These topics include the scope of virtue, the power of consent, and the risks of hospitality. Although Arendt's concepts seem easy to deconstruct, her formulations exhibit a care that lends them an unexpected resilience. As Bonnie Honig argues, labor, work, and action should be construed in Arendt not as essences that belong to particular classes or genders, but as attitudes, modes of "performative production," that "constitute *all* subjects to some extent."[35] Reading Arendt with Shakespeare allows us to mount a biopolitical critique of liberalism in its collusion with capital, while still remaining open to aspects of the civic humanist tradition, stretching from the Greeks to the Italian communes, that are not commensurate with Marxism and that remain vital resources for the Anglo-American political discourse that Arendt joined, and to which Shakespeare bears substantial if not exclusive affinities.

Take the concept of power. Whereas Foucault reads power as a quasi-autonomous energy that tends to disperse and neutralize human agency, spawning a whole generation of materialist Shakespeares, Arendt reads power (which she always opposes to violence) as "what keeps the public realm, the potential space of appearance between acting and speaking men, in existence."[36] In a line of thought that Agamben also picks up, Arendt returns power to "its Greek equivalent *dynamis*," potentiality. "Power," she writes, "is always, as we would say, a power potential and not an unchangeable, measurable, and reliable entity like force or strength."[37] Arendt's "dynamic" account of power always returns to the presence of distinct human

33. Paul Kottman speaks here of the "elemental horizon of interaction" that joins actors and audience together in a single scene (*Politics of the Scene,* 186).

34. Arendt, *Men in Dark Times,* 162.

35. Honig, "Towards an Agonistic Feminism," in *Feminist Interpretations of Hannah Arendt,* ed. Honig, 143.

36. Arendt, *Human Condition,* 200. Compare Agamben, *Potentialities,* which also develops the Aristotelian vocabulary of the potential and the actual in relation to emancipatory and totalizing forms of power.

37. Arendt, *Human Condition,* 200.

actors in the public space that their actions bring about: "The only indispensable material factor in the generation of power is the living together of
people."[38] Such a vision is inherently dramatic, involving the contingency
of human expression in scenarios constituted by the unpredictable plurality
of one's fellow actors. And it is also dramatic in a specifically Shakespearean
mode, insofar as Shakespeare's plays cast a wider net than Greek tragedy in
their pursuit of the varieties of political speech that humans are capable of
broaching. Shakespeare and Arendt, in other words, are heirs to a certain
line of questioning, first Greek and then Roman, that takes the exercise of
virtue in concert with others as an exemplary subjective possibility and discovers in the resources and impasses of that questioning the outlines of the
good life. This line of questioning, which is also a form of living, teaching,
and reading, is the matter of this book.

Thinking with Shakespeare

In his classic study, *Shakespeare Our Contemporary*, Jan Kott wrote of *Hamlet*,

> Shakespeare had written, or rather re-written, an old scenario, and the parts
> in it. But he did not distribute the parts. This has been done anew in every
> age. Every age has its own Poloniuses, Fortinbrases, Hamlets and Ophelias.
> Before they enter the stage, they have to go to dressing rooms. But let them
> not stay too long. They may put on huge wigs, shave off their moustaches, or
> stick on beards, put on medieval-looking tights, or throw Byronic capes over
> their shoulders; they may play in armour or in tails. This does not really make
> a difference, on condition that their make-up is not overdone; for they must
> have modern faces. Otherwise they would perform a costume piece, instead
> of *Hamlet*.[39]

Kott insists that theatricality be limited when it comes to the face, the expressive organ through which actors communicate their own subjective
stakes in the characters they have consented to assume. The same is true
of criticism. We can choose any number of conceptual environments to
refresh our sense of the plays. Historicism provides vast menus of possible
settings (law court, shipyard, news stand, apothecary shop), while theoretical discourses such as feminism, Marxism, and psychoanalysis continue
to provide resilient and provocative ideational architectures. All readings,

38. Ibid., 201.
39. Kott, *Shakespeare Our Contemporary*, 59.

however, risk turning into what Kott calls "costume drama," productions constrained by the corsets and laces of their own apparatus, whether the interpretation is flooded by too much context or left high and dry by too much concept. *Thinking with Shakespeare* aims to return to Kott's project: to engage Shakespearean drama with a sense of playfulness, experiment, and historical awareness, but *without too much make-up*, in order to touch what is timely in Shakespeare.

Like Kott's book, *Thinking with Shakespeare* attests to the universality of Shakespeare's plays, not as a thesaurus of eternal messages but in their capacity to establish real connections with the successive worlds shared and sustained by actors and audiences over time. Shakespeare's universality is animated by the *dynamis* of potentiality rather than constrained by the facticity of actualization, insofar as his plays continue to solicit new readings in relation to associations that border on without belonging fully to his historical moment. Shakespeare's universality is open, not closed: open to figures of complaint and exclusion such as Shylock, but also open to the challenges of repeat performance, epochal reinterpretation, and global translation.[40] Needless to say, the vast majority of texts fail this challenge; those that survive it, like Shakespeare's, are made stronger by the process.

Thinking with Shakespeare is an exercise in neither presentism nor reception history. Rather than reconstructing the significance of Shakespeare for later traditions of thinking or staging his uncanny echoing of current events, I am concerned with constellations that *persist*, that appear in, before, and after Shakespeare. Such ensembles of meaning, character and setting resonate across periods by dint of becoming urgent in the successive situations that reframe them, but also by virtue of losing their original grounds of authority and hence seeking new moorings in relation to emerging orders of value. The play text itself, as Kott demonstrates, is an instance of such persistence, dispatched from a previous time and place whose parameters continue to challenge us as maps of lost worlds, yet exposed to the terror and contingency of new life each time it is performed, read, taught, edited, translated, or sold back to the bookstore. It is no accident, moreover, that the central ideas pursued in this book—election, consent, hospitality, sociability, and personhood—are *configurations* as much as *concepts*, social scripts

40. On the open universality of theater, see Alain Badiou: "The great text of theatre, because it is open and incomplete, because it will be played through the ages and by human beings . . . who have changed gods, whose city no longer has the same form, and whose loves no longer have the same law, this text must possess the powerful simplicity of the atemporal, it must bespeak a *generic* humanity, capable of passing from actor to actor, from body to body, from State to State, all the while preserving its fundamental meaning" ("Rhapsody," 227).

governed by formulas, requiring an audience, and subject to the hazards of performance. Each case of election, or consent, or the giving of a dinner party, involves what Kott calls the *distribution of parts*: roles handed out to living beings whose acts of speech have the power to bring something novel into the space of *Öffentlichkeit* that they convene together.

To grasp the persistence of such designs for living, Arendt had repeated recourse to the image of the pearl fisher, harvested from Ariel's song in *The Tempest*. First appropriating the Shakespearean figure in a letter to her friend and mentor Karl Blumenfeld in 1960, Arendt developed it further in her introduction to Walter Benjamin's *Illuminations*, a piece that also appeared in the *New Yorker* in 1968 and in her collection *Men In Dark Times* in 1970.[41] In the Benjamin piece, a full citation of Ariel's song heads the essay's final section, "The Pearl Fisher," where Arendt uses the phrase to describe Benjamin's decontextualizing manner of citation, a form of retrieval exercised in the face of the breakdown of tradition. She ends the essay with an explicit commentary on the Shakespearean epigram:

> And this thinking, fed by the present, works with the "thought fragments" it can wrest from the past and gather about itself. Like a pearl diver who descends to the bottom of the sea, not to excavate the bottom and bring it to light but to pry loose the rich and the strange, the pearls and coral in the depths, and to carry them to the surface, this thinking delves into the depths of the past—but not in order to resuscitate it the way it was and to contribute to the renewal of extinct ages. What guides this thinking is the conviction that although the living is subject to the ruin of the time, the process of decay is at the same time a process of crystallization, that in the depth of the sea, into which sinks and dissolves what once was alive, some things "suffer a sea change," and survive in new crystallized forms and shapes that remain immune to the elements, as though they waited only for the pearl diver who one day will come down to them and bring them up into the world of the living—as "thought fragments," as something "rich and strange," and perhaps even as *Urphänomene*.[42]

41. I would like to thank Paul Dahlgren for first pointing out to me Arendt's use of the pearl-fishing metaphor. On the letter to Blumenfeld, see Young-Bruehl, *Hannah Arendt*, 95. Hanna Fenichel Pitkin provides a penetrating gloss of the motif and its significance for Arendt's thought, and catalogues Arendt's uses of the image in a helpful footnote in *The Attack of the Blob*, 274–76 and 324–25, n. 78.

42. Arendt, "Introduction," 51.

Her signature directly follows: HANNAH ARENDT. After all, she has spoken of and for Walter Benjamin, whose writings she had ferried out of France and seen into publication, but she also speaks of and for herself, holding up to public light the image of the pearl fisher first disclosed in the intimate space of her letter to Blumenfeld. In retrieving such classical "pearls" as the *vita activa*, citizenship, power, and the polis for twentieth-century political philosophy from the crystallizing sedimentations of the postclassical tradition and its catastrophes, Arendt saw herself not as writing intellectual or political history, but as salvaging potentialities within democratic thought for unknown futures. She calls these potentialities *Urphänomene* in order to grasp both their originary and their enduring character as well as their vulnerability to sea changes to come. In her (self-) portrait as the pearl-fisher, Arendt demonstrates a kind of thinking with Shakespeare: not analyzing Shakespeare per se, but following the rhythm and images of thought in Shakespeare in order to achieve original interpretive ends, effecting a kind of renaissance in and through them. Indeed, it is at the level of argumentative habit rather than topics of analysis that Arendt strikes me as salutary for Renaissance studies. Arendt's style of writing and thinking was philosophical and journalistic, deeply historical yet suspicious of all historicisms, faithful to the call of antiquity yet always responding to present crises and developments, and penned with great learning but without beholdenness to the academy. As such, her model of the intellectual life, beyond the details and values she discerned within it, partook of, indeed repeated, the historical-recreative impulses of Renaissance humanism, and may be ready for its own renaissance in the humanities today.

Chapter 1, "Animal Husbands in *The Taming of the Shrew*" takes up Hannah Arendt's passing distinction between *zoē* and *bios* in order to examine the environments formed by people, animals, and things in Shakespeare's early comedy. I read the play alongside the writings of Gervase Markham, a younger son and lesser poet who left his tracks on the English literary landscape by writing about farming, horsemanship, and housekeeping. I am interested in the extent to which the taming motif in the play *is not a metaphor*—the extent to which, that is, Kate's animal virtues really are tapped and rechanneled under Petruchio's "husbandry," expanding our sense of what virtue might be in the tradition of ethics, psychology, and physics inherited from Aristotle. In the scenario of taming, the animality of both husband and wife is not overcome or negated so much as purified and instrumentalized. On the one hand, the play stages an early instance of biopower, in which *zoē*, as creaturely life, becomes directly subject to sovereign rule. At the same time, I also attend to the ways in which animal existence comes to appear in a distinctively human world that seeks ways to honor its covenants with createdness.

Chapter 2, "The *Hamlet* Elections," places Hamlet among his peers, Horatio and Fortinbras, who represent distinct alternatives in the political tradition. Horatio instantiates the classical circle of political friendship, while Fortinbras enters the play from the states of emergency that both precede the opening of the drama and are escalated by its actions. At the end of the play, Horatio and Fortinbras share the stage, suggesting opposing yet interdependent destinies of politics in a future organized by election. The key companion text for this investigation is the commentary on *Hamlet* by Carl Schmitt. In reading *Hamlet* Schmitt was concerned to defend the "elective" character of Denmark's monarchy against any "liberal" appropriations. What is Schmitt scared of? I use Schmitt's antiliberal reading of election in *Hamlet* in order to unlock the constitutional potentialities of the play.

Chapter 3, "*All's Well That Ends Well* and the Futures of Consent," examines the staging of medical, sexual, and political consent in *All's Well*, combining a fundamental concept from political theory with an essentially narrative and performative problem: when, and how, does consent need to be inferred or retroactively determined? What are the verbal, gestural, psychological, and legal-contractual elements of consent, and how are these distributed in literary enactments and investigations of consent? What continuum obtains between consent and coercion in the early modern period and in our own? By using a combination of texts taken from contemporary legal theories of consent, along with texts from the period broadly conceived (including Hobbes, Locke, and their predecessors), this chapter aims to be an exemplary staging of "thinking with Shakespeare," taken as the association of Shakespearean texts with contemporary problems, conducted via key concepts from the Western political tradition that receive new point and purpose in the Renaissance.

Chapter 4, "Job of Athens, Timon of Uz," reads *Timon of Athens* in tandem with the Book of Job, one of the Biblical texts most cited by Shakespeare. *Timon of Athens* presents Shakespeare's philosophy and pathography of the gift. In Timon's world as in our own, gifts have the capacity to build and break human bonds, to establish and confound selfhood, and to address and avoid the divine. Timon's search for a pure instance of the gift is closely related to Job's complaint in despite of all consolation: both Timon and Job are good men who refuse to submit their virtues to economic itemization and calculation. Suddenly cast out of the social structures that they had previously administered, these abandoned masters find themselves reduced to a minimal existence that opens them to new forms of politics, in the form of rant, plaint, and protest. The Book of Job is theology bordering on drama, while *Timon of Athens* is drama bordering on theology. Both works share traits with the philosophical dialogue, and hence provide test cases for reading literature with philosophy. Harshly satiric on the subject of human nature yet refusing to relinquish the dream of an achieved sociability, Timon's Athens bears revisiting by anyone concerned with the social, cognitive, and ritual dimensions of hospitality and gift-giving.

The party continues in Chapter 5, "Hospitality and Risk in *The Winter's Tale*." Here I track the sudden appearance of politics, like a ghost or a guest, within the more normative scenes set by hospitality in *The Winter's Tale*, events that also render visible the phenomenological affinities and differences between entertainment and drama. The play discloses hospitality as the zone in which domestic life reveals its capacities for political speech, above all through the reluctant actions of Hermione, who is forced to perform her discretion and publish her modesty in a public space both erected and deformed by her husband's tyrannical imagination.

Chapter 6, "The Minority of Caliban," reads Caliban in relation to juridical categories of childhood and nonage. The minor is the bearer of equality *in potentia*, an unrealized capacity for independence sheltered and supported by the institutions of family life and protected when necessary by law. Reading the figure of the minor in Locke's critique of absolutist patriarchalism back into Shakespeare's play delivers both a counter-Jacobean Prospero, chastened by his imperfect exercise of paternal duty, and a rights-bearing Caliban worthy of a care that puts us, not him, to the test of humanity. Caliban's passage through the disparate conditions of the orphan, the foster-child, the slave, and the accidental citizen establishes his irrevocable participation in personhood.

In Chapter 7, "Paul Shakespeare," I argue for the centrality of Paul's Epistles to Shakespearean drama. I read Paul not in terms of his concrete reception in the English Reformation, but as a figure whose legacy is dynamically divided among Protestant, Catholic, Jewish, and philosophical articulations. Reading Shakespeare's plays for these four faces of Paul—faces disclosed in part by twentieth- and twenty-first-century readings of the Epistles in both New Testament studies and critical theory—expands our sense of the pluralist, creaturely, and universal elements of Shakespeare's explorations of politics and life.

An epilogue, "Defrosting the Refrigerator with Hannah Arendt," visits the Arendtian triad formed by thinking, making, and doing in order to examine their disposition in contemporary life. I look to education and the D.I.Y. ("do it yourself") movement for scenes of action and activity in which the humanities have a chance to help shape a culture currently undergoing a sea change in its cognitive, productive, and democratic platforms.

This book in part affirms a return to theory, especially to the frameworks proffered by philosophy, psychoanalysis, politics, and theology. I am not, however, primarily interested in the internal logics of specific methods and debates, nor do I pursue the afterlife of Shakespeare in later instances of thought.[43] Instead, I try to use the orienting scenarios, compelling subjectivities, and object worlds of the plays—Petruchio's animals, Kate's laundry, Timon's rage, Hamlet's friends, Helena's recipes, Caliban's constraints, Hermione's reticence—to stage the philosophical and political questions that continue to engage Shakespeare's audiences. To think with Shakespeare is, ideally, not to instrumentalize the plays in the service of an ideological program (as one drives in a nail "with" a hammer), but rather to think alongside Shakespeare about matters of shared concern (as one speaks "with" a friend). At the same time, my chosen topics of politics and life, hitched as they are to the development of Arendtian thought in the direction of biopower and political theology, tend to pull these interpretations in certain thematic directions. My challenge has been to approach the texts with a light touch, using the frameworks provided by Arendt and her readers in order to respond freshly to the texts rather than simply discover my preoccupations there.

Although my own proclivities are conceptual and exegetical rather than historical, I have tried to execute my readings with an awareness of Shakespeare's historical possibilities. To return to the terms from design theory that I served up earlier on Arendt's table: history offers both affordances and constraints that together help direct the project of thinking with Shakespeare. History *affords* this enterprise by delimiting sets of themes, affiliations, discourses, and ways of knowing that resonate in Shakespeare's plays. History also *constrains* this enterprise by excluding or discrediting some readings as less valid than others. Throughout this book, I try to read concepts with a strong contemporary currency (consent, citizenship, animality, minority, hospitality) against their earlier instantiations in classical, biblical, and early

---

43. For genealogical accounts of Shakespeare and theory, see, for example, Halpern, *Shakespeare Among the Moderns*; Wilson, *Shakespeare in French Theory*; Kottman, ed., *Philosophers on Shakespeare*; as well as Lupton and Reinhard, *After Oedipus*. A. D. Nuttall reads Shakespeare as a philosopher in his deep yet accessible book, *Shakespeare the Thinker*. Agnes Heller is another philosopher reading Shakespeare within a broad humanistic frame; see *The Time Is Out of Joint: Shakespeare as Philosopher of History*. On Shakespeare and the new cognitive sciences, see Davis, *Shakespeare Thinking*. On Shakespeare and phenomenology, see Witmore, *Shakespearean Metaphysics*.

modern discourses. But if history both affords and constrains interpretation in this book, history is also not the object of my study, which remains rather the plays of Shakespeare. *Thinking with Shakespeare* is ultimately in search of ways to *live with* Shakespeare, as one might learn to live with AIDS, with cats, or with children. This means acknowledging the sources and the scope as well as the limits of Shakespeare's several discourses on virtue, not in order to declare our greater wisdom concerning human arrangements, but in order to recover their potentialities for the project of living well.

ONE

Animal Husbands in *The Taming of the Shrew*

In his *Cheape and Good Husbandry* of 1614, agriculturalist Gervase Markham describes the role of the capon in the sociology of the poultry yard:

> These Capons are of two uses: the one is, to lead Chickens, Ducklings, young Turkies, Peahens, Phesants and Partridges, which hee will doe altogether, both naturally and kindely, and through largenesse of his body will brood or cover easily thirtie or thirty and five; he will lead them forth safely, and defend them against Kites and Buzzards, more better than the Hennes; therefore the way to make him to take to them, is, with a fine small Briar, or else sharpe Nettles at night, to beate and sting all his brest and neather parts, and then in the darke to seate the Chickens under him, whose warmth taking away his smart, hee will fall much in love with them, and when so ever he proveth unkinde, you must sting or beat him againe, and this will make him hee will never forsake them.
>
> The other use of Capons is, to feede for the Dishe, as eyther at the Barne dores, with craps of Corne and the chavings of pulse, or else in Pennes in the house, by cramming them, which is the most daintie.[1]

The capon serves up an instance and allegory of what I call in this chapter the "animal husband." He is a creature with immense domestic responsibilities, caring in the scene set by Markham for "thirtie or thirty and five" smaller birds drawn from several types of domestic fowl. The capon's immense bulk suits him to "brood and cover" the little ones and to defend

---

1. Markham, *Cheape and Good Husbandry*, 116. This essay is indebted to work by my student Nichole Miller, "The Sexual Politics of Pain," and to Richard Halpern's readings of Arendt, Shakespeare, and performativity, in "Eclipse of Action."

them against birds of prey, "more better than the Hennes" could do. The capon does all of this "naturally and kindely," from his being and out of species-love, yet no capon is found in nature, since he is the product of animal husbandry. Once castrated, the cock grows large in size and gentle in temperament; but his paternal bonding with little chicks, who by definition cannot be his offspring, requires the supplemental stinging and beating of his "brest and neather parts" with nettles, followed by the nocturnal tucking of the chicks beneath him for warmth and comfort, a barnyard bed trick to be repeated whenever he "proveth unkinde." More than kind and less than kin, the capon is manufactured in and for the farm and the table, a figure whose larger-than-life capacities issue from a fundamental subtraction, and whose promised end is ultimately "the Dishe," a goal enhanced through force-feeding.

According to the *Oxford English Dictionary*, "husband" means "master of a household," "a man joined to a woman by marriage," "one who tills and cultivates the soil," or "the manager of a household or establishment; a housekeeper; a steward"; behind the primary, modern, marital sense lies a series of agricultural and administrative meanings, stemming from animal husbandry as the art of raising domestic beasts for food, labor, transportation, and sport.[2] I use the phrase *animal husband* to demarcate those moments when the different senses of husband hybridize, doubling meanings and offices. Often the effect is simply to magnify masculine authority: thus the husband as householder is also husband to a wife, duties that authorize man's jurisdiction over woman as chattel. Yet convergences can also cross and tangle proper lines of mastery: to be an effective domesticator of animals, the husbandman must learn to participate in animal psychologies and ecologies, mortgaging a bit of his humanity in order to channel the virtues of the environment. To be caught up in the world of labor is not simply to take control of one's milieu, but also to enter into relations of dependence, attention, physical intimacy, self-limitation, and even self-loss. Finally, the animal husband finds his mate in the animal housewife, who submits to her husband's governance while also husbanding her precious goods and charges, exercising her own knack for thrift, remedy, increase, and ordering in relation to household stuff both animate and inanimate. It is she who sauces the capon, and perhaps manufactures it, too.

2. *Oxford English Dictionary*, 2nd ed. The *Medulla Grammatice* (c. 1480, Pepys MS 2002) translates *Iconomus, maritus,* and *coniunx gis* as "husbond." See Huntsman, *Pepys MS 2002.* On husbandry in its sexual, economic, and agricultural senses in Shakespeare, see Greene, "Pitiful Thrivers."

Shakespeare harbors many animal husbands in his stable of characters. Closest in name and spirit to Markham's capon is Shakespeare's Capulet, a man of the pantry and the trestle table whose brooding, solicitous hospitality nurses an ancient grudge; later, greater instantiations include Shylock, Antonio, and Timon, all marked by the terror of bodily subtraction and the burden of household management, vocations that affiliate them with a range of animal avatars. The play in which Shakespeare most assiduously cultivates the bond between husband and husbandman, however, is *The Taming of the Shrew*. It has been a staple of *Shrew* criticism to read the play in relationship to discourses of falconry, horsemanship, and home economics, and my reading borrows heavily from these ventures.[3] What distinguishes my approach here, however, is my interest in the phenomenological and existential fruits of animal husbandry in Shakespeare. I have labored to avoid either a rhetoric of praise and blame or a hermeneutics of suspicion in favor of piecing together some features of human-animal cohabitation broached in Shakespeare's play, as well as the modes by which Shakespeare makes them appear in the space of theater. My goal is not to historicize *Shrew* but to probe the possibilities for experience, cognition, interaction, imagination, and subjective disclosure that we continue to share with Shakespeare, which means marking in chalk, not stone, the differences between his world and ours. I conduct my domestic investigations with Gervase Markham by my side. As the seventeenth century's most prolific writer on household stuff (and a one-time candidate for the office of "rival poet" to Shakespeare), Markham is not only a purveyor of Renaissance domestic ideologies, but also a phenomenologist of the farmyard: an acute observer of animal behavior and vegetable virtues, and an avid trainer of human beings, both male and female, to be apt and able respondents to an environment that solicits both their cruelty and their kindness.[4]

The Taming of the Shrew harbors within it the demands and duties of creaturely life, including the ligaments tying humans to nutritive needs, to labor and work, and to the order of the *oikos*. Moreover, the play adamantly yokes these concerns to the life of the city and thus to the piazzas of

3. On animals in *Shrew*, see especially Benson, "'If I do prove her haggard'"; Berry, *Shakespeare and the Hunt*; Hartwig, "Horses and Women in *The Taming of the Shrew*"; Ranald, *Shakespeare and His Social Context*; and Jean Addison Roberts, "Horses and Hermaphrodites." On things in *Shrew*, see especially Korda, "Household Kates," reworked in her book *Shakespeare's Domestic Economies*; and Orlin, "The Performance of Things."

4. On Markham as rival poet, see Gittings, *Shakespeare's Rival*. On the nation-building elements of Markham's georgics, see Wall, "Renaissance National Husbandry." Wall also discusses Markham's contributions to household theory in *Staging Domesticity*, 26–42.

human appearing, the space of action cultivated by drama as the art of self-manifestation in the scene of plurality. The central taming motif cross-couples human husbanding (the man-wife relationship) with animal husbandry (the man-animal relationship). Both man and woman's animal affinities come forward in the play, not simply as signs of base or irrational instincts that must be controlled by reason or excluded from the body politic, but as players in a multidimensional discourse of virtue that includes the plant and animal kingdoms as well as the *bios politikos* in its reach. The tamed wife produced at the end of *Shrew*, as the play's animal readers have long pointed out, is not cowed so much as falconed. In Shakespeare's play, to tame a wife is not to break, expel, or subdue her animal capacities, but rather to perfect them, to render them newly visible in a human world they help to build and sustain, calling her to demonstrate those capacities on the stages of their shared world, in this case the boards provided at the end of the play by the theater of hospitality. The taming of Katharina most decidedly yields a wife "conformable as other household Kates" (2.1.270), a program that engineers forms of life conceived as less than fully human (female, animal, thingly) in relation to the instrumental needs of man. It is thus biopolitical in the most brute sense: the sequestering, shaming, and torment of a vitality forcibly separated from its autopoetic capacities in order to expand and support a governing instance conceived on the narrowest of class, sex, and species terms. Yet Petruchio, too, by submitting to the yoke of marriage, has undergone a certain *caponage* by the end of the play. *Shrew* remains starkly biopolitical with respect to both sexual and creaturely divisions of labor, but that fact should not blind us to the variety of life forms and the politics they might breed, including styles of stewardship, curation, and tendering, hosted in the more experimental sectors of the play's topography. In dramatizing the actualization of *one* potentiality in Katharina—that of the conforming wife—the taming scenario unveils the vista of potentiality as such, as a scene for the ongoing political and dramatic investigation of virtue. (We know that the experiment continues, as Kate molts into Beatrice, and Lady Macbeth, and Emilia, and Paulina.) In this early play, I argue, Shakespeare taps a landscape of human, animal and artifactual resources, not in order to deplete them, but in order to open their entanglement up for further inquiry.

Although I focus on animals, I am also interested in the copious object world of *Shrew*. Divided between urban Padua and Petruchio's rustic ranch, the play is at least as concerned with the proper curation of apparel and appliances as it is with the maintenance of the animal kingdom. Here, too, much work has been done, especially in groundbreaking essays by Natasha

Korda and Lena Orlin. Once again, however, I would like to shift focus from the rise of mercantilism and modern consumption in Shakespeare's England to the kinds of company that persons, objects, and animals might keep in the imaginative inventories of Shakespeare's plays. Although I pay attention to the disposition of objects over time, my interests lie more in phenomenological affordances than historical constraints, and my ultimate aim is to draw out points of possible affirmation and assonance among texts, epochs, and life forms rather than submit Shakespearean blind spots to contemporary critique.

Phenomenon means "appearance." By *phenomenology*, I intend here not only an attentive description of Shakespeare's household stuff, but also some account of the conditions under which animate and inanimate things appear as such to human consciousness.[5] To bring biopolitics to bear on the appearances made by things in *Shrew* entails recalling the debts of the biopolitical critique to this book's heroine, Hannah Arendt. In *The Human Condition*, Hannah Arendt delineates politics as the arena of a specifically human appearing, a platform that depends for its existence on the extraordinary labor expended by artisans, women, slaves, and beasts of burden to make the pressures of biological life step back for a moment so that public action can take place. If Foucault is the animal husband of biopolitical thinking, Hannah Arendt is most decidedly its animal housewife, first wary cultivator and severe hostess of the distinctions and dependencies between *zoē* and *bios* in the modern era.

Shakespeare's Book of Virtues; or, Arendt in Italy

Lucentio's sojourn in Padua begins under the sign of virtue:

> And therefore, Tranio, for the time I study,
> Virtue and that part of philosophy
> Will I apply that treats of happiness
> By virtue specially to be achieved. (1.1.17–20)

Lucentio speaks here of ethics in the Aristotelian vein, in which happiness is achieved through the exercise of the moral virtues as their own reward.

---

5. There is a phenomenological dimension to Derrida's late work on animals, *The Animal That Therefore I Am*. Gail Kern Paster calls her work on Renaissance humoral psychology "historical phenomenology." See Paster, Rowe, and Floyd-Wilson, eds., *Reading the Early Modern Passions*, 111; see also Floyd-Wilson and Sullivan, eds., *Environment and Embodiment in Early Modern England*, and Bruce R. Smith, *Phenomenal Shakespeare*.

For Aristotle, the virtues of courage, temperance, or friendship exist not as attributes or qualities of the "friendly," "courageous," or "temperate" man, but only in and through their habitual practice. Happiness is not a reward given to the actor in exchange for doing the right thing, but the state of well-being that accrues to the exercise of virtue itself, as the harmony between virtues as particular excellences (courage, friendship, etc.) and their actualization in the practice of living well. Lucentio touches on the practical and performative dimension of virtue when he speaks of "applying" philosophy and of "achieving" happiness through virtue.

In *The Human Condition*, Arendt addresses virtue as the practice of the good life:

> Aristotle, in his political philosophy, is still well aware of what is at stake in politics, namely, no less than the *ergon tou anthrōpou* (the "work of man" *qua* man), and if he defined this "work" as "to live well" (*eu zēn*), he clearly meant that "work" here is no work product but exists only in sheer actuality. This specifically human achievement lies altogether outside the category of means and ends; the "work of man" is no end because the means to achieve it—the virtues, or *aretai*—are not qualities which may or may not be actualized, but are themselves "actualities."[6]

Since virtues only exist in, through, and as their performance, politics (and ethics as a prolegomenon to politics) are comparable to the arts of "healing, flute-playing, play-acting," the occupations that "furnished ancient thinking with examples for the highest and greatest activities of man" but were denigrated by Adam Smith as "unproductive" labor, since they do not yield a durable product.[7]

Arendt follows Aristotle in linking ethical and political *action* to the *acting* achieved in drama and music, where indeed there is no product, no "end," apart from the performance itself. In this sense, we might say that virtue is *virtual*, existing only as performance. Action is above all exercised in speech, in situations of deliberation, adjudication, witnessing, or contestation that unfold in the presence of others; to act in public for Arendt is to let something of oneself appear to others, and to become oneself, to become a subject, through this revelation. In Arendt's political phenomenology, the polis is "the space of appearance in the widest sense of the word, namely, the space where I appear to others as others appear to me, where men exist

6. Arendt, *Human Condition*, 207.
7. Ibid., 85–86.

not merely like other living or inanimate things but make their appearance explicitly."[8] She quotes Dante: "For in every action what is primarily intended by the doer, whether he acts from natural necessity or out of free will, is the disclosure of his own image [*propriam similitudinem explicare*]."[9]

As Paul Kottman and Richard Halpern have recently reconfirmed, such a vision is dramatic through and through, for what is drama if not the appearing of actors in public, in scenarios of self-exposure and interpersonal liability that generate a story in excess of any one character's will or intention?[10] It is also a vision that traces a certain separation between the properly human form of life produced in virtuous action and the existence of "other living or inanimate things," which do not, according to Arendt, make their appearance on the human stage in the same way. In a passage I cited in the introduction, Arendt writes that the specifically human life of action "is itself always full of events which ultimately can be told as a story, establish a biography; it is of this life, *bios* as distinguished from mere *zōē*, that Aristotle said that it 'somehow is a kind of praxis.'"[11] Although Arendt follows Aristotle and the civic humanist tradition in valuing the self-disclosing processes of the *vita activa* over the efforts of the *animal laborans*, she by no means degrades or debases creaturely life, and she includes its relentlessly responsive maintenance through the labor of the *oikos* and the work of the artisan in her overall conception of the human condition. The phenomenological language of appearance continues to mark the manifestation of natural life in human experience: "While nature manifests itself in human existence through the circular movement of our bodily functions, she makes her presence felt in the man-made world through the constant threat of overgrowing or decaying it."[12] Arendt speaks of natural life neither as "bare" (stripped of all human structuring) nor as "constructed" (a fabrication of human systems of culture, meaning, or ideology), but as that which makes itself known through the metabolic rhythms of digestion and through the tendency of human artifacts to fall into disrepair under the incessant flourishing and decomposition of organic growth.

The flexible crease between *bios* and *zoē*, broached essayistically and in passing by Arendt, has taken center stage in contemporary critiques of biopower, above all in the work of Giorgio Agamben, whose writings on sovereignty, bare life, and states of exception have become a touchstone in recent

---

8. Ibid., 198–99.
9. Ibid., 175.
10. Kottman, *Politics of the Scene*, 23–26; Halpern, "Eclipse of Action," 456–59.
11. Arendt, *Human Condition*, 97.
12. Ibid., 98.

Shakespeare criticism.[13] What is not usually noted in this criticism is the extent to which Agamben, along with other Italians writing on biopolitics, takes Arendt as his point of departure and remains in many ways attuned to her central critique of the housekeeping mission of the modern state. In his essay "The Work of Man," Agamben returns to the same virtue complex that Arendt addresses in *The Human Condition*. In Agamben's gloss of Aristotle, happiness is *"psukhēs energeia . . . kat' aretēn,* the being-at-work of the soul in accordance with excellence."[14] Agamben sees Aristotle as opening the possibility of a "work of man" that would not be defined by any function and that would not force the breaking up of life into different grades of existence (nutritive, sensitive, and rational). Agamben is reminding us that for the Aristotle of the *Physics*, virtue characterizes every substance, as the perfection of its particular form, and not just human action. Yet Aristotle, in Agamben's reading, finally binds the work of man, and hence human virtue, to that feature of life—rationality—that is *not* shared with nutritive plants and sensitive animals, thus forever identifying properly human being with "'a certain kind of life' (*zoē tis*), life that is in accordance with *logos*."[15] The life left over—*zoē*, bare life, creaturely life—originally excluded from what is properly political, has returned in the modern era as the main object of politics, assiduously calculated, managed, and manipulated by the bureaucratic state. Here Agamben echoes Arendt: even while the modern state takes the biological safety of the people as the normative object of a benevolent public policy, that same state also sequesters and concentrates extreme, aberrant, or superfluous quantities of life in spaces conceived as juridically outside the body politic—encampments where the rule of law can be suspended.

Whereas Arendt, however, honors the Greek virtualization of political virtue—its phenomenal separation from other forms of life in the act of man's self-appearing through action—Agamben records that same moment as a catastrophe, a constitutive exclusion of *zoē* from politics that can only be

13. On Shakespeare and questions of life and the creature with reference to Agamben, see Höfele, "Humanity at Stake." On states of emergency in Shakespeare, also approached through Agamben, see Kuzner, "Unbuilding the City." In *Rethinking the Turn to Religion in Early Modern English Literature*, Gregory Kneidel develops Agamben's encounter with St. Paul. On Agamben, Benjamin, and the creature, see Eric Santner, *On Creaturely Life*. For a wider set of recent critical responses to Agamben, see Ross, ed., *The Agamben Effect* (Durham: Duke University Press, 2007), especially Benjamin, "Particularity and Exceptions," which proceeds by way of Renaissance iconography (71–77), and Kaufman, "Saturday of Messianic Time." See also Calarco and DeCaroli, eds., *Giorgio Agamben*.

14. Agamben, "Work of Man," 2.

15. Ibid., 5.

recovered through moments of what he calls the inoperative (*inoperosità*): not the *ergon* or work of man, but the *argia* or inactivity of man—the not-working, the remaining-potential, the unactualized. We might look to *art* as a key scene of the inoperative (the work of art works by not-working), but also to holiday and festival—to the Sabbath, for example—as moments when work is interrupted and forms of life can enter into new relations with each other. The inoperative effects a further virtualization of virtue; rejecting actualization as already too end-oriented, the inoperative names forms of performance that repel ends altogether.

For Paolo Virno as well, these passages in Aristotle and Arendt are crucial. Whereas Agamben tracks the unmediated emergence of bare life in the sphere of the political, Virno focuses on the contemporary draining of labor from work and the infusion of work with the spirit of action, thought, and play in the information economy. Virno reads Aristotle through Arendt:

> In the *Nichomachean Ethics* Aristotle distinguishes labor (or *poiesis*) from political action (or *praxis*), utilizing precisely the notion of virtuosity: we have labor when an object is produced, an opus which can be separated from action; we have praxis when the purpose of action is founded on action itself. . . . Implicitly resuming Aristotle's idea, Hannah Arendt compares the performing artists, the virtuosos, to those who are engaged in political action. . . . One could say that every political action is *virtuosic*.[16]

In the contemporary workplace, "the virtuoso punches a time card," and "the informality of communicative behavior, the competitive interaction typical of a meeting" have becoming defining features of the software sweat-shop.[17] The motto of the new economy is "Everyone does everything," from the mysteries of Photoshop to making coffee, or at least drinking it (branded brew being the symbolic gasoline of post-Fordism).[18] A workplace that demands virtuosity of its employees puts a premium on youth and adaptability; today's in-house service becomes tomorrow's outsourced skill, while labor itself occurs in camplike settings operating under the most extreme conditions in countries far, far away. Virno suggests that "the intermingling of virtuosity, politics, and labor has extended everywhere," remaking all

16. Virno, *Grammar of the Multitude*, 52–53.

17. Ibid., 58–59.

18. On the phrase "Everyone does everything" as the new motto of newsrooms, design studios, and software companies, see Ellen Lupton, "Everyone Does Everything," available online at http://design-your-life.org/index.php?id=71 (accessed 6 August 2010).

"industrial sectors" in the image of the "communication industry."[19] The result is not only to transform work (rendering it at once sexier and more transient), but also, Virno argues, to sap traditional politics of their interest and affect.

Arendt discovers in the Greek separation of the work of man from the labor of the *oikos* and the fabrication of the workshop a space of freedom where the virtuality of virtue can appear through public action. Agamben, on the other hand, puts forward the inoperative precisely as a way of re-integrating diverse forms of life, including animal ones, on the other side of modern biopower. For Virno, the inoperative is already here, in the guise of the work-as-play agenda of the information-age virtuoso, who trades in various forms of virtuality, whether it's social media, junk bonds, or iPod apps. Virno's interest lies in neither separating out the political from the socioeconomic (Arendt), nor in ending *zoē*'s debilitating internment within politics (Agamben), but in creating the conditions for a "nonservile virtu-osity," symptoms of which are visible in internet activism as well as in the resurgence of handiwork, urban farming, and garage branding in the new *oikoi* of the D.I.Y. ("do it yourself"), slow food, fair trade, and green move-ments.[20] I venture that we can "think with Shakespeare" about these three positions in their genealogical conversations, their moments of consensus, and their variations in emphasis and interest. In *The Taming of the Shrew*, Shakespeare evokes Aristotelian lines of thinking about forms of life, styles of virtue, the nature of work and labor, and the world of persons, animals, and things in a manner that not only reflects the *historical conditions* of the late sixteenth century, but also bears on the *human condition*, in Arendt's existential sense.

Our Lucentio, all sophomoric enthusiasm, seeks virtue of the classical sort, his own aims close to those articulated by Aristotle for the civic hu-manist tradition, yet voiced in a manner that remains naively and comi-cally academic, not yet tied to any real practice or conduct of life. His man Tranio, on the other hand, urges a broader, more integrated curriculum:

I am in all affected as yourself,
Glad that you thus continue your resolve
To suck the sweets of sweet philosophy.
Only, good master, while we do admire
This virtue and this moral discipline,

19. Virno, *Grammar of the Multitude*, 59.
20. Virno, "Virtuosity and Revolution:," 199.

Let's be no stoics nor no stocks, I pray,
Or so devote to Aristotle's checks
As Ovid be an outcast quite abjured.
Balk logic with acquaintance that you have,
And practice rhetoric in your common talk;
Music and poesy use to quicken you;
The mathematics and the metaphysics,
Fall to them as you find your stomach serves you.
No profit grows where is no pleasure ta'en.
In brief, sir, study what you most affect. (1.1.26–40)

Tranio counters the classical vision of happiness and the good life as the exercise of virtue with a more expansive program that draws the inoperative—"music and poesy"—into a *paideia* that supplements happiness with pleasure, understood to involve body and heart as well as mind. This amatory agenda lays out the course of what will become Shakespearean romantic comedy, its motives undergoing an initial groping exercise in the play's Bianca subplot. Urging a course of learning and living that is "somehow a kind of practice," Tranio urges his master to extend his studies from the classroom to the street and the table: "Balk logic with acquaintance that you have, / And practice rhetoric in your common talk." Although Tranio's language, like Lucentio's, is learned, his motto remains "Let's party." When Lucentio falls in love with Bianca in almost the next instant, we see displayed before us both the appeal and the shallowness of the Ovidian syllabus picked up along with the French disease by young men studying abroad. The interchange between master and man serves to announce virtue as the problem of the play, but also to dramatize a certain limit, both intellectual and experiential, in these first two modes of approaching it.

Tranio and Lucentio are soon sidelined by the arrival of Petruchio, whose brash worldliness and overtly economic calculus displaces this first contest between programs of virtue (ethico-political versus amatory-erotic) with a whole other discourse of virtues, namely, those pertaining to marriage, household, and husbandry. Petruchio belongs more to the world of Gervase Markham than he does to that of Aristotle or Ovid, and the taming motif that accompanies him like a horseman's riding crop draws nutritive and sensitive forms of life into the orbit of virtue, without, however, excluding questions of performance, virtuality, and virtuosity.[21] And this other

21. Natasha Korda notes the parallels between Petruchio and Markham in *Shakespeare's Domestic Economies*, 65.

discourse has preceded him: it is no accident that *The Taming of the Shrew* opens not directly with Lucentio's humanist curriculum, but with that Renaissance course of action and acting known as the hunt, an elaborate biosport accompanied by its own argot, ceremonies, and manuals.[22] The Lord, entering his lodge weary from a day in the forest, tends first to his dogs:

> Huntsman, I charge thee, tender well my hounds.
> Breathe Merriman, the poor cur is embossed,
> And couple Clowder with the deep-mouthed brach.
> Saw'st thou not, boy, how Silver made it good
> At the hedge corner, in the coldest fault?
> I would not lose that dog for twenty pound. (Induction, 1.12–19)

To "tender" the hounds is to *tend them* but also to *attend to* them, to treat them with tenderness, to acknowledge their special identities, to call them by name. The dogs exist for the Lord's use and pleasure: "But sup them well, and look unto them all / Tomorrow I intend to hunt again" (24–25). Yet this economy, though unabashedly serving human interests, requires care for the hunter's nonhuman companions. The dog that is out of breath ("embossed") needs time and space to rest, perhaps in a kennel like the elaborate affair that Markham sketches in *Countrey Contentments*.[23] Berry points out that Clowder may be "coupled" with the "deep-mouthed brach" (mature bitch) because young hounds were often introduced to the hunt through their senior colleagues in the pack, the social order among dogs being a key component of their integration into the economy of human needs and wants.[24] At the end of the play, the beta-bitch Bianca will be coupled with

---

22. See Edward Berry's excellent monograph, *Shakespeare and the Hunt*. The most influential Renaissance handbook for hunters is *The Noble Art of Venerie or Hunting*, by George Gascoigne and George Turberville (1575 and 1611), based on a French guide by Jacques du Fouilloux (London: Thomas Purfoot, 1611). Gervase Markham's *Countrey Contentments* begins with a hunting guide that draws from this same material, linking it to the lesser arts of husbandry.

23. The ideal kennel, Markham advises, should be placed "a pretty distance from your dwelling house, near som river, pond, spring, or fresh water." Eastern exposure "will be a great refreshing and comfort unto the *Hounds*, which love naturally to stretch, trim, and pick themselves in the sunne" (Markham, *Countrey Contentments*, 14–15). Here and elsewhere, Markham's verbal blueprints for an animal architecture manifest an attention to canine habits and creature comforts that, like the Lord's language of concern, extends beyond mere utility or the exercise of mastery, though that surplus functions primarily as a luxury characteristic of aristocratic privilege, an impasse that continues to haunt the largely privileged character of modern environmentalism.

24. Berry, *Shakespeare and the Hunt*, 116.

the alpha-bitch Katharina in order to manage the younger sister's emergent shrewishness.

Virtue is at stake here: the virtues of proper care ("tendering"), virtues that in turn consist in the practical knowledge of the capacities or virtues of the natural world. In *The English Huswife*, Markham treats "the inward and outward Vertues which ought to be in a compleate Woman: as her Phisicke, Cookery, Banqueting-Stuffe, Distillation, Perfumes, Woole, Hempe, Flaxe, Dairies, Brewing, and all other things belonging to an Houshold."[25] The housewife exercises "outward virtues" when she uses her knowledge of the virtues of things to meet the manifold physical demands of the household; thus "gentleness" is a virtue in dairy kine, and Markham expends considerable praise on "the excellency of oats, and the many singular virtues and uses of them in a family."[26] The Friar in *Romeo and Juliet* taps this naturalistic conception of virtue when he avers of his morning collation of baleful weeds: "Many for many virtues excellent, / None but for some, and yet all different" (2.3.13–14). These "virtues excellent," a phrase that doubles the translations of the Greek *arête*, consist in the form that makes each substance itself, giving "plants, herbs, [and] stones" "their true qualities" (2.3.16). Such virtues also bear a relational dimension, dependent on their use in specific situations: in the Friar's pharmaceutical terminology, "Virtue itself turns vice when being misapplied" (2.3.21–22).

Modern ecologists would speak here not of "virtues" but of "affordances." Environmental psychologist James J. Gibson in 1977 first coined the word *affordance* to conceptualize the potentialities of objects, surfaces, and materials in complex natural systems: "The *affordances* of the environment are what it *offers* the animal, what it *provides* or *furnishes*, either for good or ill."[27] Certain plants afford nourishment to some species but are a poison to others, and the ecologist, the apothecary, the husbandman, the housewife, and the hunter must all become students of these diverse potentialities. Such "outward virtue" has a performative dimension, insofar as the practitioner exercises his or her own virtue or practical knowledge by actualizing the virtues of the natural world. Throughout his tracts, Markham speaks of "knowledges" in the plural, in order to indicate the way in which the outward virtues of both husbandry and huswifery bear their fruit close to

---

25. From the title page of *Countrey Contentments*, a double edition that reprinted *The English Huswife* after a volume on husbandry, published in 1615 and reprinted in facsimile.

26. Oats join "virtue and value together"; see Markham, *English Huswife*, ed. Best, 68, 199–203.

27. Gibson, *Ecological Approach to Visual Perception*, 127.

the ground, in and for specific ecologies of habitation and use.[28] The plural knowledges of the husbandman and the housewife are "active," not in the full Arendtian sense of political speech in the public sphere, but in the more local sense of actualizing what is potential in the creaturely world they tend, for human use but in service of those needs and wants that affiliate humans with other creatures. These "outward and active knowledges," that is, are closer to the Aristotle of the *Physics*, concerned with the "virtues" of substances, than to the Aristotle of the *Ethics* and the *Politics*, aiming at the exercise of excellence for its own sake in the public sphere.[29] Or rather, what come forward in these household manuals are the strange assonances, still felt in the ancient and the early modern worlds, that link moral virtue, practical knowledge, and the special capacities of things (animal, vegetable, and mineral) across the divide of their enduring differences.

The Lord's animal discourse shifts abruptly when he encounters the sight of Christopher Sly, drunkenly sprawled on the cold threshold of the lodge:

> Oh monstrous beast, how like a swine he lies.
> Grim death, how foul and loathsome is thine image.
> Sirs, I will practice on this drunken man.
> What think you if he were conveyed to bed . . . (Induction, 1.30–34)

The Lord's mood swings from tender attention to the needs and virtues of his hounds to his marked disgust at a human instance of life reduced to its nutritive minimum, deprived even of sense and movement. The Lord apostrophizes the sleeping Sly as a "monstrous beast" and a "swine," images of animality that translate the gap between man and animal onto the divide between lord and beggar, the latter's life quite a bit "barer"—more exposed to both want and abuse—than that of the Lord's well-kenneled canines.[30] The Lord goes on to describe the jest that follows as a kind of husbandry: "It will be pastime passing excellent, / If it be husbanded with modesty" (Induction, 1.63–4). Here Shakespeare compares directing a play to husbanding an estate, both involving managerial skills and prudential judgment. Meanwhile, the contrast between the tendering of the dogs and the

---

28. The heading to chapter 1 of *The English Huswife* proposes to speak of "her general knowledges of both in physic and surgery" (5). Later in the same text, he refers to "the outward and active knowledges which belong to our English housewife" (60).

29. In the *Physics*, Aristotle declares that "excellence is a perfection," and he refers to "bodily excellences such as health and fitness" (246a). *Arete* can also be translated as "virtue."

30. Berry notes debates about the treatment of dogs versus servants among aristocratic households (*Shakespeare and the Hunt*, 116).

debasement of Sly manifests the troubling link between the more creative biopolitics of canine companionship and the brutality of class warfare, a confluence emblematized by the memory of St. Christopher bearing the head of a dog.[31]

The frame tale has often been compared to the central taming episode of *Shrew*; in a certain line of thinking about the play, Shakespeare uses the parallel between the Lord's duping of Sly and Petruchio's taming of Kate to reveal that both class and gender identities are culturally constructed. Thus Frances Dolan in her comprehensive Bedford edition of the play suggests that "the Induction teaches viewers that characters form their identities by playing roles and that they can switch roles and thus identities and that characters also form their identities in relation to other characters."[32] I agree that performance and metatheater are key to understanding the true scope and depth of the taming motif in the play, but I would caution against lifting that motif too completely from the animal-human interface from which it takes its orientation. Sly, though apostrophized by the Lord as a swinish beast, is tricked, not tamed; once awakened from his man-made dream, he will not continue to play aristocrat. To tame a horse, a dog, or a falcon is to sculpt and fashion the natural capacities of the animal, to bring forward and perfect its special forms of intelligence and sociality for human enjoyment and employment. Although one may teach the dog tricks (to sit, heel, fetch, or hunt; to sniff for bombs, marijuana, or Jews; or to perform acts of oral pleasure), one is not actually *tricking the dog* (Fido really is sitting, heeling, fetching, hunting, or pleasing). These acts are most definitely performances, which involve the intelligence, communication, and cooperation of both tamer and tamed, often in tandem with an entourage or audience; but they are not fictions, in the way that Sly's man-made lordship is a fiction, nor can they properly be called "roles" in the dramatic sense, capable of being donned and cast off at will like a mask.[33]

Just because *The Taming of the Shrew* is a play does not mean that every form of performance described in it is fully theatrical or theatrical in the same way. So too, if there are parallels between Sly and Kate, I would contend that they are ultimately false parallels. Sly, for all his swinishness, is

---

31. Hobgood-Oster, *Holy Dogs and Asses*, 101. My thanks to Drew Daniel for this reference.

32. Dolan, "Introduction," in Shakespeare, *The Taming of the Shrew: Texts and Contexts*, 6.

33. See Donna Haraway on the "behaviors" solicited in the training of dogs: "A behavior is an inventive construction, put together by people, organisms, and apparatus all coming together in the history of animal psychology. Out of the flow of bodies moving in time, bits are carved out and solicited to become more or less frequent as part of building other patterns of motion through time. A behavior is a natural-technical entity" ("Training in the Contact Zone," 448).

human, all too human, capable of the most outrageous duping, a fool and not a knave, while Kate actually does participate, in a way that continues to shock us still, in the world of animals and things and thus exhibits a canniness that may be more truly "sly" than the Christopher who precedes her on stage. In Catholic hagiography, St. Christopher is he who bears the whole world on his shoulders when he ferries the infant Christ across the river. Our Christopher, too, bears the world for an instant during the interim of his phantasmatic induction. Kate may be more like the fox who swims the gingerbread man across the river; we do not know if her cate (cake) of a husband will make it intact to the other side. Both Christopher and Kate are human animals; but the tricking of the one operates at a purely theatrical level, as a passing performance, whereas Kate's transformation remaps her being at a more environmental or ecological level, crafting a new assemblage of properties that link her to embodied networks of attention, response, and technique.

In *Shakespeare and the Hunt*, Edward Berry, using the husbandry literature of Gervase Markham as evidence, lays out one set of political-theological terms that corral the relations between men, women, and animals in *The Taming of the Shrew*,

> As a play about "taming," and especially taming in the context of hunting, the *Shrew* is implicitly about "man's" dominion over nature. The right to tame animals, like the right to hunt them, derives from God's exhortation in Genesis to "subdue" the earth and to "rule over the fish of the sea and over the foule of the heaven, and over everie beast that moveth upon the earth." As Gervase Markham rather smugly notes, in defending the legitimacy of recreational hunting, "a man so good and vertuous as the true *Husband-man* is, should not be deprived of any comfort, or felicity, which the earth, or the creatures of the earth can affoord unto him, being indeed the right Lord and Master (next under God) of them both."[34]

Certainly this normative view of masculine authority governs the official morality of Markham's guides to living, tempered somewhat by his ambition to narrow the gap between husbandman and aristocrat, which does some small violence, akin perhaps to poaching a deer, to the ideology that identified hunting above all with royal prerogative and seigneurial

34. Berry, *Shakespeare and the Hunt*, 97.

right.[35] Yet Berry's account by no means exhausts Markham's appreciation of man-animal dependencies and cohabitations in a God-created cosmos. Thus Markham's description of hunting as the "curious search or conquest of one Beast over another" sets a dramatic scene of creaturely life extended between earthly and heavenly coordinates: "In this recreation [of hunting] is to be seen the wonderfull power of God, in his creatures, and how far rage and pollicie can prevaile against innocence and wisdome."[36] In the hunt, domesticated animals exercise "rage and pollicie" against the "innocence and wisdome" of wild beasts. This scene of orchestrated carnage evinces "the wonderfull power of God" not only by demonstrating the diversity of his creation but also by revealing nature's innate capacity for a violence that is extra-moral, even immoral. The "pollicie" of the beasts who hunt is of course cultivated in them by the men who run them; hunting is a "recreation" (sport, pastime, game) that feeds on and amplifies a natural drama unfolding among God's "creatures." The bio-drama of the hunt involves the human *as animal* in the act of engaging the human *with* the animal, in a scene in which neither party holds a monopoly on either violence or intelligence.

Markham's hunt is a scene of *creaturely life*, a term I use in this book to indicate the way in which the Jewish and Christian traditions of the Middle Ages and Renaissance saw the needs of life as capturing humanity within an animal and indeed vegetable continuum that linked all of existence to both the whims and standards of a sublime Maker. Such life could be "bare" in its radical exposure to the exigencies of sheer want (see Lear adrift in his terrible storm), but such life was also always caught up in narratives of creation and codes of covenant that infused even the most reduced of circumstances with an element of intelligibility, commitment, attention, and purpose.[37] In her study of animal life in Shakespeare, Laurie Shannon counters the dominion mandate of Genesis 1:25–27 with the Bible's sublime encyclopedias of creaturely life; such catalogs, she argues, attribute "rights of sustenance to animals" and imply attitudes of stewardship, care, covenant, and wonder not encompassed by the mandate of *dominium*.[38] Walter Benjamin writes of

---

35. See Berry on the politics and carnival of poaching, as well as Shakespeare's possible involvement in such acts of rioting (ibid., 19–21).

36. Markham, *Countrey Contentments*, 3.

37. On creaturely life, see especially Santner, *Creaturely Life*, and my essay, "Creature Caliban."

38. Shannon, "Eight Animals in Shakespeare," 475. She addresses the same issues at greater length in "Poor, Bare, Forked," 181–85.

the Baroque sovereign, "He is the lord of creatures, but he remains a creature."[39] What is true of the sovereign is also true of the hunter and the husbandman: *dominium* over the natural world not only places humans above animals, but also necessarily submerges them in the metabolisms, drives, and pleasures of the beasts on whose flesh, hides, milk, and labor their lives have come to depend. One figure for this dependency, in *Shrew* and in the period, is the centaur.

Sick Centaurs

The significance of the centaur to the bestiary of *Shrew* was established by Jeanne Addison Roberts in her 1983 essay, "Horses and Hermaphrodites." In the words of Biondello in *Shrew*, "A horse and a man / Is more than one, / And yet not many" (3.2.76–78). The centaur is a classic figure of man's division between the bestial and the rational, often moralized with a view to "taming" or "bridling" animality in order to create a more civil society, a theme beautifully represented by Botticelli for the Medici circle in his painting of a mournful, pacific centaur under the guidance of Minerva, a red bridle laced about his upper form as a sign of her ability to control him.[40]

Whether read as a political allegory or a marriage gift, the painting taps the normative reading of the Centaur as a "symbolum . . . humane vitae," divided between animal and rational souls and requiring domestication for proper civic life.[41] At the same time, the melancholy submission of the male centaur (perhaps a wayward Medici husband) to the severe direction of the armed virago communicates just a whiff of *caponage*. In another life, Athena was a shrew.

Machiavelli took the monstrous body of the centaur up as a figure animated by a caesura in virtue itself, internally divided between moral and extramoral, human and creaturely, domains. In chapter 18 of *Il Principe*, Machiavelli writes,

---

39. Benjamin, *German Tragic Drama*, 85.

40. The painting has been read as an allegory of Chastity overcoming Lust. Whether the female figure is Pallas or Camilla, she is an "armed woman representing Chastity who is clearly associated with the Medici." Randolph refers to her as the "centaur-tamer"; see Randolph, *Engaging Symbols*, 221–24.

41. E. H. Gombrich cites F. Licetus, *Hieroglyphica*, Patavii, 1653: "Quem admodum ergo biformis natura Centauri Sagittarii symbolum est humanae vitae, quae constitutur ex parte rationali superiore, ac irrationali inferiore, tanquam ex voluntate et appetitu, ex intellectu et sensu"; see Gombrich, "Botticelli's Mythologies," 52.

1. Sandro Botticelli, *Minerva and the Centaur* (fifteenth century). Tempera on wood. 207 × 148 cm. Uffizi, Florence, Italy. Photo: Erich Lessing/Art Resource, New York.

There are two ways [*dua generazione*] of fighting: either with laws or with force. The first is peculiar to men, the second to beasts. But because the first often does not suffice, one often has to resort [*conviene*] to the second. Nevertheless, a prince must be expert in using both. This has been taught to princes allegorically, by ancient writers, who tell us that Achilles and many other ancient princes were sent to Chiron the Centaur to be raised and tutored. What this means is that the ancient princes, whose tutor was half man and half beast, learned to use both natures, neither of which can prevail without the other.[42]

Machiavelli reaches back through the Christian and neo-Platonic commonplaces that shape the iconography of the moralized centaur in order to find a hidden figure for the dual nature of the prince and his counselors. Rather than prescribing that one aspect dominate the other, a ratio that would identify the sovereignty of reason with the sovereignty of law, Machiavelli suggests instead a reciprocity and dependency between them [*l'una sanza l'altra non è durabile*]. Reason is not sovereign over passion, nor is law sovereign over force; instead, something like an uneasy commonwealth between divided principles organizes the brute yet canny *virtù* of the new prince.[43] Thus the motif of the centaur swiftly divides again, flowing into Machiavelli's equally infamous yoking of the lion and the fox as the arsenal of force and fraud required by the prince in the Florentine's bestiary.[44] Reason also belongs to the animal kingdom, but it is a practical, on the ground, cunning—the intelligence of the hunting dog, the camouflage artist, and the multitudinous swarm—that distinguishes it from the higher *logos* of the normative Christian-classical synthesis that Machiavelli undoes throughout his treatise. As a civic humanist, Machiavelli emphasizes virtue activated in performance, but he also insists on keeping virtue firmly leashed to its animal resources, its amoral capacities captured and channeled in his handling of the word *virtù*.[45]

42. Machiavelli, *Il Principe*, in *Essential Writings*, 68.
43. Compare Miguel Vatter, who emphasizes "Machiavelli's intuition of the conflictual basis of political life" in *Between Form and Event*, 16.
44. As Victoria Kahn comments, "Machiavelli begins the chapter by distinguishing between human law and bestial force, but he then abandons the first pole of his binary opposition and proceeds to locate the range of political invention and imitation within the second term of force"; see Kahn, *Machiavellian Rhetoric*, 23. In other words, the bestial side of the prince is itself subject to a splitting that mirrors that between man and beast, but within the domain of the animal.
45. Thus Arendt writes of Machiavelli on courage that he was the "only postclassical political theorist who, in an extraordinary effort to restore its old dignity to politics, perceived the

Petruchio's most dramatic tapping of husbandry discourse under the sign of the centaur occurs when he enters Padua on a sick horse:

> Why, Petruchio is coming, in a new hat and old jerkin, a pair of breeches thrice turned; a pair of boots that have been candle-cases, one buckled, another laced: an old rusty sword ta'en out of the town armory, with a broken hilt, and chapeless; with two broken points; his horse hipped, with an old mothy saddle, and stirrups of no kindred, besides, possessed with the glanders and like to mose in the chine, troubled with the lampass, infected with the fashions, full of windgalls, sped with spavins, rayed with the yellows, past cure of the fives, stark spoiled with the staggers, begnawn with the bots, swayed in the back, and shoulder-shotten, near-legged before, and with a half-cheeked bit, and a headstall of sheep's leather, which, being restrained to keep him from stumbling, hath been often burst and now repaired with knots; one girth six times pieced, and a woman's crupper of velure, which hath two letters for her name, fairly set down in studs, and here and there pierced with packthread. (3.2.41–57)

Read with Markham's manuals in hand, the sorry creature appears saddled with a whole heap of the diseases that a horse can pick up if improperly husbanded. Wind-galls ("little blebs or soft swellings on each side of the Fetlocke") are "procured by much travel on hard and stonie wayes."[46] "Hipped," "swayed in the back," and "shoulder-shotten," the beast shows signs of "intemperate riding,"[47] perhaps "ingendred by surfets and unreasonable labour."[48] Some of these diseases reflect the same humoral system that maps human psychology and physiology in the Renaissance; the yellows, for example, comes from the "overflowing of the Gall, which is the vessel of choller," the humor whose excess catches Petruchio and Katherine in their ill-humored duet.[49] Moreover, this catalogue of diseases, likely culled from Markham's first horsemanship book, taps a landscape of natural virtues or affordances that flower just beyond the maladies themselves. Infected with the fashions? Slit those troublesome knots of flesh and then apply an ointment of "fresh grease, and yealow *Arsnicke*," which can later

---

gulf and understood something of the courage needed to cross it." The Condotierri were for Machiavelli those who rose "from privacy to princedom, that is, from circumstances common to all men to the shining glory of great deeds" (*Human Condition*, 35).

46. Markham, *Cheape and Good Husbandry*, 35.
47. Ibid., 17.
48. Ibid., 19.
49. Ibid., 18.

be removed with a mixture of "old pisse and salt boyled together."[50] It is not only physical ailments that plague Petruchio's sick stallion; this bad husbandman has allowed the equipage that networks horse and human to fall into a state of disrepair and over-repair ("one girth six times pieced").[51] A "half-cheeked bit" disturbs communication by distorting the rider's directive tugs; the "head-stall," part of the bridle system, has apparently burst from overuse ("being restrained"). "Equus," Jeanne Addison Roberts reminds us, is linked to "equal"; when the equipment loses its balance, so does the delicate horse-human partnership.

Petruchio's horse staggers and stumbles into Padua from a domestic ecology of outward virtues and active knowledges that knit horse and horseman together, inserting their biform being into a dense ensemble of plant, animal, and mineral dependencies, affordances, and appliances. The centaur is not only an emblem of man's divided being, but a distillation of the merging of man with animal in the communicative phenomenology of riding. If there is a delirious character to Biondello's inventory, it is not only Biondello, but Shakespeare himself who is suddenly "stark spoiled with the staggers," drunk on the curious argot of husbandry and its fantastic pharmacy of brisk and earthy words. Markham, a third-rate poet and a first-rate husbandman, loves the words of his world; *Cheape and Good Husbandrie* begins with an astounding "SHORT TABLE expounding all the hard words *in this booke*," logging the names and virtues of useful plants and minerals, and sometimes producing the most lovely definitions.[52]

Shakespeare taps Markham's world, however, in order to measure Petruchio's imperfect meshing with it; Petruchio presents the figure of a husbandman who has mismanaged his household stuff. Petruchio himself, of course, is engaging in theatrics; we are not meant to believe that he always rides in such low style, but that he is flaunting decorum in order to put Katherine, the wedding party, and the festival script as such on the defensive.[53] Petruchio's wild and mangy entrance is, in its own way, a kind of virtuoso performance, a concerted and deliberate enactment of the stable

50. Ibid., 30.

51. Frances Dolan notes, "Almost all the diseases here are described in Gervase Markham's *How to Choose, Ride, Train and Diet both Hunting Horses and Running Horses . . . Also a Discourse of Horsemanship*, probably first published in 1593"; see Shakespeare, *Taming of the Shrew: Texts and Contexts*, 93n.

52. "*Adraces* or *Adarces* is that Salt which is ingendred on the salt marshes by the violence of the Sunnes heat after the tide is gone away" (Markham, *Cheape and Good Husbandry*, frontmatter).

53. LaRue Love Sloan suggests that Petruchio stages his entrance as a village Skimmington, in which hen-pecked husbands were made to ride backwards on their overbearing wives, humiliating both members of the marriage; see Sloan, "'Caparisoned like the Horse.'"

of virtues associated with husbandry, actualizing the defects rather than the excellences of the animal husband in all of his piss and vinegar splendor. Petruchio's devolution from "bridegroom" to mere "groom" (3.2.146) measures the extent to which the animal husbandman himself has become animal, tumbling down the ladder of estates and beginning to merge with the beasts he tends. Entering the wedding scene as a sick centaur, Petruchio's send-up of husbandry (and of his own capacities as a husband) is above all great comedy. His self-staging does not make Petruchio a nicer guy; indeed, this particular bio-pageant depends on the physical neglect of his horse. (The abuse, however, occurs off stage; "no animals were harmed" in producing this play.[54]) It does have the effect, however, of qualifying any easy identification of rationality, masculinity, sovereignty, and the human over against an animal planet populated by beasts, women, and things.

Petruchio's most famous taming speech begins under the sign of the political:

Thus have I politicly begun my reign,
And 'tis my hope to end successfully.
My falcon now is sharp and passing empty.
And till she stoop, she must not be full-gorged,
For then she never looks upon her lure.
Another way I have to man my haggard,
To make her come, and know her keeper's call,
That is, to watch her, as we watch these kites
That bate and beat and will not be obedient.
She eat no meat to-day, nor none shall eat.
Last night she slept not, nor to-night she shall not.
As with the meat, some undeserved fault
I'll find about the making of the bed,
And here I'll fling the pillow, there the bolster,
This way the coverlet, another way the sheets.
Ay, and amid this hurly I intend,
That all is done in reverent care of her,
And in conclusion, she shall watch all night;
And if she chance to nod, I'll rail and brawl,
And with the clamor keep her still awake.
This is a way to kill a wife with kindness,

---

54. The same was not true of the bear-baiting that occurred nearby. See Steven Dickey, "Shakespeare's Mastiff Comedy."

And thus I'll curb her mad and headstrong humor.

He that knows better how to tame a shrew,

Now let him speak. 'Tis charity to show. (4.1.168–91)

As many critics have demonstrated in depth, Petruchio draws in his "poli-tic" speech primarily on falconry, not horsemanship.[55] Edward Berry has masterfully mapped the three stages of falcon taming—"manning" (accus-toming the bird to her human handler), training to the lure (sending the bird out on a line), and finally, "the test of unrestricted flight," in which the falcon is allowed to follow her prey and return to her master—onto the progress of the play.[56] We might sense the proximity of biopower in the yok-ing of this animal discourse to the word *politicly*, which activates the region shared by the "policie" of Markham's hounds, the "politics" of Machiavel-li's centaur, and the politics of the household state. Petruchio announces his sovereign mastery (his "reign") over Kate, and in this sense his policy is authoritarian in the most coercive vein possible; the crudest reading of the speech would line up man, sovereign, and human over against woman, subject, and animal.

Biopower, however, does not simply oppose man to animal, but forces animal life into the very field founded on its exclusion. In being tamed "like" a falcon, Kate is also literally tamed, her animal being made to appear in the human world as both what is other than politics and what becomes politics' object. The taming motif is more than a metaphor, since the status of crea-turely life as such—as both obstacle and resource for a properly "human" conception of both marriage and state—is at stake. As Nichole Miller has argued, Petruchio's taming program is biopolitical insofar as the techniques of privation and surveillance initiated here suture sovereignty directly onto the needs of life. And it is biopolitical in a manner distinct from source texts and analogues like "A Merry Jeste," the ballad that parallels the taming plot in many key ways.[57] In "A Merry Jeste," the husband slaughters and flays his old horse Morrel, whips his wife until she bleeds, salts the hide, and then binds her in it and throws her in the "seller," part pantry, part prison, until she promises obedience. Petruchio, on the other hand, deprives Kate of sex,

55. On falconry in *Shrew*, see especially Ranald, "'As Marriage Binds, and Blood Breaks'"; Berry, *Shakespeare and the Hunt*; and Benson, "'If I do prove her haggard.'"

56. Berry, *Shakespeare and the Hunt*, 101–9.

57. In both works, there are two sisters; in both, the shrew is tamed by her new husband and then displays her obedience before her assembled family at a final feast. The "Merry Jeste" is reprinted by Dympna Callaghan, 106–19, and by Frances Dolan, 24–87, in their editions of the play.

food, and sleep, and eventually of fine clothing and of rational conversation, but he does not physically mar or mutilate her. Whereas the Joan of the "Jeste" is physically merged with the carcass of the horse in a kind of grotesque, literalized metamorphosis, Petruchio's falcon imagery literally soars; as Edward Berry notes, "The whole point of taming a falcon is not to break its spirit but to attract, focus, and control its wild energy."[58] The systematic deprivations are designed not simply to break, constrain, or reduce Kate, but to bring out new behaviors and capacities, to solicit new forms of affiliation between her animal being and a civil society brought into focus through the manifestation of these forms of relation.

The "modernity" of Petruchio's taming techniques does not consist simply in an amelioration of cruelty, indicative, say, of a new humanist decorum that moderates medieval extremes. Petruchio's methods are different *in kind* as well as *degree*, closer to both Abu Ghraib and basic training than to the iron maiden, and depending on a certain isolation and humiliation, but also a cultivation and refinement, of animal life within the woman.[59] Petruchio's farmhouse outside the city is a retraining or reeducation camp, enclosing a kind of violent biopolitical pastoral.[60] If the normative function of the *oikos* or household is to satisfy the needs of life, and thus to keep bare life at bay and out of sight, Petruchio's taming turns the functions of the *oikos* inside out by refusing to meet the needs of life and thus forcing life as such to lurch into view.[61] Vitality comes forward—like a falcon to its trainer—as the result of Petruchio's systematic privations, each of which involves both real and symbolic dimensions, linguistic as well as physical manipulations of affect and expectation. It is a schooling based on shame, not pain, and on exposure to need rather than bodily mutilation, sealing Petruchio's sovereignty as a power funded by and founded on the energy of a vitality that it masters through *exposure*: both exposure to the humiliating exigencies of bodily need and exposure to the public eye. Shame flushes the needs of life out into the open, making them appear as such, like hares driven from the bushes by village beaters in preparation for the aristocratic hunt.

58. Berry, *Shakespeare and the Hunt*, 105.

59. Roberto Esposito might speak here of taming as a form of immunization, in which privation is used not only to control life, but also to strengthen it: "*Immunitas* is revealed as the negative or lacking [*privativa*] form of *communitas*" (*Bíos*, 50).

60. On camp architecture and the biopolitical pastoral, see Hailey, *Camps*.

61. See Miller, "Sexual Politics of Pain," for an exemplary reading of the significance of bare life for this play.

Shame, of course, belongs to the primitive world of rural ritual. The public shaming of Kate at her wedding in Padua resembles the village rites of skimmington, cucking, and charivari that continue to link Shakespeare's play to archaic forms of disciplining the scold, as demonstrated by Lynda Boose and Gary Schneider.[62] The play does not simply substitute the diversity of modern Italian urban life for the homogeneity of the English village; rather, centaurlike, it embodies and incorporates that split into its own dramatic texture and generic experiment. The play shuffles topoi from humanist education like so many souvenirs from the European tour while drawing on native archetypes of wedding ritual, holiday, and public shaming. Might we indeed say that just as the falconer needs his falcon, so too, the urban dramatist needs his village festivals? Shakespeare does not suppress, neutralize, or destroy festive culture, any more than Petruchio destroys the animal in Kate. Rather, the dramatist *tames* it: he harnesses the bio-anthropological energies of ritual performance for modern theater; he teaches it new tricks; he makes it soar in the sky and return to his hand, carrying messages from the living and the dead.

Biopolitics here is a double-edged discourse (or, like the spur and the riding crop, both an instrument of pain and a communication device). On the one hand, biopolitics names, sequesters, and diagnoses all that is abhorrent in the modern politics of internment, concentration, military rape, and ethnic cleansing, as well as the economics of child labor, sex slavery, and industrial farming that have accompanied globalization with the dogged fidelity of a German shepherd following his police handler. The biopolitical critique, as mounted for example by Agamben and Esposito, brings into focus just what makes *Shrew* such a disturbing and compelling play, not as a document of gender relationships past, but as a diagnosis of all that is unwell in states present and future. Yet these writers also hint at positive biopolitical constitutions, a *bio-politeia* that would integrate diverse forms of life in less coercive and destructive scenes of action and interaction. Agamben uses the hyphenated phrase "form-of-life" to imagine such an integration: "By the term *form-of-life* . . . I mean a life that can never be separated from its form, a life in which it is never possible to isolate something such as naked life."[63] Actualizing Aristotelian virtue discourses, *The Taming of the Shrew*, I have been suggesting, allows us to think with Shakespeare about both the negative and the positive faces of biopower. If the tactics of

62. Boose, "Scolding Brides and Bridling Scolds"; and Gary Schneider, "The Public, the Private, and the Shaming of the Shrew."
63. Agamben, "Form-of-Life," 151.

quarantine and brainwash affiliate Petruchio with the politics of the camp, animal husbandry suggests other forms of engagement with creaturely life. It is not that Petruchio does not declare his sovereignty, but that in proclaiming it through the language of husbandry, he renders his own power at least partially contingent on the self-organizing complexity of the creaturely world. Thus "policy" implies a form of reason that does not separate man from animals so much as connect them, not only because they share certain forms of intelligence (the sociality of the pack, the cunning of the predator, the escape art of the prey), but because it is precisely those forms of intelligence that are "tamed," rendered into "policie," by the horseman, the falconer, and the husbandman, who must develop his own cunning in response to theirs. The husband is cruel in order to be kind (using techniques of privation to render the shrew manageable and marriageable). The husbandman is kind in order to be cruel (becoming animal in order to domesticate his fellows for the yoke and the table). As both husband and husbandman, Petruchio juggles these two distinct biopolitical ratios, finding his sovereignty at their crux.

When Petruchio speaks of curbing Kate's "mad and headstrong humour," he describes his own temperament as well as Katherine's.[64] Later he will restrict both their diets based on their shared humors. Burnt meat, he declares,

> engenders choler, planteth anger,
> And better 'twere that both of us did fast,
> Since of ourselves, ourselves are choleric,
> Than feed it with such overroasted flesh:
> Be patient, tomorrow 't shall be mended,
> And for this night we'll fast for company. (4.1.152–57)

It is a marriage not just of true minds, but of true humors, their bodily dispositions binding them together in an economy of choler that places man and wife not only in the "company" of each other, but in the circuit of creaturely life as such, as beautifully demonstrated by Gail Kern Paster for Shakespearean drama more broadly.[65] In Markham's world, rabbits are "melancholie in their natures," and the "Night-Mares" that really do plague

---

64. On humors and *Shrew*, see the classic study by Draper, *Humors and Shakespeare's Characters*, 52.

65. Paster writes, "Emotions were also shared by humans and animals, thanks to their common possession of a sensitive soul." See Paster, "Melancholy Cats," 111, 115, 129.

some horses as they sleep stem from "cold, flegmaticke humors, ingendered about the Braine."[66] If the lord of creatures remains a creature, the animal husband remains an animal. The wedding fast marks the choleric commonality shared by husband and wife with the very flesh they abstain from eating.

What Markham calls the "ordering" and "governance" of cattle, chickens, rabbits, and other domestic beasts requires the husbandman to attend to each species' habits of feeding, sleeping, and breeding, its humoral constitution, and its special forms of intelligence and sociability, all within a seasonal calendar measured by the ancient feasts of Michaelmas in the fall and Candelmas in the spring.[67] To learn to "order" one's chickens is not (as in industrial farming) to destroy their emergent relationships, but to discover the forms of autopoeisis that exist within their world and to adapt those patterns for human purposes, adding technical innovations (such as the castration of the capon, or the architecture of the connie house) in order to bind animal to animal as well as man to animal in new ways. The more concerted and artful "taming" of domestic animals for demanding acts of service like the hunt does not, in Markham's books, primarily involve violence, but verbal and physical forms of communication. The horseman communicates through body as well as voice; Markham tells the trainer to use "changes in the calves of your legs" as well as the "secret pleasing and cherishing of a horse with the bridle," forms of communication that occur "with such an unperceived motion, that none but the beast may know it."[68] In Markham's account, horse and rider share an extraordinary intimacy; not only their backs and butts but their very beings are bound together, centaurlike, by the prostheses, ligatures, and communication devices of spur, bridle, saddle, rod, and shoe.

In *Shrew*, we might look here to the kinds of verbal cues given by Petruchio to Katherine that measure their journey back to Padua. Language is his bridle, his spur, and his rod, a means of ordering her actions not through reasoning or discussion but through a form of prompting—massage more than message—that serves above all to indicate directionality as such. He urges her forward as he would urge a horse: "Come on, i' God's name, once more toward our father's" (4.5.1). Although she is exasperated by his coercive game, some critics at least have detected a certain pleasure here as well,

66. Markham, *Cheape and Good Husbandry*, 99, 31.

67. On Michaelmas and Candlemas in traditional English culture and the Reformation, see Duffy, *Stripping of the Altars*, 15–22.

68. Markham, *Country Contentments*, 45, 46.

especially in her exuberant apostrophe to old man Vincentio as "Young budding virgin, fair, and fresh, and sweet" (4.5.37). Perhaps animal husband and animal wife have come to share the "secret pleasing and cherishing" that Markham senses between horseman and horse. Their more orderly ride corrects the miry and bemoiled mess of their journey to the homestead (4.1.62–63), implying better horsemanship as well as improved husbandry. Petruchio's verbal techniques in this scene keep Kate firmly within the stable of animal virtues—taming rules the play from beginning to end—but it is a taming that has begun to keep just a little time with the gentler measures of husbandry. We owe it to Shakespeare to learn how to listen to a range of tempos.

Petruchio's animal husbandry makes the creaturely outlines of the human condition come forward as such, reminding us that Petruchio's mastery is only provisional, that his techniques embed him in the world he aims to control, and that the animal in Kate is here to stay, in all its candor and canniness. Meanwhile, Petruchio's "politic reign," intersecting with Machiavelli's cultivation of the centaur's ambiguous *virtù*, manifests the negative features of biopower: the bad pastoral of encampment, detention, and quarantine that transforms the needs of life into weapons of humiliation, brainwashing, and the disassembly of personhood. At the same time, their choleric commonalities, secret cherishings, and the forms of autopoeisis they imply begin to suggest the extent to which an affirmative biopolitics might find some fodder in early modern husbandry's mobile network of persons, animals, and things. In *Shrew*'s georgic sojournings, Shakespeare tests the full expressive bandwidth of biopolitical technique, from torture to tendering, implying not only their constitutive coimplication, but also the possibility of redistributing their kindnesses and their cruelties.

Things Are Creatures, Too

Objects have been at least as prominent as animals in recent criticism of *Shrew*, as evidenced by two truly shelf-clearing efforts, Lena Orlin's "The Performance of Things in *The Taming of the Shrew*" and Natasha Korda's *Shakespeare's Domestic Economies*. Orlin demonstrates the extent to which the play "is cluttered with references to and displays of objects, and especially household furnishings," while Korda brilliantly follows the path of commodities in the play, including Petruchio's aim to "tame" Kate by attempting to render her "conformable as other household Kates."[69] Whereas

---

69. Orlin, "Performance of Things," 167; Korda, *Shakespeare's Domestic Economies*, 58–61.

animal analysts tend to closet the role of things in the drama in favor of its pastoral vistas, commodity critics tend to assimilate animals to the world of objects: thus Orlin analyzes the Lord's dogs as bearers of value, and Korda associates Kate's "wildness" not with animal life but with the unruliness of the commodity.[70] Where can we look for paradigms that can help us think animal and thing together, not as twinned forms of reification that together serve to dehumanize and subjugate the wife, but as more active and integrated contributors to a life world constituted by variable relations among animals, humans, and artifacts?

Let's recall the emergence of affordance theory from the field of ecology. James J. Gibson coined the term *affordance* to describe the forms of potentiality—what I have called, following Aristotle, the virtues—that reside in different features of any given environment, thus supporting or constraining various forms of life as well as nonlife; wood, for example, affords "burning," which resembles life in its energy, and works on biological life, but is not itself organic. For Gibson, responding to affordances is a "process of perceiving a value-rich ecological object."[71] Although affordance theory took shape in the study of environments, it gained momentum in design research when psychologist and engineer Don Norman repurposed the word *affordance* in order to describe "the perceived and actual properties of the thing, primarily those fundamental properties that determine just how the thing could possibly be used."[72] The ecological origins of the term should call us back to an environmental view of the object world—"environmental" not only in our contemporary sense of stewarding resources, but also in the sense of engaging interconnected networks of meanings and uses by multiple constituencies. Thus Jane Bennett has argued for a "political ecology of things" that maps human and nonhuman interaction from the view of the worm and the sardine can.[73] Affordance theory sketches scenarios in which things and animals share properties through both routine use and creative repurposing.[74] I am suggesting that the Renaissance discourse of

70. Orlin writes, "Things construct a system of value . . . the possessions of the Lord that we first encounter are his hounds" ("Performance of Things," 174). Korda writes, "'cates' may themselves be 'wild'; . . . there is something unruly, something that must be made to conform, in the commodity form itself" (*Shakespeare's Domestic Economies*, 60).

71. Gibson, *Visual Perception*, 140.

72. Donald Norman, *Design of Everyday Things*, 9. For an account of the relevance of affordance theory to the humanistic study of objects, see Julka Almquist and Julia Lupton, "Affording Meaning: Design-Oriented Research from the Humanities and Social Sciences."

73. Bennett, *Vibrant Matter*.

74. Bonnie Nardi and Vicki O'Day develop the ecology metaphor, which, they argue, combines the holistic frame of systems analysis with an attention to locality, diversity, and change.

husbandry, with its intensive attention to household things in their artifactual as well as their animal, vegetable, and mineral virtues, offers an early instantiation of these later accounts of affordances.

Take, for example, the great word fight of Katherine and Petruchio's first encounter:

PETRUCHIO: Myself am moved to woo thee for my wife.
KATE: Moved? In good time. Let him that moved thee hither
    Remove thee hence. I knew you at the first
    You were a movable.
PETRUCHIO: Why, what's a movable?
KATE: A joint-stool.
PETRUCHIO: Thou hast hit it. Come, sit on me.
KATE: Asses are made to bear, and so are you.
PETRUCHIO: Women are made to bear, and so are you.
KATE: No such jade as you, if me you mean. (2.1.192–99)

Kate calls Petruchio "a movable" (a piece of furniture, or *mueble*), which she then specifies as a "joint-stool," the lowest form of seating in medieval and Renaissance houses. Denying him the dignity of a chair, reserved for great lords, she reduces him to an object designed to bear the rump of anyone in the house, and to be moved about at will for the frequent rezonings of shared space that characterized the minimalist choreography of Renaissance furnishing.[75] Joint-stools afford sitting; they also afford rapid transport from one space to another; and they can, under certain circumstances, afford hurling. In the verbal hurling that follows, the joint stool rapidly metamorphoses into a beast of burden—first an ass, and then a jade. What lubricates these shape changes are two affordances shared by stools, mules, and horses: the ability to bear a human butt, coupled with some connection to locomotion or transport. In their bawdy repurposings, both man and woman are caught up in this world of animals and things; in a dour mood, we could call it reification, were it not that their exchange grants so much

---

Nardi and O'Day critique Norman Holland's "tool" model of affordances for limiting the scope of human participation in technological adoption and adaption, and they propose ecology as a more capacious metaphor that "stimulates conversations for action." See Nardi and O'Day, *Information Ecologies*, 28–30, 50–51.

75. On joint stools in Shakespeare, see Korda, *Shakespeare's Domestic Economies*, 197–200. On the migration of furniture (*muebles, mobilia*) between estates for aristocrats and within public rooms in bourgeois homes, see Rybczynsi, *Home*, 26–27. On the ubiquity of stools and the paucity of chairs in the Middle Ages and Renaissance, see Florence de Dampierre, *Chairs: A History* (New York: Abrams, 2006), 52.

motion and connectivity to objects that the charge is in danger of losing its bite.

One of the most notorious couplings of woman with both animals and things occurs in Petruchio's recitation of the Tenth Commandment at the end of the wedding scene:

> I will be master of what is mine own.
> She is my goods, my chattels. She is my house,
> My household stuff, my field, my barn,
> My horse, my ox, my ass, my anything. (3.2.221–23)

Here "chattels" encompasses both domestic animals and moveable property, a collection restated in the phrase "household stuff" that has become something of an emblem for the reification of women in the play's domestic economy.[76] Yet the biblical prooftext, along with the husbandry discourse with which it is here so promiscuously mated, presumes a more teeming view of createdness that collects things, beasts, and persons in its cosmic environs. The Tenth Commandment's household catalogue, "Thou shalt not covet thy neighbours house, nether shalt thou covet thy neighbours wife, nor his man servant, nor his maid, nor his oxe, nor his asse, nether any thing that is thy neighbours" (Ex 20:18), echoes the intensive reach of the Fourth Commandment,

> But the seventh daie is the Sabbath of the Lord thy God; in it thou shalt not
> do anie worke, thou, nor thy sone, nor thy daughter, nor thy man servant, nor
> thy maid, nor thy beast, nor thy stranger that is within thy gates. For in six
> daies the Lord made the heaven and the earth, the sea, and all that in them is,
> and rested the seventh daie: therefore the Lord blessed the Sabbath daie, and
> hallowed it. (Ex. 20:10–11)

Because God is the God of Creation, Sabbath rest is granted to the cattle as well as to all who dwell or labor inside the household. Thus Agamben speaks of "the *Shabbat* of man in Kojève" as an example of the inoperative,

---

76. Orlin comments that Petruchio incorporates Katherine "into the comprehensive catalogue of domestic objects that constitute his little kingdom," and she cites Coppélia Kahn: "'His role as property owner is the model for his role as husband; Kate, for him, is a thing'" (Orlin, "Performance of Things," 179). Similarly, Korda argues that the list transforms Kate "from an object of exchange into the home-grown materiality of mere stuff, into a thing defined by its sheer utility, a beast of burden ('my horse, my ox, my ass')"; see Korda, *Shakespeare's Domestic Economies*, 65.

the Sabbath being observed precisely by not working.[77] The Tenth Commandment's reduction of persons to property should be read against the Fourth Commandment's extension of rights to strangers, servants, and animals. The patriarchal intentions of Petruchio's declaration are undeniable. We just might, however, be able to limit the negative impact of the Tenth Commandment by referring it back to the Sabbatarian *bio-politeia* of the Fourth, in order to convene a gathering of persons, animals, and things more emancipatory than that afforded by garden-variety patriarchy alone. If the two tablets were first written on stone, their almost immediate shattering predicts their iterative reinscription, their *deutero nomos*, in response to new arrangements of politics and life.[78] The Decalogue offers a primal scene of latency, a discourse *on virtue* whose *own virtues* (of adaptability and inclusiveness, for example) remain potential in relation to the often sorry history of their actualizations.[79] Each reader must decide whether such efforts at hermeneutic repair are appropriate or exorbitant, a decision that will likely reflect the layout of her own commitments to literature, scripture, feminism, and creaturely life. Here it is not to Shakespeare that we owe an extra channel of attentiveness (his intentions are clear enough), but rather to the ensemble of our own fidelities.

Almost equally notorious is Gremio's household inventory, which the rich old man offers in frank exchange for the hand of fair Bianca:

First, as you know, my house within the city
Is richly furnishèd with plate and gold,
Basins and ewers to lave her dainty hands;
My hangings all of Tyrian tapestry;
In ivory coffers I have stuffed my crowns;
In cypress chests my arras counterpoints,
Costly apparel, tents, and canopies,
Fine linen, Turkey cushions bossed with pearl,
Valance of Venice gold in needlework,
Pewter and brass, and all things that belongs
To house or housekeeping. Then at my farm
I have a hundred milch kine to the pail,

77. Agamben, "Work of Man," 6.
78. *Deuteronomy*, meaning "second law," translates the Hebrew *devarim*, which simply means "words" and refers to Moses' retelling of Exodus, including the Decalogue, which makes up the bulk of the fifth book of the Torah.
79. On latency as a juridical, psychic, and dramatic principle, see Haverkamp, *Shakespearean Genealogies of Power*.

Six score fat oxen standing in my stalls,
And all things answerable to this portion. (2.1.338–51)

Korda emphasizes the urban character of Gremio's possessions and rightly calls attention to the play's contrast between Petruchio's frugal farmstead and Gremio's palazzo in Padua. Yet Gremio goes on to parade his country holdings as well, consisting primarily of livestock. "All things that belongs / To house or housekeeping" ends the sequence of objects, but the phrase also borders on Gremio's cattle, which require their own forms of "keeping" or curation. Indeed, Gremio is a type of the curator, the collector and keeper of goods. As we will see in later chapters, the curator and the tutor were two aspects of the office of guardian in Roman law. The curator was responsible for the estate and physical well-being of his ward, while the tutor was in charge of education. Gremio, unlike his rival Hortensio, outsources tutoring duties to his delegate (Lucentio disguised as Cambio), as if to dramatize the juridical split between the curation of life and education for citizenship.

While Gremio's objects seem to us like "superfluous expenditure," "imported luxuries" designed to provoke competition in the marketplace of status, we might also want to consider their disposition in Renaissance domestic spaces in a more magnanimous manner.[80] What happens, for example, if we place Gremio's "cypress chests" stuffed with "arras counterpoints" next to the elaborate *cassoni*, or wedding chests, produced in Quattrocento Florence, on whose boxed surfaces and raised backs (*spalliere*) so many early mythological images first appeared? As Malcolm Bull comments, "It was probably easier to kick a mythology than to see one, for the most likely place to find representations of scenes from classical myth was not at or above eye-level, but just above the floor, on the front of a *cassone*."[81] Although the *cassoni* were destined for the marriage chamber of the new couple, they played an important role in the wedding celebration itself; they were carried in the bridal procession that wound through the city streets from the paternal house of the bride to the abode of her new husband. The orchestrated yet riotous movement of persons, costumes, horses, and props remapped the streets of the city. Even peasant weddings activated abduction motifs: the groom is a bandit "raping" his bride and carrying her person and her profits off to his lair.[82] In any case, "scenes of rape and abduction

---

80. Korda, *Shakespeare's Domestic Economies*, 63.
81. Bull, *Mirror of the Gods*, 37.
82. Witthoft, "Marriage Rituals and Marriage Chests."

had long featured on the fronts of *cassoni*"; carried through the streets in a ritual enactment of *raptus*, the chests often displayed similar stories on their sides.[83]

Stuffed with luxury goods along the order of Gremio's shopping list, the *cassoni* passed through the streets with their lids closed, in order *not* to display the wealth within, in accordance with sumptuary laws that forbade the kinds of overexpenditure that weaken neighborhoods, economies, and 401K accounts. The *cassoni* were at once prominent symbols of status in a commercial urban economy and storage units designed to shelter and curate, preserve and protect. They hold, withhold, reserve, but they also open, pour forth, manifest, and they performed these virtues of closure and disclosure both *in situ* in the marriage chamber and *en route* through the streets of the city. The *cassoni* put *reserve on display*; so, too, the interiors of the chests often contained intimate, even erotic pictures, to be seen only by the bride and groom.[84] *Shrew* is scattered with allusions to the kinds of mythological stories that found their way onto *cassoni* and other marriage articles in Renaissance Italy, including icons of wifely virtue such as "Grissel / And Roman Lucrece" (2.1 287–88), erotic images of Venus (Induction, 2.47–51), elegiac and pastoral themes such as Daphne and Apollo (Induction, 2.55–58), and wedding scenes both orderly and riotous.[85] Shakespeare likely knew nothing of painted *cassoni*, which belong largely to Quattrocento Florence and Siena. By 1550, Vasari already found them old-fashioned.[86] Yet chests of all sorts played a role in marriage rituals throughout premodern Europe, and Shakespeare was by no means immune to their dramatic and symbolic resources.[87] In England, mythological stories were more likely to appear on painted arrases and embroidered seating cushions—that is, on the kinds of

83. Fermor, *Piero di Cosimo*, 59.

84. Witthoft, "Marriage Rituals and Marriage Chests," 52.

85. Botticelli's Lucretia sequence was originally designed for a *cassone*, as was his *Venus, Mars, and Cupid*; the *Primavera* was likely a *spalliera* for a *lettucio*, or daybed; see Dempsey, *The Portrayal of Love*, 20–24. Daphne and Apollo appear on wood panels of *cassone*-like proportion in paintings by the "Master of the Apollo and Daphne Legend," his very anonymity suggesting the workshop quality of his panels (David and Alfred Smart Museum of Art, University of Chicago, Chicago).

86. The *cassoni* entered English consciousness in the nineteenth century, thanks to an art dealer named William Blundell Spence (1814–1900) who busied himself with Florentine primitives through a gallery in Florence. American collectors of *cassoni* panels included Thomas Jefferson; see Callmann, "William Blundell Spence." Vasari describes (and to a certain extent disparages) *cassone* painting in "The Life of Dello," in *Stories of the Italian Artists from Vasari*, 37–38.

87. Witthoft, "Marriage Rituals and Marriage Chests," 43.

textiles housed *inside* Gremio's chest.[88] Gremio's collection of household goods, caught between the play's Italian setting and its English performance space, invites our own creative curation of objects culled from several worlds.

Piero di Cosimo's *spalliera* painting of the battle between the Lapiths and the Centaurs sits close to the mythic world of *Shrew*.[89] A wedding picnic is thrown into chaos by disorderly centaurs who drag animal life into the scene of civility. Jeanne Addison Roberts compares Petruchio's mad appearance on his neglected horse to the same narrative tapped by Cosimo: "Petruchio has come, not like a proper bridegroom, but like a parody of the centaur at the wedding feast."[90] Echoes of the mythic narrative of rape and adduction are close to the surface in *Taming of the Shrew*, where Petruchio forcibly removes his new bride from the wedding scene with the help of his entourage, skipping the banquet and pretending to defend himself against her family members. He tells his man Grumio, "Draw forth thy weapon, we are beset with thieves. / Rescue thy mistress if thou be a man" (3.2.227–28). Katherine's father, of course, does nothing to stop him. "Nay, let them go," he says, expressing his relief in being rid of a problem daughter, while enunciating the ritual pattern of marriage as rape and abduction. Traditionally, the father did *not* accompany his daughter in the marriage procession, since she had, symbolically speaking, been forcibly snatched from him. In *Shrew*, Shakespeare tames the customary scripts of ritual in order to bring forward their psychological dimensions without denying or dissolving their basis in traditional rites of passage.

The *cassoni* belong only imperfectly to Shakespeare—we must import them into his plays through the devious alleys of innuendo and association. Yet the Padua of *Shrew*, as several recent critics have pointed out, maps the same fluid urban space occupied by the *cassoni*, a space in which art and craft, commodity and fetish, thing and representation, mix, mingle, and perform their virtues, generating new forms of objecthood, personhood, and signification. The not-so-secret life of marriage chests in *Shrew*, encasing in their silent depths whole worlds of ritualized space and time, not to

---

88. For a sampling, see Levey, *Hardwick Hall Textiles*.

89. Dated between 1500 and 1515, the subject matter of Cosimo's *spalliera* bears a striking resemblance to Alberti's formula for an effective *istoria* or narrative painting: "It would be absurd for one who paints the Centaurs fighting after the banquet to leave a vase of wine still standing in such tumult"; see Alberti, *Of Painting*, 75.

90. Roberts, "Metamorphoses," 165. Sharon Fermor analyzes the painting in *Piero di Cosimo*, 54–56.

2. Piero di Cosimo, *Battle between the Lapiths and the Centaurs* (ca. 1500–1515). Oil on wood. 71 × 260 cm. Bequeathed by Charles Haslewood Shannon (1937) (NPG4890). Photograph © The National Gallery, London.

say gloves, arrases, handkerchiefs, and other assorted Shakespearean laundry—demonstrates how an ecology of affordances presents new handles for understanding the dependencies among things, persons, and environments, in both designs from the past and designs for the future. The Renaissance thing-world invites not only an integrative mode of inquiry toward human artifacts and their users but also an attitude of concern, care, and engagement—let's go ahead and call it housekeeping—in response to the interlocking habitats of persons, animals, objects, rituals, and resources that surround and sustain us still.

What we glimpse in Gremio's apparently static inventory is the extraordinary and unexpected mobility of objects as elements of interior décor in spaces that existed not simply to display status, but to perform multitracked biographical and biological libretti. Perhaps his collection of "basins and ewers" cupped images of women giving birth, like the extraordinary birth trays and birth bowls of Renaissance Italy.[91] Just as "things" must be conceived not as disarticulated entities but as dynamic elements in an environment composed of both meanings and affordances, so too, "housekeeping" should be taken up in its full verbal sense, as a curatorial and indeed directorial relationship to the built environments of both house and homestead, from joint stool to milch kine. In the stitched, enameled, and painted world of Renaissance furnishings, stories were not just for books, images were not just for walls, and on the boxed and rounded surfaces of Renaissance *objets d'art*, humans make room for beasts.[92]

---

91. Musacchio, *Art and Ritual of Childbirth in Renaissance Italy*. Orlin speaks of objects in *Shrew* as "ritual adjuncts" and refers specifically to hand-washing ("Performance of Things," 176).

92. Speaking of Renaissance painting, Laurie Shannon writes, "Hardly an urban, rural, or domestic scene was painted without [animals]"; see "Eight Animals in Shakespeare," 472.

The Animal Housewife

Enough about husbands. This is a play ultimately about the fate of wives. The play's interpretation turns on how one reads (or performs, or reads Katherine as *performing*) Kate's final speech.[93] Do we read it "straight," as the sign of her complete submission to the authoritarian ideology of marriage impressed upon her by Petruchio's program of deprivations? Do we read the speech ironically, so that her sarcastic parroting empties out the truisms of tradition even as she mouths them? Or does the truth hibernate somewhere in between, with Katherine "Sly" learning to voice patriarchal commonplaces in order to survive in a world run by men, but retaining some margin for maneuver within the rules of the game? Not surprisingly, this middle ground has proved the most productive and most convincing in recent readings of the play; Edward Berry in particular has crafted a satisfying rendition of this argument that marries well with a biopolitical account of the play. Arguing against "liberal" readings of the play that decide the drama in favor of mutuality, he insists that the taming metaphor

> actually enables us to imagine the very Katherine who appears in productions and critical essays of the romantic kind. She is not brutalized in body or cowed in spirit. She is vibrant, alert, so ready for competition that she performs far beyond the expectations of her master or the demands of the occasion. She carries with her a sense of play, as if in following orders she herself is achieving the fulfillment of her own desires, as if her very freedom were to be found in obedience itself.[94]

The tamed falcon takes pleasure in flight, the very symbol of freedom becoming the sign of her submission. Accordingly, Katherine's final speech is like the free flight of the falcon, in which she takes up the topoi of masculinist authority all on her own, executing the rhetoric of patriarchy with flawless skill. She delivers a miniature book of virtues for the new wife—"love, fair looks, and true obedience" (5.2.157)—that transmits the most normative version of the *dominium* paradigm: "Thy husband is thy lord, thy life, thy keeper, / Thy head, thy sovereign" (5.2.150–51). If on their walk into the city, she had learned to respond to her trainer's coded promptings, now she is able to reproduce the script with no cues at all. This makes her not less

---

93. For performance traditions read in the light of feminism, see Hodgdon, "Katherina Bound."

94. Berry, *Shakespeare and the Hunt,* 113.

of an animal, but more of one. It is no accident that the language of puppetry, existing between animate and inanimate forms of nonhuman being, begins to follow Katherine in the final movement of the play. In the puppet, the refined and reliable automatism of the trained animal, suddenly possessed of new affiliations with the human world, becomes the perfected automatism of the feminine machine, who speaks the master's discourse better than the master himself.

Paolo Virno would call this a virtuoso performance: "The pianist and the dancer stand precariously balanced on a watershed that divides two antithetical destinies: on the one hand, they may become examples of 'wage labour that is not at the same time productive labour'; on the other, they have a quality that is suggestive of political action. Their nature is essentially amphibian."[95] Kate is a virtuoso because she perfectly performs the discourse of wifely virtue. Yet the virtuoso is not simply virtuous; there is an element of superfluity, like high-gloss paper or vanilla vodka, in her performance, which presses her discourse and her being beyond morality, not unlike the "policie" of Markham's Machiavellian hounds. Although Virno is not by and large interested in animals, it is interesting that he speaks here of the "amphibian" character of the virtuoso, able to breathe in air as well as water, afloat in both politics and labor. The centaur is also a kind of amphibian, divided between human and equine worlds and thus doubling in his person the brands of virtue that dwell in these different realms. Katherine grants all productive labor to the husband, who "cares for thee, / And for thy maintenance commits his body / To painful labor both by sea and land" (5.2.151–53). The work of the wealthy wife is simply to *perform wifeliness*, to make "our soft conditions and our hearts . . . well agree with our external parts" (5.2.171–72), a couplet that echoes Aristotle on virtue as the actualization of excellence through its exercise and on happiness as the alignment between the soul and virtue achieved in such performances.

Katherine is working, oh yes, but she is not stewing a lamb's head,[96] making jumbles,[97] or brewing malt.[98] All of these products would count for Markham among the "inward offices" of the housewife; Katherine is engaged here in something closer to what Markham calls the "ordering" of banquets and feasts: "the manner of serving and setting forth of meat," the "skill to marshal the dishes," and giving "precedency according to fashion

---

95. Virno, "Virtuosity and Revolution," 191.
96. Markham, *Country Huswife*, 82.
97. A kind of macaroon; ibid., 113.
98. Ibid., 180–98.

and custom"—in short, the virtue of hospitality, which differs from the knowledges of cookery precisely in requiring a certain virtuosity, an element of pure performance above and beyond the tastiness of any item being served.[99] Hospitality is a labor of display: not only the laying of foods on trenchers of wood, plate, or sugar, but also the display of self and household for the assembled company. Lucentio welcomes the guests:

> Feast with the best, and welcome to my house.
> My banquet is to close our stomachs up
> After our great good cheer. (5.2.8–10)

A banquet was a dessert service, designed to "appear delicate to the eye, but invite the appetite with much variety thereof."[100] Bianca's father has hosted the wedding feast; now the groom, perhaps in temporary lodgings, is hosting the dessert. The after-dinner entertainment, however—the dessert after the dessert—is provided by Katherine in her final performance. She is not herself the hostess, of course; she is what we would call the "maid of honor," the young woman closest to the bride and the member of the wedding party most vulnerable to the barbed arrows of comparison, having just narrowly missed the spinster's fate of dancing barefoot at her sister's wedding (2.1.33–34). Katherine's final speech plays some of the same function as the best man's toast at weddings today. Such rhetorical confections must overflow with equal parts of wit and wisdom, while the truly "best" of them hit on some difficult truth about the nature of both *this* union in its trembling and overpresent singularity and *all* unions that join person and person in one flesh. The capon always lurks nearby, if not served for dinner under an "excellent sauce" of claret wine and orange juice,[101] then brooding in the barnyard as a living icon of the contractions imposed by marriage.

Hospitality is a form of "unproductive" work, linked to the labor of the household yet itself a form of theater that labors by not laboring, by appearing effortless (hence the importance of sugar and alcohol in the arsenal of good cheer). Hospitality is also a form of politics, if we follow Arendt in defining action as "the disclosure of 'who' in contradistinction to 'what' somebody is . . . the 'who,' which appears so clearly and unmistakably to others, remains hidden from the person himself, like the *daimōn* in Greek religion which accompanies each man throughout his life, always looking

99. Ibid., 121–24.
100. Ibid., 121.
101. Ibid., 89.

over his shoulder from behind and thus visible only to those he encounters."[102] In Shakespeare, as we will see again in chapter 6, dinner is always theater, a scene of exposure to the scrutiny, laughter, or amorous glances of other people, or simply to the long wind of too much conversation. When Katherine delivers her after-dinner speech, she gives a homily on marriage, but she reveals something above, beyond, or beneath the commonplaces that she distributes like so many Renaissance fortune cookies. What flutters behind her shoulder is the daemon of creaturely life—the horse, the falcon, and the centaur who have trailed just behind her throughout the drama, and whose special powers Petruchio has not destroyed or expelled, but sequestered, trained, and released. Her daemon flickers in the figure of Pegasus, the name of the lodgings in Genoa where Signior Baptista stayed twenty years earlier (4.4.5), a mythic image of sublime transport whose amphibian biform melds the attributes of *equus* and falcon. There is a bit of Pegasus in Katherine, too, as, both "cunning and tractable," she uses her shrewdness to perform her husband's teachings while flying in circles about his bewildered head. Smitten, tongue-tied, and earth-bound after Kate's heady flight, he can only respond in ardent monosyllables, "Why there's a wench! Come on and kiss me, Kate" (5.2.184).

Although Arendt corrals the daemon within the pale of political life, the figure originally dwelled in the frontiers shared by animal and psychic phenomena.[103] Katharina's speech says submission, but the daemon behind her shoulder reveals something more: it speaks of intelligence and agility, of the "policie" of hounds and the wisdom of hares, of the social life of bees and the beastly affordances shared by joint stools, asses, women, and husbands, too. Her daemon also remembers the dark horse of confinement and privation, the unkind crucible in which this marriage has been forged. The daemon of creaturely life manifests itself in the provisional public space constituted by the virtue of hospitality, which summons *zoē* to appear on the stage erected by *bios*. *Appears* is a key Arendtian term here; *zoē* has not been dragged onto stage in unmediated form, as the terrorized and hounded object of detention, quarantine, and abuse, but is present only phenomenally, as a similitude that transcribes animal spirits within a distinctly human frame, displaying the creatureliness of human life without ever becoming

102. Arendt, *Human Condition*, 179–80.

103. In her study of selfhood in Greek tragedy, Ruth Padel links the *daemon* to animal life: "Any animal, at any moment, might be alive with *daimōn*. A god might be manifest in an animal in the woodshed or kitchen. Animal epiphanies were a normal part of imaginative and lived experience." The *daemon* helps unlock what Padel calls "the animal code" in Greek tragedy; see Padel, *In and Out of Mind*, 142, 148.

fully naked. Unlike the scold's bridle of village shaming rituals, Petruchio's taming program, far from silencing Katharina, has sent her off into an unprecedented flight of speech.

Kate, whose life has become the consummate "work of man" under Petruchio's schooling, might also come to embody the inoperative, the nonproductive element in virtuoso performance—if not at this table of sweet meats, then perhaps at meals yet to be served, their recipes still in the making and the ordering of their appearance still to be determined. If she demonstrates animal virtues at the end of the play, she is not a beast pure and simple, but a *zoon politikon*, translated by Adriana Cavarero as "'an animal of the polis,' just as the bee is an animal of the apiary."[104] This final performance is by no means a moment of emancipation, but it is not silence either, and Katherine does accede in these moments to something like subjectivization, coming into speech before others, though not on terms she has drawn herself.

In the forefront of Piero de Cosimo's centaur *spalliera*, surrounded by the bustle of riot and food fight, nestles a calmer, quieter image: a female centaur, Hylonome, cradles her husband Cyllarus, who has been mortally wounded in the melée. Behind them wine jugs have been tipped over; the one jug still standing appears to be shaped like a cat ("Kate), its tail arching backward into a handle. Cosimo's painting sports one of the few extant images of a female centaur; whereas centaurs are often depicted raping nymphs or women, here we have the marriage of two biform beings, both split between human and equine species.[105] Hylonome's head hovers lovingly above her dying husband's in a graceful figure eight, their bodies at once splayed and entwined in provisional symmetry, together composing a serpentine circle of restfulness spiraling in on itself in the bottom center of the panel's busy composition. As marriage gift and ceremonial ark, Cosimo's *spalliera* presents an image of festive disorder that manifests the element of ravishment encrypted in marriage rituals, while also proffering an emblem of erotic union that swirls together human and animal as well as male and female virtues into an environmental ensemble. Poured into Hylonome's embrace like Samson into Delilah's lap, Cyllarus's hands have released the javelin at his side, and he lies fully disarmed in her love. The translucent veil Hylo-

---

104. Cavarero, *For More Than One Voice*, 183.

105. Sharon Fermor notes that there is little contrast in the painting between reason and bestiality, but instead between lust and married love, the latter crystallized in the embrace of the centaur couple. Vasari associates Cosimo with *bestialità*: he "followed a way of life more like that of a brute beast than a human being; . . . he was content to let everything run wild like his own nature"; see Vasari, *Lives of the Artists*, 107.

3. Piero di Cosimo, *Battle between the Lapiths and the Centaurs* (ca. 1500–1515) (detail of Hylonome cradling Cyllarus). Oil on wood. 71 × 260 cm. Bequeathed by Charles Haslewood Shannon (1937) (NPG4890). Photograph © The National Gallery, London.

nome wraps around his chest recalls the red bridle used by Pallas Athena to lead the centaur into the city in Botticelli's painting. (Lest we wax too romantic, the shallow diagonal cut by Cyllarus's abandoned weapon leaves a signature of cruelty in the landscape of kinds, reminding us that the phallus is most powerful when cut off.) Making a beast with four backs, could this marriage of two centaurs offer us a possible map, a design for living, of the union between Petruchio and Katherine, animal husband and animal wife, whose disrupted wedding just might turn into a settlement of sorts, with the woman gracefully, even submissively, yet most definitely on top?

TWO

The *Hamlet* Elections

In a book largely impelled by an engagement with the writings of Hannah Arendt, it may come as a surprise, even an affront, to encounter the clouded figure of Carl Schmitt. The conservative Catholic jurist, sometime Nazi, and critic of pluralism seems worlds away from the young Zionist, defender of the Greek polis, and refugee from National Socialism. Whereas Schmitt identified politics with the possibility of war, Arendt insisted that war and politics were mutually exclusive. Yet their work uncannily converges on certain points. Both Arendt and Schmitt rigorously distinguished politics and society, whose rapid integration under modern liberalism they saw as a tremendous threat to the human condition. Both were, in this sense, early critics of what Foucault would call "biopolitics"—the absorption, economization, and technocratic management of every aspect of human life under the increasingly administrative functions of the state, whether in its social-democratic or its totalitarian manifestations. Challenging the regime of bio-politics, both Arendt and Schmitt counterposed strong conceptions of the political. Arendt insisted that plurality, "the fact that men, not Man, live on the earth and inhabit the world," is "*the* condition . . . of all political life," since the singularity of each person elicits the startling synapses of narration, deliberation, and action.[1] Schmitt, on the other hand, reduced the

---

1. Arendt, *Human Condition*, 7. Paul Kottman and Adriana Cavarero have mounted Arendtian readings of *Hamlet*. See Kottman, *Politics of the Scene*; and Cavarero, *Stately Bodies*. On Schmitt and *Hamlet*, see especially Kahn, "Hamlet or Hecuba"; Türk, "The Intrusion"; Galli, "Presentazione dell'edizione italiana," 7–35; and Santner, *Royal Remains*, chap. 5. A series of essays on *Hamlet or Hecuba* is forthcoming in a special issue of *Telos* edited by David Pan and myself; see especially Trüstedt, "Hamlet against Hecuba"; Daniel, "'Neither Simple Allusions nor True Mirrorings'"; Frank, "Between Idol and Icon"; Wong, "Steward of the Dying Voice"; and Strathausen, "Myth or Knowledge?"

essence of the political to the distinction between friend and enemy, a collective but most definitely not a pluralist situation in which people adhere
into cohesive bodies based on acknowledged antagonisms with another
group. Although the democratic plurality of Arendt is fundamentally opposed to the hostile coherence of Schmitt, both attribute a strong existential
power to politics that places them at odds with the privatized neutralities
of official liberalism.

Whereas Arendt's references to Shakespeare are scattered and passing,
Schmitt dedicated an entire small monograph to Hamlet. *Hamlet oder Hekuba: Der Einbruch der Zeit in das Spiel* ("Hamlet or Hecuba: The Intrusion of
the Time into the Play"), was published in 1956 after Schmitt led a seminar on the topic at the Volkshochschule in Düsseldorf the year before.[2] Although I ultimately find my way to an understanding of politics in *Hamlet*
closer to Arendt's than to Schmitt's, I do so by taking seriously the moments
of affinity as well as antagonism between their equally vigorous thinkings
of the political. Moreover, Schmitt's delimitation of political theology, itself
produced by his encounters with sixteenth- and seventeenth-century texts, is
absolutely essential to any reading of Renaissance drama that aims to map
the passage of exegetical rhythms and sacral figures into the modern zones
of civil society, national citizenship, and secular literature. For this reason
alone, I want to put place Schmitt's oeuvre on the Renaissance Studies table
for sustained engagement as well as necessary critique.

My argument about *Hamlet* centers on the status of friendship in the play
and its relation to the act of election. Schmitt's theory of the friend and enemy comes out of international law, beginning with the Roman concept of
the *justus hostis*, or just enemy, and is clearly relevant to both the internal
and external states of emergency in Shakespeare's play. At the same time,
however, friendship discourse in the play, especially as it gathers around the
figure of Horatio in concert with Hamlet, also stems from humanist and
classical sources that take their sustenance from moments in republican and
democratic theory, and thus draw friendship closer to Arendt's world than
to Schmitt's. What kind of enemy is Fortinbras to Hamlet and to Denmark?
And how does the election of Fortinbras as new prince rework the earlier

---

2. Schmitt, *Hamlet oder Hekuba*. An early version of segments of this chapter was published
as "Hamlet, Prince." This chapter grows out of years of discussion of *Hamlet or Hecuba* with Jennifer Rust, conversations partly recorded in our joint introduction to the English translation of
Schmitt's *Hamlet* essay, and evident in these pages as well. See also my essay, "Invitation to a
Totem Meal." For an earlier version of *Hamlet oder Hekuba*, see Carl Schmitt, "Vorwort."

election of Horatio as friend? The translation among friendship discourses in the play—which reflects the theoretical translations I am effecting between Schmitt and Arendt—provides a path to understanding the concept of the political in *Hamlet*, which, I argue, unfolds on a horizon uneasily defined by statist sovereignty on the one hand and constitutional possibilities on the other. *Hamlet* is a play both in mourning for frustrated patrimony and aroused by the dream of forms of succession to come. *Election*, moreover, borrowed from theological, juridical, and ethical discourses, and thus forming a theological-political knot, is the term that funds this translation, creating an opening within the waning sacral sovereignty of *Hamlet* for new forms of political thinking, affiliation, and embodiment. Although Schmitt tries to neutralize the force of election in the play, his very identification of it as a source of hermeneutic and juridical difficulty itself confirms the importance of election to the play's deliberative processes and indeed to his own reading.

At stake here in part are the legacies of Machiavelli: Fortinbras is a type of the new prince, seizing the opportunity to found a new order in a moment of constitutive violence, whereas Horatio, as Hamlet's "elected" representative, is concerned with the deliberative speech of *I Discorsi* and the new beginnings it can bring about. In new work on Machiavelli and Renaissance political theology, Graham Hammill emphasizes the necessary relationship between the founding violence of *Il Principe* and the constitutional structures of *I Discorsi*.[3] In effect, what we witness in the Machiavellian world of *Hamlet* is the proximity and even the alliance of Horatio and Fortinbras, the friend and the enemy, in a world in which the king is, increasingly, a "thing of nothing," his mystic body dissolving into new forms of psychic and political life in the disorienting space created by crises in succession—not only from one monarch to the next, but from one order to another.[4]

Meeting Schmitt's Hamlet

In *Hamlet or Hecuba*, Schmitt diagnoses Hamlet's inhibitions as well as the play's wavering on the question of Gertrude's guilt by mapping the play's scenario onto the family romance of James I. The essay is governed by

3. In current work, *The Mosaic Constitution from Machiavelli to Milton*, Graham Hammill examines the role of constitutive violence in the founding of covenantal or contractual forms of government. See also Kalyvas, *Democracy and the Politics of the Extraordinary*; and Bonnie Honig, *Emergency Politics*.

4. On these dissolutions and transformations, mapped as the movement from political theology to biopower, see Santner, *Royal Remains*.

a kind of primitive historicism that single-mindedly and even simple-mindedly strives to identify Hamlet with James. Yet Schmitt's search for sovereign stabilities repeatedly reveals disturbances at the heart of kingship itself, insofar as Shakespeare's tragedy brings England's geopolitical exceptionalism, confessional traumas, and unique succession woes into contact with the possibility of "election" carried by the monarchical forms peculiar to Denmark, but delivered to an England to come. By reading the play for the real sovereign lurking behind the theatrical arras, Schmitt ends up disclosing the force of the play's own ambivalence towards kingship, an ambivalence that ultimately carries the name "election" in both Shakespeare's play and Schmitt's essay.

James VI of Scotland and Hamlet, prince of Denmark both suffered the murder of their fathers by men who would then marry their mothers. Schmitt argues that the sovereign presence of James enters the play not as a mere allusion but as an *Einbruch*—an intrusion, a break-in, an interruption. The subtitle of *Hamlet oder Hekuba* is *Das Einbruch der Zeit in das Spiel*; the accusative "into" *[in das]* syntactically dramatizes the violent breaking of history *into* the aesthetic universe of "das Spiel": the play *Hamlet*, but also the self-referential enclosure of artistic play more generally. *Spiel* evokes here both the *Trauerspiel* of Walter Benjamin and the aesthetic education of Schiller and German Romanticism, whose reflexive accounts of drama Schmitt rejects in favor of the existential reality marked by historical intrusion. Schmitt writes,

> It is then all the more crucial to recognize that this drama, which never ceases to fascinate as a play, does not completely exhaust itself as a play. It contains components that do not belong to the play and, in this sense, it is imperfect as play. It has two major openings through which historical time breaks into [*einbricht*] the time of the play . . . Both intrusions—the taboo surrounding the guilt of the queen and the distortion of the avenger that leads to the Hamletization of the hero—are shadows, two dark areas. They are in no sense mere historical and political connections, neither simple allusions [*Anspielungen*] nor true reflections [*Spiegelungen*], but rather two given circumstances [*Gegebenheiten*] received in and respected by the play and around which the play timidly maneuvers. They disturb the unintentional character of pure play and, in this respect, are a *minus*. Nevertheless, they made it possible for the figure of Hamlet to become a true myth. In this respect they are a *plus*, because they succeeded in elevating *Trauerspiel* to tragedy.[5]

5. Schmitt, *Hamlet or Hecuba*, 44; *Hamlet oder Hekuba*, 46.

Schmitt distinguishes what he calls an intrusion (*Einbruch*) from the historical impress of "simple allusions" or "true reflections" by virtue of its intimate yet dangerous association with the "realities" suffered by an actual sovereign and the function of taboo in keeping the allusion both present and at bay. The *minus* or negative space formed by these intrusions becomes a *plus* in so far as they interrupt the pure "*Spiel*" of the *Trauerspiel* with the "tragic" weight of a genuine historical presence whose unspeakable content generates imaginative responses in the audience. The *Einbruch*, in short, functions as an *exception* to the normative order of representation as *Spiel*, or play. Far from damaging the play, the *Einbruch* of history intensifies *Hamlet*'s dramatic effect by raising the existential stakes for the audience, that is, their sense of active complicity in the real issues both hidden and displayed before them.

The analogies themselves are relatively uncontroversial.[6] More important is what Schmitt wants to gain from asserting the identity of Hamlet and James and what he needs to do in order to maintain its systematic, rather than merely topical, significance. First, in making this argument, Schmitt attempts to infuse the play with the presence of the sovereign, who now haunts the drama not only as kingship's ghost, but also as England's future king. *Hamlet* was probably written and first performed in 1601, near the end of Elizabeth's reign, when the succession issue inspired uncertainty and unrest, involving not only competing personalities, but also the specter of confessional and even constitutional mutation, as evidenced in the diverse anxieties and ambitions associated with the Essex rebellion. Schmitt's identification of Hamlet and James serves to assert not only Hamlet's claim to the throne, but also *the throne's claim to sovereignty*, the appropriateness of the sovereign solution instantiated by the political writings and leadership of James I, the philosopher-king of an English absolutism that never really

6. Andrew Hadfield summarizes the debates concerning Hamlet and James in "The Power and Rights of the Crown," 566–70. See also Kernan, *Shakespeare, the King's Playwright*, 31–44. Suggesting that *Hamlet* was played during James's first Christmas at Hampton Court Palace, December 1603, Kernan mounts an argument similar to Schmitt's: "The pattern fits loosely: a legitimate king murdered by his wife and a usurper who would soon marry, a son on whom lies the responsibility for revenge. And although young Darnley and Old Hamlet appear to have little in common, there is a great deal of the clever Machiavel in Bothwell and in Claudius; and a Gertrude whose only way of dealing with men is seduction is not a world away from Mary, queen of Scots. If this left James to play the part of the educated and philosophical Hamlet, no one would have been surprised" (43). Drew Daniel, in "Neither Simple Allusions nor True Mirrorings," takes up the analogies between Hamlet and James as drawn by Schmitt; Anselm Haverkamp rejects both Kernan's and Schmitt's readings of Hamlet as James (*Shakespearean Genealogies of Power*). On Mary Queen of Scots in the English imaginary, see Lewis, *Mary Queen of Scots*, and *The Trial of Mary Queen of Scots*.

took root. Thus Schmitt writes that "Hamlet's direct, unequivocal right to succeed to the throne" arises from "sacred blood right. In other words: from the divine right of kings that James always appealed to."[7] To identify Hamlet with James is not only to discover an unhappy family romance behind both figures, but also to identify Shakespeare's prince with James's principles of sovereignty. Returning Hamlet to his origins in a primal mirroring of James has the further effect of de-psychologizing and de-aestheticizing Hamlet, not unlike Margreta de Grazia's recent study, *Hamlet without Hamlet*.[8]

At the same time, however, James himself, even for Schmitt, represents religious schism and political anachronism rather than the timely installation of personal rule. Schmitt forcefully insists on James's painstaking balancing act "between his Catholic mother and her Protestant enemies," and he makes the evidentiary uncertainty surrounding the Ghost a question of confessional allegiances.[9] Schmitt's reading of the play is political-theological in the very precise sense of addressing itself to England's religious divisions and their symptomatic effects in Shakespeare, an area that has become a major topic in Shakespeare studies today. James himself defended his theories of personal sovereignty to Jesuit interlocutors such as Suarez and Bellarmine, who were, in Schmitt's estimation, "more modern than James."[10] As Eric Santner argues, Schmitt's James is a living anachronism, "a remainder of a royal conception of kingship that has, however, not yet been reorganized into the political entity Hobbes would later theorize as the theologically neutralized administrative state and that was at some level already in existence on the continent."[11] To identify Hamlet with James, then, is not to stabilize the political ambivalence of the prince in a unified design, despite Schmitt's desires for such a solution, but to confront the specter of a sovereignty out of joint with itself. Hamlet, like James, begins to suffer the death throes of kingship as such: the play is the "dramatized reality of a king who has overthought and overdiscussed [*zerdenkt und zerredt*] the sacred substance of his kingship, but who at least still dies on the stage like a king."[12] Here we witness both Schmitt's effort to identify the prince with the king once and for all, and his recognition that kingship itself can-

7. Schmitt, *Hamlet or Hekuba*, 58.

8. De Grazia, *Hamlet without Hamlet*.

9. Ibid., 28. For a beautiful reading of these problems, see Drew Daniel, "Neither Simple Allusions nor True Mirrorings."

10. Schmitt, *Hamlet or Hecuba*, 29.

11. Santner, *Royal Remains*, chap. 5 (cited from typescript).

12. Schmitt, "Vorwort," 17 (translation mine).

not survive intact the corrosive thinking to which it is subjected in the play and in the century of revolutions in which it was born.

It is ultimately the disturbances generated by kingship in crisis rather than the referential coherence granted by historical allusion that render Schmitt's reading of Hamlet critically productive. Although Schmitt strives to de-Hamletize Hamlet by returning him to his origins in the political actuality of the succession crisis, his acknowledgment of sovereignty's interregnal dissolutions ultimately re-Hamletizes the hero, but on grounds other than the purely subjective or aesthetic. This double move suggests the rapprochement, beyond the horizon of Schmitt's own anti-psychoanalytic reading, between political theology as an investigation of the symbolic structures of sovereignty and Freud's account of the social contradictions at the heart of unconscious formations. Although Schmitt dismisses the Oedipal reading of Hamlet as "the death spasm of the purely psychological phase of *Hamlet* interpretation," what affiliates Schmitt with Freud, and political theology with psychoanalysis, is the negative operation of taboo.[13] Schmitt entitles a section "The Taboo of the Queen," in which he defines the forces of knowing disavowal that keep these topical references at the edge of direct representation. The prohibitory energies of taboo expose the link not only between Hamlet and James, but also between drama and history, not as a positive content, but as a region of ongoing darkness and contradiction, and hence also of imaginative address and possible transformation. Schmitt's Hamlet is always off-center, insofar as both James and Hamlet are suffering a sea change that concerns more than their persons alone, or rather concerns their persons as precisely that which no longer holds in the shifting sands of sovereignty. As Carlo Galli, Johannes Türk, and Adam Sitze have argued, "the time" that breaks into the play itself embodies conflict and schism, and thus communicates a negativity and not a positivity to *Hamlet*'s truant disposition.[14]

At the scholarly core of Schmitt's Hamlet analysis lies Lilian Winstanley's 1921 book, *Hamlet and the Problem of the Scottish Succession*.[15] In 1952,

13. Schmitt, *Hamlet or Hecuba*, 50. I address the formative role of taboo in Schmitt's negative engagement with Freud in "Invitation to a Totem Meal."

14. Jennifer Rust and I summarize these positions in "Schmitt and Shakespeare," xxiii–xxxv. Victoria Kahn criticizes Schmitt for opposing "real action" to "mere literary invention" ("Hamlet or Hecuba," 69). Johannes Türk argues in "The Intrusion" that the aesthetic in Schmitt ultimately serves to capture and display the difference between politics and play. Carlo Galli argues that Schmitt's Hamlet is not a myth of origins but a figure of fissure ("Presentazione"). Adam Sitze has translated Galli's *Hamlet* essay into English along with a helpful commentary; both are forthcoming in Hammill and Lupton, eds., *Points of Departure*.

15. Winstanley, *Hamlet and the Scottish Succession*.

Schmitt's daughter Anima Schmitt translated Winstanley's book into German, under the title *Hamlet Sohn der Maria Stuart*, with a preface by her father that lays out many of the central motifs of what would become *Hamlet
oder Hekuba* a few years later.[16] The change in title from the English text to
the German itself provokes literary-historical readjustments. Whereas Winstanley's title emphasizes succession as a political process and problem, the
Schmitts (*père* and *fille*) fuse Hamlet and James into a single body: "Hamlet
Sohn der Maria Stuart." Is there also a reference here to Friedrich Schiller?
Schmitt opposes the concrete tragedy of his heavy *Hamlet* to Schiller's neo-
Kantian philosophy of aesthetic education. Yet the title for the Winstanley
translation veers close to that of one of Schiller's own historical dramas,
Maria Stuart. If the force of Schmitt's Hamlet interpretation is to de-Schillerize
Hamlet by diagnosing an undigested kernel of historical reality resistant to
playful metabolism, the Winstanley translation also effectively re-Schillerizes
Hamlet on a higher plane, by acknowledging the German playwright as
one of Shakespeare's most astute respondents, precisely in the region where
history and drama are joined by political-theological motifs of sacrifice,
martyrdom, and constitutional contest.[17]

A similar dynamic of apparent simplification that both wards off and
reveals a deeper complexity governs the title of Schmitt's Hamlet essay. The
phrase "Hamlet oder Hekuba" comes to pose for Schmitt the choice between what he sees as the immediacy of Elizabethan drama ("Hamlet") and
the artifice of continental Baroque drama ("Hecuba"). To weep for Hecuba
is to embrace a fundamental theatricalization of experience, whereas to find
oneself, as Hamlet does, unable or unwilling to weep for a Trojan queen
from the distant past is to insist on an existential link between drama and
historical actuality within a "common public sphere" in which the problems presented on stage are still quite literally alive—occurring on an open
stage where contact among audience, players, roles, and contemporary poli-

16. See Schmitt, "Vorwort," 7–25. What is lacking from this early sketch of the problem is
Schmitt's later account of taboo, and hence of a negative or "intrusive" allusion, that becomes
central to *Hamlet or Hecuba*. I would like to thank Stefan Hermanns for calling my attention to
Anima Schmitt's Winstanley translation.

17. On Schiller and early modern political theology, see Jacques Lezra, "The Instance of the
Sovereign in the Unconscious." Lezra's prooftext is *Don Carlos*, not *Maria Stuart*, but both plays
concern "the tragic sacrifices that attend the encounter between the political and the theological
domains," and both do so via an engagement with Shakespeare. Schmitt's uneasy dance with
Schiller supports Katrin Trüstedt's reading in "Hamlet against Hecuba" of the unsolicited return
of *Spiel* (and *Trauerspiel*) within Schmitt's conception of modern tragedy, as well as Carsten
Strathausen's argument for the deeper, ontological Romanticism that animates Schmitt's critique of aspects of Romantic aesthetics and politics ("Myth or Knowledge?").

tics remains raw and unpredictable.[18] Schmitt's most acute formulations involve those moments where he is able to recover an existential punch in typically Hamletian instances of distancing and framing. The play-within-the-play, he argues, is no Baroque hall of mirrors but "the real play itself repeated *before* the curtains."[19] The doubling and indeed tripling of the drama's primal scene, Schmitt suggests, amplifies rather than aestheticizes the continuity between art and reality forged by the Elizabethan theater and embodied by Hamlet's affiliations with James, in part because those affiliations unfold under the black sun of taboo and hence involve a life that is already canceled by the forces of inhibition and repression. If Schmitt brings politics into contact with life in his reading of *Hamlet*, their conjunction is not brute, naive, or unmediated, but tightly knotted around crises in representation, succession, and the opacities that issue from them.

James I would be succeeded by his son, Charles I, whose execution in 1649 represented the central trauma motivating England's constitutional settlements for the next century and beyond.[20] Schmitt places the play on the main stage of European and English history: "This is then the century of the English Revolution (1588–1688), whose first phase saw the dramas of Shakespeare," a period, Schmitt argues, in which "the island of England withdrew from the continent of Europe and took the step from a terrestrial to a maritime existence . . . without going through the constricted passage of continental statehood. . . . Following the lead, first of seafarers and pirates, then of trading companies, England appropriated the lands of a New World and carried out the maritime appropriation of the world's oceans."[21] Echoing the arguments he makes at greater length in his major postwar work, *The Nomos of the Earth*, Schmitt argues that England skipped over the "constricted passage of continental statehood" by jumpstarting an industrial economy inclined toward the sea, whose unregulated vastness opened a region free from law within the increasingly legal ordering of European territory. Such a geopolitics eschews the *politesse* of continental courtiers in favor of the barbarism of pirates, but they are modernist bandits from the commercial future, not primitive ambassadors from the Viking past. The rough character

18. Schmitt, *Hamlet or Hecuba*, 35. On the conceptualization of the public sphere in Schmitt's Shakespeare essay, see Stephanie Frank, "Between Idol and Icon."

19. Schmitt, *Hamlet or Hecuba*, 43.

20. In *The Constitution of Literature*, Lee Morrissey has meticulously demonstrated the role of this trauma in what he calls "the constitution of literature" in the eighteenth century: both the creation of literary criticism as a modern vocation and the exploration of constitutional forms appropriate to the English situation.

21. Schmitt, *Hamlet or Hecuba*, 64–65.

of Shakespeare's dramaturgy—mixed with respect to modes and genres, dismissive of classical unities, and refusing to weep for Hecuba—reflects in Schmitt's analysis England's contribution to the epochal drama of modern spatial ordering. Schmitt's Hamlet—rogue, peasant slave, and pirate too—is inhibited not by thinking too precisely on the event (4.4.41) but by his terrifying proximity to the very wellsprings of contemporary action and geopolitical reorientation.

Schmitt's Shakespeare reading is marked, then, by both the drive to resolve the problems of the play through the specific gravity of topical allusion and the need to design complex and inherently self-divided scenarios organized by taboo, schism, and anachronism in order to achieve those regulatory ends. Choosing English historicism over German Romanticism, Schmitt's *Hamlet* reading polemically de-psychologizes and de-Schillerizes *Hamlet*, in order, however, to establish deeper affiliations with both psychoanalysis and Romantic dramaturgy than he is willing to acknowledge.

Election Trouble

Schmitt's effort to determine the play in a monarchic direction is most explicit in "Excursus I" to the *Hamlet* book, "Hamlet as Heir to the Throne." Here he poses the question of election in the play: the Hamlet-James equation only makes sense in the context of a monarchy ruled by dynastic succession, since Hamlet must both deserve and desire kingship if the pathos of succession is going to carry the drama. Yet Shakespeare, to the chagrin of Schmitt and other royal-watchers, does indeed demonstrate knowledge of the elective character of the Danish monarchy.[22] In sixteenth-century Denmark, the king was elected by the Council, consisting of the major nobles of the land, a choice then ratified by representatives of the common people. The reigning monarch played a substantial but not decisive role in scripting the election of his successor, giving not only his "dying voice" to his choice, but also influencing the opinions and interest blocs of the councilors.[23] One sixteenth-century case involved contested elections first of the brother and then of the son of a dead monarch. Gunnar Sjögren describes the more felicitous coronation of Christian IV in 1596: "At the most solemn moment the Ordinator, the Bishop of Sjælland, asked the twenty Councilors to come

---

22. For an excellent recent reading of *Hamlet* that takes contemporary royal-watching into account, see Charnes, *Hamlet's Heirs*. Schmitt builds his own anti-elective reading on arguments made by J. Dover Wilson, *What Happens in Hamlet*.

23. Sjögren, *Hamlet the Dane*, 36.

forward and join simultaneously in putting the crown on the head of the King. . . . The King was crowned with the following words: 'Your Majesty, accept *from us* the Crown of this State in the name of God the Father, the Son, and the Holy Ghost.'"[24] Neither a classical republic nor a hereditary kingdom (though closer to the latter than to the former), the elective monarchy of Hamlet's Denmark could hold a mirror up to England's own succession worries while also prophesying more distinctive forms of constitutionalism that just might emerge from a genuine crisis in the crown. As Harold Jenkins argues in the Arden edition of the play, when the play opens, there is no question about the legality of Claudius's rule; as the play proceeds, Claudius is delegitimated by the fact of murder and the further actions it requires, but not because he has displaced Hamlet in the succession.[25] And Hamlet's dying act, of course, is to "prophesy th'election" (5.2.360) of Fortinbras, installing an erstwhile enemy of the state on its vacated throne.

In the face of such internal and external evidence concerning the character of the Danish monarchy, Schmitt feels compelled to distinguish elective monarchy from "free election" in the modern sense. Unlike a liberal election, the "dying voice" of the monarch, he notes, plays a major role in the choice of a successor. Moreover, Schmitt insists on the *volkisch* character of these elections: the king is "bound to name a member of his own royal clan, a son or brother or some other kinsman. The 'dying voice' is, in other words, ordained by the old blood right, which originally had a sacred character . . . still . . . recognized in James' writings on the doctrine of the divine right of kings."[26] Finally, although Hamlet elects a foreigner to be king, the exception proves the rule: when "the Saxon Duke Heinrich" was named "by the dying King Konrad, who was a Frank," the negotiations that ensued demonstrate the authority of blood right as a principle, Schmitt argues.[27]

It is not clear, however, that election in *Hamlet* can or should be kept so firmly apart from its liberal post-history. I would suggest to the contrary that the theme of election forms another temporal *Einbruch*, a "minus" that becomes a "plus" in the play's political disposition. Indeed, election functions precisely as what intrudes or breaks into the hereditary succession of kings, lodging procedural alternatives within the biopolitical drive of primogeniture. *Election* is a term strung among several discourses, including politics, classical friendship, and theology. To understand its force in the play, we

24. Ibid., 38 (his italics).

25. "The play does not question the legality of [Claudius's] title, even though it also regards the Prince of Denmark as the future king" (Shakespeare, *Hamlet*, ed. Jenkins, 433–34).

26. Schmitt, *Hamlet or Hecuba*, 58.

27. Ibid., 60.

must read Hamlet's election of Fortinbras against its earlier instantiations in the drama.

The first instance of the word *election* in the play occurs in a private interchange between Hamlet and Horatio, just before the play within a play:

HOR. Here, sweet lord, at your service.
HAM. Horatio, thou art e'en as just a man
    As e'er my conversation cop'd withal.
HOR. O my dear lord.
HAM.   Nay, do not think I flatter
    [. . .]
    Since my dear soul was mistress of her choice,
    And could of men distinguish her election,
    She hath seal'd thee for herself. [3.2.53–65; emphasis added]

Horatio adapts a courtly language of deference, placing himself at Hamlet's service, but Hamlet responds, graciously, by asserting their parity in friendship. Hamlet's "conversation"—his dealings, his social experience—have never met the match of Horatio, who in turn has become his partner in the familiar arts of civil conversation.[28]

Here and throughout the play, the Hamlet-Horatio couple draws its energy from the classical discourse of friendship. The play alternates between thinner and thicker measures of friendship: between the conveniences of fellowship among a group and the tighter, more intimate bond between Horatio and Hamlet. In the opening of *Hamlet*, the changing of guards on the ramparts of Elsinore establishes equivalence among the men who take turns guarding the castle. The citizen, writes Aristotle, is he who rules and is ruled in turn.[29] What makes citizens equal to each other is not identity of qualities, attributes, skills, or wealth, but the offices that they share. Barnardo names Horatio and Marcellus as the "rivals of my watch," rivalry here implying not competition but exchange, as rendered in Q1's "partners." Schmitt might argue that these bonds of equivalence coalesce in response to the state of emergency represented by the approach of the public enemy

28. For a perceptive reading of this exchange in terms of the occlusion of class in the play and its criticism, see Christopher Warley, "Specters of Horatio." I follow Warley in linking Horatio to democratic vistas in the play and to the argument that "some changing of the guard has been enacted, some historical shift accomplished" (1043).

29. "In most constitutional states the citizens rule and are ruled by turns, for the idea of a constitutional state implies that the natures of the citizens are equal, and do not differ at all" (Aristotle *Politics* 1259b).

Fortinbras; yet they also take their bearings from the humanist discourse of offices and duties that form an outer precinct of friendship literature. As Paul Kottman has argued, when Horatio joins their circle in order to bear witness to the Ghost, the purely formal fellowship among guards is resealed through the act of shared testimony: "The relation between these three might be fairly taken as something like an emergent polity—a nascent company that will soon include Hamlet and that will come to be bound by an oath."[30]

As if affirming the political nature of their association, Horatio works to secure consent from the sentries concerning Hamlet's membership in their group: "Do you consent we shall acquaint him with it / As needful in our loves, fitting in our duty?" (1.1.177–78). And Hamlet, having joined this team on their night watch, will ask his company to "consent to swear" to secrecy concerning the Ghost (1.5.159). Hamlet prefaces his request with topoi from the discourse of friendship: "And now, good friends, / As you are friends, scholars, and soldiers, / Give me one poor request" (1.5.146–48). This band of "friends, scholars, and soldiers"—a cohort bound by education, vocation, conversation, affection, and consent—shelters and supports Hamlet's loneliness as he grudgingly shoulders the burden of the paternal past. The play's awful longitudinals—parent-child, sovereign-subject, divine-human—are crossed by an equally dense network of civic latitudinals: brothers and sisters, comrades and sentries, foils and rivals. In both performance and criticism, the play's sublimely vertical relationships often take center stage, but the horizontal strands provide an alternative scene— for Hamlet and for criticism—to the drama of sovereignty played out on center stage.

Classical friendship both pre- and postdates the institutions of democracy, yet it received a decisive philosophical and political imprint during the rule of the Athenian *demos*, forever binding friendship (*philia*) and citizenship (*politeia*) in Western discourses of sociality. In his chapter on friendship in the *Nicomachean Ethics*, Aristotle cites the proverb, "*philotês isotês*," "friendship is equality";[31] although he accounts for friendships among unequals, equality is the norm. David Konstan documents the deep affinity between friendship, citizenship, and reciprocity in the ancient world. Unlike the lover/beloved dyad, Konstan notes, there is no designated active or passive partner in friendship; each is a *philos*, exchanging benefits

---

30. Kottman, *Politics of the Scene*, 146–47.

31. Aristotle *Nicomachean Ethics* 1168b. Laurie Shannon cites Erasmus's *Adagia* for the Latin equivalent: "*Amicitia equalitas*" (*Sovereign Amity*, 3).

as equally as possible, in order to model equality as "the primary value represented by friendship in the ideology of the classical democracies."[32] Laurie Shannon has argued that Renaissance friendship inserted an experimental space defined by parity and likeness into the hierarchical scaffolding of early modern life. Friendship, Shannon suggests, crafted "a virtually civic parity not modeled anywhere else in contemporary social structures" by creating a "consensual social bond or body that is not inherently subordinating."[33] Classical friendship forms a kind of lozenge that emerges out of Homeric bonds of reciprocity, swells into properly political definition in response to democratic institutions, and then tapers off into Hellenistic imperial and monarchical formations, carrying echoes of its egalitarian ethos into Roman and Judeo-Christian scenes of sociability.[34] Contrary to Schmitt's oppositional definition of friendship in *The Concept of the Political*, the classical tradition emphasizes the positive social and civic gains derived from identification and affiliation, without any reference to an enemy. In the classical discourse, the opposite of the friend is not so much the enemy as the false friend on the one hand (flatterers or "fair weather friends"), and the spouse or romantic partner on the other. Whereas the language of romance is ruled by imagery of involuntary passion, the language of friendship courts deliberation, choice, and consent. (This is not to exclude sexuality from friendship; indeed, one might speculate that the idea of "sexual consent" originated in same-sex relationships based on parity rather than in heterosexual relations that presume permanent inequality and the mediation of a father.)[35] If *The Merchant of Venice* struggles to differentiate the qualities and purposes of friendship and love, *Timon of Athens* probes the continuum among true and false friends in the public sphere. Both plays, set in cities associated with constitutional rule, demonstrate the political dimensions of classical friendship; Aristotle categorizes citizenship as a species of political friendship, whose forms of free and equitable affiliation (what will later be called "civil society") support and fill out the institutional and legal architecture of the polis.

When Hamlet professes his soul's election of Horatio, he may appear to confuse friendship and romance, feminizing "my dear soul" as a "mistress"

32. David Konstan, "Reciprocity and Friendship."

33. Shannon, *Sovereign Amity*, 2.

34. On the Homeric origins of friendship and reciprocity and the egalitarian strains within the aristocratic ideal, see Donlan, *Aristocratic Ideal*.

35. For a philosophical and legal analysis of sexual consent, which touches on homosexual consent, see Archard, *Sexual Consent*.

who has "seal'd" Horatio "for herself." The word *election*, however, carries the sense of conscientious choice that distinguishes friendship from love. In his *Letters*—early essays on friendship—Seneca advises his familiar addressee to deliberate before choosing a friend: "Think a long time whether or not you should admit a given person to your friendship."[36] *Thinking* and *friendship* are doubly bound: to think *about* one's friends (to "elect" with care) is a precondition to thinking *with* one's friends (to share in conversation); friendship, Aristotle writes, is realized by *philoi* "living together and sharing in discussion and thought."[37] In the dedicatory letter to *The Discourses*, Machiavelli opposes the Prince and the Friend as the addressees of two very different forms—or *discorsi*—of political writing: "Accept [this book], then, in the manner in which things are accepted amongst friends. . . . I seem in this to be departing from the usual practice of authors, which has always been to dedicate their works to some prince."[38] Machiavelli's dedication decisively associates friendship and citizenship as part of what makes this particular book a set of "discourses": a commentary on Livy, but also a civil conversation with his contemporaries.

Returned from the ghostly encounter, Hamlet announces to Horatio, "There are more things in heaven and earth, Horatio, than are dreamt of in your philosophy" (1.5.174–75). The Folio reads "*our* philosophy," situating their discourse in the conversational sphere of amity. The "more things" that represent the rational limit of philosophy bear not only on matters supernatural, but on the untested resources of philosophy itself. Hamlet's philosophical language repeatedly touches on this "more," a potentiality caught between the social and the subjective, between civil publicity and psychic inwardness. Hamlet "eats the air, promise-crammed" (3.2.93–94), a phrase that binds a *soupçon* of the stage Machiavel with the promissory language of friendship in order to hollow out an inward space of pure expectancy. Although Schmitt might want to read this passage as proof of Hamlet's thwarted ambitions, the language of aborted potential troubles rather than props up the potency of sovereignty by finding in frustrated *virtù* new linguistic, imaginative, and dramatic resources. If the netherworld contains "more things" than philosophy, philosophy, too, is always more

36. In the words of Seneca, "Think a long time whether or not you should admit a given person to your friendship" (*Letters from a Stoic*, 35).
37. Aristotle, *Complete Works*, 1170b.
38. Machiavelli, *Discourses*, 93–94.

than itself, a discourse of social and political dreaming that overflows its own actualizations.

The kind of election that Hamlet exercises in relation to Horatio is reserved for the intimate bond between two people: Aristotle contrasts the "comradely way of friendship" *(hetairikê philia),* "always between two people," and the wider ties of political friendship *(politikê philia).*[39] Though linked to political friendship by the measure of parity, the "best friends" couple is exclusive; in Laurie Shannon's formulation, "friendship discourse offers no comportment or affect to be generalized beyond the pair, no pattern to link all political subjects to one another."[40] In modern parlance, we would say that intimate friendship is not "scalable"—incapable of generalization or replication behind its existential instance. Yet Hamlet's elective affinity with Horatio is *still political* in an Arendtian sense, locating the prince on a horizontal plane defined by genuine instances of equitable encounter, its distributions of affect both distinguishing and sheltering him from the terrible specter of a sovereignty that bears the name of revenge. As Paul Kottman has argued, the intimacy of their relation, in life and in death, ultimately leaves us, as Horatian witnesses to the play, in a situation of renewed human plurality.[41]

Election also, of course, delivers a theological punch: Hamlet "elects" Horatio much as the sovereign deity elects Israel as a sacred nation in the Hebrew Bible, or his saints in the New Testament. Although we could tap this dynamic from countless points of greater proximity to Shakespeare himself, our focus on Schmitt invites us to access this theme via the extraordinary set of lectures, published in English under the title *The Political Theology of Paul,* by the Jewish intellectual historian Jacob Taubes, who had engaged in

---

39. Seneca develops both the distinction and the dependence between political and comradely friendship, with a cosmopolitan emphasis absent in Aristotle: "The assiduous and scrupulous cultivation of this bond, which leads to our associating with our fellow-men and belief in the existence of a common law for all humankind, contributes more than anything else to the maintenance of that more intimate bond I was mentioning, friendship. A person who shares much with a fellow human being will share everything with a friend" *(Letters from a Stoic,* 97).

40. Shannon, *Sovereign Amity,* 18.

41. On Hamlet and Horatio, Kottman writes, "Hamlet does not simply perish alone, after all, but dies *to* Horatio, who, it is decided, must survive him. Indeed, Hamlet is able to grasp his death only in terms of his living, dying relation to Horatio: 'Horatio, I am dead, / Thou livest' (5.3.343–4), 'O, I die, Horatio' (5.3.357)." On the creation of the conditions of human plurality through drama, Kottman writes, "From the raw material of this ontological plurality [the sheer gathering of people in a theatre], the scene fashions a new plurality, a singular 'those' who were on the scene, a unique 'they' who are distinguished from all others in the world inasmuch as they alone can address one another as witnesses" (Kottman, *Politics of the Scene,* 165).

a series of interchanges with Carl Schmitt on the subject of Paul's Epistles.[42] Taubes tunes into the brutality of election as Paul experiences it in Romans, where he writes of Jacob and Esau that one was already elected in the womb, before "the children were borne, and when they had nether done good, nor evil" (Rom. 9:11). Taubes exclaims, "So it can't be a matter of the deeds. It's already determined in the womb, that's election! Dreadful thing, one would say in a modern vein—how can it be decided already in the womb, where is God's righteousness here."[43] To be elected is to be chosen by God, apart from one's merit, in a manner "which completely escapes from ethics—for these aren't deeds, works, but elections!" (48). In Taubes' account, Paul expresses the brute character of election—much closer to Schmitt's sovereign decision than to Arendt's narrative plurality—in relation to Israel itself, to the remnant within Israel, and to his own election as a prophet.

Hamlet undergoes the terror of election in the play. When he receives his mission from the Ghost, he writes "thy commandment all alone" on his "tables," echoing the terrible singularity of the revelation of the law at Sinai. Hamlet plays Moses to the Ghost's God, becoming, in Lyotard's telling phrase, the "Jewish Oedipus," "possessed by an Other who has spoken" and hence "dispossessed of origin," subjected to a command that comes from outside.[44] Yet the scene at Sinai is not one of complete heteronomy, since the covenant instituted there implies at least some form of consent, even if imbalanced or coerced. Covenant, moreover, institutes civic relations among Israel, transforming the mixed multitude in flight from Egypt into a body politic. To be elected by God as a nation is to enter into forms of election and representation among the Jews as a covenanted group.[45] So, too, in *Hamlet*, the prince returns from a precipice overshadowed by the Ghost to rejoin and reconfigure his circle of friends. Entreating them to "consent to swear" to secrecy, he alerts them to his antic disposition, in

42. In 1987, Taubes gave a series of lectures on Paul at the Protestant Institute for Interdisciplinary Research in Heidelberg. The lectures were published posthumously and recently translated into English by Dana Hollander under the title *The Political Theology of Paul*.

43. Ibid., 48.

44. Lyotard, "Jewish Oedipus," 402. For other readings of the Mosaic connotations of this scene, see Battenhouse, "The 'Ghost' in 'Hamlet,'" 174–77; Garber, *Shakespeare's Ghost Writers*, 149–53; and Rust, "Wittenberg and Melancholic Allegory," 273.

45. In Spinoza's account of the covenant at Sinai, "as in a democracy, [the Hebrews] all surrendered their right on equal terms, crying with one voice, 'Whatever God shall speak, we shall do,' [Ex 24:3] (no one being named as mediator), it follows that this covenant left them completely equal" (Spinoza, *Theological-Political Treatise*, 196). On covenant and contract in the Jewish tradition, see Walzer, Lorberbaum, and Zohar, eds., *Jewish Political Tradition*. Graham Hammill's current work on the Mosaic constitution is relevant here as well.

order to carry out, but also to test and attenuate, to create an easement from, the Ghost's commands. Hamlet is doubly lonely: trapped by the secrecy and questionable legality of the Ghost's commandment, and isolated still again by the subjective terror of his own resistance to revenge. Yet this double loneliness–so definitive for the Hamlet that we know and love—is nonetheless from the beginning circled by a fellowship of friends who lighten and lessen this isolation.

And the key figure is Horatio. When Hamlet "elects" Horatio as his friend, he repeats, reverses, and renders horizontal Hamlet's own terrible election by the commandment of the Ghost. His name implying *ratio* or reason as well as Horatian decorum and public *oratio*, Horatio supports Hamlet's experimental path. If Hamlet is the object and mirror of our imaginary fascination, Horatio directs the symbolic dimension of our subjective capture within the scenes before us. A late remnant of the classical chorus, Horatio performs this work in the mode of public opinion formation, testing, weighing, and summarizing the state of the union throughout the drama.[46] As such, Horatio is another figure for us, the audience, an emblem of normative consciousness within the play, between the play and its audience, and in the constitution of tragedy as a genre with a history. Hamlet has "elected" him to this representative function—representative of Hamlet, but also representative of us. It is out of this complex of friendship, politics, and theology that the word *election* recurs in its constitutional sense in act 5, and it is here, at the temporal and conceptual reaches of the play, that we must follow it.

The Girlfriend, Unelected

But first, a few words for Ophelia. If the male friend is freely chosen as a partner in evidentiary experiments and perhaps the occasional consensual circle jerk, the girlfriend subsists at the far reaches of election. Thrown together by their grim Elsinore childhoods, the love affair between Ophelia

---

46. Analyzing the scholarly position that Horatio has come to represent in academe, Christopher Warley argues that "the claim to universality—to objectivity, disinterest, and 'justness'— is never really universal" ("Specters of Horatio," 1024). Warley's class analysis of Horatio is beautifully executed, but I would resist simply rejecting as ideological the space of judgment and testimony that Horatio clears in the drama. Such acts do aim at universality, but only through the iterative and situated nature of their actual utterance and performance. They produce a fragile or provisional universality that must continually be retested collectively. These are the processes that drama both stages and performs, if and when we participate in its public sphere. On Horatio and constituent sovereignty, see Wong, "Steward of the Dying Voice."

and Hamlet seems accidental and unplanned, like Ophelia's own death by drowning or the pregnancy that some critics have intuited in her ballads of abandonment. Whereas Hamlet elects his madness, transforming his temperamental melancholy into a politic mask, Ophelia is swept away on the weeping brook of her own distress. Even the "snatches of old tunes" that sing her to her rest are not of her own design (4.7.176). Yet Shakespeare does limn some possibility of action for Ophelia. Act 1, scene 3 is, strikingly, composed of two parallel interviews, the first with Laertes, and the second with Polonius. In both exchanges, the men urge Ophelia to repel Hamlet's advances. Why risk such repetition in a play that far exceeds the "within's two hours" of appropriate performance (3.2.125)?

The purpose of the doubling, I'd like to argue, is to open, in the aperture created by the narrow difference in Ophelia's responses, a field of action that might have been. To Laertes, she replies,

I shall th' effect of this good lesson keep
As watchman to my heart. But good my brother,
Do not as some ungracious pastors do,
Show me the steep and thorny way to heaven,
Whiles like a puff'd and reckless libertine,
Himself the primrose path of dalliance treads
And recks not his own rede. (1.3.45–51)

She accepts his advice, but not without turning it back on him. What she manifests here is some capacity to push back, to produce a counternarrative out of the bantering script of sisterly familiarity. If Laertes identifies feminine virtue with the rigors of an extreme chastity ("The chariest maid is prodigal enough / If she unmask her beauty to the moon" [1.3.36–37]), Ophelia begins to practice a broader virtue in the act of speaking up. Leartes's coercive commonplaces inadvertently toss virtue into her court not only as the straitjacket of femininity, but also as a spring of potential action, taken up and revealed as such in her playful yet pointed rejoinder. By holding him to the same standard, Ophelia calls attention to the inequities that govern male and female virtue. In the process, she transforms the brother-sister couple into the template for a possible polity: a scene governed by the lateral exchange between peers whose deliberation *on virtue* becomes itself an exercise *in virtue*, in the civic sense of an excellence only articulated in practice.

In Arendt's terms, Ophelia's response to Laertes manifests the "space of appearance" that "comes into being wherever men are together in the manner of speech and action."[47] By talking back, even in this mild manner, Ophelia flashes her possible kinship with other, more assertive Shakespearean heroines; through her hesitant leap beyond the personal to a consideration of something like justice, the polity she assembles begins between brother and sister, but extends Antigone-like to a community of witnesses and precedents. The entry of Polonius, however, almost instantly deflates this space of appearance. ("Wherever people gather together," Arendt writes, publicity "is potentially there, but only potentially, not necessarily and not forever."[48]) The exchange between father and daughter ends in the almost-mute finality of a response that seals the tragedy to come: "I shall obey, my lord" (1.3.136). Between the pertness of her reply to Laertes and the resignation of her response to Polonius unfolds Ophelia's own terrible "To do or not to do": whether to resist conscription in the surveillance plans of father and king, or to accept her role as a piece of bait set out to trap the symptom of her lover.[49] In repeating these scenes of advice, Shakespeare reveals the slimmest possible margin of action for Ophelia, a steep and thorny way not to *heaven* (virtue in the moralized Christian sense) but to *politics* (virtue in the civic sense).

Ophelia, however, does not and perhaps cannot muster the resources to travel that path. When Laertes warns his sister that "the canker galls the infants of the spring / Too oft before their buttons be disclos'd" (1.3.39–40), he means to describe the danger of Hamlet's advances, but he predicts instead the mortal effects of his father's predatory projects. Laertes proffers the bud as an image of virgin virtue, all tight and self-enclosed around its tender button, yet the same bud also hides within its infant petals the still-birth of Ophelia's own capacity for action. When in the infamous nunnery scene Hamlet submits Ophelia to his own abusive virtue discourse ("Are you honest? . . . Are you fair?" [3.1.103–5]) , she has already mortgaged the honesty she protests to uphold by accepting her part in the plot of the lurking elders. When Hamlet asks her, "Where's your father?" (3.1.130–32), he gives Ophelia the chance to choose doing over not-doing. When she responds, "At home, my lord," she tells what we know is a bald lie, neither honest nor fair. Polonius and Claudius witness the lie from behind the arras; we in the audience witness their witnessing, as well as the horror of Ophelia's fatal complicity. The point is not to blame Ophelia for her own

---

47. Arendt, *Human Condition*, 199.

48. Ibid.

49. On "that piece of bait Ophelia," see Lacan, "Desire and the Interpretation of Desire," 77.

victimization, first by Polonius and then by Hamlet, who could have asked after her father in a manner directed toward her predicament, not his. We have all found ourselves telling such lies, simply by virtue of inhabiting scenes where the public sphere is constrained and distorted from the start by the crippling phantasms of sexual gaming or the uneven distribution of power. In mapping these deformations in *Öffentlichkeit*, Shakespeare allows us to glimpse a possible polity *even where it has no chance of flourishing,* where election finds itself least elastic, and thus invites us to begin the work of identifying the conditions of action. Even for Ophelia.

Hamlet, Prince

Whereas Ophelia's chances for action rapidly close down, Hamlet's expand as the play draws to a close. As critics have long pointed out, when Hamlet returns from his aborted trip to England, he expresses a new sense of purpose in relation to a divine plan that is larger than the vengeful spirit of his father. This new Hamlet apprehends "a divinity that shapes our ends" (5.2.10) and "a special providence in the fall of a sparrow" (5.2.215–16), the latter recalling Calvin's account of predestination in the *Institutes*.[50] Christopher Pye puts special emphasis on the Messianic "interim" that Hamlet claims as an opening for subjectivity in act 5: "It will be short. The interim is mine. / And a man's life's no more than to say 'one.' (5.2.73–74).[51] In and through this interim, Hamlet transforms the passivity of delay that he suffered under the commandments of his father into the activity of an anticipatory deadline, a call to action that allows the prince to become a subject: "The 'interim' that Hamlet speaks of is the split and pause that haunt the male revenger's act, now miraculously transformed into the enabling measure of his life."[52] This is not a Christian conversion so much as a political-theological reorientation of the vertical sovereignty at Sinai towards its horizontal axis in collective covenant. In act 5, defined by the gap of this interim, Hamlet's princeliness is put to the final test. Does he remain a prince in the limited sense of a sovereign-in-waiting? Does he attain a measure of fulfilled sovereignty in the moments between the death of Claudius and his own? Is he a *principe* in the Machiavellian sense of negotiating his own ascendancy? Or does he institute a different kind of principality, becoming, to echo the Roman phrase, a *princeps* in the sense of First Citizen, understood not as the

50. See Fernie, *Spiritual Shakespeares*, 199.
51. I develop the Messianic theme in chapter 7, "Paul Shakespeare."
52. Pye, *Vanishing*, 112.

imperial terminator of representative rule but as the initiator of the chance for constitutionalism, an emperor in reverse?

The word *election* occurs twice in this final act. Within the arc of his return to Denmark, Hamlet declares to Horatio that Claudius "hath kill'd my king and whor'd my mother, / Popp'd in between th'election and my hopes" (5.2.64–65). It is the moment when Hamlet comes closest to subscribing to the Machiavellian persona that he elsewhere assumes as a pose, in the same moment that he calls our attention to the elective character of the Danish monarchy. It is not his *succession* to the throne by primogeniture that has been stymied by Claudius, Hamlet tells Horatio, but rather his *election* to it. If this prince suffers from frustrated ambition, his foiled hopes reach beyond inherited blood right to include the chance for some form of political self-actualization on a broader public stage.

When he returns to the word again in his final speech, it is to *elect* Fortinbras:

> O, I die, Horatio,
> The potent poison quite o'ercrows my spirit.
> I cannot live to hear the news from England,
> But I do prophesy th'election lights
> On Fortinbras. He has my dying voice.
> So tell him, with th'occurents more and less
> Which have solicited—the rest is silence. (5.2.357–63)

Schmitt insists that Hamlet's act is fully intelligible within the terms of England's own monarchy: "This is the 'dying voice' with which Hamlet names Fortinbras, with which Elizabeth will name James and which, in the year 1658, the English attempt to attribute to Cromwell at his death in favor of his son Richard."[53] In electing Fortinbras, Hamlet, I would argue, does not choose his own successor, but rather begins to speak from the body politic, called to give its minimal consent to the new king. *Pace* Schmitt, Hamlet, unlike Elizabeth, is not sovereign when he gives his dying voice to Fortinbras, for he himself has not been elected. In the last moments of the play, Denmark is effectively headless. Hamlet "prophesies" the election of Fortinbras, not naming his successor outright but rather initiating a political process by which Fortinbras will likely come to power. Election is distinct here from what Schmitt calls the political decision. Whereas decision names the singular extralegal judgment of the sovereign in a state of emergency,

---

53. Schmitt, *Hamlet or Hecuba*, 56.

"election" implies deliberation, rationality, and choice, not carried out by one person but pursued by a political collectivity.[54] "Election" itself belongs to the people through its representatives, not to the monarch; if Hamlet predicts Fortinbras's election here, his voice issues from a place somewhere between that of the dying sovereign and that of the body politic that must ratify any new king. Turning to the phalanx of doubles and foils that have assembled around him in the course of the drama's last scene, the *princeps* as sovereign-in-waiting becomes the First Citizen, initiating an election that by definition exceeds the scope of his own life and will.

Moreover, the man whom Hamlet names, far from being a Danish clansman, comes from *out of state*. Schmitt writes, "a word like *Wahl* or 'election' must only be understood in the context of and in connection with the concrete order of an individual people and its ruling house."[55] For Schmitt, a "people" is a *Volk*, defined nationally if not ethnically.[56] But the English word *people* has two competing roots in Greek thought: the people as *ethnos* represents the national idea emphasized by Schmitt, while the people as *demos* suggests a group constituted by its institutions, not its blood lines. While in many national formations (including ancient Athens), these two forms of the people effectively overlap, the difference between them becoming invisible, citizenship steps forward as a discourse and a problem precisely at the moment when the two circles separate out around an alien element that requires naturalization.[57] Fortinbras, a new prince in the Machiavellian paradigm, introduces a measure of heterogeneity into the state, which cannot simply remain identical to itself under his rule.

A mixed social body shows up symptomatically, as a specter of election gone wrong, throughout the play. Laertes returns to England "in a riotous head," the possible candidate of a popular election: "They cry: 'Choose we!

---

54. In a helpful critique of Schmitt, political philosopher and sometime-Shakespearean Agnes Heller distinguishes between decision as will (the model she attributes to Schmitt) and decision as choice (which she derives from the Aristotelian tradition): "Greek philosophy knew nothing about will. In Aristotle, decision is interpreted as choice and it follows the act of deliberation. . . . If the act of decision is not the act of will but the act of choice, *popular sovereignty is possible under the conditions of social diversity and heterogeneity*" (Heller and Fehér, *Radical Universalism*, 412; their italics).

55. Schmitt, *Hamlet or Hecuba*, 56.

56. Schmitt himself, as his biographer Joseph Bendersky notes, came from French Catholic stock and identified with Latin culture, and, though he was a German nationalist, avoided racial thinking, at least until joining the Nazi Party; see Bendersky, *Carl Schmitt*, 64–83.

57. Etienne Balibar distinguishes between "*ethnos*, the 'people' as an imagined community of membership and filiation, and *dēmos*, the 'people' as the collective subject of representation, decision making, and rights" (*We the People of Europe*, 8). See also Honig, *Democracy and the Foreigner*.

Laertes shall be king!'" (4.5.101, 106). Meanwhile, "the distracted multitude" loves Hamlet (4.3.4), though "the people" is also "muddied"—mixed
up and adulterated, rendered untransparent to itself—by the death of Polonius (4.5.81). And then there is "a certain convocation of politic worms":
equal among themselves, they sublimely level "your fat king and your
lean beggar" in the common communion of corpses (4.3.19–23). Hamlet
thinks of the world itself as a "foul and pestilent congregation of vapors,"
an uncivil society composed of heterogeneous elements (2.2.302–3). Along
with references to "the late innovation" (2.2.331) and "fine revolution"
(5.1.89), the play assembles a mixed multitude of phrases and images concerning political and social change. These motifs never cohere into a positive program of constitutional reform or popular rule, instead convening
distractedly around the undiscovered country of the play's potentialities,
"th'occurrents more and less" that Hamlet bequeaths unenumerated to Horatio (5.2.362).

Schmitt would like Hamlet to represent Denmark in the *volkisch* sense:
"Hamlet's direct, unequivocal right to succeed the throne arises from only
one factor in the Nordic order of succession to the throne, the sacred
blood right."[58] Yet the declamatory energy of Schmitt's claim indicates that
Hamlet's rights, as well as his commitment to those rights, may not be so
unequivocal after all. Throughout the play, Hamlet commits the most extraordinary verbal abuse on the tropes of political theology: more than kin
and less than kind, the king is a thing of nothing; Claudius, wed to the body
politic through his marriage to Gertrude, is Hamlet's obscene mother (and
the nation's, too). With the office of kingship already contaminated by the
dubious virtues of Hamlet's father and further violated by the usurpations
of Claudius, the prince takes sardonic pleasure in finding something rotten
in the state of sovereignty.

Yet perhaps it is in the negation of these tropes of kinship, divine right,
and sacramental contract—the "thing of nothing" disclosed at their center—
that Hamlet eventually finds the space for his own subjectivization, the "interim" he calls his own when he returns to Denmark. This interim—what
Lacan calls with reference to Greek tragedy the zone between two deaths—is
defined by the punctual character of its appearance.[59] Opening up only to
close again, life in and as the interim lasts no longer, Hamlet says, than a
man can say "one." The *princeps* is the One (the "first") who can find himself, claim his own life, in and as the time of that single beat. Hamlet, like

58. Schmitt, *Hamlet or Hecuba*, 58.
59. Lacan, *Ethics of Psychoanalysis*.

Orestes before him, passes through but also out of the modality of revenge, discovering something like citizenship on the other side of reciprocal violence and sacral sovereignty. The subjectivizing "interim" marked by the act and fact of election orients Hamlet in a sequence of equivalent figures, his foils and doubles, his friends and his successors. If he accepts the beat of "one" as the space of his own life, it is not to remain apart, but rather to enter into a sequence of fellows, to become *primus inter pares*, to be counted as part of a collective. Hamlet's final words, I would argue, announce not his accession to kingship in the moment of death, but rather his passage into the chain of friendship that will survive Hamlet and take up his story: "Horatio, I am dead, / Thou livest. Report me and my cause aright / To the unsatisfied" (5.2.343–45). If so, he joins an uncommon commonwealth, sutured out of a grab bag of friendship types exhibiting conflicting social energies and competing conceptual provenances. Hamlet can only address himself to the world through the singular voice of Horatio, their deep but irreplicable intimacy forming an impossible measure for the weaker forms of fellowship that sometimes support, but ultimately destroy, Hamlet in the play.

The election of Fortinbras takes shape on the other side of the debasement of the corporate metaphors that help buttress traditional sovereignty. Fortinbras stages the play's final tableau:

> Let four captains
> Bear Hamlet like a soldier to the stage,
> For he was likely, had he been put on,
> To have prov'd most royal; and for his passage,
> The soldier's music and the rite of war
> Speak loudly for him.
> Take up the bodies. Such a sight as this
> Becomes the field, but here shows much amiss.
> Go, bid the soldiers shoot. (5.2.400–408)

Here the pomp and circumstance of princely elegy put Hamlet to rest, marking "his passage" from the stage of life before he could make his formal passage from minority to majority. Cut off in the flower of his youth, he was "likely . . . To have prov'd most royal." Fortinbras muscles Hamlet's legacy into the mold of the soldier manqué, borrowing capital from the prince's lost future in order to fund his own military campaign. At the end of the play, *princeliness equals potentiality*, urged in a "royal" direction by the weight of history, narrative, and blood right, yet never fully disclosed or realized, and hence acting as a kind of promissory note for a politics to come.

In Greek tragedy, these final lines were called the *exodos*, the brief "exit ode" delivered by the Chorus on its way off the stage. Recall the ending of the *Oresteia* and the *Antigone*: in each case, the vacuum left by the terrible destruction of the royal house opens onto a scene in which political institutions stand to gain new scope and momentum, the scandalous *minus* of familiacide becoming the *plus* of a possible politics.[60] Shakespeare's Denmark is, of course, no Athens, and constitutional conditions and outcomes hang very far on the horizon indeed. At the end of *Hamlet*, the monarchy remains a monarchy, and a brutalized and debased one at that, in the hands of a foreign strong-arm who is more thug than scholar, more dictator seizing the occasion of emergency than either an anointed king or an elected magistrate. The political possibilities that attend election disappear even before they are named. Yet an interim has opened up in a scene in which royal primogeniture is fundamentally haunted by the suspect ghost of sovereignty past and displaced by the ambiguous call of elections future.

At the beginning of the play, Fortinbras is an enemy in the political sense that Schmitt establishes in *The Concept of the Political*: "The specific political distinction to which political actions can be reduced is that between friend and enemy. This provides a definition in the sense of a criterion and not as an exhaustive definition or one indicative of substantial content."[61] The distinction between friend and enemy, Schmitt insists, has no content; it is not correlative with "good" and "bad" or "beautiful" and "ugly," which belong instead to the domains of ethics and aesthetics. *Friend* and *enemy* are terms of pure affiliation and disaffiliation, terms that bind together the constituencies of one group, in opposition to another, on the existential plane of life and death. The friend is not a character type, not a personality infused with a set of likeable attributes or elective affinities; the friend is simply the one with whom I throw my lot when together we face a common enemy. And the enemy is not a bundle of negative features, an embodiment of devilish villainy or ethnic monstrosity who could be identified as such according to a preestablished set of norms, but simply the collective other whom I oppose with my friends in a genuinely political situation.

---

60. On the end of *Antigone* and its civic potentialities, see Tyrrell and Bennett, *Recapturing Sophocles' "Antigone."* On Hamlet and Orestes, see Murray, *Hamlet and Orestes*; Kott and Taborksi, "Hamlet and Orestes"; and Schleiner, "Latinized Greek."

61. Schmitt, *Concept of the Political*, 26.

Fortinbras is an enemy in this formal sense, the *justus hostis* or "just enemy" against whom the emergency powers of the state are mobilizing in the opening scene, but without embodying any intrinsically negative qualities; indeed, one might even say that he fails to embody qualities of any kind, save those derived from the friend-enemy distinction itself. In response to the enmities of Norway *père* and Norway *fils*, the collectivities of two nations assemble, a conflict free of any content beyond the fact of pure antagonism, yet whose intensity seems more than enough to explain the pitch of martial preparation at the onset of the play. The enmity between Norway and Denmark merges the chivalric protocols of feudal honor with modern sovereignty's emphasis on territorial integrity, the mutual recognition of borders, and rules of engagement.

At the end of the play, two types of the friend remain on stage: the enemy-turned-friend of the European state system represented by Fortinbras, and the philosopher-friend of a more civic tradition represented by Horatio. Both have been elected to represent Hamlet, and each represents a face of princely potentiality, one a commissarial dictator in the line of Schmitt (and Machiavelli's *Il Principe*), the other a public speaker and deliberator in the line of Arendt (and Machiavelli's *I Discorsi*). Hamlet prophesies the election of Fortinbras, entrusting the task of campaigning to Horatio, and thus enunciates a more plural, Arendtian, concept of the political. In naming Fortinbras as king, however, he deposits as the end of the political process a more Schmittian solution, whose conceptual strength lies in his insistence on the purely relational positioning, apart from any cultural, national, or ethnic affiliation, of friends and enemies. Although Shakespeare leaves Denmark in the hands of Fortinbras, he leaves Hamlet's story with Horatio, who in turn leaves it with us. The rest is *not* silence. We are enjoined rather to continue to essay matters of ongoing interest: to think with Shakespeare about the shapes, origins, costs, and limits of political community.

THREE

All's Well That Ends Well and the Futures of Consent

In the previous chapter, a consensual oath founds the fellowship of peers that buffers Hamlet from the sublimity of his father's command. In chapter 6, I demonstrate that *The Tempest* revolves in part around the legal disabilities that attend the consent of minors. Elsewhere I've argued for the significance of consent to the action of both *The Merchant of Venice* and *Measure for Measure*.[1] Yet *All's Well That Ends Well* is, Helena-like, so keen in its quest for consensual solutions that we might dub it Shakespeare's anatomy of consent. The play stages consent from several angles and within several discourses, binding its often labored trains of thought around consent as a political, ethical, sexual, and dramatic factor. In contemporary political theory, consent concerns not only the founding myths of the liberal state, but also daily life in liberal societies. In civil and criminal law, the presence or absence of consent helps determine the validity of contracts (including marriage) as well as the criminality of certain acts (including sexual assault and harassment). In a related area of the law, the "age of consent" refers to the moment at which minors can enter into binding contracts or agree to intercourse. Finally, medical consent comprises the rights of patients to understand, accept, and refuse medical treatment.

All's Well That Ends Well, somewhat astonishingly, engages all of these forms of consent, albeit in a premodern frame that intersects unevenly with modern accountings. The king is ill when the play begins, and Helena must persuade him to consent to treatment. Her reward is the choice of a husband, Bertram, who, as a ward of the king, is subject to an exaggerated form of minority that effectively debars him from the rights associated with the age of consent. Under duress, Bertram grudgingly yields to Helena's wish

---

1. Lupton, *Citizen-Saints*, chapters 3 and 5.

and the King's command, but refuses to consummate the marriage; the ever-resourceful Helena uses the bed trick in order to procure nonconsensual sex from him. At the socio-symbolic level, the play allegorizes the marriage between Bertram and Helena as the contest between aristocratic Nobility and bourgeois Virtue, or between "descent" and "consent" as competing principles of political authority and membership. The play assiduously tests consent as a means of moderating human interaction and constituting civil society and the body politic, as well as oiling the real and metaphoric transitions and translations among existential, economic, and sovereign planes.

Throughout this chapter, I probe the *futures of consent*: both the temporal perplexities of consent as a speech-act and the special momentum carried by consent in liberal philosophy and social arrangements. Like promising, consent commits its speaker to a future, its terms negotiated in advance by the contracting parties yet never fully predictable by them. Moreover, consent often must be inferred backward from the present, from the realized future of a past moment that may or may not have occurred as such; the temporality of consent, in both its ideal linearity and its labored reconstructions, forms much of the dramatic and literary as well as legal interest of consent.[2] Consent itself balances precariously between medieval formulations of ritual assent and liberal procedures for collective deliberation; this transitional character describes not only the state of consent in Shakespeare as a figure between epochs, but, more deeply, affects *consent as a concept always in process*, always casting a possible future out of a set of coordinates whose antiquity disappears into the modernity they deliver. Consent exercises its special rights at the infolded border between political theology and liberalism, between medieval conceptions of the body politic as a mystical unity and liberal conceptions of the social contract as a consensual document among secular persons. In both the dramatic and the symbolic vistas of the play, Shakespeare investigates the peculiar futurity of consent, its relation to politics to come, while also holding before us consent's diverse sources and idioms. In the process, Shakespeare exposes consent as both problem and promise, as a formula that can only imperfectly hold together

---

2. As Lisa Hopkins argues, the play's "very title suggests a teleological and forward-oriented perspective" ("Paris Is Worth a Mass," 369). Garrett Sullivan has explored the play as an exercise in Renaissance "self-forgetting" ("Forgetting, Memory, and Identity in *All's Well That Ends Well*.") See also Patricia Parker on the drama's temporality of dilation: "The intervening space introduced by Bertram's farewell becomes . . . the generative space of Helena's project" (*Shakespeare from the Margins*, 190). A new collection of essays edited by Gary Waller, *All's Well That Ends Well: New Critical Essays*, includes an excellent piece by Michele Osherow on Biblical paradigms of radical maternity ("'She is in the Right'").

the various settlements it brokers, yet one that also provides a conceptual commons for political speculation, experiment, and action. When *All's Well* was written, the liberal futures of consent still lay before it, to be forced into modernity by the writings of Hobbes and Locke. Thinking with Shakespeare about consent places his plays in dialogue with both the prehistories and the mature expressions of liberalism, broadening our sense of the experimental field of Shakespearean drama.

The Literature of Consent

In "Locke, Haywood, and Consent," Jonathan Brody Kramnick proposes to study "the literature of consenting agency"; Kramnick goes on to demonstrate consent's special relationship to modern and early modern literature, its motifs animating the founding fantasies and hypothetical fictions of liberal philosophy while clinging intimately to the romantic plots and subplots of marriage, courtship, seduction, and rape.[3] Although Locke's *Two Treatises of Government* (the starting point of Kramnick's essay and the focus of chapter 6) clearly mark an epochal moment in the consensual binding of politics and literature, fluid exchanges between political and sexual consent certainly predate Locke and form a distinctive stratum of Shakespearean drama. Studies by Victoria Kahn, Gillian Brown, and Holly Brewer demonstrate the ubiquity, variety, and resilience of contractual themes in seventeenth-century literature and life; together, these works constitute a genuine opening into what I am calling *the literature of consent*: the tracking of both real and symbolic consent in and between political writing and dramatic and narrative fiction.[4]

The mother of the contemporary literature of consent is surely the feminist political philosopher Carol Pateman.[5] Although other scholars had connected acts of consent in the real world to the socio-symbolic function of consent as the legitimating fiction of the liberal state, Pateman was the

3. Kramnick, "Locke, Haywood, and Consent," 453.

4. Kahn, *Wayward Contracts*; Brewer, *By Birth or Consent*. For a study of consent in nineteenth-century novels, see Jones, *Consensual Fictions*. Catherine Belsey has written about consent in *Lucrece*; see "Tarquin Dispossessed," 329. The word *consent* appears three times, always with reference to popular affirmation, in Shakespeare's poem.

5. Pateman's 1980 article "Women and Consent" led to her book, *The Sexual Contract* (1988), a sustained feminist critique of liberal contract theory as enunciated by seventeenth-century political philosophers and their heirs; see "Women and Consent"; and *Sexual Contract*. Pateman's work was preceded by the excellent work on seventeenth-century patriarchalism by Gordon Schochet; see *Patriarchalism in Political Thought*. Pateman cites her own debts to Freud, John Stuart Mill, and Mary Astell.

first political scientist to consider systematically the strange and persistent role of sexual and marital consent in contract theory for feminist purposes. In Pateman's argument, the sexual contract names the originary moment in which women consent to submit to masculine authority, a permanent service agreement implicit in, but forgotten by, the social contract that institutes civil society. In everyday life, the marriage contract replays and renews the sexual contract, requiring that women participate as equals in an agreement that seals their legal subordination.[6] Pateman concludes that consent must be rejected as a principle for both social life and political philosophy: "An egalitarian sexual relationship cannot rest on this basis; it cannot be grounded in 'consent.' Perhaps the most telling aspect of women and consent is that we lack a language through which to help constitute a form of personal life in which two equals freely agree to create a lasting association together."[7]

My own project unfolds in the conceptual, historical, and narrative space cleared by Pateman, but I do not accept her categorical rejection of consent as a viable locus for the creative and emancipatory expression of human relationships and social formations. Pateman's argument is ultimately claustrophobic in its construal of a world in which the truth of the employment contract is slavery, and the truth of the marriage contract is rape. Her own reconstructions are largely negative, functioning to diagnose the coercive lies embedded in contract's story of freedom; only rarely does reconstruction imply a more positive program that might scan the liberal tradition for moments of bravery and insight—and engage literary texts as allies in such a campaign.[8] I would insist, contra Pateman, that the relationship between consent and inequality is, historically and conceptually, not simply one of false consciousness or ideological ruse. Indeed, consent is often elicited precisely in situations of inequality, in order to redress imbalances of authority acknowledged as necessary yet potentially debilitating. Medical consent laws, for example, do not claim to make patients into doctors, but

6. In Blackstone's unforgettable formulation, marriage suspends "the very being, or legal existence of the woman" by incorporating her into the person of her husband (cited by Pateman, *Sexual Contract*, 91).

7. Pateman, "Women and Consent," 164.

8. Pateman is not always clear on the extent of her rejection of consent, contract, and the classical tradition. Although in general her readings of Locke, Hobbes, and Rousseau as well as Pufendorf and Grotius are conducted with a dogged attention to their failures with respect to women, occasionally she applies the language of speculative reconstruction toward a more positive program; for example: "To begin to work towards such a reconstruction of [the liberal state and sexual life] is to *begin to transform the legacy of the early contract theorists*" ("Women and Consent," 163; emphasis added).

to create conditions that actively address the patient as the guardian of her own well being.[9] Similarly, laws concerning the consent of minors do not deny children's legal disabilities, but borrow from the minor's future contractual capacities in order to protect her interests in the present.[10] Nor did marital consent claim to make wives equal to their husbands. In an uneven status landscape in which women were presumed to need the protection of men, consent inserted an element of provisional autonomy and self-determination into an unequal relationship. The consensual moment could have real consequences in a court of law as well as in the rights and rituals of courtship, and it provided a conceptual wedge for rethinking the relations between the sexes when new forms of equality became viable social goals.

If Pateman is the mother of the contemporary study of consent in literature, its grandmother is another political philosopher, Hanna Pitkin, who published a lengthy article in 1965–66 entitled "Obligation and Consent."[11] Pitkin reasserts the importance of obligation in political life in response to liberalism's romance with consent. Whereas Pateman finds consent *insufficiently consensual* (belying its own ideal of free and voluntary agreement), Pitkin faults consent for an *excessive voluntarism* that fails to account for the call of political obligation. What Pateman takes to be the scandalous truth of consent—namely, that it uses the rhetoric of equality to validate subjection—constitutes for Pitkin its philosophical and political interest: "We are both superior to and subject to *all* our obligations, and *that* is what requires an accounting."[12] Pitkin's significance for the *literature* of consent lies in her attention to the language and grammar of consent, which she derives from a reading of Wittgenstein on language games and Austin on speech-acts.[13] Citing Austin, Pitkin argues that "'promise' is not just a word. Promising is a social practice, something we *do*, something children have to learn *how*

9. "On a micro-level, the relationship between doctor and patient has been presented as a negotiation in which the parties are not equal. . . . Traditionally, the law has a role in reducing this imbalance of power" (Montgomery, "Power/Knowledge/Consent," 247).

10. David Archard describes the temporal dynamic of the "caretaker" thesis, which he sees as the major theory of children's rights and parents' duties in liberalism, with its origins in Locke's accounts of childhood: "The caretaker, if you like, chooses for the child in the person of the adult whom the child is not yet but will eventually be" (*Children*, 53). For a Kantian development of the caretaker thesis as it relates to medical consent, see Ross, *Children*.

11. Hanna Pitkin, "Obligation and Consent." pts. 1 and 2. Pitkin is best known for *The Concept of Representation*, a landmark application of language philosophy to the political concept of representation. Pitkin is also the author of an insightful critique of Arendt, partly on feminist grounds, *The Attack of the Blob*.

12. Pitkin, "Obligation and Consent," pt. 2, 49.

13. Pitkin developed her investigations into Wittgenstein, Austin, and politics in *Wittgenstein and Justice*.

to do." Promising is "a self-assumed obligation," and "to the question why obligations oblige the only possible answer would seem to be that this is what the words mean." Contract theorists have long associated consent with promising; both are forms of agreement that commit the subject to a future course of action. Piktin is notable for analyzing both consent and promising as language games whose meaning turns on conventions and social practice rather than on an *a priori* logical or legal ground. Citing Wittgenstein, she writes that there is no "absolute, deductive answer to the question, 'why does any promise ever oblige?' . . . It is, to be sure, related to any number of other principles, obligations and values; but the relationship is more like a network (or patchwork) than like a hierarchical principle."[14]

Piktin uses Wittgenstein and Austin in order to construct a political scene that tips the consensual see-saw between freedom and obligation toward the latter, but in a post-foundationalist setting of laterally networked conventions that can be neither rationally deduced nor divinely authorized. Moreover, she is interested in something like the existential element of promising: not simply its contractual terms, but the way in which consent pledges the speaker to an unknown future, building an ethical world out of speech-acts that create bonds between distinct persons and moments.[15] "The person who makes a promise," she writes, "seems to recognize and commit himself to the institution of promises."[16] Promising "is not socially useful; it is indispensable to the very concept of society and human life."[17] When *Hamlet*'s Player-King argues against promising, he does so by denying the intersubjective connectivity of consent: "Purpose is but the slave to memory, / Of violent birth, but poor validity . . . Most necessary 'tis that we forget / To pay ourselves what to ourselves is debt" (3.2.183–88). In *Timon of Athens*, the Painter subjects promising to a similar cynical analysis: "To promise is most courtly and fashionable; performance is a kind of will or testament which argues a great sickness in his judgment that makes it" (5.1.26–28).Yet promising becomes a debt and a testament only via our obligations to others, and to the future itself. Securing the "validity" of promising in a future by definition cut off from its inception is, in Pitkin's analysis, an ethical as well as a legal and political venture, and one grounded in the very grammar of commitment.

14. Pitkin, "Obligation and Consent," pt. 2, 47.
15. Pitkin marks the link between her Wittgensteinian investigations and a certain existentialist project in *Wittgenstein and Justice*, xl.
16. Ibid., 46.
17. Ibid., 48.

In these reflections, Pitkin begins to expose the extent to which consent is not identical with contract. Derived from the Latin *consentire*, literally, "to feel together," consent is both *speech* and *act*, both expressed content, in which I agree *to* a course of action or state of affairs, and the sheer fact of connection and coordination, the coinciding of sensibilities that creates a social moment. Renaissance poetry expresses this extralegal sense of consent most often in lyric. In "Love's Ecstacy," Thomas Heywood represents sexual consent not as the mutual agreement to intercourse that constitutes modern consent laws, but as the ecstatic coincidence of desires, souls, and bodies:

> Crown our wishes with content,
> Meet our souls in sweet consent,
> And let this night, this night, be spent
> In all abundant pleasures.[18]

"Consent" and "content" reconnoiter frequently in Renaissance verse; consent produces its own form of contentment by aligning subjects with each other and with a social order that coalesces out of their harmony. In lyric poetry, the choreography of consent—what Shakespeare calls "the marriage of true minds"—purports to synchronize the parts of the person (heart to hand or soul to word) in relation to the sensibilities of others in the echoing consensus drawn by eros, civility, and the cosmos itself.[19] When Hobbes writes that the Leviathan is "more than consent or concord," being a "real unity of them all in one and the same person, made by covenant of every man with every man," he posits the political equivalent of this deep synchronization, diverting its sexual energy in order to fund a socio-symbolic force of extraordinary power. Hobbes's "more than consent" measures the difference between consent in its contractual dimension, as a formal relation between distinct legal persons, and consent as the quasi-atomic fusion of elements into a new political body.[20]

18. See Bullen, ed., *Lyrics from the Dramatists of the Elizabethan Age*, 148–49.
19. Sonnet 116, in Shakespeare, *Sonnets*. Other examples include Milton's "At a Solemn Music," where Voice and Verse join in a cosmic "undisturbed Song of pure consent"; see Milton, *Complete Poems of John Milton*, 4:41. In "Discipline," George Herbert aspires to a "full consent" with God, where the goal is the complete coincidence of their "desires" rather than adherence to a specific content: "For my heart's desire / Unto thine is bent : / I aspire / To a full consent" (*Complete English Poems*, 168).
20. Hobbes, *Leviathan*, 128.

But consent can miss its mark, coming forward as problem rather than solution when its terms, sincerity, or free exercise are found lacking in the courts of law or public opinion. The construal of consent as a speech-act has become a touchstone of contemporary legal theories of consent, though Pitkin is rarely cited as its source. David Archard's *Sexual Consent* and Peter Westen's *The Logic of Consent* offer the most sustained philosophical accounts of contemporary consent law conducted from within legal theory circles. Each begins with the "morally transformative" character of consent, whose presence or absence makes the difference between romantic union and date rape, between theft and loan, or between surgery and mutilation.[21] Archard writes that "the giving of consent is an act rather than a state of mind. Consent is something I do rather than think or feel. . . . [This] view of consent . . . is usually expressed by the statement that consent should be understood in 'performative' and not 'psychological' terms."[22] Yet for both Archard and Westen, performance does not exhaust consent, which always points inward toward a psychological state of acquiescence, affirmation, or general willingness, and also outward to the conventions in which consent is understood and processed, as well as to any conditions of undue influence, persuasion, or force that might impeach its free exercise. The publicly expressed instance of consent mediates between internal and external spheres of meaning and validity, between a prior intent and a ratifying context that delivers its witnessing amen to the act in question. In many legal cases, no formal speech-act or equivalent gesture of consent has actually occurred, or it has taken place in the most private corners of human interaction and experience; instead, consent must be retroactively imputed or disputed on the basis of circumstances and conventions, themselves subject to individual construal and collective transformation. Consent is thus subject to strange temporalities: as a species of promising, consent commits me to an unknown future. Yet sometimes the future is now, a state of affairs from which the act of consent itself may have to be inferred, reconstructed, withdrawn or invalidated. Both the law and the literature of consent take shape in the rifts between the interiority of intention, the expression of consent, and the public web of expectations and memories that confirm consent in the public sphere.

---

21. Westen, *Logic of Consent*, 15; Archard, *Sexual Consent*, 3. Neither cites Pitkin, since her interests are quite different, their touchstone being instead Hurd, "The Moral Magic of Consent." Nonetheless, Pitkin initiated the performative reading of consent, and I would like to credit her here. On the limits of speech-act theory for understanding consent in criminal law, see Westen, *Logic of Consent*, 89–91.

22. Archard, *Sexual Consent*, 4.

In the case of "tacit consent," Locke's contribution to the liberal theory of political obligation, consent subsists in a kind of permanent present tense, implicitly proffered in every act of civil belonging; such consent, Kramnick notes, "burrows into our 'very being'" in liberal theory and life.[23] Adriana Johnson associates tacit consent with the function of ideology: "It concerns the way in which everyday material practices become naturalized, so that standing in line for a passport, going to school, acquiring a marriage certificate, affixing a number to one's house, or measuring a pound of wheat becomes as ordinary or banal as sweeping a floor or eating bread."[24] Yet Johnson goes on to posit negative consent—the possibility of a refused, withdrawn, or reserved consent—as a more emancipatory future for consent, designating "not so much a free rational choice on the part of the subordinate populations but the fragility or instability of hegemony, the possibility for struggle and contention."[25] While Johnson would agree with Pateman that consent generally supports the status quo, she also suggests that negative consent riddles the quotidian present tense of consensual governance with possible futures. Hannah Arendt makes a similar point, but posed closer to the core of the democratic tradition: "All political institutions are manifestations and materializations of power; they petrify and decay as soon as the living power of the people ceases to uphold them."[26] Consider the role of withheld consent in *Measure for Measure*, where both Barnardine's vocal refusal and Isabella's inscrutable reticence suspend the rubber stamp of consent, summoning the chance for political transformation.[27]

In the Renaissance, the discourse of consent flows among sexual, civil, and political instances, inmixing protoliberal and theological trends. As Arthur Monahan has amply demonstrated, consent was not a new idea on the early modern scene.[28] Medieval rulers, as well as bishops, popes, and abbots, usually took office through some public demonstration of popular consent. These expressions, however, were often ritual in nature, proceeding by acclamation rather than formal balloting. In the early modern period, consent, along with the sister concept of political representation, underwent a sea change from a largely ritual and symbolic understanding involving public assent to right rule to a procedural one involving collective deliberation by a people organized through representatives.

---

23. Kramnick, "Locke, Haywood, and Consent," 454, 457.
24. Johnson, "Everydayness and Subalternity," 23.
25. Ibid., 24.
26. Arendt, *On Violence*, 41.
27. See Lupton, *Citizen-Saints*, 154.
28. Monahan, *Consent, Coercion and Limit*.

The Roman civil formula *quod omnes tangit ab omnibus tractari et approbari debet* ("what touches all must be approved by all") provided one touchstone for considering consent; through the Roman legacy, private law expanded and democratized public institutions on an economic model that would privilege liberal over republican political tendencies.[29] Yet Monahan also asserts the roots of consent in Jewish and early Christian concepts of authority and community.[30] The Decalogue borrows its covenantal models from both suzerain-vassal treaties, "where one party transparently imposes its will on another" following a military conquest or liberation, and from milder narratives of courtship and marriage, in which God woos Israel as His bride.[31] In medieval Christendom, the community of the faithful represented the *corpus mysticum*, or body of Christ, a conception subject to both hierarchical and horizontal mappings in the unfolding political scenes of European politics.[32] Thus the "election" of a ruler could simultaneously point upward, to his special election by God, as well as downward, to his appointment by a council or *populus*, with a circuit of collective inspiration seamlessly connecting upper and lower founts of legitimacy.[33] Liberalism does not simply shed these theopolitical origins. Gordon Schochet speaks of "gratitude" as a forgotten form of consent in Hobbes's contract theory; such covenants "presuppose no equality. . . . Because they depend on largesse and there-

29. Monahan dedicates a full chapter to the formula abbreviated as *q o t* (*Consent, Coercion and Limit*, 97–111). On the Greek tradition of man as a political animal versus the Roman tradition of the citizen as a legal person, see Pocock, "The Ideal of Citizenship," 31–42.

30. *The Jewish Political Tradition*, edited under the direction of Michael Walzer, places the concept of covenant at the base of its archive. The selections on covenant begin with Moses at Sinai and end with Spinoza's *Theological-Political Treatise*, where the Biblical motif of covenant comes face to face with liberal consent theory. See (Walzer, Lorberbaum, and Zohar, eds., *Jewish Political Tradition*, vol. 1, *Authority*, 3–46. See also Novak, *Jewish Social Contract*.

31. Such treaties were written in duplicate on tablets of stone, one for the suzerain and one for the vassal; following this convention, a tradition dating from the Palestinian Talmud avers that each tablet of the Decalogue contained the full text of the agreement, with one copy for God and one for Israel (Sarna, "Exodus," 108n). I develop the tension between sovereign and marital metaphors of covenant in the Decalogue and the political traditions it spawned in my essay, "Rights, Commandments, and the Literature of Citizenship."

32. On the *corpus mysticum* and the genealogy of political representation as a concept, Hanna Pitkin writes, "The Latin *repraesentare* was gradually extended in Christian religious literature to signify a kind of mystical embodiment 'applied to the Christian community in its most incorporeal aspects'" (Pitkin, ed., *Representation*, 2). For the political implications of the *corpus mysticum*, see Kantorowicz, *King's Two Bodies*, 193–272; Oakley, "Natural Law, the Corpus Mysticum, and Consent"; and Rust, "Political Theologies of the *Corpus Mysticum*."

33. Monahan cites John of Salisbury: "He actually employs the terms 'election' (*electio*) and 'to elect' (*eligere*), but the context shows that he is speaking of the ruler as chosen (elected) by God"; see *Consent, Coercion and Limit*, 65.

fore on goodwill, they may be withdrawn at the pleasure of the grantor."[34] Schochet cites Hobbes: "'As Justice dependeth on Antecedent Covenant; so does GRATITUDE depend on Antecedent Grace.'"[35] Evoking archaic gift economies rather than modern contract law, gratitude reflects the inequality between conquering suzerain and his subjects that backlights the pact at Sinai. Although Locke's contract is more bilateral and less routinely subject to coercion than Hobbes's, it reroutes rather than extinguishes the theological commitments that accompany contract in the medieval tradition. In the classical Lockean triad of "life, liberty, and property," the inaugural term *life* embodies the self-possession of the person associated with possessive individualism, yet also manifests the limits of a purely economic definition of property by repeatedly instantiating itself as something other than property in the alienable sense.[36] Locke has recourse to theism in defining the peculiar obligations that self-possession brings with it: since men are "the Workmanship of one Omnipotent, and infinitely wise Maker, . . . they are his Property" and each man is thus *"bound to preserve himself."*[37] Life, unlike liberty or property, cannot be temporarily alienated, since death is permanent; the laws that govern medical consent engage the exceptional character of life in the norms of liberal law, developing the consequences of Lockean political theology in a post-theological vein.[38]

The vicissitudes of covenant within the legacies of contract haunt the history and futures of consent. By mapping a fundamental inequality within the scene of contract, covenant smuggles a retrograde, feudal tendency into apparently equal relations. Yet the gift character of covenant, bearing an element of surplus in relation to equivalence, can also deposit an existential

34. Gordon Schochet, "Symposium on David Novak's *The Jewish Social Contract,*" 595.

35. Schochet, "Intending (Political) Obligation," 69.

36. On the relation between Locke's broad definition of property as "life, liberty and estate" versus his narrower definition of property as alienable land and goods, see Gordon Schochet, who concludes, "Given the historical and political differences between property in land and material possessions, on the one hand, and property in one's self, on the other, it is doubtful that a single theoretical doctrine could contain them both" ("'Guards and Fences,'" 377). It is this gap, a gap designated by "life," that interests me, and which continues to generate some of liberalism's political-theological urgency.

37. John Locke, *Two Treatises of Government* (*Second Treatise,* §6; his emphasis). Compare also his statement that parents are accountable to God for the welfare of their children, whose lives are not the product or property of their parents, but of God as creator (*Second Treatise,* §56).

38. See Terrance McConnell on life and "inalienable rights" as they affect medical consent laws. He specifically distances his project from the theism of Locke, while also developing the exceptionality of life already disclosed in Locke's philosophy (McConnell, *Inalienable Rights,* x, 11–19).

possibility within or at the borders of liberal consent. When that surplus remains with the sovereign, as it does in Hobbes, or justifies expropriation and slavery, as it can in Locke, it becomes an illiberal moment within liberalism, funding some of the nasty work done in liberalism's name. But that surplus can also become a reservoir in and for the one who consents, a political-theological element that accrues not to the state but to singular subjects, equal to each other in the scene of liberal contract yet unequal to themselves, in possession of or possessed by an excess of consensus. And all of these issues bear on *All's Well*, where covenantal and contractual ideas of consent meet around questions of life and death.

The Consent to Experiment

When *All's Well* begins, the Countess of Rossillion has lost her husband, and her son Bertram has now become a ward of the king. Worse than losing a father is gaining a guardian; as Bertram complains, "I must now attend his majesty's command, to whom I am now in ward, evermore in subjection" (1.1.4–5). Meanwhile, Gerard de Narbonne, a gifted physician of modest means, has also died, leaving his daughter Helena in the custody of the countess. Helena, not unlike Bertram himself, cares more about the young man's departure for court than about the death of her father, and she resolves to follow him there, bringing with her the "prescriptions" and "receipts" that form her precious dowry of medical knowledge (1.3.216; 2.1.104). The king of France suffers from a "fistula," or abscess, and the "congregated college" of "our most learned doctors" has been unable to cure him (2.1.115–16). In the eruption of this fistula Helena intuits a possible ingress for her designs: "The king's disease—my project may deceive me, / But my intents are fix'd, and will not leave me" (1.1.224–25).

At court, Helena's first task is to persuade the king to submit to her ministrations. She offers her services with a double flourish of bravado and modesty:

> And hearing your high majesty is touch'd
> With that malignant cause, wherein the honour
> Of my dear father's gift stands chief in power,
> I come to tender it and my appliance,
> With all bound humbleness. (2.1.109–13)

Helena credits her father with any success, but supplements his transmitted knowledge with the necessary action of her "own appliance" (2.1.112).

The word *appliance*, like its cousins *compliance* and *suppliance*, suggests the fundamental *plier* of service in a feudal scene of hierarchical obligations, while also naming the instrumental or "applied" character of her medical knowledge. She is, throughout the play, a figure of both dedicated service and applied knowledge, of *phronesis* as that form of pragmatic virtue exercised in order to achieve desired ends. Her knowledge of plant, animal, and mineral virtues affiliates her with Markham's husbandmen. Yet this "sweet practiser" (2.1.184) cannot apply her recipes unless the king complies with her proposal. At his first refusal, Helena—with anticipations of Isabella—seems willing to exit without further ado, but the king—with intimations of Angelo—keeps the conversation going. Helena, not needing the prompting required of her Viennese sister, eagerly waxes more eloquent, arguing that any remedy will flow not from her own skill but from God's grace. In a key couplet whose resonances will occupy us throughout this chapter, Helena momentarily weds the discourses of contract and medicine through the sweet coincidence of rhyme: "Dear sir, to my endeavors give *consent*; / Of heaven, not me, make an *experiment*" (2.1.152–53; emphasis added).

The king begins to acquiesce, but wants to know the terms of their agreement. "Upon thy certainty and confidence / What dar'st thou venture?" (2.1.168–69), he demands; in response, she offers not only her "maiden's name" but also her very life (2.1.171–73). He finally agrees, "Sweet practiser, thy physic I will try, / That ministers thine own death if I die" (2.1.184–85). Helena, however, who never lets modesty interfere with her negotiating skills, wants both sides of the contract spelled out: "Not helping, death's my fee; / But if I help, what do you promise me?" (2.1.188–89). He asks her to name her terms, and she suggests as a reward the husband of her own choosing. The king gives his hand—a conventional gesture of formal consent:

> Here is my hand; the premises observ'd,
> Thy will by my performance shall be serv'd;
> So make the choice of thy own time, for I,
> Thy resolv'd patient, on thee still rely. (2.1.200–203)

As her "resolv'd patient," the king finally places himself in her care, and he promises the "performance" of her will if she succeeds in curing him. Despite her humble pose, Helena is determined to gain something from this transaction, and the king too is not so desperate for good health that he lacks interest in the terms of engagement. Not unlike *The Merchant of Venice*, the language of contract operates at the political-theological interface, building the scene of consent out of archetypal formulas from myth and folktale.

The exchange is an extraordinary one, especially when read through and against the modern template provided by medical consent. The unexpected rhyme of "consent" and "experiment" precociously affiliates the discourses of contract and medicine; since their engagement will only be consummated in modern medical consent laws, it is fitting that "consent" and "experiment" form only a half rhyme, an imperfect echo whose discrepancies are as telling as their assonance.[39] Thus the scene is fundamentally structured by the inequality of sovereign and subject, their disproportion of power heightened by the gender difference between "Doctor She" and her male monarch. In this interaction between subject and sovereign, the word *consent*, far from implying relations between formal equals (as in a contract) or between functional non-equals (as in the modern doctor-patient couple), instead serves at least in part to reaffirm the sovereignty of the king. The king's consent functions more like an act of grace, as when a parent grants a child a special privilege, than like the signing of a contract between equal parties. In the late feudal context, the king's consent resembles a *deed of gift* more than a *deed of sale*, an unequal covenant rather than a balanced contract.

Nonetheless, from within the arc of sovereign gratitude, both the king's majesty and the king's body appear subject to decay and transformation. The king's "consent" to treatment opens onto the space and time of what Helena calls "experiment." Consistent with modern medical consent, the king knowingly submits himself to the risk of an uncertain course of treatment, manifesting consent's special relationship to an unknown future, its commitment to contingency. And the risk is mortal: they bargain not in francs and centimes, but in life and death. If the king dies, so shall Helena, and if he is cured, she can choose a husband, ticket to new life. We should note here that medical consent, which concerns the dignity as well as the knowledge of the person submitting to a course of treatment, unfolds on a completely different plane from that of any financial agreement. As such, I would insist that medical consent inhabits and holds open a certain nonidentity between consent and contract, mobilizing the subjective and

---

39. Institutional Review Boards, which govern the informed consent of research subjects, trace their origins to the Nuremburg trials. Consent to medical treatment is older, avowed as part of English common law by twentieth-century judges. Most precedents, however, appear to date from the late nineteenth century, when unconsented procedures were tried as a form of battery. For contemporary bioethical analyses of medical consent, see especially Brennen, *Just Doctoring*; and McConnell, *Inalienable Rights*.

existential dimensions of consent that entail affirming uncertainty as a condition of existence. Although most exercises of medical consent, scripted by regulatory and liability concerns, fall far short of such an existential affirmation, the roots of informed consent norms in the Nuremberg trials reveal the extent to which medical consent continues to reflect and respond to a kind of trauma suffered by the body of the medical profession itself as it struggles to reconcile liberal rights talk with older discourses of beneficence, service, and care.[40]

To return to Arendt, we might say that medical consent exemplifies the modern regime of *biopolitics*, the management of life processes by the administrative state and the consumer economy, but it also shelters the chance to enter the *bios politikos*, the conduct of living that Arendt associates with the Greek polis and with the human condition as such. Under the regime of biopolitics, the bureaucratic state appropriates and reorganizes the sovereign's unique jurisdiction over the life and death of his subjects. Medical consent law is an instance of biopolitics insofar as informed consent protocols extend and stabilize the agreement to treatment into a system of procedures that are themselves neither medical nor ethical. Yet medical consent, by harboring at its core the patient's subjective performance of her own responsibility in relation to the hazards of embodiment, does not simply disappear into the paperwork that regulates and records it. Whereas signing on the dotted line exemplifies the global navigations of biopolitics, actively exercising my rights and dignity in the medical scene can reopen the *bios politikos* from within the regulatory precinct that appears to have foreclosed it.[41]

I would argue that this existential moment of medical consent also partakes in political theology, now understood not in the negative sense of a biopolitical economization of life by the state, but in a more positive,

40. On Nuremburg and informed consent, see Weindling, *Nazi Medicine*, which meticulously reconstructs the legal, political, and ethical dimensions of the trials in relation to informed consent: "Informed consent permeates modern medicine: an understanding of its meaning and implications in the political ordering of human life requires critical historical analysis of the Nuremberg medical maelstrom" (8). The connection between Nuremberg and modern consent is a commonplace in biomedical discourse, substantiating my claim that medical consent includes a political-theological dimension. In a helpful though somewhat dated summary of the debates, Bradford H. Gray makes passing reference to the Nuremberg Code, which established patient rights in the wake of the Nuremberg trials, and he goes on to address the gap between the regulated procedures of consent and the conditions of a more genuine act of consent (Gray, "Complexities of Informed Consent"). The Nuremberg Code opens with the following declaration: "The voluntary consent of the human subject is absolutely essential." The code is available online at http://ohsr.od.nih.gov/guidelines/nuremberg.html.

41. Arendt, *Human Condition*, 25.

emancipatory sense of a scene that allows the subject to confront embodiment as something other than the object of a determinate knowledge or possession, as a surplus vitality that solicits a care deeper and more beholden
than the techniques of actuarial management. The point is not to theologize
life as a gift of God, as occurs in the fundamentalist strain of the "right to
life" movement, but to see life as an overdetermined quantity that survives
the death of God in order to constellate and animate modern discourses of
rights, responsibilities, and civic action. Eric Santner captures this positive
quotient of political theology in modernity: "What is *more than life* turns out
to be, from the post-Nietzschean perspective, imminent to and constitutive
of life itself."[42] In a related project, William Connolly makes room for what
he calls the "visceral register of subjectivity and intersubjectivity" largely ignored by modern secularism.[43] Following Santner and Connolly, I am interested in capturing how acts of consent respond to life as that which exceeds
both theistic and secular determinations. Medical consent as the *consent to
experiment against the horizon of a receding heaven*—as the agreement to venture into an unknown future—is one route by which life renders manifest
the productive limit shared by liberalism and political theology.

The France of *All's Well* is undergoing a crisis in sacral sovereignty.[44] The
king's body mortal has been pathologically perforated, opened up internally and externally to dangerous flows and exchanges, compromising the
viability of the king's two bodies. The Royal Touch was attributed to the
kings of France and England, who were believed to be able to cure scrofula.
In the scene's thaumaturgic dramaturgy, it is as if the king profanes the aura
of his office by consenting to Helena's appliances. High and low come into
mysterious contact, the Royal Touch of magical kingship brushing against
the feminine hands of a lay healer.[45] Gratitude rather than parity may still
govern the scene, but the direction of debt has shifted. Whereas scrofula
is a skin disease, the fistula burrows inward; indeed, fistulation is one way
that advanced scrofula manifests itself. Afflicted at least associatively with
the very ailment his office is purported to cure, the royal physician cannot
heal himself, and must open his sores to the ministrations of Helena. The
weary mood of gentle decline that characterizes the speech of the play's

42. Santner, *Psychotheology of Everyday Life*, 10. See also Bonnie Honig's account of life, liberalism, rights, and futurity, including the ambiguities of the right to die movement, in *Emergency
Politics*, 41–64.

43. Connolly, *Why I Am Not a Secularist*, 3, cf. 24–26.

44. As M. C. Bradbrook put it, "The metaphor of the sick king was always something more
than a metaphor for Shakespeare"; see "'Virtue Is the True Nobility,'" 294.

45. See the classic study by Bloch, *Royal Touch*.

older generation—the Countess of Rossillion, the Count Lafew, and the king himself—implies a general aging and exhaustion of the political order as such: its mounting impotence, its need for new transfusions and infusions of "life"—through fertile marriages between young people most certainly, but also through new alliances between social classes or estates.[46] Helena has the power to revive the king, but such reanimation also suggests a transformation in kingship itself, exposing the monarchy to its mortal dependence on middle-class energy and to a form of public housekeeping that will, as one of the futures of consent, expand and reorient the domestic projects of the modern state. Gone: the Royal Touch. On the horizon: the Office of Public Health. Required: the consent of all parties. Still at play: "life" as both the object of biopolitical administration and the tremulous frontier of political expression and emancipation struggles.

As a slew of recent critics have argued, the play takes place against the backdrop of the Reformation, the French setting implying both nostalgia for England's Catholic past and the religious uncertainties of contemporary France.[47] Lisa Hopkins argues that "the splitting of Christendom effected by schism can only be healed . . . by reversion to a much-older, quasi-magical mode of thought and worship that preceded the splitting of the faiths and the theological controversies that consequently ensued."[48] Yet there is also a sense that the monarchy itself, along with its sacred tropes, is in decline, requiring a new set of metaphors and institutions in the face of a changing social body. Insofar as consent in its covenantal dimension exists in some tension with consent in its contractual dimension, consent becomes both a bridge and a battleground between competing conceptions of sovereignty. Such a transition involves not so much a replacement of political theology by secularism as a refunctioning of political-theological resources in order to accommodate and legitimize new forms of civil society. Signs of this transformation already shape the scene of medical consent in *All's Well* in order to come to the fore in the play's main action, which struggles to make marital and sexual consent do the work of reconciling class, gender, and generational tensions. When the king returns from his treatment, Lafew declares him "Lustique," highlighting the reinvigoration of the king as a sexual

46. Lisa Hopkins, citing Richard Levine, notes the sexual nature of the King's dysfunction ("Paris Is Worth a Mass," 370).

47. See for example, Hunt, "Helena and the Reformation Problem of Merit," and Hopkins, "Paris Is Worth a Mass." Peggy Munoz Simonds also studies the theological metaphors that animate the play, though her emphasis is not on Reformation controversies but on a more generalized Christian heritage; see "Sacred and Sexual Motifs."

48. Hopkins, "'Paris Is Worth a Mass,'" 378.

one. But the real sex must occur in the next generation, as part of the cost as well as the benefit of the king's cure. The *consent to medical treatment*, performed between subject and sovereign, precedes and frames the *social and marital consent* between persons and classes that unfolds with so many fits and starts in the marriage of Bertram and Helena. These social exchanges are part of the experiment to which the king consents, allowing the body politic itself to enter into a zone of risk and potential transformation.

The Trouble with Bertram

Having cured the king, Helena must now make her choice. Bidding her sit, queenlike, by his side, the king presents his wards:

> Fair maid, send forth thine eye. This youthful parcel
> Of noble bachelors at my bestowing,
> O'er whom both sovereign power and father's voice
> I have to use. Thy frank election make;
> Thou hast power to choose, and they none to forsake. (2.3.52–56)

His life now in her debt, the king shares a bit of his sovereignty with her, proclaiming his double power—as both king and guardian—over the young men lined up before them. Lisa Hopkins links the use of the term *election* here to "the Calvinist doctrine of double predestination," an allusion that would, by association with the king and his own divine right, render Helena in the image of God, insofar as she chooses a saint at her own pleasure and without regard to his will.[49] *Election*, like consent, is part of an entrenched theopolitical vocabulary that conceptualizes the simultaneously divine and popular legitimacy of preliberal polities; in chapter 3 we witnessed Hamlet undergoing the brutality of election from above and struggling to disperse and depressurize its power into other conduits of affiliation and attachment.[50] The sexual and sovereign "frankness" of Helena's election indicates the unusual scope of her own will and the corresponding unfreedom of her prospective spouse, launching a vertiginous set of domestic and political questions. If Helena is free to choose her domestic sovereign, how much control will her elected husband have over her in marriage? If her free

49. Ibid., 378.

50. Arthur Monahan cites Godfrey of Fontaines, a thirteenth-century commentator: "The whole community *(tota communitas)* either 'elects' *(eligens)*, 'institutes' *(instituens)*, 'accepts' *(acceptans)*, or 'consents' *(consentiens)*" to its ruler, a sequence of political speech-acts that tellingly places election in a continuum with consent *(Consent, Coercion, and Limit,* 186).

choice of spouse is related to the frank election of a sovereign, what might such election reveal about the monarch's own power? Finally, how does "frank election," unconstrained by the will or wishes of the chosen object, compete with the cognate idea of consent, whose language of reciprocity is deeply embedded in marital discourse?

The questions only continue to mount. Helena herself takes the stage with a show of modesty, always strategic in her careful display of virgin virtues. When she finally stands before Bertram, she tries to couch the exceptional activity of her frank election in the most passive, indeed feudal language possible:

> I dare not say I take you, but I give
> Me and my service, ever whilst I live,
> Into your guiding power. This is the man. (2.3.102–4)

The king's impatient response implies discomfited silence on Bertram's part: "Why, then, young Bertram, take her; she's thy wife" (2.3.105). Bertram, of course, would prefer not to:

> But follows it, my lord, to bring me down
> Must answer for your raising? I know her well:
> She had her breeding at my father's charge—
> A poor physician's daughter for my wife! Disdain
> Rather corrupt me ever! (2.3.112–16)

The king, roused but not yet furious, responds to Bertram's priggish snobbery with his famous speech on virtue, setting into play the allegorical contest between virtue and nobility that M. C. Bradbrook identified as "the governing idea of the whole composition."[51] The king identifies virtue with Aristotelian praxis, distinguished from all marks of birth: "From lowest place when virtuous things proceed, / The place is dignified by the doer's deed" (2.3.124–25). Virtue belongs to the field of action, including the actions that Helena has already performed; it also belongs to the bourgeoisie, of which she is a member. Although Bradbrook's analysis is thematic rather than political—"virtue" and "honor" remain ideational contents rather than symptoms or players in structural change—she aptly nails the strained romance of the play's plot to an intellectual debate that in turn reflects social

51. *All's Well*, she writes, juxtaposes "the social problem of high birth versus native merit and the human problem of unrequited love" (Bradbrook, "Virtue Is the True Nobility," 289).

and economic trends in the Renaissance. Can the "virtues" of the emergent middle class, with its new educational, economic, and professional aspirations and capacities, produce a "true nobility" that will supplant feudal and aristocratic honor codes?

The issues are political as well as economic, involving the terms and criteria of civic membership. Modern theorists of citizenship would translate "virtue" versus "honor" into "consent" versus "descent" as competing paradigms for group membership and political legitimacy. *Consent* names the equalizing agreement to a social contract that requires the new citizen to exchange prior ethnic or regional identifications for the shared traits of civic belonging. *Descent,* on the other hand, designates inclusion or exclusion based on birth, whether conceived in caste, aristocratic, or ethnocultural terms.[52] Intermarriage is a classic path into the polity from a location outside it, in both the lived histories of peoples and in the symbolic architecture and mythology of citizenship protocols. The party who enters the commonwealth through marriage is doubly *a figure of consent*: consenting to romantic union and consenting to membership in a new group at the expense of prior affiliations. Shakespeare dramatizes such scenes of civic naturalization through intermarriage in the unions of Othello and Desdemona and of Jessica and Lorenzo in his Venetian plays. *All's Well*, along with its sister play, *Measure for Measure*, is also a story of intermarriage, now between social classes rather than racial or religious groups. The duke aims to *marry down* in proposing to Isabella; Helena aims to *marry up* in electing Bertram. In both cases, consent is a political factor, not only because the chosen partners withhold their consent, but because *consent itself is at stake* as a legitimating principle for political and social relations. In other words, if Descent and Consent as civic criteria consent to marry each other, Consent appears to win the game by virtue of the nature of the agreement itself, signaling a fundamental swerve—the swerve we call liberalism—in the European investment in bloodlines. Both plays hesitate, like shy lovers just released from the magic towers of feudal childhoods, before the prospect of such modernity. Shakespeare limits any scandal, however, by placing his female citizens under the sovereign coverture of their noble husbands, reserving a head start on the liberal playing field for nobility's avatars, such as old money, good schools, racial privilege, and the charisma of celebrity.

52. On consent versus descent, see for example Klusmeyer, *Between Consent and Descent.* Werner Sollors emphasizes the special status of consent in American civic culture and its implications for U.S. ethnic literatures in *Beyond Ethnicity.* See also Bonnie Honig's analysis of the role of intermarriage in consent-based citizenship paradigms that incorporate foreigners into the body politic (*Democracy and the Foreigner*, 92–98).

Shakespeare places the most sustained exposition of virtue's superiority to nobility in the mouth of the king, the crowning apex of the noble pyramid. Sovereign is he who can declare bourgeois exceptions to the laws of aristocratic nature:

> If thou canst like this creature as a maid,
> I can create the rest. Virtue and she
> Is her own dower; honour and wealth from me. (2.3.142–44)

Exercising a classic trope of political theology, the king claims that he, like the Creator above, has the power to new-create his subjects by endowing them with titles and wealth.[53] If this claim flows from his most traditional attributes of sovereignty, it is at the same time an argument and instrument for the bourgeoisification of the ruling class. Hobbes will sketch a similar topology when he declares that "in the sovereignty is the font of all honour." Using the same creationist discourse employed by Shakespeare, Hobbes writes, "The dignities of lord, earl, duke, and prince are his creatures. At the presence of the master the servants are equal and without any honour at all, so are the subjects in the presence of the sovereign. And though they shine some more, some less, when they are out of his sight; yet in his presence they shine no more than the stars in the presence of the sun."[54] The sublime singularity of the sovereign renders equivalent the subjects who have covenanted among themselves to create the artificial person of the Leviathan; the equality of citizens (the liberal moment in Hobbes) both produces and is produced by the dazzling light of sovereignty (the absolutist moment in Hobbes). So too, in claiming his right to create nobility, the king ends up making a place for the consensual discourse of what will become bourgeois liberalism, but he does so in the sacred precincts of the sovereign exception, which, as an act of grace, elaborates the covenantal rather than the contractual formulae of consent.[55]

Bertram, in any case, will have none of it, holding true, as Bradbrook notes, to the old proverb, "The King cannot make a gentleman."[56] Helena wants out (or says she does), but now the king, tyrantlike, insists: "My honour's at the stake, which to defeat, / I must produce my power" (2.3.149–50).

---

53. On sovereign as creator, see Schmitt, *Political Theology*, 47.

54. Hobbes, *Leviathan*, 137.

55. We might even scent an anticipation of neoliberalism here, with its double commitment to free enterprise and executive privilege. On neoliberalism and biopolitics, see Foucault, *Birth of Biopolitics*.

56. Bradbrook, "Virtue Is the True Nobility," 296.

Threatened with disinheritance, Bertram finally yields to the king, in an acceptance speech read by some critics as bitterly ironical:

> Pardon, my gracious lord; for I submit
> My fancy to your eyes. When I consider
> What great creation and what dole of honour
> Flies where you bid it, I find that she, which late
> Was in my nobler thoughts most base, is now
> The praised of the king; who, so ennobled,
> Is as 'twere born so. (2.3.167–73)[57]

The king chooses to take Bertram's speech as a sign of acquiescence; bidding Bertram to "take her by the hand, / And tell her she is thine" (2.3.173–74), he asks the groom to provide both the physical and the verbal markers of consent. Bertram, as Hunter notes, performs only half: "I take her hand" (2.3.176), Bertram replies, but conspicuously fails to make a verbal pledge. For the king, eager to be out of Helena's debt and to restore his public control over Bertram, it is enough: "Good fortune and the favour of the king / Smile upon this contract" (2.3.176–77).

We are meant to see trouble. In English marriage law, consent was the definitive criterion of a valid marriage. Gratian's *Decretum* of 1140 defined marriage as consent plus consummation; in the thirteenth century, Pope Innocent III declared oral consent alone to be required for a valid marriage. The vesting of property, however, required a church ceremony, so common-law or "handfast" marriages, conducted solely between two individuals, were more common among unpropertied than among propertied couples. In 1563, the Council of Trent prohibited handfast unions; although this ruling had no legal jurisdiction in England, it ran alongside the renewed emphasis on church ceremony promoted by the Church of England in the sixteenth and seventeenth centuries, material familiar to readers of *Measure for Measure*.[58] In any case, consent remained at the heart of the marriage contract. In sixteenth-century English marriage law, for example, consent was required of both parties (and *not* of their parents), even for very young spouses; Holly Brewer studies cases involving marriage between children as young as two or three years old. Consent could be retracted at puberty,

---

57. Maurice Hunt describes Bertram's speech as a "sarcastic rephrasing" of the king's argument in favor of virtue ("Helena and the Reformation Problem of Merit," 346).

58. Jacobs, *Marriage Contracts*, 1–11. On marriage law and the Tridentine precedent in *Measure for Measure*, see Scott, "'Our Cities' Institutions'"; and Ranald, "'As Marriage Binds, and Blood Breaks.'"

again at the initiative of the couple, and the conditions of consent could be probed for undo force or influence, though coercion and consent were not such oppositional terms in the early modern period as they generally are today.[59] When such marriages were contested, usually by one or both parties after puberty, "The main questions of the court focused on consent, as discerned through both behavior and words. Did they exchange love tokens (like rings) or kisses? Did they consummate the marriage? Did they reaffirm after puberty in any way the vows they had made when younger?"[60] Although consummation was not required to validate a marriage, its occurrence, even when it involved force, was a major sign of consent, and there was a strong popular association, reinforced by drama, between consummation and marital contracting.

Bertram does consent, but his consent occurs under serious public pressure from the king. Giving his hand without his words, Bertram pointedly marks his consent as incomplete before the assembled court; though he then goes through with a ceremony off stage, he not only refuses to consummate the marriage, but even, in an especially poignant moment, to kiss the bride. When he tells Parolles, "Although before the solemn priest I have sworn, / I will not bed her" (2.3.265–66), he officially launches the period of delay between vow and consummation, and then between consummation and its public recognition, as the experimental intervals that measure the ensuing dramatic action.

In modern law, Bertram might be said to have acted "under volitional duress"—not physically coerced into consenting, but rather consciously making an unwelcome choice whose terms and alternatives have been fixed by another party.[61] In the judgment of Kathryn Jacobs, "An actual court, faced with an indisputed church ceremony such as Bertram's and Helena's, would almost certainly have ignored the issue of consummation altogether, either ordering Bertram to live with his wife or voiding the marriage as coerced."[62] There was one type of marriage, however, in Renaissance England that did not require the consent of one of the partners: the marriage of wards. Wardship originated as a feudal institution that placed the orphaned

---

59. On children and the consent to marriage, see Brewer, *By Birth or Consent*, 288–337.
60. Ibid., 299.
61. See Alan Wertheimer's philosophical analysis of legal coercion in his *Coercion*: "Nonvolitional contracts are said to be *void*; contracts made under volitional duress are said to be *voidable*" (46–48). Bertram's consent would fall under the second: he is not physically forced to marry Helena; he is mentally competent when he chooses to do so; but he acts under pressure from the king.
62. Jacobs, *Marriage Contracts*, 126.

minor heirs of deceased knights under the guardianship of the father's lord; since the dead knight owed military service that the surviving son could not provide, wardship allowed the lord to take back the land in order to obtain military service elsewhere. "Wardship of the land" was accompanied by "wardship of the body"—the child went into custody, too—a distinction dating from the Norman period.[63] Wardships of land and body repeat and project onto feudal scenery the "curatorial" and "tutorial" duties of the guardian under Roman civil law: as curator, the guardian cared for the estate of his charge, and as tutor, the guardian was responsible for his education (distinctions played out in *The Tempest*'s drama of minority and in *Shrew*'s commerce with things). Under Henry VIII, wardship underwent a major renovation; in order to raise money for the crown, Henry sold monastic lands to members of the nobility, but required that they hold it "by knight service of the crown," subjecting their estates to possible wardship; in 1540, the Court of Wards was created in order to protect these revived and expanded feudal rights of the king in an increasingly postfeudal political and economic environment.[64] By the end of the sixteenth century, wardship of the body had become almost exclusively identified with the right of the guardian to choose the spouse of his charge; wards could make their own matches if they paid their guardians a fine. "Feudal marriage," writes Joel Hurstfield, "was up for sale."[65]

There was one situation, however, in which a ward could turn down the choice made by his guardian: namely, if the match was considered a "disparagement," that is, lower in rank, or old, crippled, or past childbearing years.[66] Bertram appears to claim this right when he exclaims, "A poor physician's daughter my wife! Disdain / Rather corrupt me ever!" (2.3.115–16). Bertram's complaint is not only a peevish reflex of his sense of aristocratic self-worth, but also a declaration of his limited but well-recorded legal rights as a ward. Shakespeare presents us with a complex legal scenario. In any other union, the fact of coercion would tend to invalidate the marriage. The ward, however, is the one partner whose consent *can* be coerced, a factor that in turn supports the legality of the union. In still another turn of the legal screw, however, Shakespeare chooses to dramatize the one situation in which a ward *could* refuse his guardian's choice. G. K. Hunter, noting the disparagement clause in wardship, writes, "The whole tenor of the play . . .

63. Hurstfield, *Queen's Wards*, 8–9.
64. Ibid., 10–17.
65. Ibid., 18.
66. Brewer, *By Birth or Consent*, 295–96.

seems to indicate that Shakespeare did not intend Bertram to have this good
ground for his refusal of Helena."[67] I respectfully disagree: it seems rather
that Shakespeare wants us to see this marriage contract as under siege from
several quarters. Throughout the scene, we are certainly led to deem Helena
more than worthy of Bertram, but we are also asked to consider the constraints under which his consent is procured.

Our sense of Bertram's immaturity—his sexual panic, his credulity, his
military enthusiasm—finds its legal coordinates in the condition of wardship, which confines its subjects to a hyperbolic minority. When we first see
Bertram at court, the king has just denied him the chance to go to war with
his fellows: "I am commanded here, and kept a coil with / 'Too young', and
'The next year' and ''Tis too early'" (2.1.27–28). The institution of wardship
itself, as a remnant of feudal practices reanimated by modern monetary
interests, shapes the scope and flavor of Bertram's ethical competence. His
heightened identification with the aristocratic markers of blood, birth and
honor—tokens of descent under revision by the social forces associated
with Helena's Machiavellian *virtù*[68]—is not simply a temperamental failing,
but a symptom of his own situation as a feudal ward in a modern world.
For Bertram, orphanage means *enforced childhood*, trapping him in a world
of fossilized institutions that come to signify and limit his personhood,
to arrest his development. Because he is a ward, "the age of consent" is effectively diminished and deferred for Bertram, crippling his emotional as
well as legal capacity for consent. For Helena, on the other hand, *orphanage
means precocity*, her aloneness freeing her to enter the age of consent ahead
of her time, understood both developmentally (as a reflection of her youth)
and epochally (as an unusually "modern" heroine).[69]

At the end of act 2, the marriage contract has neither been definitively invalidated by the evident facts of coercion and disparagement, nor has its permanence been sealed by consummation, cohabitation, or the exchange of
tokens. It is the work of the remainder of the play to make Bertram's consent
retroactively binding by securing one or more of these missing pieces. Consent comes forward as the means of reconciling the two classes represented

---

67. Shakespeare, *All's Well*, 53n.

68. As Lars Engle points out, there is something distinctively Machiavellian in her "resolve to
act boldly, maximize [her] own freedom, seek out and follow liberating historical examples of
improbable successes achieved by merit and cling to [her] purposes despite adversity" ("Shakespearean Normativity," 271).

69. On the age of consent in contemporary law, especially with regard to sexual consent,
see Waites, *Age of Consent*. See also Archard, *Children*, which begins with a chapter on Locke and
childhood.

by honor and virtue, yet, through the infelicities of its performance, consent
is also the grounds of their initial divorce. What *All's Well* must try to effect
is *consent between two forms of consent*. The play, that is, struggles to reach a
settlement that would join a more archaic, ritualized consent based on the
inviolability of status and the gift-economy of gratitude to a more modern, contractual notion of consent founded on formal equality between rational parties. The marriage contract provides the perfect template for such
a reconciliation, since, as Victoria Kahn has demonstrated, marriage weds
equality and submission in a fundamentally romance movement.[70] Helena's apt application of the rhetoric of service to her courtship of Bertram
certainly confirms the classic model of sexual contract disclosed by Pateman, in which the wife freely submits to her legal subordination. Yet, what
makes Shakespeare's staging of this consensus between freedom and service
so innovative is his insistence on the woman's sexual initiative, which is
also the initiative of an emergent social class. Pateman writes, "Consent
must always be given *to* something; in the relationship between the sexes,
it is always women who are held to consent to men."[71] Not so in *All's Well*,
where it is the nobleman whose consent is constrained at every front: first,
as ward of the king, second, as the unwilling object of a woman's frank election, and finally, as the object of nonconsensual sex. For, in another turn in
the play's quest for consent, Helena will begin to secure Bertram's retroac-
tive consent to marriage not by trying to win him over on the equal ground
of wit (like Beatrice and Benedict), but through still another act of missed
consent, namely, the bed-trick.

The Consent Trap

In act 3, Helena receives the letter from Bertram spelling out the terms of
their separation: she must get the ring from his finger (the token that failed
to pass hands at their wedding), and she must become pregnant by him. He
ends by declaring, "Till I have no wife I have nothing in France" (3.2.74).
In flight from matrimony and patria, Bertram's attempted seduction of
the Florentine virgin Diana is a desperate effort at reversing the predation
to which Bertram has felt himself subjected. Whereas Helena's pursuit of
Bertram is a modern tale of social mobility fueled by active female desire,

---

70. Cf. Kahn: "According to both the domestic and the royalist rhetorics of obligation, the
political subject consented to his natural subordination out of love and affection for the sovereign, just as the wife consented to her husband" (*Wayward Contracts*, 10–11).

71. Pateman, "Women and Consent," 164.

Bertram's infatuation with Diana rehearses the medieval genre of the *pastourelle*, in which a nobleman rapes or seduces a maiden who is socially beneath him. He aims to take charge of the battle between the sexes, which is also a class war, by deflowering a middle-class girl. And he proceeds by conspicuously avoiding any consent talk. When Diana reminds him of the duties he owes his wife, he responds,

> I prithee do not strive against my vows;
> I was compell'd to her, but I love thee
> By love's own sweet constraint, and will for ever
> Do thee all rights of service. (4.2.14–17)

Rejecting his own bond to Helena as "compell'd," Bertram substitutes "love's own sweet constraint" as the antidote to the bitterness of that first coercion, insistently preferring feudal "rights of service" to any contractual language. Bertram appears temperamentally unable to speak the idiom of consent—its discourse is simply too bourgeois for him—and any inkling of a consensual imagination has been brutalized out of him by wardship and coerced marriage. In this, Bertram may unexpectedly share something with Caliban; as we'll see in chapter 6, both the noble and the savage suffer extended and extreme minorities that damage their capacities to listen for consent.

Bertram's behavior in Italy is purely reactive, his frantic vigor a form of passivity, inherently antimodern—like wardship itself—in its generic precedents and social momentum.[72] Helena, on the other hand, seeks a meeker mode, but ends up only aggrandizing her sphere of action. She embraces the antiquated narrative forms and figures of hagiography, aiming to mortify her own outspokenness through ascetic discipline:

> I am Saint Jaques' pilgrim, thither gone.
> Ambitious love hath so in me offended
> That barefoot plod I the cold ground upon,
> With sainted vow my faults to have amended. (3.4.4–7)

Yet her pilgrimage route to Spain passes by way of Florence, and Shakespeare remains coy as to the exact ratio of providential circumstance and calculating intent that lands Helena in the inn run by her husband's new beloved.

---

72. Cf. Lars Engle: "Male honour manifests itself normatively as a form of passivity, not agency" ("Shakespearean Normativity," 276).

The bed-trick, distasteful to Victorian readers on grounds of both morality and realism, has been rehabilitated in recent years by reference to sacred exemplars, especially the story of Tamar from Genesis, which plays the same role in this drama that the Annunciation plays in *Measure for Measure*. By making modernity and miracle coincide, Shakespeare is able to lend gravity and legitimacy to Helena's stratagem. Yet the moral paradox remains: her ruse circumvents Bertram's consent to sex, but with the goal of procuring his consent to marriage. A few readers have gone so far as to call it rape, and well it might be by modern standards of sexual assault and harassment.[73]

We might also evaluate the bed-trick as a form of unconsented medical treatment; after all, Helena is not simply consummating the union but, like Tamar, also impregnating herself. David McCandless, who reads the bed-trick as deeply erotic, wonders why Bertram is asked to "remain there but an hour" (4.2.58). "What, must one ask, is the point of this detention? What takes place during that hour? Does the dilation of the trick create a space for the operations of a less propulsively phallic, consumptive sexuality?"[74] I'd propose a less sexy reading. Helena, after all, is a "Doctor She" with great knowledge of many "appliances." Even a less-educated woman might intuit that postcoital cuddling increases the chances of conception. Read this way, the bed-trick is an early case of assisted reproduction, in which Helena loses her virginity "to her own liking" (1.1.147) and without asking her mate if she can use his sperm.

Neither the rape nor the medical readings of the bed trick are normative with respect to the world of *All's Well*, which more readily accommodates our backward burrowings into Bible and folklore than our more forward forays into liberalism's late innovations. Yet harassment and medical consent, areas mapped out by modern bioethics and feminism, form key domains of the *future* of consent, the experimental territory whose early traces in Shakespeare's plays can only become visible retroactively, and not without exerting some hermeneutic duress. In his brilliant essay, "Shakespearean Normativity in *All's Well That Ends Well*," Lars Engle argues that the play tests sexual norms by placing them under "strain."[75] By the play's end, Engle concludes, "We can see chastity as something that for some, needs elaborate and daring management if it is to coexist with satisfaction. If this is normative, it is a kind of normativity that insists we think about the relations between norms and the social situation of the agent attempting to live ac-

73. See, for example, McCandless, "Helena's Bed-Trick."
74. Ibid., 463.
75. Engle, "Shakespearean Normativity," 270.

cording to them, a version of the normative that insists on its embodiment in particular bodies and particular situations."[76] *All's Well*, I argue, performs a similar experiment with norms concerning consent. Stretching the speech-act of consent—to reveal its constituent parts and moments, to examine its mixed genealogy, to test its capacities for social and sexual conciliation—is part of what the play does. The medical and rape readings of the bed-trick impose additional strain, beyond the efforts exerted by the play itself, and readers may feel coerced by such advances into the futures of consent. Yet the play, I'd suggest, invites us to essay its own elasticity, to see how far it can stretch before it snaps back to its comfort zone.

The last act of the play assures Bertram's consent, but at considerable cost: consent has exacted Bertram's public humiliation, even his taming, and the tenor of his love and desire remain fundamentally in question.[77] The *fact of consent* has been established, but what bioethicists call the *quality of consent* remains poor.[78] Helena, on the other hand, has achieved her ends, but at the cost of the very autonomy and ambition that got her there in the first place. As McCandless puts it, "Ever in thrall to Bertram, she wins him only by putting him temporarily in her thrall so that she may put herself permanently in his."[79] Does the only emancipation in the play lie in the public shaming of a boy-man? And is the only end of marriage the subjection of women? If so, *All's Well* finishes quite badly, and Pateman is right after all: consent cannot be a scene for ethical and political action. But perhaps we can take other truths about consent with us from the play. When Helena declares in the final scene, "'Tis but the shadow of a wife you see; / The name and not the thing" (5.3.301–2), she calls attention to the gap between formal consent and its existential instantiation, a non-coincidence reasserted more than denied by the iterative beat of Bertram's "Both! Both! O pardon!" (302). Diana and Helena figure forth the two bodies of the wife (name and thing, office and woman), but also the two bodies of the citizen-subject, as both member of the polity and subjective being.[80] By

76. Ibid., 275.

77. Janet Adelman reads the scene as a shaming ritual, performed on Bertram but also on Diana; see *Suffocating Mothers*, 83–85.

78. Weindling contrasts the total occlusion of consent by Nazi researchers and the Allied medical establishment, which did secure consent from prisoners and other populations, but achieved an inadequate "quality of consent" by post-Nuremberg standards (*Nazi Medicine*, 8).

79. McCandless, "Helena's Bed-Trick," 457.

80. On the citizen-subject in relation to the rights of "man and citizen," the two bodies of the person in modern political formations, see Balibar, "Citizen-Subject." I would like to thank Donald Pease for linking Balibar's analysis to the doubled figure of the citizen embodied by the Diana-Helena couple.

holding consent out as unfulfilled, as imperfectly suturing the social and sexual orders, *All's Well* homes in on the incomplete identity of consent and contract. In the process, the play submits for our deliberation the existential and affective dimensions of consent as not simply a legal assenting-to, but an ethical sensing-with (*consentire*), a moment of creative relationship irreducible to a specific content, its willed future not identical with a set of predetermined terms or conditions.

Recall our encounter with medical consent as the creative binding of political theology and liberalism around "life" as a quotient that both enters into and escapes liberalism's economies of self-possession. The most visible embodiment of life at the end of the play is the unborn child whose quickening presence in Helena's womb helps assure her husband's consent to their marriage. Certainly the baby completes the conservative arc of the marriage plot, simultaneously guaranteeing Helena's taming and Bertram's *caponage*. Divine comedy is neater, of course, than profane life, and Shakespeare knew this, too. Then as now, the child may provide a welcome object of attention and care, but it cannot in itself make up for the lack of a sexual relation between husband and wife. And a single intermarriage, happy or not, might serve to bring a comedy to a satisfying close, but it cannot resolve the social and sovereign tensions that will continue to strain the English polity, often around questions of consent.

Yet the coming child is also the play's most visible incarnation of the *future of consent*. After all, Helena's pregnancy, classic icon of futurity, is the fruit of the act of nonconsensual sex that serves to backdate Bertram's consent, the realized outcome that delivers to these earlier acts their final meaning. Read in terms of the play's atmosphere of generalized decrepitude, the child dispenses another remedy to decline, repeating the cure of the king in relation to the future rather than the past. Just as the king had exposed his abscess to treatment from a middle-class lay physician, so the child of Helena and Bertram, itself secured as recompense for that remedy, springs from the intermarriage of Honor and Virtue, Descent and Consent. Its presence knits together the various non-coincidences gathered up by the play—between intention and action, between deed and knowledge, between contract and covenant, between status and parity, between past and future—and presents their gloriously ingathered discrepancies to us as a knot of sexual and political speculation.

It is not enough to either reject the bed-trick as an ethical error that reveals the violence of all consent discourses (along the lines of Pateman) or to reclaim the bed-trick as a victory for liberal equality, in which the abused woman finally gets her own, establishing the chance of equity between the sexes. For this child, in all its ambiguity, is meant to stir us, as something real, and new, and true. The child materializes the fact that Bertram's consent has occurred on another stage and without his knowledge, and yet consent has indeed taken place, and, though fashioned out of lies, nonetheless has achieved a certain validity. Consent has managed to suture human relationships without hitting—indeed *precisely by bypassing*—a full, conscious, perfectly achieved concordance of moments, faculties, and persons. It stages *consent as event*: as the advent of a novelty that requires commitment and fidelity on the part of those who participate in it, partaking in gift as well as deed.[81]

Consent is not equal to contract. Such a formula points on the one hand toward the magical coincidence of subjects imagined by both erotic verse and absolutist politics. There is something frightening about such fusion, and we might well prefer the discontented proceduralism of liberal citizenship to such fantasmatic union. But consent as a temporal complex nestles gaps as well as identities. Circles of agreement can overlap incompletely, creating regions of distinction among parties and persons, and the act of consent can suffer jet lag, leaping ahead or falling behind itself. The dissent within consent includes possibilities of resistance to the endless iterations of tacit consent. Such rifts also invite us to consider the unconscious in consent, the extent to which consent always involves bed-tricks in black boxes, moments of trust and self-abandonment that solicit consent in despite of ourselves, on planes other than that of conscious deliberation.

Politically, think here of my consent to throw my lot with the fortunes of another group whose interests do not coincide with mine, not out of altruism or charity but because a signifier such as freedom or equality gathers together our dreams for emancipation around a common point that carries the weight of revelation.[82] Existentially, consider the consent to enjoy, not in terms of the regulation of harassment, but rather as the intersection of two separate fantasies whose paths cross as they rotate around different centers of gravity. Some notion of the consent to enjoy is implied by Freud's idea of object-choice *[Objektwahl]* and the choice of neurosis *[Neurosenwahl]*. The word *Wahl*, translated as "choice" but also as "election," implies for Freud not a deliberate and conscious decision to take on a particular sexual identity or set of symptoms, but an unconscious commitment to a path of desire

81. On the event, see Badiou, *Manifesto for Philosophy*.
82. On this basic structure, see Laclau, *Emancipation(s)*.

that precedes and helps birth subjectivity as such.[83] The bed-trick names the real space of frank election in *All's Well*, the shuttered closet, both tunnel and tower, where groom and bride furtively agree to let the new appear.

In *All's Well*, the final coverture of virtue by honor and wife by husband achieved by the conclusion of the marriage plot predicts the shell games that liberalism will play with privilege. Yet fistulation may accompany coverture, abscessing liberal equivalence with pockets of exceptionality and grace. And the child as gift, as increscent growth, represents such an embedding of the new within the transmission of the old. Recall Hannah Arendt's concept of natality. Arendt associates the fact of human birth not, as one might expect, with labor or the *oikos*, but with action and the polis: "The new beginning inherent in birth can make itself felt in the world only because the new-comer possesses the capacity of beginning something new, that is, of acting. In this sense of initiative, an element of action, and therefore of natality, is inherent in all human activities."[84] Action, including the act of consent, sets into motion unpredictable responses that lead not only to self-disclosure and storytelling, but also to world-conserving efforts on the part of the guardians of public life.

It is important to note here that Hannah birthed books, while Helena births children. Arendt borrows natality from physical parturition but immediately tropes it as the "second birth" of action.[85] Arendt, *in* her life and *as* her work, chose *gravitas* over *gravidas*, the contingencies of speech, action, and thought over the exigencies of maternity, even while allowing her own femininity to draw birth into the orbit of philosophy. That the choice between *gravidas* and *gravitas*, not only for married heterosexual women like me, but for single women, gay people, and adoptive parents, is no longer drawn so sharply has something to do with the insemination of consent throughout liberal society, in concert with reproductive and judicial technologies at the intersection of politics and life. If Helena's pregnancy signals the end of her public life, it is also the trophy of her active virtue, delivering the promised end of her situational intelligence, her medical savvy, and her tactical virginity. Helena's pregnant person announces the future set into motion by the play's interlocking consent concerns, which include, in their order of appearance, medical consent, marital consent, the age of consent,

83. See Kenneth Reinhard on the theopolitical and biopolitical implications of *Wahl* in Lacan and Freud: "Even before the constitution of a body politic, the subject's body is *already* political, insofar as it is the site of a crisis that requires a determining *choice*" (Žižek, Santner, and Reinhard, *Ethics of the Neighbor*, 34).

84. Arendt, *Human Condition*, 9.

85. Ibid., 176–77.

and sexual consent. Moreover, the exhibition of her swelling figure on stage also manifests the symbolic reconciliation, residual survivals, and cryptic energies of the play's major tensions—between genders, generations, social classes, and sovereign metaphors. *All's Well* may indeed end badly, but it also does not end where it began, insofar as it has indeed effected a mingling of estates, a redistribution of sexual norms and potentialities, and an opening of sovereignty to new impulses, insuring, without fully imagining, a future for consent.

FOUR

Job of Athens, Timon of Uz

Shakespeare's poetic responsiveness to the Book of Job has been demonstrated anew in recent work by Kenneth Gross, Steven Marx, Eric Malin, and Hannibal Hamlin.[1] Although *Lear*, *The Merchant of Venice*, and *Othello* all testify to Shakespeare's lifelong dialogue with the man from Uz, I would contend that his most developed dramatic encounter with the Book of Job takes place in *Timon of Athens*.[2] In both plays, rich men with good hearts lose everything, and both engage in fruitless dialogue with a parade of inadequate friends. Falling out of the social networks that had sustained their great households, these cast-off lords find themselves subjected to private need and public scorn, a situation that raises them to new heights of anguish and ardor. Both Timon and Job place virtue beyond itemization and calculation, a resistance that ends up driving them past the verge of civility and community, in order, however, to essay new forms of public speech on the barren stages cleared by privation.

The environment of Job, I argue, is zoned by the interface of creation and covenant that shapes the patriarchal economy of Genesis. *Creation* encompasses God's work, as manifested in the mysteries, beauties, and terrors of

---

1. Kenneth Gross, *Shylock Is Shakespeare*; Steven Marx, *Shakespeare and the Bible*; Hamlin, "The Patience of Lear"; Malin, *Godless Shakespeare*. See also my forthcoming essays, "The Wizards of Uz," and "Job in Venice." The first of these essays touches on Timon; my thanks to the editors of these projects for their feedback. According to Richmond Noble, Job, along with Ecclesiasticus, Proverbs, and Isaiah, is among the most allusively recurrent books of the Bible in Shakespeare's plays (*Shakespeare's Biblical Knowledge*, 43). Jonathan Lamb notes the contiguities between Lear and Job in the writings of James Barry (*The Rhetoric of Suffering*, 295, 298).

2. In the Oxford edition of *Timon*, John Jowett notes two allusions to the Book of Job in *Timon* (3.2.89 and 4.3.300). Many critics have noted parallels between Timon and Job; see Michael Dobson and Stanley Wells, eds., *Oxford Companion to Shakespeare*, 45. See also Fielitz, "Learned Pate and Golden Fool," 192.

nature, a nature never simply opposed to art because it is itself the product of divine *poiesis*. *Covenant* signifies God's law, imposed above all on an Israel brought into being as such through the revelation at Sinai, but shadowing backwards, in a kind of reverse typology, to the looser affiliations associated with the clan of Abraham, and further back still to the Noahide commandments, a *bio-politeia* that addresses all mankind as well as relations among species. The patriarchal arrangements exercised and dismantled in the Book of Job help map the precincts of a primitive universality hospitable not only to neighboring peoples, but also to other, nonhuman forms of creaturely existence. Thus the horizon of Job is traced by the sideways burrowings of the worm, while its vertical dimension is marked by the singular cut of a God who covenants with creation itself, addressing the human as an instance of the creaturely. In the greekjew world of Timon's Athens, *covenant* reappears in the play's concern with "bonds," that quintessentially Shakespearean word for contract, affiliation, and obligation, while *creation* coalesces around the discourse of animals and the diet of roots in the wilderness outside Athens. Exiting the city of bonds and entering the desert of creatures, Timon, like Job, serves to reassert the minimal claims of the social relation when more elaborated institutional forms have been stripped away, destroyed, or exposed in their ideological dimension. Both the Book of Job and *Timon of Athens* occupy the deserted margin between politics and life in order to reassemble provisional fellowships out of the remains of friendship and hospitality.

The Man from Uz

The Hebrew Bible groups the Book of Job with the *Kethuvim*, or Holy Writings—works of wisdom literature, including Psalms, Proverbs, and the Song of Songs—with Job appearing between the latter two. In the Geneva Bible, Job falls after the romance book of Esther and before the lyric Psalms and Proverbs. Both arrangements indicate the book's status as something other than history, a work of literature that does not fill out the story of Israel or salvation, but directs itself toward ethical and poetic reflections on and for everyday life. Victoria Kahn has argued that the Book of Job became a model of secular literature for Milton, and Eric Malin takes Job as the starting point for a Shakespearean antitheology in his book *Godless Shakespeare*.[3] The Book of Job subsists at the borders not only of distinct religious dispensations (pagan, Jewish, Muslim, and Christian) but also, through the extremity of

3. Kahn, "Job's Complaint."

its theodicy, at the shifting shoreline where revelation surges into poetry and the Bible breaks into literature.

This neverland bears the name of Uz: "There was a man in the land of Uz called Job, and this man was an upright and juste man, one that feared God, and eschewed evil" (Job 1:1). The great medieval commentator Maimonides, aiming to reconcile Job and Judaism with Aristotelian philosophy, avers that Uz "can be read as the imperative form of the verb 'uz, 'to reflect' or 'to meditate.'"[4] Whether lying to the north, the south, or nowhere at all, Uz, as commentators from several traditions agree, is not in Israel, and Job was not a Jew. For Jewish commentators, this meant that Job could become an emblem of suffering available to all people and peoples, while still remaining open to more particular allegorization as a figure of Jewish tribulations.[5] For Christians, Job's nativity outside Judaism made him into a placeholder for Gentile conversion; Job's references to a Redeemer and to the possibility of resurrection (Job 19:25–26) reinforced the Christian reading of Job as a type of Christ.[6] For Muslims, Job (or "Ayyub") hailed from the pre-Mohammedan canon of holy prophets shared by Judaism, Christianity, and Islam; his name occurs four times in the Koran (4:163; 6:84; 21:84; 38:41–44), and a series of legends, based on the Hebrew pseudoepigraphal Testament of Job, develops themes of testing, patience, illness, and divine healing that overlap significantly with Job's treatment in medieval Christendom and rabbinic Judaism. All three religions link Job to the family of Abraham; thus Theodor Beza, in his 1589 commentary on Job, concludes that the hero of patience was an Idumean, a descendant of Esau.[7] Indeed, the adjective Abrahamic rather than Gentile may best capture the form of regional universality manifested by Job in his passage through neighboring traditions, including the three monotheisms and Near Eastern pagan wisdom cults.[8]

4. Maimonides, paraphrased in Robert Eisen, Book of Job, 48. For Maimonides, the ensuing text is an allegory of the imperfect human intellect that manages to achieve philosophical illumination by the end of the dialogue. Maimonides points out that the text identifies Job as "righteous" but not, he insists, as intelligent; the same could be said for Lear, Shylock, Othello, and Timon, each of whom, in his own distinct precinct of affection, loves not wisely but too well.

5. Robert Eisen examines the universalist and particularist dimensions of Jewish medieval commentators in a separate subsection of each chapter of his excellent study, Book of Job.

6. See the marginal comment in the Geneva Bible: "For as muche as he was a Gentile and not a Jewe, & yet pronounced upright, and without hypocrisie, it declareth that among the heathen God hath his" (Job 1:1, gloss b).

7. Beza, Job Expounded, 3.

8. The Geneva Bible notes the young friend Elihu's affiliation with Abraham (33:2, note a). Both Jews and Muslims traced Job's lineage to the family of Abraham. Theologically, Abraham and Job were linked as objects of divine testing (Eisen, Book of Job, 23). Lawrence Besserman

The Book of Job is divided between the archaic prose narrative that frames the book and the long poetic dialogue between Job and his three friends, which cuts between Job's iconoclastic outbursts and his friends' attempts to master the extremity of his situation through theological truisms. The speech of Elihu, followed by the declamation of God himself out of the whirlwind, is likely even later than the central interchange. We thus have a text mixed both generically and temporally, consisting of several layers of prose and poetry that span an ideational spectrum from the naive to the sophisticated. Whereas the miraculous restorations of the prose frame imply a simple ethics of virtue tested, exonerated, and rewarded, the more difficult and substantial interior sections grapple with the fact that good people can suffer without cause—the position put forth by Job and largely contested by his friends.

If wisdom literature is normative, the Book of Job, in a famous phrase coined by Biblical scholar Gerhard von Rad, expresses "wisdom in revolt," becoming a case of "anti-wisdom wisdom."[9] In its movement from wisdom to antiwisdom, the Book of Job allows exceptional forms of life to appear within conventional ones. I say "appear" because such manifestations of life, though carrying the terrible force of immediacy, remain shaped by the social, rhetorical, and poetic conventions that support and render them legible. Some of Job's most powerful statements are those that both manifest and visualize the visceral intensity of his speech-acts, expounded at the agonized edge of body and voice, as when he asks, "Wherefore do I take my flesh in my tethe, and put my soule in mine hand?" (Job 13:14). Here Job exercises the rituals of mourning not only to manage but also to capture the quotient of life that is now inflamed and provoked by the fact of privation. What gives the Book of Job its enduring power—which is also its translatability—is its movement, "swifter than a weaver's shuttle" (7:6), between normative and exceptional forms of life, and the reflective processes that

---

refers to Aramaic, Coptic, Arabic, and Hebrew legends of Job (*Legend of Job in the Middle Ages*, 9). Modern Biblical scholars emphasize the fertile contexts of other Near Eastern religious traditions, including Egyptian and Akkadian (see Perdue, *Voice from the Whirlwind*). The Muslim exegete and narrator Ibn Kathir (b. 701) gives the following genealogies: "Ibn Ishaaq stated that he was a man of Rum. His name was Job Ibn Mose, Ibn Razeh, Ibn Esau, Ibn Isaac, Ibn Abraham. Someone else said he was Job, Ibn Mose, Ibn Rimil, Ibn Esau, Ibn Isaac, Ibn Jacob. There have also been other statements on his lineage. Ibn Asaker narrated that his mother was a daughter of Lot. It was said, also, that his father was one who believed in Abraham when he was cast into the fire" (*Stories of the Prophets*, 92).

9. Marvin Pope, cited by Lawrence Besserman, *Legend of Job*, 7. See also Gerhard von Rad on Job and the limits of wisdom, *Wisdom in Israel*, 97–110, 206–25, and 237–39.

vibrate at the elastic membranes connecting theology, poetry, philosophy, and drama.

Life in Uz is distinctively patriarchal, preceding the Mosaic covenant and the institutions of cult and sacrifice associated with Exodus, Leviticus, and Deuteronomy. Job hails from the era of Abraham, with whom he is genealogically and theologically associated, and even further back to Noah. Job is "an uprighte and juste man [*ha eish . . . tam v'yasar*]"; Noah was a "juste and upright man [*eish tsaddik tamim*] in his time" (Gen 6:9). Noah and Job are both *tam*, "perfect," "blameless," a word used of sacrificial animals in a ritual context.[10] The attributions, though laudatory, place the men just outside the covenantal bonds that will constitute Israel as a nation in relation to God, at once asserting the virtue of Job and Noah and suggesting a certain historical and conceptual limit to their moral capacities. As a righteous Gentile, Job lives outside God's covenant with Israel, both spatially and temporally; his primitive world, like Noah's, is that of creation as it devolves after Eden and before Sinai. In a tradition of both rabbinic and Christian commentaries recently reconstructed by Jason Rosenblatt, Job was conceived as a "virtuous Gentile who kept the Noahide laws," the seven commandments given to Noah after the Flood as the legal requirements for all humanity.[11] Moreover, the animal references will continue to accompany him, two by two, as it were. It is no accident that the Book of Job is heavy with reminders of creation, whether proclaiming God's powers as architect of the cosmos (creation taken as a whole [e.g., 26, 28]), or cataloguing the fashioned character of natural things (creatures taken in their infinite variety [e.g., 12:7–9]). Job casts himself as such a creature: "Remember, I pray thee, that thou hast made me as the clay, and wilt thou bring me into dust again? Hast thou not powred me out as mylke? And turned me to cruds [curds] like chese?" (10:9–10). What Job grasps in these passages is his own participation in what Eric Santner calls creaturely life, the conditions of beholdenness that suddenly surface in the disturbance of the routines that had sustained him in the days of his prosperity.

Yet the God that speaks to Job out of the whirlwind is nonetheless the Lord of covenant (Yahweh, the Tetragrammaton, the God of the J-Text), not the God of creation (Elohim, the subject of the first sentence of Genesis, the

---

10. Chaim Potok and the Jewish Publication Society, *JPS Torah Commentary*, 1:50. Robert S. Fyall notes the association of Job and Noah as well as the sacrificial language: "He is 'blameless' (*tām*), a word used of clean animals offered for sacrifice (e.g., Lev. 22:18–20), a word with ominous nuances in light of what follows" (*Now My Eyes Have Seen You*, 35).

11. Rosenblatt, *Renaissance England's Chief Rabbi*, 154–57.

God of the E-text).[12] If creation is God's architecture, covenant is his public policy: "I layed the fundacions of the earth. . . . I established my command-ment upon [the sea], and set barres and dores" (Job 38:4, 10). Covenantal moments mark various points of the text: in Job's oath of innocence, he declares his marital fidelity by averring that "I made a covenant [*brit*] with mine eyes; why then should I thinke on a maid?" (31:1). Earlier he insists not only that he, like Noah, has followed the "steppes" and "ways" of God, but that he has never "departed from the commandement[s] [*mitzvot*] of [God's] lippes" (23:11–12), implying adherence to some form of revealed law. Job is a creature, yes, but a creature who attends to God's law, hearken-ing to the impress of his word as well as his hand. Again, the case of Noah is resonant: the Noahide laws are the pre-Sinaitic set of seven commandments applicable to all mankind, not just to Israel, while the Flood story itself culminates in a covenant not between God and Noah, but between God and creation itself (Gen 9). The Noahide laws include prohibitions against idolatry, adultery, theft, and murder, but also, more mysteriously, against eating the limb of a living animal—bearing thus on the proper relations between people and animals as one involving respect and obligation, not just sovereignty and consumption.

This theopolitical moment, at the archaic juncture of creation and cov-enant, zones the peculiar form of universality in which Job participates. It is a universe delimited by the canopy of a common cosmos inhabited by a plurality of peoples and creatures, yet set up by a single God (note the prohibition against idolatry) and therefore consecrated to the future poten-tialities of monotheism, whose promise to transcend national differences will also fund a whole history of culture wars and antitranslation projects. The God of Job, like the God of Noah, is he who covenants with creation, addressing man as the denizen of a landscape shot through with the fact of jurisdiction but not yet divided into nations or polities. Covenant brings forward creation as itself a form of inscription and of exposure to inscrip-tion. Covenant puts the creature into writing, redelivering as codified com-mandment the human creature's primal relationship to language, kinship, and sociability.

Not unlike Homer's world, Job's is ruled by the ritual hospitality of the rotating feast: "And his sonnes went and banketted in their houses, everie one his day, and sent, & called their thre sisters to eat & to drinke with them" (Job 1:4). Meanwhile, Job remains in his own quarters, making sacri-

12. See Fyall, *Now Mine Eyes Have Seen You:* "It is Yahweh, the Lord of the Covenant, who answers Job from the storm" (33).

fices on his sons' behalf; he is an oddly distant father, at once content in his prosperity and removed from its most conspicuous blessings in a nomadic settlement characterized by dispersal and decentralization. In any case, Job became a type of hospitality in a number of medieval texts, grouped along with Abraham, Isaac, Jacob, and Lot as one who has "given hospitality to strangers," deserving "an inheritance in the city of God."[13] Hospitality knits the cluster of households into a neighborhood through reciprocity; meanwhile, marauding bandits can disrupt the eminence of the patriarch by destroying his cattle, suggesting the fragility of prepolitical communities (1:15). The physical conditions of hospitality—namely, the house in which Job's children feast—literally come down around their heads: "And beholde, there came a great winde from beyond the wildernes, and smote the four corners of the house, which fel upon the children, and they are dead" (1:19). This loss differs in both magnitude and kind from the demise of Job's livestock, annihilating whole households of progeny, the intimacy they embody, and the promise of memory and succor that they represent. These losses, however, Job initially bears with proverbial patience, turning to the routines of ritual for support: "Then Job arose, and rent his garment, and shaved his head, and fel downe upon the grounde, and worshiped" (1:21). What pushes Job from prose into poetry is not the death of his children, but his affliction with skin disease: "So Satán departed from the presence of the Lord, and smote Job with sore boyles, from the sole of his fote unto his crowne. And he toke a potsharde to scrape him, and he sate downe among the ashes" (2:6–8). After sitting shiva with his wife and his friends for seven days and seven nights, "Job opened his mouthe, and cursed his day," initiating the central dialogue of the book.

Images of psychic and bodily incursion through disease abound in the interchanges that follow, forming some of the most powerful and memorable poetry in the Book of Job, and forever associating him with illness, especially diseases of the skin, in Judaism, Christianity, and Islam. The plague of sores violates Job's bodily integrity, rendering him loathsome to sight and smell as well as subjecting him to intense pain.[14] Job is "vulnerable" in the existential and political sense developed by James Kuzner, for whom the *vulnus* lodged in "vulnerability" is a mouth as well as a wound, an orifice for orisons, and thus a place where history passes.[15] The Geneva commentary

---

13. Besserman quotes the pseudoepigraphal *Apocalypse* (*Legend of Job*, 66–67).

14. On his noxious smell, Job laments, "My breath was strange to my wife, thogh I praised her for the childrens sake of mine owne body" (19:17).

15. Kuzner, "Unbuilding the City," 26.

compares Job's affliction to the plague of boils visited against the Egyptians. Indeed, we could say that Job's situation smacks of Egypt, since he suffers the death of his cattle and his children as well as skin disease, placing him once again at the outskirts of the covenant at Sinai. The loss of his substance had already rendered him naked (1:21); the rain of sores, however, breaches nakedness itself, punching apertures into the bodily envelope that release Job's vociferous complaint. In a cry with enough thrust to become proverbial, Job exclaims, "My bone cleaveth to my skin & to my flesh, and I have escaped with the skinne of my teeth" (19:20)—surviving with only his gums intact, the only tissue not subject to leprosy according to one rabbinic gloss.[16] In chapter 15 he declares, "I have sowed sackecloth upon my skin"—meaning, according to another rabbinic gloss, that his rough clothes of mourning and poverty have adhered to his sores. Becoming one with his scabs, his garb hardens into an exoskeleton, devolving into a new and more terrible form of nakedness.[17]

The figure of the worm binds disease with creatureliness in the text. The worm is a quintessential creature: slimy and swarming, it breeds at the slippery threshold of life and death. Lacking the dignity of the higher animals, it is one of those "creeping things that creep on the earth" (Gen 1:26; KJV) that the rabbis classed as *sheretz*, "'any living being that is not higher than the ground—like flies, ants, beetles, worms, rats, mice and all fish.'"[18] Job, like Hamlet after him, is obsessed with the worm-eaten destiny of corpses (Job 19:26, 21:26, 27:14).[19] But it is the company that worms keep with the living that forms Job's most powerful gift to vermicular iconography. In an evocative passage that would spawn a wealth of cult and commentary, Job represents his living flesh as teeming with worms: "My flesh is clothed with worms and clods of dust; my skin is broken, and become loathsome" (7:5; KJV). Later legends from rabbinic, Christian, and Muslim traditions would recount the transformation of Job's sores into veritable worm-factories, extruding parasites from the ulcerated openings of the flesh like so much vermicelli. In some cults of Job, the worms themselves were considered magical, curing those who suffer from skin diseases, syphilis, and parasites. In Job and his legends, the worm becomes a kind of livid incarnation and inverse image of the negative space of the sore itself: have the sores given birth to the worms, or have the worms created the sores, piercing Job's flesh

16. *Soncino Book of Job*, ed. Rev. Dr. A. Cohen, note to 19:14.

17. Ibid., note to 16:15.

18. On *sheretz*, see Zornberg, *The Beginning of Desire: Reflections on Genesis*, 7–10.

19. See also Bildad's comment, "How muche more man, a worme, even the sonne of man, *which is but* a worm?" (25:6).

by burrowing into it? The worm is the tongue of the wound. The worm is the word made flesh, in and as the dimension of the creature. Supine and serpentine, the worm is the opposite of everything human, yet the worm also becomes the emblem of human being itself in its creaturely aspect, figuring the body politic as a rank and disordered collectivity, as swarm not state, its horizontal order always emergent, associative, and self-organizing.[20]

This life, however, is not bare. Like the pricked flesh of Shylock, Job's sores become the occasion of provocation and protest. The loss of his substance and the dismantling of his social identity subtract Job from the minimal public sphere of the patriarchal *oikos*, but his reduction to creaturely life immediately incites a politics of litigation within a new form of publicity. In the life of Job, the lesser drama of hospitality gives way to the greater drama of the trial. Covenant is there to provide the transition, placing the trembling, lesioned Job in a scene of dissent and accountability that draws on the scripts of trial, disputation, and testimony. In this drama, Job serves in his own defense against friends who are also prosecutors masquerading as witnesses and jury members, a scene of plurality that renders Job's complaints political. God, too, is put on trial: the fact of covenant means that not only the creature, but also the Creator can be subpoenaed. Covenant asserts relationship, establishes obligation, and invites dispute. It is not because Job suffers that his case becomes universal, but because he protests; rezoning his dung heap into a stage and a soap box, Job's great gift is to summon the conditions of publicity out of the terror of privation. Job is he who subjectivizes his sufferings without symbolizing them, turning them into a political possibility for others.

In the Book of Job, creaturely life, always tattooed by covenant, appears as both the condition and the remainder of the forms of sociability that had sustained Job's patriarchal prestige in the long summer of his content. One etymology derives the word *religion* from the language of binding; establishing obligations among members of a community or between the community and God, religion as re-ligature always bears the signs of the constitutive incompleteness of collective life.[21] In the final dramatic movement of the dialogue, God storms into the gap left not by the destruction of Job's substance but by the dismantling of social identity that has occurred in the wake of those privations. Job's God appears in response to civil impasse rather than natural disaster, drawing attention to the limits of communal self-repair on the one hand and the subterfuges of theology on the other.

20. On the political ecology of worms, see Jane Bennett, *Vibrant Matter*, 95–109.
21. See Hammill and Lupton, "Sovereigns, Citizens, and Saints," 3.

Religion in the land of Uz, hazy region of translation and exchange, comes forward not as the legacy of a particular culture or faith, but as the iterative attempt to make sense of trauma's refusal to make sense.[22] In the process, the Book of Job yields religion as a "form of life" taken in a universal rather than a cultural direction: as life acknowledging the fact of its own formation, put to the test by catastrophe, and published as protest. Job's singular sores become mouths through which others, including Shylock, Lear, and Othello, can howl, rant, or rage. The central dialogue of the Book of Job invites repeat rehearsals in the performance spaces of liturgy, litigation, and drama, indexing Job's translatability across languages, traditions, and subjective possibilities.[23]

A Misanthropology of Religion

Timon of Athens is both a later and a lesser work. *Timon* has been called Shakespeare's most "intellectual" play; with its radical dearth of female characters, family ties, and romantic interest, it reads like a kind of academics' bachelor party after the keg has run dry. Whereas the poetic sequence of the Book of Job verges on drama by exercising legal rites of disputation and testimony, the drama of *Timon* turns into emblem and allegory through the static character of its declamations. *Timon*'s textual status remains uncertain: is it unfinished? does it show the hand of a collaborator? would it have survived at all if *Troilus and Cressida* had been ready for printing? And its genre, too, is perplexed: M. C. Bradbrook, in a passionate defense of the play's "broken and uneven magnificence," calls it "an experimental scenario for an indoor dramatic pageant," a description that grasps its allegorical and cerebral character as well as its felt divergence from the tested forms of public theatre. She notes that it is the only play in the "Tragic" section of the Folio to lack the word *tragedie* in its title, presenting itself purely and simply as *The Life of Timon of Athens*.[24] The word *life* flags the drama's origins in the biographical writings of Plutarch, who provides one source text of the play in the brief account of *Timon Misanthropos* tucked into his "Life of

22. Slavoj Žižek compares the scenario of Job to the dream of Irma's injection, in which three doctors cover over the inadequacy of their own response when confronted with the image of Irma's wound: "The function of the three doctors is the same as that of the three theological friends in the story of Job: to obfuscate the impact of trauma with a symbolic semblance" (*Monstrosity of Christ*, 53).
23. On the universality of protest in Job, see Negri, *Il Lavoro di Giobbe*.
24. Bradbrook, *Tragic Pageant*, 1–2.

Marcus Antonius."[25] *Life* in Plutarch means biography, the central sense the word carries into Shakespeare's title. Yet the drama is also a discourse on life, living, and even what we now call *lifestyle*; like the Book of Job, it tracks the effects of bankruptcy on a social world defined by the magnificence of a master, pursuing the reduction of the "good life" as exhibited by the liberality and munificence of a host to the "bare life" of an enraged hermit who turns against every social tie that had previously defined his prestige. If the play indeed addresses itself to the paradigm of Job, it does so by suspending Job's traumas of bereavement and illness in order to focus exclusively on the ethics and economics of substance. The scope of *Timon of Athens* is thus narrower and more trivial, and yet it manages—and here lies its own "magnificence," in the ethical and the stylistic senses—to wring existential themes from these economic concerns.

Like the Book of Job, *Timon of Athens* suffers a split. Whereas the Book of Job is divided between prose and poetry, patience and complaint, *Timon* falls into two movements. The first half of the play is overseen by *Timon philanthropos*, a wealthy man dispensing favors to his friends; its central setting, like that of Job's prose frame, is the banquet hall, a site of conviviality, communion, and gift-exchange. The second half, which, like the central section of the Book of Job, follows the host into his precipitous bankruptcy, is dominated by *Timon misanthropos*, a creature given over to hatred, subsistence, and the dogged pursuit of a language capable of capturing their terrible rudiments. The critical histories of both works largely consist of efforts to comprehend the vast stylistic, cognitive, and emotional spectra scaled by each text as it follows its hero and his language into the devastation of sociality.

As an analyst of forms of life in their extremity, the Timon of the play's second movement is not simply a misanthrope; he is a *misanthropologist*. If anthropology is the science of man, increasingly taken as the study of human cultures, misanthropology is the overturning or undoing of anthropology, its de-particularizing antidote. The student of misanthropology might begin by observing the cultural habits of misanthropes—which include, if we take *Timon* as an accurate case study, speaking in curses, playing hangman with Athens, and eating alone. Beyond such an inventory, however, misanthropology would also take issue—cantankerously of course—with "culture" itself as the proper conceptual framework for analyzing the misanthropic habitus. If the misanthrope finds himself at odds with culture, then

---

25. The Arden edition provides the appropriate excerpts from North's translation of Plutarch; see Shakespeare, *Timon of Athens*, ed. H. J. Oliver, 141–43.

his gestures of withdrawal cannot simply be reduced to forms of cultural expression, even if such gestures are only visible through formulas of the familiar. Whereas *anthropology* is intimately invested in the particulars of individual cultures, Timon's *misanthropology* indexes universals, if only because it maps those regions of rage and isolation where customs and manners have been violated. The creaturely curses of Timon describe a world in which man is no longer the measure, not because animals are people too (a green misanthropology), but because humans have broken their own norms and have thus challenged the grounds of citizenship in a common species.

Timon lives in a city far, far away from the land of Uz. Athens is an established polity, not a nomadic neighborhood, its representative institutions signaled by the parade of senators through the halls of Timon's house, which sits within the walls of the city. Despite its advanced stage of development, the world of munificence on display in the first long movement of *Timon* resembles in certain ways the primitive economy of the world inhabited by the Job of the prose frame tale. As Coppélia Kahn notes, Timon himself is oddly bereft of office; his prestige is defined purely by his capital, no longer the pastoral plenty of Job but the money bags and credit lines that will make this play a touchstone for Marx.[26] The contractual nature of the money economy, however, is supplemented and concealed by the more primitive gift economy that governs the decorous interactions of the characters, both distinguishing and intertwining *financial capital* and *social capital*. Whereas financial capital concerns the generation of surplus through the advantageous exchange of goods in a monetary economy, social capital encompasses the formation and maintenance of personal bonds through the reciprocal gifting of favors and services. The financial capitalist gains by getting more than he gives; the social capitalist, on the other hand, gains by giving more than he gets, by producing gratitude in those who receive his beneficence. Yet the gift still promises return, even if deferred in time, displaced along the chain of friends, or reciprocated only in the form of permanent beholdenness. Thus the classical emblem of beneficence is defined by *three* graces, not two, their interclasped hands indicating not only the flow of the gift back to the giver at a later date, but also its indirect return, via a third party in an interlocking chain. In Seneca's famous gloss in *De Beneficiis*, as rendered by Arthur Golding in 1578, "Some would haue it ment thereby, that the one of them bestoweth the good turne, the other receiueth

26. Coppélia Kahn, "'Magic of Bounty.'"

it, and the thirde requiteth it." As a result, benefits are that form of virtuous action that "most of al other knitteth men togither in fellowship."[27]

John Wallace emphasizes the classical sources of Timon's concern with beneficence and reciprocity, convincingly demonstrating that the play's primary models of the gift are Roman.[28] In the classical world, gifting was part of the literature and theory of friendship, an odd and powerful mix of political philosophy, ethics, sociology, and manners. A vast edifice of affiliated terms—including *kindness* (*beneficientia*), *hospitality* (*xenia*), and *generosity* (*liberalitas*)—dictated the basic moves in the social dance of friendship (*philia* or *amicitia*). Yet gifting is not simply classical, as Marcel Mauss demonstrated in his anthropological study.[29] Although classical friendship was both more far-flung in its social maneuvers and more saturated with erotic energy than our contemporary conceptions of friendship, the basic formula of the gift—the reciprocal exchange of kindnesses, services, or stuff—continues to resound in gift-economies both ancient and modern. Timon and Job are both in their way social capitalists. They are men defined not simply by their wealth but by their willingness to distribute it freely to those around them, in turn securing their prestige in the communities of hospitality that they oversee. Job lives before the advent of monetary capital, which will translate covenant into contract in and for modernity. Timon lives in a city where ritualized gift exchanges keep at a distance the starker transactions of financial debt that subtend monetized relations. In both cases, we confront heroes defined by neither military prowess nor political leadership, but by their habitation within fundamentally domestic dispensaries founded on hospitality and gift-giving. In the terms of chapter 1, Job and Timon are "animal husbands" by virtue of their initial status as hosts and their later fall into creaturely life, understood as the scene of our capture within forms of kinship and care that render us reliant on others.

"What need we have any friends," asks Timon the Greek, "if we should ne'er have need of 'em?" (1.2.93–94). Friendship, Timon tells us, exercises itself most perfectly in moments of services rendered and services received. Gifts given in response to needs create proximity between friends: "Why, I have often wish'd myself poorer that I might come nearer to you" (1.2.98–99). The true friend, Timon suggests here, not only helps his friends,

27. Seneca, *De Beneficiis*, 1.3, 1.4.
28. Wallace, *"Timon of Athens* and the Three Graces."
29. Mauss, *The Gift*. Nuttall also notes the relevance of Mauss as well as Christian theories of grace to the world of Timon (*Shakespeare the Thinker*, 314).

but allows himself *to be helped*, strengthening the bonds of friendship by exposing himself to the special burden of obligation. Yet *Timon philanthropos* is almost pathological in his resistance to accepting gifts; or rather, he accepts gifts only in order to return them manifold, refusing to accrue any excess obligation. As such, he becomes an impediment in the classical gift economy, not simply failing to live up to its standards, as John Wallace has argued, but manifesting a more fundamental difference from it.

Ken Jackson argues that we must think donation in *Timon* beyond the classical gift economy, a reading he goes on to execute under the rubric of Abraham as interpreted by Kierkegaard and Derrida.[30] Scriptural allusions abound. Apemantus, the play's cynical philosopher, evokes Christ's sacrifice when he describes the banquet as a Last Supper: "What a number of men eats Timon, and he sees 'em not! It grieves me to see so many dip their meat in one man's blood" (1.2.39–41). Like Jesus, Timon finds himself abandoned by those he would redeem: "They have all been touch'd and found base metal, / For they have all denied him" (3.3.7–8). If Timon has borrowed from Peter in order to give to Paul, his friends reveal themselves as Peters indeed in the hour of need. Job presents an analogue and supplement to Jackson's theological reading of Timon as a type of Abraham. As we saw earlier, both Job and Abraham were figures of divine testing as well as heroes of hospitality in several exegetical traditions; Job, hailing from the period of the patriarchs, partakes in a regional universality that might well be called "Abrahamic." *Timon of Athens* is certainly closer to the dramatic structure of the Book of Job than to the story cycles associated with Abraham, while the chromatic and somatic intensity of Timon's speeches in the second half of the play, which aggravate philosophy into curse, rant, and cry, is closely affiliated with the plaints of Job.

It is odd perhaps to consider *Timon of Athens* a religious play. Yet the word *religion* recurs three times in *Timon*, more than in any other play by Shakespeare.[31] Timon seems to echo the roots of religion in acts of collective binding and unbinding when he says of gold, "This yellow slave / Will knit and break religions" (4.3.34–35). Suddenly let loose, unbound, from the chain of beneficences that had earlier sustained his world, Timon must *re-ligare* himself to the gods and to humanity, an act he executes in a negative mode. In the words of the Steward, "Now all are fled / Save only the gods" (3.3.37–38). "The gods," like the creature, are what remain when human sociality has been disassembled. Timon's gods, like Lear's, thus belong

30. Jackson, "'One Wish.'"
31. See 3.2.78, 4.3.16, and 4.3.35.

to *misanthropology* rather than *anthropology*; these are gods drawn into the framework of civility not by trauma but by the failure of the social body to meet its own needs when disaster strikes.

Yet the most absolute nonrelation can also become a means of relation. Thus we see the Steward and the servants reforming a fellowship in honor of the terrible breach in the social order made by Timon's bankruptcy. The Steward tells the disbanded household, "Good fellows all, / The latest of my wealth I'll share with amongst you. / Wherever we shall meet, for Timon's sake, / Let's yet be fellows" (4.2.22–25). Released from the bonds of service by the failure of their master's finances, they reaffiliate as "fellows" (the term recurs four times in the short scene) by dividing the Steward's last paycheck, the dissolution of the very conditions of service becoming the means of a new form of commitment among them.

Timon's misanthropology is religious not in the sense of presenting a positive program to which Shakespeare might ask us to subscribe, but by transforming a singular tear in the social fabric into an opening onto something larger, an existential encounter with the limits of friendship as a form of life and hence a means for us to rethink, and re-link, our social relations. "Religion" appears not as the legacy of a particular culture or faith, but as a more primal function of human connection and its failures. Seneca's treatise *De Beneficiis* includes an extended reflection on the benefits conferred by God on man and cosmos, casting debt and gift, binding and unbinding, as features of a primal economy and universal architecture.[32] As a misanthropologist of religion, Shakespeare's interests in Timon would seem to include patterns of sociality and thought that subtend cultures even while reflecting diverse times and places. *Timon* draws on the religious syncretism of Roman philosophy as well as Biblical paradigms in order to manifest the acts of *de-ligare* that motivate religion's insistent *re-ligare*.

Greek friendship links men in a chain of ultimately equal and equivalent relationships: in Greek political theory, citizenship is friendship rendered public, the reciprocity of gift-giving becoming the rotation of offices. The Judeo-Christian gift, on the other hand, as Ken Jackson argues, is one of radical disparity: all giving, no return. In brushing off reciprocity, in spending without thought of resources or hope of repayment, Timon in effect strives to remove himself from the social fabric of friendship, to refuse absolutely the moment of parity that defines the classical ideal. Timon's distinctive and definitive *misanthropy* realizes the principle of separation already visible in Timon's acts of extravagant *philanthropy*, above and beyond the call

32. Seneca, *De Beneficiis*, 4.5.

of (classical) friendship, that mark out the social rhythms of the first half of the play. When Timon declares, Lear-like, his isolation from all human company, even from himself,

> Therefore be abhorr'd
> All feasts, societies, and throngs of men!
> His semblable, yea himself, Timon disdains (4.3.20–22),

he expresses the full force and consequence of his desire to use the gift as a means of transcending rather than sustaining the normalizing ties of ordinary social obligation. Timon aspires to a kind of economic martyrdom, crashing through the credit economy in order to discover a standard other than gold.

Friendship fails for two reasons in the play. The first is objective, involving the deep shallows of Timon's social circle. Compare here *The Merchant of Venice*, where *friendship* (an informal relation among social peers who share values and manners) comes into conflict with *contract* (a formal bond between parties from distinct and even hostile social realms).[33] Bankrupted by his own extravagant generosity, Timon finds only creditors recalling their loans in a world where monetary capital has devoured social capital, its benign and humanizing supplement. Timon is Antonio bereft of Bassanio's willing friendship most certainly, but he also lacks the honest enmity of a Shylock. Timon's false friends are drugged on rationalizations distilled from the very language of friendship they so readily abuse. Thus one friend says that he would gladly have reciprocated, if only Timon had approached him first: "I was the first man / That e'er received gift from him. / And does he think so backwardly of me now, / That I'll requite it last?" (3.3.18–21). Haughtily standing on ceremony, he sends Timon's servant away empty-handed and is rightly accused of a "politic love" (3.3.36).

But it is not only a failure in the world that confounds Timon. It is also the non-Greek element in Timon's own philanthropy that upsets the Greek ideal. Unlike Job, who is initially surrounded by wife and offspring, Timon has been single from the start, and he never quite fits into the social world he has built, ever subject to exceptional extravagance rather than regulated giving. His acts of themselves tear a hole in the fabric woven by the give and take, warp and woof, of reciprocity; both borrowing and lending at

---

33. Compare C. Kahn on contractual and social friendship traditions in *Timon* ("'Magic of Bounty,'" 48).

subprime, he is his own Adversary, and he needs no bandits or tornados to destroy him. Both Job and Timon come to inhabit the pits and heaps of a wasted landscape, but Timon, as Coppélia Kahn puts it, "literally and figuratively digs his own grave."[34] Through the exorbitance of his philanthropy, he digs the cavern of his future misanthropy into the classical landscape of friendship, and in so doing creates subterranean synapses with the world of Job.

Kahn chastises Timon for the aggressivity of his giving; like a guilt-tripping parent or a pushy date, he is trying to create obligation by doing too much. If this is true, he only gets what he deserves when his dependents reject the emotional blackmail of the excessive gift. Yet this seems too harsh and "cynical" a reading. Even the play's professional Cynic, Apemantus, sees Timon as a fool, not a knave. If Timon is a fool, he is a *holy* fool, truly sublime, though never exemplary, in both his philanthropic and his misanthropic outpourings. The fount of munificence wells up out of the classical setting with the brutal singularity of monotheism. Timon, as Ken Jackson argues in the line of Kierkegaard, is a figure of religious but not ethical heroism. As Apemantus puts it, "The middle of humanity thou never knewest, but the extremity of both ends" (4.3.301–2). Like Job, Timon travels the extremes of human living and giving; Shakespeare, however, unlike the redactors of Job, refuses to deliver his exceptionalism into any form of exemplarity. Maintaining "the extremity of both ends" gives the play the schematic character that banishes it from the mimetic successes of *echt* Shakespeare, while also delivering the poetic punch that continues to affiliate Timon with Shakespeare's other tragic heroes.

Timon makes universal claims for his misanthropy:

> The gods confound—hear me, you good gods all—
> Th'Athenians both within and out the wall;
> And grant, as Timon grows, his hate may grow
> To the whole race of mankind, high and low!
> Amen. (4.1.37–41)

Phrased as a prayer to the pagan gods, Timon's declaration ends with the Hebrew "amen" familiar from Christian liturgy. Timon's assault begins with the Athenians, gyrating out beyond its walls to include all mankind; in a parody of Pauline inclusiveness, there is neither Greek nor Jew, neither slave

---

34. Ibid., 41.

nor free in the great circle drawn by Timon's mounting hatred.[35] This is not a universalism to which any nation or culture could subscribe; it is a platform without a party, a vista of negative infinity projected from within the deeply situated place of social exclusion. It takes shape as Timon's subjective response to his betrayal by his social circle, his way of assuming as his own the position of creaturely life to which he has been casually relegated by the reflexes of his neighbors. It is, in a phrase used twice by Knight, a "peculiar universality."[36] This peculiar universality—rotating around a universe of one—describes the set produced when the pocket occupied by Timon in Athens, conceived as a specific space, time, and culture, is turned inside out, not deprived of its specific texture but stretched, exposed, and inverted to the point of becoming something else.[37] In the first half of the play, Timon is "of Athens" in the sense of residing within it; in the second half, he is "of" Athens only in the ablative sense of having moved "out of" and beyond it, *ex* Athens. The act of self-banishment, in tracing the physical movement from *oikos* and polis into wilderness, explodes the local habitation of name and place into the extremity of exposure to the universe and the universal, but a universe of one, a universe that does not brook companionship.

For both Timon of Athens and Job of Uz, friendship is a resilient social arrangement that nonetheless has failed to provide from within its own supply of customs and resources the means that would repair the tears in the fabric of fellowship. Job's comforters are not the worst of men; they sit shiva with Job and then try to engage him in reconstructive conversation; others, apparently, have abandoned Job more completely to his sorrows. But the comforters' reliance on ordinary ethical frameworks, their parroting of a moral vernacular, is inadequate to Job's situation, and their uneasy and embarrassed efforts serve to heighten rather than to ameliorate Job's isolation. Misanthropology is phenomenological inquiry into the negative theophany of God out of a neighbor-love that, perplexed to the extreme, has become incapable of attending to its own distress.

---

35. G. Wilson Knight seems to echo the Pauline scope of Timon's hatred when he notes, "The whole race of man is his theme. His love was ever universal, now his hate is universal, its theme embraces every grade, age, sex, and profession" (*Wheel of Fire*, 221).

36. Ibid., 207–20.

37. C. L. Barber and Richard P. Wheeler tap a similar insight when they suggest that the play is "an extreme social history" that uses its satiric situationalism to "deal with something far more fundamental" (*Whole Journey*, 306).

Forms of Life in *Timon of Athens*

The dramatic core of Job is the visitation by friends; Shakespeare had already floated a variation on this scene in the opening to *The Merchant of Venice*, when Antonio entertains a stream of well-wishers pondering the causes of his sadness. In *Timon of Athens*, as in the Book of Job, the better friends show up to make amends. Apemantus, the Steward, and Alcibiades had each made attempts earlier in the play to break through or be other than the flatterers who abandon Timon in his credit crisis. Whereas the Bandits, the Painter and the Poet, the Whores, and the Senators emblematize economic principles (theft, the culture industry, prostitution, the political machine), Apemantus, the Steward, and Alcibiades visit Timon having already taken exception to the generalized economy of Athens from within their specific spheres of activity. Apemantus voices the consolations of cynical philosophy, manifesting the margins of thinking. The Steward, like Kent, proffers the comforts of pure service after its contract has been broken, figuring the cares of the *oikos*. Finally, Alcibiades represents the violence of exile, coup, and dictatorship, testing the concept of the political. Apemantus predicts the misanthropy that delivers Timon to a poetics of hatred beyond that achieved by the professional Cynic. The Steward's "care of . . . food and living" (4.3.220–21) anticipates Timon's subsistence menu. Finally, Alcibiades figures the states of emergency that Timon now inhabits outside Athens. Each friend draws out a facet of Timon's own exceptionalism as it opens onto the human condition as such: the life of the mind; the life of work, labor, and bodily care; and the *bios politikos*, the life of the polis.

Hannah Arendt would insist that "life" in each case manifests a distinct aspect or profile of a single vitality. The *oikos* shelters life in its biological dimensions, as feeding, birthing, dying, and the acts of care and labor they require; both the Book of Job and *Timon of Athens* make their homes in this prepolitical sphere. Arendt defines the *bios politikos* as freedom from the nutritional concerns of the *oikos*, the life whose *res gestae* can be gathered up into the kind of biography popularized by Plutarch.[38] Finally, the life of the mind is no life at all in either the biological or the political senses, but a radical subtraction of the subject from the forms of appearing that characterize both the polis and the *oikos*. Arendt writes that "the thinking ego is sheer activity and therefore ageless, sexless, without qualities, and without a life story"—not because there is no body supporting the thinking being,

---

38. Arendt, *Human Condition*, 84.

but because thinking involves the temporary withdrawal from those very attributes and the forms of privacy and publicity they condition.[39]

Timon of Athens tests the extremities of each of these forms of life. The Timon of the first half of the drama is master of his house but not liberated into the exercise of citizenship by the labor of his servants; he is an animal husband, a caponlike captive to the nutritive necessities that he appears to transcend through wealth and its management. At home, Timon is neither a citizen nor a philosopher, his difference from the latter conspicuously marked by his impatient exchanges with Apemantus. In the second movement of the play, paralleling Job's habitation on the dung heap, Timon exchanges the *oikos maximus* of Athenian luxury for the *oikos minimus* of the cave—not a denial but an intensification of and confrontation with the needs of life that subtend domesticity.[40] For Timon as for Job, this exodus to the very edges of the *oikos* transforms the ordinary intellect into that of a philosopher, his misanthropic maxims voiced in the ritualized genres of retort, curse, and invocation.

Finally, though more obscurely (here the imperfect character of the text yawns most loudly), Timon's self-exile brings him into a new relationship with the *bios politikos*, the political life of the city. The final visitation to Timon's cave before his death is extended by the delegation of Senators, led unwillingly by the Steward. The Senators "with one consent of love / Entreat thee back to Athens" (5.1.139–40), a return intended to stave off Alcibiades' imminent destruction of the city. The Senators' "consent" articulates the representative nature of government at Athens, though the editor notes, following Malone, that the Latin *concentus*, meaning harmony of voices, overrides the secondary origin in *consensus*. This harmonically unified "public body" (5.1.144) has agreed to offer Timon the "captainship," to head that body "with absolute power" (5.1.160, 161). Timon, who before had been master of his house but not a senator in the city, is now offered an extraordinary political position as dictator, a sovereign figure both in and beyond the constitutional order. Already living outside the walls of the city, he is now invited back into the city in order to assume an exceptional role within it.

An unlikely candidate for *condottiere*, our misanthropologist declines public office of any kind. Yet he does not really escape publicity. The real *bios politikos* of both Timon and Job lies in the scene of visitation itself, whose

39. Arendt, *Life of the Mind*, 43.
40. What James Kuzner writes of Coriolanus applies to Timon as well: "In seeking to exist outside Rome's fictions, as I believe Coriolanus does, he also stands for other, more habitable forms of unprotected existence" ("Unbuilding the City," 175).

assembly of interlocutors erects the space of *Öffentlichkeit* in which the needs of life as well as the disconsolations of philosophy are put on trial. Both dung heap and desert become primitive theaters, unlikely rostra drafted into the service of human appearing by what remains from the script of hospitality when bankruptcy and abandonment have unraveled social ties. In the clearing outside Timon's cave, the rudiments of philosophy, politics, and economics take root and intertwine, displaying their dependencies. What *Timon* reveals, in concert with Job, is our terrifying incompleteness with respect to other people, the world, and our own vitality, as well as our shaping and scarring by the signifying practices through which we manage as well as avoid our connectivity.

Apemantus mocks Timon's exposed state by recreating nature as a fawning household of caregivers and flatterers:

> Thou hast cast away thyself, being like thyself,
> A madman so long, now a fool. What, think'st
> That the bleak air, thy boisterous chamberlain,
> Will put thy shirt on warm? Will these moist trees,
> That have outliv'd the eagle, page thy heels
> And skip when thou point'st out? Will the cold brook,
> Candied with ice, caudle thy morning taste
> To cure thy o'ernight's surfeit? Call the creatures
> Whose naked natures live in all the spite
> Of wreakful heaven, whose bare unhoused trunks,
> To the conflicting elements expos'd,
> Answer mere nature: bid them flatter thee.
> O thou shalt find—
> TIM.   A fool of thee. Depart. (4.3.222–33)

Apemantus contrasts what Timon was (coddled and cared for, supported in both his bodily being and his sense of self by an entourage of stewards, servants, and sycophants) and what he is now: as "bare," "unhoused," and "expos'd . . . to the conflicting elements" as the "creatures" that surround him. Apemantus at once confronts Timon with the fact of his own creatureliness and, Orpheus-like, reassembles a ghostly household out of the cheerless landscape. Timon is to Apemantus as Lear is to his Fool; indeed, the parts were likely written for the same pair of actors, Richard Burbage and Robert Armin.[41] Timon, however, unlike Lear, is no madman. In the

---

41. Shakespeare, *Timon of Athens*, ed. John Jowett, 17.

first movement of the play, Timon is *everyone's fool*: their dupe, their mark, their sucker. In the second half, Timon becomes *nobody's fool*: he who can out-cynic the professional cynic, who sees through every gambit, and who has learned to trust no one. Yet nobody's fool is still a fool: subjected to bodily cares that recollect the ministrations of others, reestablishing in the frigid isolation of the desert the conditions of human appearing that obtain wherever others are present, if only in memory. Timon is not "unhoused" so much as encamped, since he finds shelter in the minimal architecture of the cave. His being is further canopied by his own fiercely embodied acts of speech, at once liturgical and litigious, whether he is hurling curses, gold, or stones. Arendt's formula for a portable politics, "Wherever you go, you will be a *polis*,"[42] could be reframed here as, "Wherever you go, you will be an *oikos*." Such an *oikos*, by tending the needs of life in scenes that require or recall the company of persons and the comfort of things, assures that life is never truly bare, and that it remains capable of a rudimentary politics. In both *Timon of Athens* and the Book of Job, that politics coalesces out of hospitality, the frontal encounter between guest and host that opens the household to the possibility of action.

Does Timon act? John Jowett calls this central sequence of visitations "static" and "untheatrical."[43] Any action that unfolds here is viscous, talky, and emblematic. Yet Jowett also argues that the three main interviews, characterized by "effectual conversation and communication of a kind not seen earlier in the play," offer Timon "a temptation not to hate."[44] By refusing this temptation, in a kind of grotesque parody of Jesus in the desert, Timon's action appears to be one of resolute withdrawal, an exit from the possibility of action as such, which requires commerce with others. Yet, in giving gold not only to Alcibiades, the prostitutes, and the thieves but also to the Steward, he reestablishes connections with the city despite his own exit strategy. By throwing insults at Apemantus, Timon gives the cynic a brushed-up version of his own philosophy. Even the stones he lobs at the Senators, rebuffing their offer of dictatorship, become a kind of offering; the ambassadors are able to tell Alcibiades that they had at least tried to "woo / Transformed Timon to our city's love" (5.4.18–19), effectively ameliorating the general's retributive violence. The anti-gift is still a gift, and Timon is still Timon, a continuity asserted through the risky self-birthing of action

---

42. Arendt, *Human Condition*, 198.
43. Shakespeare, *Timon of Athens*, ed. John Jowett, 3
44. Ibid., 10.

through speech and not by the flow of temperament and disposition alone. *De-ligare*, the resolute breaking of all social contracts from the vantage of a stripped and lonely creatureliness, becomes a form of *re-ligare*, the painful and precarious rebuilding of civil and civic bonds in the aftermath of their decimation. Timon's speech and gestures count as action because their effects exceed his aims, rippling beyond the cave back to the city not as the tsunami of annihilation but as the chance for repair. They also accede to action insofar as Timon's behavior yields an unintended image of himself as vulnerable, gift-giving, and still capable of covenant, a daemon visible not to the actor himself, but only to the others assembled in the provisional space of publicity constituted by cave and stage.

Whereas Job's friends struggle to reassert the economy of norms in the face of Job's singular situation, Timon's friends, perhaps more wisely, deploy their own precocious exceptionalisms in their efforts to draw Timon back into Athens. Neither Job's comforters nor Timon's are bad men, yet in both cases their consolatory projects fail. Job's friends founder by remaining trapped within the economy of retributive thinking. Timon's friends do better by meeting exception with exception, yet because their goals remain social reintegration, Timon rebuffs their advances. The dialogic mode, the remedial aims, and the necessary shortcomings of these encounters bind the dramatic scaffolding of Timon's comportment to that of Job. Unwelcome guests are still guests, and their intrusion at once betrays and publicizes the isolation of their unhappy hosts.

In both the Book of Job and *Timon of Athens*, the drama of privation, visitation, and complaint engenders a poetics of monstrosity, natality, and disease. A series of Jobean motifs come together in Timon's prayer to nature:

> That nature, being sick of man's unkindness,
> Should yet be hungry! Common mother, thou
> Whose womb unmeasurable and infinite breast
> Teems and feeds all; whose self-same mettle,
> Whereof thy proud child, arrogant man, is puff'd,
> Engenders the black toad and adder blue,
> The gilded newt and eyeless venom'd worm,
> With all th'abhorred births below crisp heaven
> Whereon Hyperion's quick'ning fire doth shine:
> Yield him, who all the human sons do hate,
> From forth thy plenteous bosom, one poor root.
> Ensear thy fertile and conceptious womb;

Let it no more bring out ingrateful man.
Go great with tigers, dragons, wolves and bears;
Teem with new monsters, whom thy upward face
Hath the marbled mansion all above
Never presented. O, a root; dear thanks!
Dry up thy marrows, vines and plough-torn leas,
Whereof ingrateful man, with liquorish draughts
And morsels unctuous, greases his pure mind,
That from it all consideration slips—
Enter APEMANTUS.
More man? Plague, plague! (4.3.178–99)

The passage resonates with classical topoi concerning a chthonic Mother Nature who generates monsters from her primitive entrails; in these lines, we hear Shakespeare exerting himself to place Timon squarely in pagan Athens. Yet the very intensity of Shakespeare's classical impulse hits on the Book of Job's covenant with creatureliness, figured in both the multitudinous swarming of worms and the monstrous rarity of the dragon, the ostrich, and the leviathan. Creatureliness itself touches on the more universalist elements of the Job story, its Canaanite sources and pre-Sinaitic affiliations, and is thus a fitting point of contact between Athens and Uz. For both Job and Timon, a *natura* ruled by mutation rather than order sets the scene of the *creatura*'s response to dereliction.

Timon, like Job, rails against the scandal of birth, impulses that lead both men into de-creative fantasies that challenge the coherence of the cosmos itself. In the desert, Timon recognizes the Steward as a "man . . . Born of woman" (4.3.497–98), a Jobean phrase familiar from both Scripture and liturgy. The worm of Job finds its comestible counterpart in the root sought by Timon: both worm and root are subterranean growths that trace the limits of the human condition, insofar as they reduce humanity to the edge of its own species identifications at the margin between life and death. To reject the fact of being born requires making war on maternity; Timon's prayer to Mother Nature is also a curse against her, echoing Lear's imprecation to a similar Nature to destroy Goneril's reproductive capacities: "Hear, Nature, hear! Dear Goddess, hear! / Suspend thy purpose, if thou didst intend / To make this creature fruitful! / Into her womb convey sterility" (1.4.274–77). Like Job, Timon expresses a misogyny derived from a deep revolt against birthing and its consequences, from within a masculinity fundamentally oriented around the husbandry of the *oikos*, not political or military heroism.[45] In an analysis developed further by Coppélia Kahn, C. L. Barber and Richard Wheeler argue that Timon "does without maternal nurturance by trying to be himself an all-providing patron," a "'plenteous bosom'" (1.2.120–21) of milky kindness.[46] Like Job, Timon's rage against maternity in the second movement of the drama expresses at least in part his anger against the very virtues of generosity, ministration, and curatorial patronage that he had earlier exercised.

Reducing the promise of natality to a bare root does not destroy natality but reclaims it by reorganizing it around the nucleus of bare beginningness that the root instantiates. A root is an origin, a *radix* (Latin) and a *rhiza* (Greek) with the power to generate new growth. Timon's more brilliant tirades, like Job's defenses, constitute such radical enunciations at the verges of philosophical, economic, and political forms of life, as in his musings on theft as a cosmic principle: "The sun's a thief, and with his great attraction / Robs the vast sea; the moon's an arrant thief, / And her pale fire she snatches from the sun . . . each thing's a thief" (4.3.439–45). Equal parts philosophy, political economy, and rant, such language, radiating from the radical of the root, is enough to assure Timon his place in the Shakespearean canon.

When he sees Apemantus enter, Timon breaks off his curse with the words, "More man? Plague, plague!" Although he does not himself suffer the disfigurations of bodily illness in the emblematic manner of Job, Timon echoes Job when he declares the unnaturalness of patience in the face of such humiliation: "Not nature, / To whom all sores lay siege, can bear great fortune, / But by contempt of nature" (4.3.6–8). Through the language of sores, Timon affiliates both the poverty of his own condition and the passionate speech it inspires with Job's categorical impatience. Whereas Job's boils function as symptoms of his own losses and the challenges they deposit in the social body, disease in *Timon of Athens* becomes a metaphor of the sickness inherent in sociality itself, which transfers its degenerative effects through the poisonous gifts and false promises of bankrupted beneficence. Timon bids the whores, "Consumptions sow / In hollow bones of man" (4.3.153–54). The play analyzes consumption in its several functions: the eating of food at the great banquets of social capital; the distribution of goods, money, and services that occurs at such affairs; and the forms of disease, real and symbolic, that accompany the profligate contacts of the

45. As Knight puts it, Timon "lives in a world of the soul where emotion is the only manliness, and love the only courage" (*Wheel of Fire*, 212).
46. Barber and Wheeler, *Whole Journey*, 305.

consumer economy. In his exit curse against Athens, Timon pictures the implosion of sociality as a symphony of symptoms:

> Plagues incident to men,
> Your potent and infectious fevers heap
> On Athens ripe for stroke! Thou cold sciatica,
> Cripple our senators, that their limbs may halt
> As lamely as their manners! Lust and liberty
> Creep in the minds and marrows of our youth,
> That 'gainst the stream of virtue they may strive,
> And drown themselves in riot! Itches, blains,
> Sow all th'Athenian bosoms, and their crop
> Be general leprosy! Breath infect breath,
> That their society, as their friendship, may
> Be merely poison! Nothing I'll bear from thee
> But nakedness, thou detestable town!
> Take thou that too, with multiplying bans! (4.1.21–34)

Timon effects his own exile from the city by cursing the exchanges of "society" and "friendship" with the rampant ravaging of contagious disease. He identifies the genre and escalating energy of his own language as "multiplying bans": curses that pile upon each other like the itches and blains he both diagnoses and casts onto what he calls "society." Such banishments delimit his own nakedness outside Athens as an index of the sins of the city. His servants had described his bankrupted state: "His poor self, / A dedicated beggar to the air, / With his disease of all-shunned poverty, / Walks like contempt, alone" (4.2.12–15). Now he willfully identifies himself with this cipher of isolation in order to convert the banned and abandoned remnant of social relations into its radical conscience and scourge. He curses Athens with the diseases spawned by its own promiscuity, yet he himself embodies the "disease of all-shunned poverty" and ultimately identifies his life as a form of sickness that only death can heal: "My long sickness / Of health and living now begins to mend, / And nothing brings me all things" (5.1.185–87).

At the end of the Book of Job, God disappears back into his whirlwind, and the friends are forgiven and restored, along with Job's wealth and a new set of offspring. In the grafting of comic novella and poetic dialogue, norms, like friends and happy endings, remain necessary if inadequate features of the social and literary world, and readers are called to bridge the gaps between divergent textual layers and ethical demands. Timon, unlike Job, never returns to his prior position of wealth and health, achieving the death wish repeatedly voiced but never realized by Job. Building his "everlasting mansion / Upon the beached verge of the salt flood, / Who once a day with his embossed froth / The turbulent surge shall cover" (5.1.214–17), his tomb will mark a space of exclusion at the mutable edge of shore and land, repeatedly appearing and submerging at "the very hem o' th' sea" (5.4.66), its margin of error traced by the cosmic thefts of sun, moon, and ocean.

Alcibiades takes over Timon's exceptionality and brings it inside the city walls, assuming the role of dictator declined by Timon. Threatening Athens with absolute destruction, Alcibiades draws back from the promise of violence in order to restore the city to its "public laws" (5.4.62). His final lines remarry the terrible emergency of military force ("war") and the normative rule of law ("peace") in an image of general physic:

> Bring me into your city,
> And I will use the olive with my sword,
> Make war breed peace, make peace stint war, make each
> Prescribe to other, as each other's leech.
> Let our drums strike. (5.4.81–85)

There is some promise here that the body politic will be restored to health. Alcibiades combines aspects of both Horatio and Fortinbras, faithful friend to Timon and hence a figure of political friendship, and extraordinary dictator, a bearer of violence beyond the law. Yet the relation between these roles remains deeply indeterminate; in a grafting of layers even more imperfect than in the Book of Job, the role of Alcibiades is especially ambiguous. In support of what unnamed man does he go to war with Athens, and how is Timon connected to both the upstart general and the scapegoat he champions? Alcibiades not only thematizes emergency in Shakespeare's play, but also incites a kind of textual emergency, an unanswerable set of questions, in the drama. He resembles the mysterious fourth friend Elihu in the Book of Job, more foreign to the unfolding of the dialogue than the other interlocutors and manifesting a distinct textual layer, perhaps a separate collaborative voice.

The play certainly brokers no synthesis among the forms of life—economic, political, and philosophical—that we associate with the legacy of Athens, in Arendt's work and in the tradition at large. Instead, it exposes their "roots" by ripping them from the grounds of social interaction and then keeping those roots raw and bare—dramatically unsatisfying, yet open to fresh encounters and new beginnings. The accidents of Timon's insertion between *Romeo and Juliet* and *Julius Caesar* in the Folio's menu of tragedies demonstrate the strange fortunes of this play, printed in order to fill a gap and forever introducing gaps of its own into the canon of Shakespearean drama. *Timon of Athens*, like Alcibiades in Plato's *Symposium*, is an unexpected guest at a philosophical party, a bit drunk and out of tune, replaying snatches of old lauds from more perfect plays (*Lear, Hamlet, Merchant of Venice*) without satisfactorily stitching them together as either drama or thought. Although I cannot concur with G. Wilson Knight that this play "includes and transcends" Shakespeare's other tragedies, it is indeed true that it refracts and reflects them, using the academic devices of parable, morality, and dialogue to render the more mimetic achievements of *Lear, Merchant,* and *Othello,* Shakespeare's greater Job plays into a schematic form that brings us very close indeed to Job's strange mingling of drama and disputation.[47]

Victoria Kahn argues that for Milton, the Book of Job became, perhaps paradoxically, a way of fashioning a secular place for literature, by which she means poetry that finally attains "an independent status as a purely human creation."[48] Shakespeare draws on Job, in all of its proto-secular literary ambivalence, in order to create a religious zone in his texts that is not strictly theological, in which God enters as an afterthought, a late addition, and thus can be imagined as not entering at all. Milton can use Job to become secular because he is already writing from such a distinctly Scriptural point of view. Shakespeare, on the other hand, is *already* writing secular literature; when he copies Job, it is not to declare poetic independence but to acknowledge moments of radical interdependence: of each human on other humans, of the human on the creaturely, and of secular writing on sacred writing. For Milton, Job may offer a way out of religion; for Shakespeare, Job offers a way in. Shakespeare's attraction to Job retains a "religious" dimension if we take religion as that which addresses human life and poetic production in their entanglement with other instances of both vitality and writing that we do not fully administer or author ourselves. Such acknowledgment—exercised through acts of allusion and imitation, for example—might then come to draft a fuller and more valid account of authorship, poetically independent precisely in its recognition of manifold dependencies.

This religion that is not strictly theological also yields a form of publicity that is not strictly political, that assembles its scenes of human appearing in the rubbish heaps of the *oikos* rather than the fora of the polis. This is a

47. Knight, *Wheel of Fire,* 236.
48. Victoria Kahn, "Complaint of Job," 644.

politics that prefers the melting moods of the animal husband to the harder virtues of the citizen-soldier. The misanthropological musings of Job and Timon harbor an *impolitical untheology*, against which they measure every missive from FEMA. In a little book entitled *The Labor of Job (Il Lavoro di Giobbe)*, Antonio Negri associates the suffering figure of Job with a creative ethics of labor, the materialism of Spinoza, and a Messianism based on the flesh, not the spirit. Negri writes of Job's social and temporal movement, "There is no finalism, but struggle, invention, and victory. *There is constitution*" (141; emphasis his).[49] *There is constitution*: this strange formulation casts "constitution" as an ongoing process of social binding and rebinding, a legislation that occurs through the burrowing work of the worms, who together create their own ever-emergent leviathan. With Job by his side, Shakespeare begins to deliver something like this constitution in the fallow wasteland of *Timon of Athens*.

49. Negri, cited and translated by Ted Stoltze in "Marxist Wisdom," 129.

FIVE

Hospitality and Risk in
The Winter's Tale

In her essay "The Crisis in Culture," Hannah Arendt finds her way to an account of judgment by contrasting culture and entertainment. Works of culture attain what Arendt calls "an objective status," indicating both the durability of objects and the generation of some consensus concerning their meanings and value. Culture, moreover, indicates for Arendt not only the objects, works, and artifacts that we deem valuable, but also the conditions of visibility and preservation that allow them to make their appearance on the human scene: "These things obviously share with political 'products,' words and deeds, the quality that they are in need of some public space where they can appear and be seen; they can fulfill their being, which is appearance, only in a world which is common to all." Situated acts of judgment, executed over time and from plural locations, generate a fragile universality that not only affirms the value of individual works of art but also the institutions that transmit them.[1] Culture builds worlds by commemorating deeds; moreover, like the deed, culture requires a space of appearing—be it museum or magazine, university or public square—that solicits culture to exercise its virtues. Entertainments, on the other hand, Arendt writes,

> serve the life processes of society, even though they may not be as necessary as bread and meat. They serve, that is, to while away the time, and the vacant time which is whiled away is not leisure time, strictly speaking—time, that

1. Arendt's "The Crisis in Culture" was first published in *Daedalus* in 1960 and then collected with other pieces in *Between Past and Future* (1961). On aesthetic judgment and Arendt's theory of culture, see Victoria Kahn, "Political Theology and Liberal Culture: Strauss, Schmitt, Spinoza, and Arendt," unpublished paper delivered at the West Coast Symposium on Law and Literature, University of Southern California, January 2010.

is, in which we are free *from* all cares and activities necessitated by the life process and therefore free *for* the world and its culture—it is rather left-over time, which is still biological in nature, left over after labor and sleep have received their due.[2]

Whereas culture is dedicated to duration, entertainment, according to Arendt, uses objects and images up as if they were food. The link between popcorn and movies is both metaphoric and metonymic: we enjoy Hollywood movies as if they were a fluffy snack, but we also view them *with* a bucket of said savory nested in our laps.

Drama for Arendt would belong to culture rather than entertainment, not only because of the public character of its performance, but also because it takes words and deeds as its medium; as she likes to note, "drama" derives from *dran*, "to do, act, perform."[3] Tragedy, drama's self-epitomizing genre, belongs to the polis, holding up its heroes and institutions for celebration, analysis, and critique. Entertainment, on the other hand, flows from the more romantic mixing bowls and drinking cups of the *oikos* and its magnificent banquets. Entertainment precedes the polis as the mainstay of aristocratic, prepolitical, and agrarian rites of hospitality, and succeeds the polis as part of the transformation of politics into society that Arendt identifies not only with modern liberalism, consumerism, and the administrative state, but also with the economic bias of Roman and Christian social theory. Entertainment, in other words, is biopolitical insofar as it clings to social arrangements organized around bodily care and wellbeing, normative routines to which the contingencies of human action pose a threat rather than a good. If risk is a tragic condition that drama shares with politics, then *risk aversion* is the sign of entertainment, understood as drama's domesticator and administrator.[4] If the wedding planner is the mistress of risk management, the theatrical director is she who is willing to "take risks"—artistic, political, and economic—in order to raise drama to the level of event.[5] The liabilities avoided by entertainment include thinking, boredom, and embarrassment, symptoms of exposure to an excess of truth (about the self, or the state, or the state of things). Drama demonstrates the existence of other minds. In mass culture, this is always risky business.

---

2. Arendt, *Between Past and Future*, 202, 218, 205.
3. Arendt, *Human Condition*, 187.
4. On immunization and biopolitics, see especially Esposito, *Bíos.*
5. On drama as event, closely allied to the political, see Badiou, "Rhapsody for the Theatre."

Yet, if the cut of Arendt's irony puts entertainment in its place next to the vacuum cleaners and vacuum tubes of the postwar boom, it also refreshes the very thing it critiques by slicing it from an unexpected angle, revealing the metabolic dimension of performances conceived as occasional and transient, sustained by wider patterns of enjoyment and hospitality. Although her analysis makes room for aesthetic judgment in the Kantian sense, the distinction between culture and entertainment is *not itself such a judgment,* since Arendt's deeper point is sociohistorical: modern life, organized around labor and consumption, gravitates against the world-making aspects of culture. Entertainment flourishes in modernity in direct proportion to the marshaling of life processes as the main concern of the state and its institutions. Entertainment defines art and media under biopolitics.

In Tudor-Stuart England, plays, masques, and interludes flowed out of the larger frame of hospitality, whose service economy was bound up with the needs for food, drink, shelter, and hygiene that Arendt associates with the labor of the *oikos* and the irksome demands of the body. As Daryl W. Palmer writes, "Under Elizabeth and James, hospitality and entertainment are nearly interchangeable terms, marking the accepted interdependence of householding and theater, domestic and political practice." Hospitality, he writes further, "was the 'first condition' of the interlude."[6] The connection drawn by Arendt between food and media also pertains to the commensal scene of Renaissance entertainment, though not, of course, on the industrial scale of modern mass culture. For Arendt, the distinction between drama and entertainment was clear, even if determined only in the acts of judgment that build consensus in the public sphere constituted by and for culture. For Shakespeare, these worlds are still in the most intimate touch with each other, their shared venues, menus, and audiences everywhere in contact and on display. First played at the Globe in 1611, *The Winter's Tale* was also performed at Whitehall, most likely in the Banqueting House, as part of the festivities associated with the marriage of Princess Elizabeth to Prince Frederick the Elector Palatinate in the winter of 1612–13.[7] Many aspects of the play, including the sheep-shearing festival and the statue scene, reflect a Stuart environment of pastime and entertainment. Yet the play is no masque or interlude, but a drama organized around the consequences

6. Palmer, *Hospitable Performances,* 3–4. The classic historical study of hospitality in the Tudor-Stuart period is Heal's *Hospitality in Early Modern England.*

7. On Shakespeare and the Stuart court, see Kernan, *Shakespeare, the King's Playwright,* as well as the excellent introduction to the Oxford edition of the play by Stephen Orgel in Shakespeare, *The Winter's Tale,* ed. Stephen Orgel, 1–83.

of the fateful actions of act 1. That action concerns above all a disruption in hospitality: the moment in which the queen, urged by the king to invite his friend to extend his stay, generates a terrible and unforeseen response in her solicitous husband.

The genesis of Leontes' jealousy has received much analysis, with especially fine readings mounted by Stanley Cavell, Ruth Nevo, Lowell Gallagher, and James Knapp.[8] I would like to reorient the play around Hermione. The queen, I argue, undergoes the trial—what she calls the adventure—of *going public*, of becoming a person in the tentative public sphere assembled by the hospitality relation at the threshold where its formal choreography dissolves into experimental intimacies. My ultimate interests lie in seeing what happens to an Arendtian definition of action, identified with both politics and drama, when it convenes its praxis in the scene set by hospitable entertainment, whose festive tempo is measured by the great wheel of the seasons, the digestive orders and disorders of the body, and the transient life suffered by objects in their passage through use. In the drama of hospitality, actors traditionally excluded from the scene of politics, including women, children, servants, and peddlers (along with sheep and the occasional bear) wander into the space of publicity by virtue of their participation in the social drama of hospitality, inevitably dragging with them the needs of life and the objects of utility, convenience, and desire that support them. Hospitality always stores a potential politics in its cellars and butteries, and Shakespearean drama, perhaps especially in its late, Stuart stages, draws out that politics in order to produce an art that attains to the status of drama while remaining at home in the world of entertainment. *The Winter's Tale* discovers dramatic action in the social theater of hospitality, reflecting the conditions of the play's own performance and revealing anew the generative knot between politics and life in Shakespearean drama.

Hospitality's Daemons

As we have seen, for Arendt human action manifests the fundamental link between drama and politics, in so far as each involves an appearing in public that issues in the contingencies of unwilled self-disclosure and the unpredictable responses of other people. In what Paul Kottman calls "a politics of the scene," action assembles persons, speech, and bodies in a public space

action in Citizenship

8. Cavell, *Disowning Knowledge*; Nevo, *Shakespeare's Other Language*; Gallagher, "Ambivalent Nostalgia"; and Knapp, "Visual and Ethical Truth."

subject to the hazards of misrecognition.[9] Arendt compares the subjectivizing effects of speech in action to the daemon of Greek religion, "which accompanies each man throughout his life, always looking over his shoulder from behind and thus visible only to those he encounters."[10] Avatars of the daemon include genius, the soul, conscience, and the unconscious, all names for the attempt to grasp that element of subjectivity that flares up in the human actor as both the essence and the limit of his or her willed identity and legal personhood, dividing the subject between the impulses of an insurgent vitality caught up in speech and the phenomenal scene of human appearing, discourse, and exchange in which such specters of life make their astonishing exits and entrances.[11] In Adriana Cavarero's gloss of Arendt, the whoness of the speaker remains "as unmasterable and invisible as the *daemon*. . . . Even on the active level of the properly human (or political) revelation, the meaning of the identity remains the patrimony of another."[12] In this book, I have put forward Arendt's daemon as a figure that, like natality, allows creaturely life to appear in and for the polis. Although the daemon belongs fully to the phenomenal world of the *vita activa*—the daemon captures the way in which humans disclose themselves to each other in their plurality—the figure of the daemon itself belongs to both the bestial and the divine, and thus suggests something in and beyond the *bios politikos* that helps constitute the human as such in relation to other life forms.

Although Arendt does not summon them directly, hospitality entertains daemons of its own. Shakespeare's plays consistently draft hospitality as the social script that opens the household to the risk of politics. Again and again, whether it is in Capulet's ballroom, Brabantio's parlor, Macbeth's guest suite, or Timon's banqueting house, hospitality chez Shakespeare harbors dangers of self-exposure that are also opportunities for action, scenes that make dinner into drama by scripting both hospitality and theater as kinds of politics. Hospitality has always housed the seeds of the political in its domestic bosom. In archaic societies like the one depicted in the *Odyssey*, *xenia* regulates the thresholds of the *oikos*, not only its gates and doorways,

---

9. A scene, writes Kottman, designates "any particular horizon of human interaction, inaugurated by the words and deeds of someone or some group, here and now, with the result that a singular relationship or web of relationships is brought into being, sustained, or altered among those on the scene" (*Politics of the Scene*, 10).

10. Arendt, *Human Condition*, 179–80.

11. I am indebted to my students Donovan Sherman (for research on the soul in early modern drama) and Rachael Hoff (for research on the conscience as a specifically public form of appearing in seventeenth century polemics and poetics). On the conscience and its links to the daemonic, see Lukacher, *Daemonic Figures*. On genius, see Agamben, *Profanations*.

12. Cavarero, *Relating Narratives*, 22.

but also the porticos where travelers would lay their temporary bedding and the hearth of supplication and sanctuary.[13] In international relations, the lack of an overarching sovereign instance renders each state into a kind of *oikos*, an entity that must determine how to greet the guests who wander into its precincts.[14] Finally, in situations anywhere and everywhere, persons normally hidden by the routines of service enter into some kind of exchange, negotiation, or deliberation with strangers to the home. What daemons emerge in the scenes set by hospitality? To whom do they belong? And what are they mumbling about? Moreover, how do these daemons invite us to modulate the more properly political images of self that accompany epic and tragic action in Arendt's account with a vision that rezones the *oikos* as a scene for comic and romance action?

Walter Burkert and John Raffan write that for the Greeks, "there is no image of a *daimōn*, and there is no cult. *Daimōn* is thus the necessary complement to the Homeric view of the gods as individuals with personal characteristics; it covers that embarrassing remainder which eludes characterization and naming." If the daemon personalizes the speaker in Arendt's account, it does so in an oddly depersonalizing way, generating an "embarrassing remainder" that belies individuation. In epic, moreover, the word *daimonie* is used "when the speaker does not understand what the addressee is doing and why he is doing it."[15] In the *Odyssey*, Penelope and Odysseus greet each other with precisely this word of reproach and surprise: "You are so strange [*daimonih*]," the returning hero, fresh from his bath, tells his wife as she remains reserved in his shining presence after their twenty years' separation. He goes on to order the nurse to make up a separate bed for him, since "this woman has a heart of iron within her." Penelope responds, "*You* are so strange [*daimonie*]," and goes on to test his true identity with the trick of the bed.[16] It is only after he has proven his knowledge of the manufacture of said bed, built around a living tree, great emblem of organic life branching at the heart of the *oikos*, that she agrees to join him in it. Husband and wife confront each other as strangers, as host-guests in a house that belongs imperfectly to both of them after the traumas of separation and household war.

---

13. On hospitality in the *Odyssey*, see Reece, *Stranger's Welcome*.
14. On the politics of hospitality, see Derrida, *Of Hospitality*; and McNulty, *The Hostess*.
15. Burkert and Raffan, *Greek Religion*, 180.
16. Homer, *The Odyssey*, 174.

Arendt might say that what appears in the space between them (he sits on a chair, we are told, "opposite his wife"), are reciprocal images of self disclosed by the fact of their facing each other, images whose outlines and effects are not shaped by the speakers themselves. All washed and glistening, purged of the blood of the suitors, Odysseus aims to present himself as the gloriously returning husband. What appears to Penelope behind his shoulder is the prospect of an imposter, of someone who plays another, a man of many ways who has *always* played another, and who, she fears, continues to do so now. What perhaps appears as well is the difference in years that Penelope sees, and that Odysseus cannot: she glimpses the specter of Odysseus *not seeing* his own aging, and all that such a self-perception reveals about the habits of his heroic masculinity. In any case, Penelope also appears *daimonih* to him: strange, inscrutable, and unexpectedly reticent. As she holds back in order to judge this man before her, to figure out whether to greet him as husband, guest, or enemy, her storied circumspection, her characteristic tactics of delay, come forward as a kind of spectral quantity, at once individuating her and rendering her uncanny.

If the daemon describes what in the gods "eludes characterization and naming," the word captures a similar remainder here. Their marriage must reconstitute itself in the scene brought into being by this double demonism. It was perhaps a union such as this, a marriage of true minds that also lies like truth, that led Aristotle to declare that the rule of a husband over a wife was political or constitutional (*politikos*), and not simply a form of despotism or mastery.[17] The scene between Odysseus and Penelope may not seem political in any straightforward sense; the only witnesses here are the nurse Eurykleia and perhaps Odysseus's faithful dog, both representatives of laborious care. What we see in such an exchange is the emergence of a political scene within a domestic one, a momentary polity that bears no direct relation to the state and yet opens up occasions for action for those convened in its sudden clearing. Such a scene for politics may seem minor or trivial, yet it is through such scenes that most of us wander, to grow, stumble, or stunt. Shakespeare's *The Winter's Tale*, a play that borrows much from Greek romance, stages a similar double demonism, its creaturely specters assembled around the breaking and making of marriage as it collides with hospitality, drawing the terrible splendor of drama from the shallow reflecting pools of entertainment.

17. "A husband and father, we saw, rules over wife and children, both free, but the rule differs, the rule over his children being a constitutional rule [*politikos*]" (Aristotle *Politics* 1259b).

Hermione on Ice

Leontes' demons are well-documented. Stanley Cavell makes the play a problem of knowledge and acknowledgment, above all, of Leontes' refusal to recognize Mamilius as his son; Ruth Nevo is similarly concerned with Leontes' horror at being excluded from the mother-child couple. The tangle of Leontes' own thought rises up behind him in a great cloud of sexual confusion. This is a man who adores the boy he used to be but cannot countenance the husband and father he has become. He takes out his rage against adulthood on his childhood friend as well as his son and his wife, whose plainly pregnant body promises further entrapment in the duties of paternity and husbandry. Refusing the role of the capon, he embraces that of the cuckold. Swarming around his head in the squiggles traced by the convolutions of his thought are the daemonic connections between paranoia and homosexual desire analyzed by Freud in the case of Schreber. "I have drunk," Leontes tells Hermione, "and seen the spider" (2.1.45). The spider is the weaver of webs as well as the bearer of poison; in Leontes' discourse, the spider dwells at the fragile fold between knowledge and belief that allows ordinary men to live with their betrayal. By believing that the veil of ignorance has been lifted for him and him alone, Leontes' knowledge of knowledge reintroduces a new and more terrible mystification in the form of his paranoid delusion. Leontes' discourse is animated by his ability both to diagnose his own jealousy and to hand himself over to its tender torments. What makes his own daemons psychotic rather than neurotic is the fact that they appear directly to him in the form of both visual and auditory hallucinations: as the adulterous dumb show that transfixes his vision and as the whispering that he hears in every hallway.

In new work, Eric Santner has brilliantly linked the structure of psychotic foreclosure in the case of Judge Schreber, studied first by Freud and then by Lacan, to the nature of sovereignty.[18] In psychosis, the subject disavows some piece of reality, withdrawing his libido from reality and thus experiencing "the end of the world." He then reconstructs the world as paranoid delusion, an attempt at healing that becomes a form of madness. Sovereignty, Santner suggests, is "structurally linked to the state of exception, the capacity, that is, to suspend the rule of law, to invoke, by way of a paradoxical legal action, a certain *nothingness of the law*, of all juridical entitlements—law at its zero degree of meaning. . . . What is abolished internally—the *shelter* of the rule of law—returns in the real of the exception as *exposure* to the

---

18. Santner, *Royal Remains*. See also Santner, *My Own Private Germany*.

pure force of law."[19] In *The Winter's Tale*, Leontes disavows his dependencies on his wife, friend, son, and unborn child. As rejected "affection" precipitously coils into inward "infection" (1.2.137,43), dragging the coordinates of his world into the annihilating vortex of divestment, his foreclosure of all attachments returns in the real as paranoid delusion. Moreover, because the husband, friend, and father is also a king, his paranoia contracts and deforms the public sphere of the court itself. His decrees subject those who stand in the circle of his command to what Santner calls "the pure force of law," no longer spaced and attenuated by the meanings of the law's statutes and the timing and decorum of its procedures (*Prozeß*).

If Leontes is Freud's Judge Schreber, then Hermione is the Witty Butcher's Wife, the woman from *Die Traumdeutung* who dreams that she was unable to hold a dinner party, inadvertently confirming Freud's theory of wish-fulfillment by desiring that her desire remain unfulfilled. Although some critics and directors sense in Hermione an abiding warmth and even flirtatiousness, I see her as inherently reserved: held back within herself and participating in a temperamental hiddenness. My Hermione is *already* the Winter Queen. Notice, for example, the way she puts off her son Mamilius in her closet scene: "Take the boy to you," she tells her ladies. "He so troubles me, / 'Tis past enduring" (2.1.1–2). A few minutes later, Leontes will take Mamilius from her, declaring that this child with mammalian vitality inscribed in his very name was not in fact breast-fed by his mother ("Give me the boy. I am glad you did not nurse him" [2.1.56]). Hermione's genius, her native talent and inner daemon, is reserve. Her pregnant body is an image of life in reserve, a *potentia* yet to unfold. She is in the late, unromantic stages of second pregnancy: no rapunzel for her, no secret cravings leading to terrifying losses, only the weary watching of the first child while waiting for the second, without much left for either husband or guest. Does a woman in this condition really *want* to entertain her husband's friend for an extra week?

Yet hers is a tremulous reserve, a reserve ever ready to go on display and thus to appear to become something other than it is, without, however, ever ceasing to index an extraordinary capacity for self-containment. Reserve breeds a set of virtues—modesty, decorum, tact, discretion—that Hermione shares with Penelope. Indeed, reserve *is* virtue, understood as the properties and capacities of a person or thing, powers or *pouvoirs* that must be practiced in order to be actual, and yet also constitute a silent ground for action, a *potentia* rendered visible as an anterior disposition only through the effort of

19. Santner, *Royal Remains*, cited from manuscript by permission of the author.

their exercise and the transience of their appearance on the human stage. As we saw in chapter 1, in the virtue discourse stemming from Aristotle, human virtues require exercise in the public space of the polis, while the virtues of things subsist as a set of dormant affordances, participating in a pregnant hiddenness at once resisting and promising actualization. "I have that within which passes show," Hamlet says (1.2.85), enunciating the virtue discourse funded by potentiality that runs through Shakespeare, often communicated through inhuman or transhuman figures, as we saw in *The Taming of the Shrew*. Arendt defines action as a second birth, its initiatory natality repeating in the arena of the symbolic the physical births that occur in the real. Hermione's second pregnancy, forming at once the pretext and the image of her reticence, is also a figure for the possibility of entry into the world of others. To be reserved is not to be half empty, but to be half full.[20] The *half-fullness* indexes her virtuous capacities; the *half-emptiness* delimits the element of lack that allows the neurotic, unlike the psychotic, to play with her desire, to make a game out of her own withdrawal and reappearance.

Faced by her reserve, Leontes urges Hermione into the space of pro-visional publicity convened by hospitality. Having failed to persuade Polixenes to extend his stay, Leontes turns to his wife: "Tongue-tied, our queen?" Hermione responds,

I had thought, sir, to have held my peace until
You had drawn oaths from him not to stay. You, sir,
Charge him too coldly. Tell him you are sure
All in Bohemia's well; this satisfaction
The bygone day proclaimed—say this to him,
He's beat from his best ward. (1.2.27–33)

"Tongue-tied" (his phrase) describes the verbal effects of Hermione's re-serve. "Holding my peace" (her phrase) expresses that reserve's binding properties, like the surface tension on a glass of water that creates a restrain-ing membrane out of the propensity to overflow. Her tongue is tied, that is, by her mouth's own fullness, by her own verbal gifts.

Leontes urges Hermione to speak to Polixenes directly. He even mocks or shames her a bit. (Listen for reminiscences here of Lear to Cordelia, or of Lu-cio to Isabella in *Measure for Measure*.) Still reserved, Hermione chooses to speak through Leontes rather than address her guest directly, demonstrating

20. Anselm Haverkamp would speak here of latency as a suspended dialectic between the potential and the actual; see *Shakespearean Genealogies of Power*.

modesty and decorum as virtues native to reserve. Yet now echoes of Lucio animate Hermione's own speech, as she criticizes her husband for "charging too coldly." As her discourse warms up, she switches from the third person to the second, venturing now to address Polixenes face to face:

> To tell he longs to see his son were strong;
> But let him say so then, and let him go;
> But let him swear so, and he shall not stay,
> We'll thwack him hence with distaffs.
> Yet of your royal presence I'll adventure
> The borrow of a week. (1.2.34–39)

After the strange gambit that hangs Polixenes' departure on the depth of his homesickness for his son, she "adventures" "the borrow of a week": on loan from money-lending, "adventure" here means venture, enterprise, the weak/ week terms of the loan that she has set. The adventure here is also, however, subjective, consisting in the shift from mediated missive to direct address, a venture that tenders her very being as collateral to the loan. That is, Hermione's subjectivity guarantees the loan insofar as she appears *as a subject* by virtue of this loan, a venture risked in the changing syntax and dramatic orientation of her enunciation.

Her initial speech to Leontes is still technically private, even if Polixenes is included in its audience. In turning now to Polixenes, perhaps even physically crossing over into his space, Hermione has *become public* by entering into persuasive speech. In her dressing room, she will accuse Leontes of "publishing" her:

> How will this grieve you,
> When you shall come to clearer knowledge, that
> You thus have published me? (2.1.96–98)

The Cambridge editors gloss "published" as "publicly proclaimed, denounced," naming the legal process that Hermione undergoes in her scandalous arrest, imprisonment, and trial.[21] Yet a more existential process of publication begins as soon as Hermione extends the invitation to Polixenes at her husband's behest. In the action that sets the drama into motion, Leontes plays both director and audience, while casting Hermione as his player queen. Hermione's doings unfold in tension with her instinct for

---

21. Shakespeare, *The Winter's Tale*, ed. Susan Snyder and Deborah Curren-Acquino, 117n.

retirement, before the eyes of a royal dictator, who amplifies the contingency of all action through the psychotic prism of his exorbitant response.

Hospitality furnishes the platform of this fateful self-publishing. On the one hand, hospitality, especially at court, transpires according to highly ceremonial protocols that allow for little free play. The opening exchange between Archidamus and Camillo, stewards to the two kings, establishes the archaic and ritualized character of the guest-host relationship as it obtains between friends who are also sovereigns.[22] At the same time, hospitality accommodates looser, more informal scripts of improvisatory banter and wit. Leontes pushes Hermione from the formal sector, where relations between men and women, servants and masters, and guests and hosts are carefully choreographed—a dance of distances measured in the ambassadorial speech that Hermione first affects—into a more experimental region of entreaty and entendre. The *less formal* mode paradoxically becomes the *more public* one, not by dint of the number of people listening, but because it requires from Hermione a more spontaneous form of speech, at once *self-authored* (produced by Hermione from out of her own verbal reserve) and *self-authoring* (she appears as a subject to those who witness her, including her husband).

The antitype of Hermione's hostessing is the shepherd's reminiscence of his dead wife in act 4:

> Fie, daughter, when my old wife lived, upon
> This day she was both pantler, butler, cook;
> Both dame and servant; welcomed all, served all;
> Would sing her song and dance her turn; now here
> At upper end o'th'table, now i'th'middle;
> On his shoulder, and his; her face o'fire
> With labour, and the thing she took to quench it
> She would to each one sip. You are retired,
> As if you were a feasted one, and not
> The hostess of the meeting. (4.4.55–64)

On loan from a Brueghel painting, the peasant hostess embodies rustic hospitality, the robust and total service of the farmwife at home in the physical duties of the *oikos* as they flower outward in feast and song. The quick cuts that track her dance across the table, "at the upper end . . . now i'th'middle, / On his shoulder, and his," resemble the *hic et ubique* energy of Ariel board-

---

22. On friendship and sovereignty, see Shannon, *Sovereign Amity*.

ing the King's ship: "Now on the beak,/ Now in the waist, the deck, in every cabin, / I flamed amazement" (1.2.197–99). The rural housewife communicates a perfect storm of entertaining energy; like Ariel, she embodies the dream of a pure laboring force, a free servility that finds its modern counterpart in robotic fantasies of the automated vacuum cleaner, the electric butler, and the smart phone.[23] Perdita, on the other hand, is the Witty Butcher's Daughter. Like Hermione, Perdita is "retired." Her modesty signals her royal birth, which precludes such tippling with her homely guests. The class distinction also shelters a phenomenological contrast between repressed and unrepressed forms of hostessing, setting the image of a hospitality without reserve (Martha Stewart returned to her roots in Central Europe) against a temperament that must overcome its own tendency to ebb, not flow. Perdita's is not a niggardly hospitality but one made more precious by the sense of exception and election: for *you* I open my house, my hand, my heart. Perdita's congenital affiliation with her mother's reserve bears further fruit in her floral displays, which are distinguished by her exquisite attention to the flowers that she *fails* to deliver, whether it is the pied carnations and streaked gillyvors that she denies to Camillo and Polixenes, or the "flowers o'th'spring" whose poignant lack she presents to Florizel (4.4.113–29).[24]

The peasant housewife projects an image of hospitality unbound and unrepressed, whereas Hermione and Perdita manifest the shaping fancies of social and psychic inhibition. In my blocking of the play, act 1 is the first time Hermione will have taken center stage in something other than a purely orchestrated gesture of hostessing. When Leontes avers that she has "never spok'st / to better purpose . . . Never but once" (1.2.87–88), he attests, not without reproach, to the history of her quietude. Those "three crabbed months" that "had sour'd themselves to death, / Ere I could make thee open thy white hand" (1.2.101) have stretched into years of tongue-tied, tight-fisted marriage that end, precipitously, in this scene of provoked speech. Here, at this moment, we might even say, *at long last*, Hermione engages directly in an act that requires her to improvise before others in

23. On Shakespeare and science fiction, with special attention to the late plays, see Maisano, *Shakespeare's Science Fictions*.

24. The class reading and the phenomenological reading are reconciled in the peasant hostess's projection of energy without expense, the pastoral operation creating a beautiful relation between rich and poor (in William Empson's classic definition) by reconciling labor and freedom in an icon of free service. Needless to say, there is a theory and practice of pastoral struggling to be articulated here that would engage with Empson's definition of pastoral as "giv[ing] the impression of dealing with life completely" (Empson, *Some Versions of Pastoral*, 29). Julian Yates has proceeded to rethink pastoral in terms of biopolitics; see "What Was Pastoral (Again)?"

the terrifying contingency of the here and now, a *Jetztzeit* defined by the acknowledging, and potentially misrecognizing, presence of others. Hermione switches, against her better instincts and her own sense of decorum, from hostessing as social role to hostessing as an existential venture. In the process, the office of hostess becomes a means of publishing Hermione's subjectivity, through an act of speech whose vulnerability before witnesses lends it the force of action.

If Hermione shakes off her virtuous reserves by actualizing them in the theater of the social, reserve remains the keynote in the subjective images birthed by her action. She tells Polixenes,

> Will you go yet?
> Force me to keep you as a prisoner,
> Not like a guest, so you shall pay your fees
> When you depart and save your thanks. How say you?
> My prisoner or my guest? By your dread "Verily,"
> One of them you shall be. (1.2.50–54)

My prisoner or my guest: Hermione presents a forced choice that is also a false choice, since in each case Polixenes must stay an extra week beyond his will.[25] In this exchange, the daemon of reserve returns again, no longer as Hermione's self-containment, but as her ability to play the jailor. When Polixenes resolves to stay, she replies, "Not your jailer, then, / But your kind hostess" (1.2.58–59). If the line communicates courtesy, it manifests, behind Hermione's shoulder, the disturbing link between internment and sojourning, varieties of homelessness that butt against each other throughout this play and that allow the micropolitics of courtly courtesy to open onto the macropolitics of tyranny, terrorism, and homelessness. (Think of the guest-worker Camillo's difficulty in wresting permission to return home from his Bohemian employer, or Hermione's own ghastly/guestly imprisonment in the house of Paulina, or the biopolitical debate that collects around the pastoral argument about grafting.) Leontes is wrong to read this truth as an erotic one, or as erotic *in this moment*, as an expression of Hermione's desire for Polixenes. Yet he is certainly not wrong to read it as a

25. See Michael Bristol on the difference between the prisoner and the guest: "To submit to the position of prisoner, to pay fees and settle accounts, would profoundly dishonor Polixenes, since it would transform the relationship into an impersonal exchange of equivalents or commodity transaction. At the same time, however, in agreeing to remain even longer, Polixenes risks another kind of dishonor in that he may not be able adequately to reciprocate the lavish generosity or 'magnificence' (1.1.12) of Leontes" (Bristol, "In Search of the Bear," 156).

truth that troubles. The eros lies rather in the revelation that the guest is always a prisoner, not fully able to determine his own departure, fundamentally at the mercy of his host. (Recall Odysseus pining on the isle of Calypso, or Aeneas fleeing from Dido in the dead of night, or Ben Stiller in *Meet the Parents*.) The host extends special privileges to the guest precisely because the visitor is so thoroughly stripped of sovereignty and dignity in the household of another; the import of the return invitation is not to repay courtesy with courtesy but to match prison term with prison term, to subject oneself to the tyranny of someone else's off-brand coffee, unfamiliar toilet, or weird, jowly hound. What Hermione reveals in the very decorum of her extended courtesy are the risks inherent in hospitality, and the terror of that revelation in turn puts *her* at risk, up for interpretive reprisal.

When she is brought from prison for trial in act 3, Hermione gives voice to the dynamic between reserve and publicity that has brought her before the court in the first place:

> You, my lord, best know,
> Whom least will seem to do so, my past life
> Hath been as continent, as chaste, as true
> As I am now unhappy, which is more
> Than history can pattern, though devised
> And played to take spectators. (3.2.32–36)

She flags "continence" as the virtue of self-containment that has characterized a "past life" now produced as evidence in the public instance of her trial. History, Hermione declares, is a kind of theater, "devised / And played to take spectators," and it is this theatricalization of existence that makes the being of the queen, pulled anew out of her reserve, into a matter for public view. As such, the trial scene repeats Leontes' initial testing of his wife in act 1; it was Hermione's very continence, I've argued, that goaded Leontes into urging her to entertain his friend against her better judgment, releasing the daemon of an untapped loquacity that in turn traps Leontes in that *jouissance* delivery system called jealousy. Hermione's daemon looms *behind her*, manifesting the symptom as the neurotic's unconscious reserve. Leontes' daemon dances *in front of him*, projecting the hallucination as the return in the real of what has been foreclosed.

Following the implications of Santner's sovereign reading of Schreber, I'd venture to say that Leontes' erratic actions not only deform the king's legal capacities in the present instant, but also expose something about his law as such. What Leontes forecloses is the very arena of recognition that

Hermione's invitation had opened up; thus the space of human action, drawn out of the intimacies of hospitality, collapses almost immediately back into a sphere organized around the policing of life. Arendt will diagnose this redistricting as the eclipse of the political by the social, and Foucault will call it biopolitics. What psychosis shares with sovereignty, and what both share with the state of emergency, is the telescoping of public space into incarceration and the abbreviation of due process into arraignment without rights.[26] In the court of the king, hospitality becomes house arrest. Because the law of the court begins as household law, with offices like Lord Chamberlain evolving out of domestic duties,[27] monarchy bears a social core, its biopolitical concerns always waiting to resurface in malignant forms.

If Leontes' catastrophic response feels oddly unmotivated compared to Othello's, we might think of his jealousy as in part structural, as no longer requiring the agency of a Iago. In a social world framed by increasingly informal and ubiquitous friendship and hospitality rites, apparently spontaneous gestures elicit extreme construals. Why wasn't my daughter invited to that birthday party, and why don't the mothers talk to me in the parking lot? Why was I not footnoted in my colleague's book, and whom should I list in my acknowledgments? Such questions arise in a world in which "life" is above all "social life," with the suspicion of collusion and betrayal constantly charging the scenarios of daily encounter with the risks of an increasingly unhidden *jouissance*. When the *oikos* is everywhere, we all become Leontes waiting to be deceived, abandoned, or simply left out of the joke.[28]

In her speech before the court, Hermione stresses the scandal of her publication:

> with immodest hatred
> The childbed privilege denied, which 'longs
> To women of all fashion; lastly, hurried
> Here, to this place, i'th'open air, before
> I have got strength of limit. (3.2.100–105)

26. For a biopolitical reading of torture in Renaissance drama, see Turner, *Torture and the Drama of Emergency*.

27. Richardson, *Tudor Chamber Administration*.

28. This paragraph is based on conversations with Paul Kottman. On intimacy, privacy, and the social, see Arendt, *Human Condition*, 38–39.

Her emphasis falls on the presencing character of publication, the fact of exposure to the contingencies of dramatic time and place as such. *"Here, to this place, i'th'open air"*: the emphatic deixis of her declaration reveals the clearing made by the nakedness of her legal appearance within it. Moreover, her speech, which is also an action, makes that clearing coincide with the openness of the stage and the assembly of an audience of witnesses summoned by the ethical force of her enacted virtue. "Strength of limit" means the physical strength owed her by a full confinement after childbirth; "strength of limit" also suggests Hermione's own virtues of self-composure, which she must exercise here in such a way that she does not betray them.

Statutory Marriage

The violence of publication, along with the news of her son's death and the seizing of her infant daughter, appears to kill Hermione. "I say she's dead," declares Paulina, the play's coroner. "I'll swear't. If word nor oath / Prevail not, go and see" (3.2.201–2). Swearing that she'll swear to Hermione's mortal state, Paulina surreptitiously reveals that Hermione is only legally dead, that she has entered into the zone that Lacan calls "between two deaths."[29] Paulina's counterfactual discourse separates out the barest indicators of life—its signs and symptoms, its colors and rhythms—while declaring death: "If you can bring / Tincture or lustre in her lip, her eye, / Heat outwardly or breath within, I'll serve you / As I would do the gods" (3.2.202–5). The death certificate is with the body, but the body is not with the death certificate. Like Juliet planted seedlike in the family mausoleum by the city's friar-pharmacist, or Antigone buried alive at the command of Creon, uncle of all tyrants, Hermione has fallen into a coma, "undertak[ing] / A thing like death" (*Romeo and Juliet* 4.1.73–74). Deprived of her good name and her children, Hermione has suffered social murder, and her morbidity embodies the most minimal form of life—so minimal it is barely form at all—left over by this series of fatal blows. Yet Hermione's dwelling among the daemons generated by a cruel and terrible publicity also returns her to that creaturely virtue in reserve, that tongue-tied continence, from which Leontes had forced his queen to exit.[30]

---

29. Lacan, *Seminar 8*.

30. See Joan Copjec on Antigone's live burial as a figure of the suspension of bare life in the state of coma (*Imagine There's No Woman*). Copjec in turn builds on Lacan's reading of Antigone "between two deaths" in *Seminar 8*.

In act 1, Hermione had reluctantly entered the space of an improvisational publicity opened up by the hospitality relation, and her performance
there had triggered the de-creating and re-creating paranoia of the king. For
both Leontes and Othello, chaos comes again when they withdraw their
love from the worlds they once knew, causing them to reconstruct those
worlds around the *ex nihilo* of delusion. When Hermione reenters the public space of the courtroom in act 3, the hostess has become a prisoner, in-
criminated by her own hesitant generosity. This trial is a show trial, and
there is no place for the Witty Butcher's Wife in the speculative house of
mirrors built by Shakespeare's Judge Schreber. Santner writes of Schreber's
condition, "When a subject is 'in foreclosure,' the shelter of the symbolic
order—its systems of credits and accreditations—collapse in on him as a series
of intrusive somatic impingements, as so many *disturbances of the flesh*."[31]
When, at the dénouement of act 3, Hermione's virtue precipitously subsides
into mere vital signs, she embodies her own reserves, but in reaction to the
tyrant's despotic destruction of the salutary spacing of the public sphere as
such. In act 1, life had unfurled its political edge through the theater of hospitality; in act 3, the newborn subject of this politics passes into and then
out of publicity in response to the preemptive rulings of the mad monarch.
Her childbearing privilege cut short by the exigencies of her trial, Hermione
now undergoes a sixteen year's confinement in the house of Paulina, coroner
turned curator, so that she can once again find strength of limit.

At the end of the play, Shakespeare translates the figure of mortified virtue encrypted in the condition of the coma into the thinglike character of
the statue mimed by Hermione under Paulina's direction. Paulina "keeps"
the statue "lonely, apart" in her "poor house" (5.3.17–18, 6). As the statue's "keeper," Paulina embodies the dual functions of hostess and jailor
that haunt the hospitality function and identify the office of the curator
with a bodily care that can mortify as well as vitalize its objects. Now it is
Paulina who bids Hermione to enter into the space of publicity: "'Tis time:
descend; be stone no more; approach; / Strike all that look upon with mar-
vel" (5.3.99–100). The language suggests here an extended and cautious
unfreezing, cued by the gradualism of "You perceive she stirs," and met in
turn by a certain stunned and frightened hesitation on Leontes' part that
requires further prompting by Paulina: "Do not shun her," she urges him,
"Nay, present your hand" (5.3.103, 107). Like Penelope and Odysseus, Hermione and Leontes are strange, *daemonie*, to each other, and their reentry
into marriage is necessarily tentative and even probationary. The statue is to

31. Santner, *Royal Remains*.

Hermione what falcon, horse, and hound are to Katharina in *The Taming of the Shrew*. The statue, that is, materializes Hermione's daemon, understood as her genius and her virtue, anterior capacities that can only appear as such through their performance in a space limned by the audience of others. The emblem of the living statue delivers a certain truth about Hermione, speaking to the strength she finds in limits. It is this character of truth that makes the image so compelling and so durable, as if she is declaring to Leontes that he must remarry her *as* the living statue, both fixed and moving, that she has always wanted to be.

Moreover, to insist on her right of return to virtue is to claim a politics for this assertive dormancy, and thus to distinguish it forever from bare life. The psychotic sovereign had rebuilt his ravaged world as an encampment for the denuded real, exposing everyone caught in its circle to the threat of exposure as such. The living statue that now reaches out her trembling hand to the quaking king extends the chance for a new drafting of the politico-domestic space, a marital *politeia* that might cultivate the inoperative latency of virtue in order that life might once more become political, on its own terms. Any marriage to be constituted or reconstituted around Penelope, or Kate, or Hermione must make room, that is, for the tree in the bedroom, the animal in the kitchen, and the statue in the garden, acknowledging both the creaturely conditions of political life and the unpredictable character of even the most domesticated action. Such remarriages would make room for several styles of virtue, in the form of both excellences realized through deed and *pouvoirs* allowed to rest. One hopes that the Hermione who consecrates this remarriage with the unclenched hand of her consent will not slip back into the coma of risk-adversity, but instead will find her own way into the theater of speech according to scripts not founded on the depletion or disavowal of her reserves.

More often than not, the advent of the accidental subject, self-authored en route between pantry and polis, discovers the occasions for her birth in the rituals of hospitality. The statue scene itself occurs as part of a hospitality exchange. Leontes and his entourage are guests in the "poor house" of Paulina. Surely a state dinner has been hosted by the king; like the dessert service hosted by the bridegroom Lucentio at the end of *The Taming of the Shrew*, the visit to Paulina's gallery serves the role of a postprandial entertainment that features a final performance by the play's forgotten heroine as its confectionary centerpiece, "as sweet / As any cordial comfort" (5.3.76–77). Here, Paulina in concert with Hermione restores that "tincture or lustre" to "her lip, her eye" that had been drained from the corpselike body of Hermione at the end of act 3. The same vital signs, the same hints of warmth, breath, and movement, that had deserted Hermione in her exit from the force of Leontes' law now kiss the statue with the possibility of life.

The statue scene is, sublimely, both a metatheatrical and an antitheatrical moment. It is *metatheatrical* insofar as Shakespeare breaks Leontes' illusion and ours in the same gesture: the statue is "really" Hermione, but Hermione is "really really" an actor playing Hermione playing a statue. But the scene is also, more deeply and more essentially, *antitheatrical*, insofar as Hermione's personifying of the statue allows her to reclaim and maintain, to distill and transmit, a quotient of that reserve she had regained in her wintry seclusion even as she hesitantly reenters the space of the living, embracing the hazards of a life that must be partially public.[32] Playing a statue that comes to life allows Hermione to reveal and confront her own antitheatrical prejudices, opening the chance for new acknowledgments and accommodations in the present, and resolving the question of whether Hermione is or isn't "really" a statue (diegetically, she isn't, but existentially, she is). As an emblem and epitome of Shakespeare's art, the moving statue at once condenses and defrosts the metatheatrical and the antitheatrical in their creative relationship with each other, bodying forth the modes of appearing that make drama something other than the society of spectacle that houses it.

That's Entertainment

But what, then, of theatricality, by which I mean that element of pure display, a virtuosity emptied of virtue, that both the *meta-* and the *anti-* are designed to qualify, disarm, or transvalue? After all, *The Winter's Tale* was performed at court, and its pastoral conceits and musical interludes as well as its living statue echo an economy and culture of entertainment that is theatrical through and through. Is *The Winter's Tale*, then, primarily drama or entertainment? Or, does it belong fully to neither *oikos* nor *polis*, but assemble a provisional public out of the risks run by hospitality, thus inhabiting the shifting threshold between the two zones?[33] The Greekness of

32. I use antitheatrical here not in the sense of the Puritan tracts, but in the sense developed by Michael Fried in *Absorption and Theatricality* to describe the way in which certain works of art stage their own absorption in order to ward off a dialectic of spectacle and voyeurism. We might speak here as well of the tension between virtue and virtuosity, between reserve and its performance, that attends Hermione and creates the sense of vibrancy and depth that accrues to her person.

33. Anselm Haverkamp speaks here of the play's division between "tragic *energeia* and spectacular *enargeia*." On the possibility of politics in the society of spectacle, see Jeffrey Edward Green, *The Eyes of the People*.

The Winter's Tale belongs more to Homer and the Hellenistic novelists than to Aeschylus and Sophocles, and this quintessentially Stuart play extends hospitality to its audience in its mode as entertainment. Entertainment, like holiday, is a social script that includes everyone in the performance, from the master of the house, the hostess of the feast, and the guests at the table to the stewards, cupbearers, children, shepherds, and rogues who support the spectacle, along with the ribbons and gloves that adorn their persons and the sheep that they shear. Drama begins to separate out the audience from the action through the fact of fiction, but as the art of *dran*, or doing, it reincludes its spectators as witness and jury, instituting what Kottman calls a politics of the scene. Entertainment embraces everyone in the *scene of life* through the script of celebration; drama drafts everyone into the *scene of politics* through the protocol of the trial and the ordeal of becoming public. Drama is organized by actions and persons. Objects are incidental to its success; a reader's theater demands no props or costumes at all. Entertainment, on the other hand, is oriented around things (marzipan and marmalade, trestle tables and joint stools, headdresses and toiletries), which in turn help define the social creatures who employ them. In *The Winter's Tale*, objects frequently allow characters and character-types normally excluded from action to enter into a politics of the scene from the more dormant resources of hospitality; objects come to mediate, that is, between entertainment and drama, providing the sprockets, hinges, and zippers that open the situation to the event.

Such things can belong to the household as a bastion of production oiled by the hierarchy of service, or they can drift in from the more chaotic world of consumer goods. Camillo is the king's cupbearer, his office defined by his relationship to an object.[34] Cups afford the holding of liquids and the pouring of libations as well as bespicing with poison (1.2.313) and habitation by spiders. Heidegger takes the similar case of the jug as his exemplary thing: "The emptiness, the void, is what does the vessel's holding. The empty space, this nothing of the jug, is what the jug is as holding vessel." Moreover, it is in response to this same jug that Heidegger calls attention to the etymology of the Old High German word *thing*, which "means a gathering, and specifically a gathering to deliberate on a matter under discussion, a contested matter."[35] Richard Halpern asks apropos of Arendt if "*things* too

---

34. "Ay, and thou / His cupbearer, whom I from meaner form / Have benched and reared to worship" (1.2.309–310). Cups were not an insignificant element in hospitality; Peter Thornton notes the "staging of the buffet with a cup-board cloth on which the lord's collection of rich plate (his 'cups') could be proudly displayed" (*Seventeenth-Century Interior Decoration*, 97).

35. Heidegger, "The Thing," 169, 174.

might possess a natality"; in *The Winter's Tale*, I think they do.[36] The cup both reserves and serves up, pouring out a path to action for its faithful steward. By refusing to drug the drink of Polixenes, Camillo abandons the routines of service for the contingency of the deed; ultimately fleeing with Polixenes into the cold night of a hasty departure, he exits not only from the house of Leontes but from the betrayed rituals of hospitality as such. And Camillo can escape with his new master by dint of his job as *janitor* or gate keeper; because he holds the keys to the palace, he can furnish the exit that his royal patrons refused their guest.[37] The objects and offices of the household define the stewardship of Camillo, and it is from the shadow cast by their familiar forms of service that Camillo stumbles into the light of action. Perhaps the cup bodies forth his daemon, his open enclosure within a suite of hospitality functions that have long supported his domestic identity but now pose an ethical decision that sends him into exile.[38]

Antigonus is the weak twin to Camillo, the counselor who succeeds only in ameliorating, not suspending, the deadly dictation of the tyrant; his exposure of the infant Perdita in Bohemia in turn exposes him to death. In new work on *The Winter's Tale*, James Kearney analyzes Antigonus's predicament as a case of what Aristotle calls a "mixed action," in which agents subject to "moral luck," including the constraints of tyranny, are not fully responsible for their actions.[39] Antigonus is dogged by the most famous stage direction in Shakespeare, "*Exit, pursued by a bear.*" We might take this bear as Antigonus's daemon, at once a brute figure of tyranny and violence, and an emblem of hibernation, the lassitude of those public virtues that Antigonus fails to enlist into practice. The bear also performs on loan from the world of entertainment, the arena in which animal life is made to run through its paces for human spectators. Yet it may finally be the "exit" itself that is the true daemon here. Exit posits the bare fact of movement from one space to another as a necessary feature of action, even if the change in position is merely moral or subjective. To *exit pursued by a bear* is at once to manifest and to suffer the conjuncture of politics and life, the former defined by transit through a scene before others, and the latter heralded by the sudden rampant roaring of animal vitality on stage.

<hr/>

36. Richard Halpern, "Theater and Democratic Thought: Arendt to Rancière," unpublished essay; cited with permission of the author.

37. "How came the posterns / So easily open?" Leontes asks. "By his great authority, / Which often hath no less prevailed than so / On your command," responds the Lord (2.1.52–55).

38. On *The Winter's Tale* as a play of service, see Schalkwyk, *Shakespeare, Love and Service*, 263–98.

39. Kearney, "Unaccountable Losses, Impossible Gifts."

If Camillo and Antigonus belong to the world of household steward-ship, the peddler Autolycus has strayed onto stage from the infant consumer economy. His bag of trinkets, promising "the bondage of certain ribbons and gloves" (4.4.219–33), supports the Stuart society of spectacle, from the renewal of Catholic mystery to the mystifications of power and the tricks of feminine masquerade. He chortles over his empty pack: "I have sold all my trumpery; not a counterfeit stone, not a ribbon, glass, pomander, brooch, table-book, ballad, knife, tape, glove, shoe-tie, bracelet, hornring, to keep my pack from fasting" (4.4.593–97). His fardel is "fasting" because all of his goods have been eaten up by his buyers, an image that taps the digestive metaphor resident in consumption. These are the things of theater, not in its status as the art of action, but in its penchant for display and its frank and garrulous celebration of its own disappearance "within's two hours" (*Hamlet* 3.2.125). Yet it is precisely his knack for disguises that allows the junk man to enter into the circuit of action, providing new identities for the eloping lovers and snatching his own exit from Bohemia. Exchanging clothes with Florizel, Autolycus's act is the prelude to Perdita's: "I see the play so lies / That I must bear a part," (4.4.650–51) she confesses, sheep-ishly donning her lover's clothing.

Is the play *the* thing (a matter concerning praxis and human assembly), or *a* thing (an artifact that builds a world), or is it not a thing at all, and simply a disposable commodity, like Kleenex and carbon credits?[40] In a recent exchange about these issues, Aaron Kunin described a scene from the 1954 film *Executive Suite*, "where William Holden stubs his cigarette and then pulls apart a chair to demonstrate its shoddy fabrication. Is a movie a refreshment like a cigarette, or is it more like a piece of furniture? One could certainly ask a similar question of Ben Jonson, who is always looking for ways to defeat theater from within, to turn plays or masques into works."[41] *The Winter's Tale* is both chair and cigarette. The play derives its power—at-tains the status of a work—precisely by dwelling so fiercely in the metabo-lisms of bodily enjoyment. Statues made of stone belong to the world of work, culture, and the artisan, promising some dose of permanence by re-flecting the deeds of heroes for an imagined posterity. Statues composed of human bodies belong rather to the royal progress, the parade route, and the theme park; that's not Alexander greeting you at the gates of the city, but an

40. Hamlet touches on the sense of "the thing" as assembly when he declares that "The play's the thing," though his thought swiftly takes him to more concrete objects like mousetraps. In Renaissance studies, Julian Yates has developed Heidegger's definition of the thing as assem-bly into an account of objects as networks; see "Accidental Shakespeare."

41. Aaron Kunin, e-mail, January 16, 2010.

Anaheim teenager dressed up as Mickey Mouse for minimum wage.[42] Shakespeare's statue scene borrows energy from both the marble statue of the public square and the living statue of pageantry and folly. *The Winter's Tale* achieves a kind of permanence through the exquisite drama of recognition and acknowledgment that plays out between Leontes, Paulina, Hermione, and their witnesses, but it also borrows freely from the kinds of entertainment that filled the Banqueting House with their epideictic kitsch.

For a hundred days in 2009, sculptor Antony Gormley invited 2,400 people to take turns standing for one hour on the giant, empty plinth that stands in the northwest corner of London's Trafalgar Square.[43] By bringing forward a random procession of human statues, who were free to strike poses, flaunt causes, or simply catch some rays during their sixty minutes of fame, Gormley's installation framed the allure of real life against the backdrops provided by the artistic wealth of the National Gallery and the built environment of Trafalgar Square as a space of assembly and promenade. Gormley's project borrowed charisma while draining pretension from the traditional resources of museum, monument, and public square. This was an art totally suited to the spectacular conditions of contemporary media, urbanism, and design, one whose popular success depended on neither ignoring the lofty alternatives provided by traditional culture nor disavowing its own approximation to reality TV. Like Giulio Romano in *The Winter's Tale*, Gormley could be said to "newly perform" his human sculptures, to allow the bare unaccommodated media of contemporary life itself to pass through the frame of art (5.2.94).

Both Gormley and Shakespeare have managed to winterize their art not by opposing themselves to entertainment but by breaking bread with it. In what remains one of the most enigmatic as well as the most compelling lines of *The Winter's Tale*, Leontes cries out in the statue scene, "If this be magic, let it be as lawful as eating" (5.3.110). Eating warms the commensal heart of entertainment. Leontes does not ask that we abandon eating in our pursuit of art, but that art be allowed to partake in some of eating's

---

42. Michael Witmore aptly links Elizabeth's coronation pageant to the entertainment constituted by the arrival of Dorothy in Oz, pointing in both scenes to the "wondrous powers of vivification and motion . . . to intensify experience within its charmed boundaries" (*Pretty Creatures*, 58–60).

43. The Fourth Plinth was vacated when the Mayor of London, Ken Livingstone, ordered two statues of Victorian generals removed from their pedestals in the square. In their absence, the city has commissioned temporary public installations from a range of artists, including Gormley (Gerstein, *Display and Displacement*). See also Cherry, "Statues in the Square." For the earlier history of Trafalgar Square, see Mace, *Trafalgar Square*.

consumptive temporality, that art allow itself to appear and disappear, to inhale and exhale, digest and expel, in order to endow such rhythms with a world-making capacity. In the final analysis, *The Winter's Tale* takes seriously the social theater of hospitality, which formed at least one condition of the play's own performance, in order to use it as a dynamic framework for considering life in its diversity of forms, from the *vita activa* of the polis, to the virulent sociality of sovereign psychosis and the active cultures gathered by the queen of curds and cream for her potluck party. In *The Winter's Tale*, entertainment is the daemon of drama, at once its origin, its remainder, and its threat, the reserve of life from which drama extricates its definitive politics and to which it always hastens to return, like a weary commuter on his drive back to nowhere. Shakespeare probes the scene of hospitality for its dramatic potential, that is, for the kinds of action and the forms of self-exposure that we risk each time we set the table. In the process, he makes room on stage for the helpmeets, hostesses, janitors, bystanders, and traveling salesmen who become actors as a consequence of their entry into such scenes, with or without the support of bears or plinths. Like Capulet presiding over "an old accustomed feast" (1.2.20), Shakespeare gives us in *The Winter's Tale* a play that is courtly, entertaining, and spectacular, a banquet worthy of the Banqueting House and a sop for the sovereign. It is also a play that is with us still, achieving an iterative universality in culture's theater of judgment by staging with such wit and grace the birth of drama out of hospitality.

SIX

The Minority of Caliban

The single mother

And what will become of this *Paternal Power*. . . . in those parts of *America*, where when the Husband and Wife part, which happens frequently, the Children are all left to the Mother, follow her, and are wholly under her Care and Provision? (§65)

The wild child

To turn the child loose to an unrestrain'd Liberty, before he has Reason to guide him, is not the allowing him the priviledge of his Nature, to be free; but to thrust him out amongst Brutes, and abandon him to a state so wretched, and as much beneath that of a Man, as theirs. (§63)

The foster father

[Paternal Power] belongs as much to the *Foster-Father* of an exposed Child, as to the Natural father of another: So little power does the bare *act of begetting* give a Man over his Issue, if all his Care ends there, and this be all the Title that he hath to the Name and Authority of a Father. (§65)

—John Locke, "Of Paternal Power," *Second Treatise of Government*

This cast of characters drawn from Locke's *Second Treatise of Government* finds its counterpart in Shakespeare's *The Tempest*:[1] the single mother Sycorax, the wild child Caliban, and the foster father Prospero. *The Tempest*, dated around 1611, and the *Second Treatise*, published in 1690, were written in the same century, but from opposite shores of the breach created by

---

1. All citations from the *First Treatise* and *Second Treatise* are from Locke, *Two Treatises of Government*, ed. Peter Laslett, and are cited parenthetically by section number.

the English Civil War. Each text works through models of political power and obligation by testing the analogy between family and state from novel angles, projects that led both authors to probe the psychology and philosophy embedded in non-normative domestic arrangements. Moreover, both Shakespeare and Locke had economic and intellectual interests in the American colonies, and they chose to stage their texts in experimental settings mapped by a mix of Old and New World coordinates, decisions that have placed the texts of both authors at the center of postcolonial rereadings of early modern letters. My emphasis, however, falls not on Locke's theories of property or just war, but on his exploration of paternal duties and filial rights. Reading the *Second Treatise* in relation to Locke's accounts of personhood and pedagogy in *Some Thoughts Concerning Education* and *An Essay Concerning Human Understanding*,[2] this chapter approaches Shakespeare's Caliban as a *minor*. I define *minor* as a child-subject in possession of certain rights, privileges, and immunities, under the care of a guardian, but presumed capable of rational autonomy and legal enfranchisement at an appointed date in the future. The minor is the bearer of equality *in potentia*, an unrealized capacity for independence sheltered and supported by the institutions of family life and protected when necessary by law. In Locke's words, children are "not born in this full state of *Equality*, though they are born to it" (§54). The very checks to a minor's freedom during his childhood serve to designate and defend his future capacity for freedom in adulthood; as the great eighteenth-century lawyer Blackstone put it, "INFANTS have various privileges, and various disabilities: but their very disabilities are privileges; in order to secure them from hurting themselves by their own improvident acts."[3]

Using Locke's discourse to conceptualize Caliban as a minor under the guardianship of Prospero allows us to consider Caliban's legal disabilities and privileges within a graduated scheme of transition from "nonage" into adulthood. This approach limits Prospero's sovereignty over Caliban and holds him accountable for unlawful infringements on the estate of the mi-

---

2. I do not attempt here a synthesis of these three complex and sometimes contradictory texts. For one such attempt, see Carrig, "Liberal Impediments." On Locke and the family, see especially Schochet, *Patriarchalism in Political Thought*. Feminists have criticized the contractualism of Locke (see especially Pateman, *Sexual Contract*); others have read the tradition more generously (see Kahn, *Wayward Contracts*, and Jordan, "The Household and the State"). On Locke and childhood (from an educational rather than a political perspective), see Ezell, "John Locke's Images of Childhood."

3. Blackstone, *Commentaries on the Laws of England*, 1.17.3. All citations, hereafter given parenthetically in the text, are from this work.

nor in his care. *The Tempest* is arguably Shakespeare's most self-consciously Jacobean play, performed before and reflecting on the sovereignty of James I. Reading Locke's critique of absolutist patriarchalism back into Shakespeare's play delivers both a counter-Jacobean Prospero, chastened by his imperfect exercise of paternal duty, as well as a rights-bearing Caliban, whose passage through the disparate conditions of the orphan, the foster child, and the slave ultimately establish his participation in personhood, understood as both a legal category and a subjective possibility. Legal personhood itself has a history, changing over time through cases, commentaries, and statutes and in reaction to social, political, and philosophical sea changes. Yet definitions of personhood, unlike accounts of culture, aim at universality even when acknowledging the localized responsiveness of their own formulations. My Lockean analysis and defense of Caliban aims to release a liberal potentiality within *The Tempest*'s romance with fatherhood, while also bringing forward emancipatory elements in Locke's discourse, supplementing current accounts of the philosopher as a colonial apologist and possessive individualist.[4] By recalibrating Prospero's absolutism from the perspective of Lockean liberalism, while also recovering from Locke a liberalism other than colonial, the speculative figuration of Caliban as a legal minor performs a "minor" variation on the major ideologies that cross *The Tempest*, the *Second Treatise*, and their trans-Atlantic afterlives. I am not concerned to establish direct textual links between Locke and Shakespeare, though the ruptured contiguity of pre– and post–Civil War England frames the project and grants it a certain chronological coherence. My larger aim is to uncover minority as a valid template for political reform and activism, as when the rights and protections of temporary minors (elite male children)

4. Colonial readings of the play are legion. Stephen Orgel summarizes some of the literature in his magisterial edition of the play, including Mannoni, Greenblatt, and Fiedler (Shakespeare, *The Tempest*, 4). More recent offerings include Hulme, *Colonial Encounters*, and Goldberg, *Tempest in the Caribbean*. Alden T. Vaughan and Virginia Mason Vaughan have argued against "American" readings of the play in *Shakespeare's Caliban*. My own reading accepts the validity of the American frame, but supplements the cultural politics of colonialism with a more universal discussion of the rights of minors. The thesis of "possessive individualism" as the essence of Locke's political theory was put forward by Macpherson in *Political Theory of Possessive Individualism*. Earlier accounts of Locke in America evaluate his influence on the Revolution; see, for example, Dunn, "The Politics of Locke." More recent accounts emphasize Locke's ideological usefulness to the economic enterprises in which Locke and his circle participated; see, for example, Lebovics, "Uses of America in Locke's *Second Treatise of Government*"; Tully, *An Approach to Political Philosophy*. The best of this work acknowledges the tension in Locke's work between colonial apology and a genuinely emancipatory and universal discourse of rights that would extend to indigenous Americans (Lebovics 579; Tully 176). Gillian Brown develops this alternative strand in *The Consent of the Governed*, to which this chapter is a Shakespearean footnote.

are transferred to other populations (to women, to prisoners, to the children of the poor, or to the disabled), a move that tests the elasticity of personhood.

My point is not to overturn patriarchal accounts of Shakespeare and Locke in favor of a liberalism that remains deeply complicit with capitalism and imperialism, but to broaden and variegate the political vocabularies and progressive potentialities of childhood in response to both seventeenth-century and contemporary horizons. It is important to assert up front, and to remind myself and my readers repeatedly, that the image of the minor has the capacity to constrain as well as to liberate, since fathers usually establish the proper shape of majority as well as the reasons for postponing its achievement, leading to the infantilization rather than the liberation of persons and populations managed under the rubric of minority. Nonetheless, the rights of the minor can also scaffold a politics of care and acknowledgment oriented not by the self-certain authority of the guardian but by the unknown futures and untested capacities of the ward. In Shakespeare's play, this politics *in potentia* is both broached by the compelling figure of Caliban and inhibited by the dark marks of original sin and proto-racialization that adhere to his emerging person. Bearing the promise of a politics belied by the subsequent history of colonialism and by the play's own arrested development, *The Tempest* remains in a state of minority with respect to enlightenments to come, but not without inviting us to read it in view of those future concerns.

Such a Wondered Father, and a Wife

Locke begins his discussion of paternal power by challenging the appropriateness of the word *paternal* itself:

> It may perhaps be censured as an impertinent Criticism in a discourse of this nature, to find fault with words and names that have obtained in the World: And yet possibly it may not be amiss to offer new ones when the old are apt to lead Men into mistakes, as this of *Paternal Power* probably has done, which seems so to place the Power of Parents over their Children wholly in the *Father*, as if the *Mother* had no share in it, whereas if we consult Reason or Revelation, we shall find she hath an equal Title. (§52)[5]

---

5. Locke's emphasis here on clarifying language use echoes key themes from the *Essay Concerning Human Understanding*; see chapter 10, "Of the Abuse of Words."

The target of the *Two Treatises* is the patriarchal theory of sovereignty, in which the unilateral and indivisible rule of the father over his household authorizes the absolute sovereignty of the monarch, in turn supported by the heavenly King and Father above. The prooftext for patriarchal theorists such as Sir Robert Filmer, as well as the garden-variety patriarchalism that permeated social, political, and religious life under the *ancien regime*, is the Fifth Commandment, "Honor thy father and mother," often conveniently shortened to the simpler formulation, "Honor thy *father*."[6] If the indivisible sovereignty of the king derives from the authority vested by God and nature in fathers, then Locke is concerned to point out that the father's power is inherently divided, shared with the mother, "who hath an equal Title." The real interest of his chapter "Of Paternal Power" lies, of course, not in reforming domestic management or defending the rights of children, but in chipping away at the paternal analogy authorizing absolutism. In order to do this, however, Locke finds his way through varieties of family life in Old and New World settings that anticipate future transformations of domesticity under liberalism. Then as now, liberal parenting and liberal politics keep house together.[7] And so we meet the single mother:

> And what will become of this *Paternal Power* in that part of the World where one Woman hath more than one Husband at a time? Or in those parts of *America*, where when the Husband and Wife part, which happens frequently, the Children are all left to the Mother, follow her, and are wholly under her Care and Provision? If the Father die whilst the Children are young, do they not naturally every where owe the same Obedience to their *Mother*, during their Minority, as to their Father were he alive? (§65)

Locke travels here a path from the most exorbitant case (wives with multiple simultaneous husbands, an idea so outlandish that he names no locale), to the more palatable "American" situation, in which indigenous women separated from their mates raise the children on their own, and the deeply

---

6. Locke never tires of pointing out the ideological convenience of the abbreviation: "I hope 'tis no Injury to call an half Quotation an half Reason, for God says, *Honour thy Father and Mother*; but [Filmer] contents himself with half, leaves out *Mother* quite, as little serviceable to his purpose" (*First Treatise*, §2.6, §2.11, §6.61). I develop the civil consequences of Locke's rereading of the Fifth Commandment in my essay "Rights, Commandments, and the Literature of Citizenship."

7. In a 1989 publication, the Population Council placed Locke's chapter in the context of "recent international efforts to codify 'the rights of the child'" (Population Council, "Locke on Parental Power").

familiar case of fatherless children who "naturally every where" obey the surviving widow "during their Minority." By insisting on the feminine instance of parental power, Locke forcefully divides it from the *"power of the Magistrate,* of which the Father hath not so much as the shadow" (§65). Having established the mother's title, he goes on to clarify the limits of the father's power: "His Command over his Children is but temporary, and reaches not their Life or Property. It is but a help to the weaknesses and imperfection of their Nonage, a Discipline necessary to their Education" (§65). The parent's command is not an independent power in its own right but a secondary supplement to the imperfect freedom of the child, filling in for and protecting the minor's potential for liberty so that it can it be effectively realized when the child arrives at "the enfranchisement of the years of discretion" (2.65). In Locke's counter-patriarchal scheme, the flow of obligation arises from the right of the child to shelter and education rather than from the absolute sovereignty of the father over his offspring.[8]

The Tempest features two single parents, Prospero and Sycorax. In the major, "Jacobean" movement of the play, Prospero's status as a widower heightens and highlights the providential character of his rule over Miranda and the island. In this reading, his absent wife might have ranked first among the "four or five women" that Miranda recollects in the dark backward and abysm of time, the mistress of her household but not an equal partner with the duke (1.2.47).[9] Miranda's mother remains unrepresented because she is superfluous; with a father like Prospero, who needs a mother past birth? As Stephen Orgel points out, such parental majesty evokes the sovereign metaphors beloved by King James I: "'I am the husband, and the whole island is my lawful wife; I am the head, and it is my body.'"[10] In the play's Jacobean self-presentation, to be a single father is to embody the

<hr/>

8. These arguments, like so much in the *Second Treatise,* are not original to Locke. Pufendorf's 1672 *Law of Nature and Nations* includes a chapter entitled "Of Paternal Power" (6.2.8) that also emphasizes alienability of parental duties to nurses and tutors, the division of sovereignty between mother and father, and the rights of children in relation to the duties of their parents. Pufendorf also uses New World as well as mythological references. Locke's accent on these themes is decidedly more "liberal": he is much less definitive on the father's superior sovereignty in relation to the mother, for example, and he seems to grant more normative value to the non-European exempla than does Pufendorf (see Pufendorf, *Law of Nature and Nations*). Peter Laslett notes the debt in Filmer, *Patriarcha,* 310n.

9. All citations from *The Tempest* are from Stephen Orgel's edition. On the question of Miranda's mother, see Orgel's essay, "Prospero's Wife."

10. See Orgel's introduction to Shakespeare, *The Tempest,* 39.

full authority, fruitfulness, and consequences of patriarchy, self-sufficient and self-contained.

Sycorax is another matter altogether. Banished from Algiers, she was "hither brought with child," where she took control of Ariel, ultimately confining him in a pine tree until Prospero liberated him, in effect giving Ariel a second birth into a new and more enlightened servitude: "It was mine art, / When I arrived and heard thee, that made gape / The pine and let thee out" (1.2.269–93). As critics have pointed out, Sycorax and Prospero sport parallel biographies: both have been exiled, both use their magic to take control of Ariel and the island's resources, and both run single-parent households. The case of Sycorax can be used simply to reinforce the Jacobean reading: fathers, not mothers, exercise right rule and thus embody the essence of sovereignty. If we bring in the Lockean frame, however, the picture changes in "minor" ways that nonetheless free up major resources for building a protoliberal interpretation of the play. Locke presents the single American mother as one instance of solo parenting within a spectrum of possible norms of domestic life; he does not judge her maternal skills, instead taking her very existence as further proof that by definition parental power can take a variety of forms.

Read through Locke, the presence of Sycorax serves to demonstrate not the singular self-sufficiency of Prospero but his qualified status as one half of a couple, always shadowed by the missing mother whose absence leaves his parenting incomplete. Prospero himself seems to acknowledge his insufficiency when he compares his tragic overconfidence in his ambitious brother to the trust exercised by "a good parent" toward his child (1.2.94). The "good parent" is *too good*; his or her propensity to trust the child requires counterbalance in another parental voice or instance of authority.[11] As Harry Berger Jr. observes, both Sycorax and Prospero "are equally antisocial, both have withdrawn into themselves, have proved unfit for, or inadequate to, social and political existence."[12] Prospero finds himself on the island because of his failures as a duke at home, and his sojourn here involves his own reeducation in the limits and responsibilities of rule in its parental and political valences.

---

11. Many of us are familiar with good cop/bad cop parenting. Locke travels related territory in *Some Thoughts Concerning Education* when he suggests that parents treat smaller children with severity and older children with familiarity: "So shall you have him your obedient Subject (as is fit) whilst he is a Child, and your affectionate Friend when he is a Man" (*Some Thoughts Concerning Education*, §40).

12. Berger, "The Miraculous Harp," 16.

Ferdinand puts the case for dual parenthood a little differently when he exclaims at the conclusion of the Wedding Masque, "Let me live here ever. / So rare a wondered father and a wife / Makes this place paradise" (4.1.122–24). The reading of "wife" in place of the Folio's "wise" (an error attributed to the breakdown of the letter *f* in the course of printing) was reintroduced in 1978, a consequence not only of advances in editorial practice, but also, Orgel argues, of changes in the political climate: "After 1895 the wife became invisible: bibliographers lost the variant, and textual critics consistently denied its existence until six years ago. . . . We find only what we are looking for or are willing to see. Obviously it is a reading whose time has come."[13] The prospect of a self-sufficient Prospero who is both wondered and wise speaks to the play's Jacobean scenario. The insertion of the "wife" into the scenario works in another direction. It reminds us again of Prospero's absent wife, and addresses Miranda not in her present condition as Prospero's dependent but in her future condition as Ferdinand's spouse. To counter the wondered father with an equally wonderful (*miranda*) wife is to suggest a distribution of authority both within and across generations, as the daughter prepares to leave her father's household for her husband's.

Preparing for this transition is one work performed by the action of the play, and it is linked not only to Miranda's sexual maturation, but also to her late education in her own life story. For Locke, the essence of parenting is education. Locke himself was never a father, but he performed the office of education for the sons of Shaftesbury and Sir John Banks, and thus participated directly in the alienability of parental obligations.[14] In the chapter on paternal power, Locke writes, "The first part then of *Paternal* Power, or rather Duty, which is *Education,* belongs so to the Father that it terminates at a certain season; when the business of Education is over it ceases of itself, and is also alienable before" (§69). Notice the qualifying movement of the sentence: Locke redefines "power" as "duty," a set of responsibilities that effectively limits rather than aggrandizes the father's authority. He then insists that education, forming the "first part" of this duty, is both *temporary* and *alienable*: transferable to a responsible delegate, as Locke well knew from his

13. Orgel, "Prospero's Wife," 13. See also Jonathan Goldberg, who comments rather differently that the eighteenth-century editors "put 'wife' there to assure the domestic relationship and the propriety of Ferdinand's remarks. They make his future wife present in order to police the male-male relations between Ferdinand and Prospero" (*Tempest in the Caribbean*, 57).

14. On bachelor Locke's experiences observing and educating the children of others, see *Some Thoughts Concerning Education*, 5–9.

tutoring jobs. Prospero, a Renaissance homeschooler, lacked the opportunity to hire a tutor for Miranda:

> Here in this island we arrived, and here
> Have I, thy schoolmaster, made thee more profit
> Than other princes can that have more time
> For vainer hours, and tutors not so careful. (1.2.171–74)

Prospero uses *tutor* in its familiar educational sense, to mean one who is "employed in the supervision and instruction of a youth in a private household" (*OED*, 1.3). In law, *tutor* designates one-half of the duties of a guardian for a minor in Roman law. As Blackstone explains, "The guardian with us performs the office both of the tutor and curator of the Roman laws; the former of which had the charge of the maintenance and education of the minor, the latter the care of his fortune; . . . the tutor was the committee of the person, the curator the committee of the estate" (1.17). Hannah Arendt develops this distinction in "The Crisis in Education" when she argues that children are born into a relationship not only to life (as animals are) but also to a world: "The child shares the life of becoming with all living things. . . . But the child is new only in relation to a world that was there before him, that will continue after his death, and in which he will spend his life."[15] Tutoring effectively de-links education from the biological instance of paternity by distributing it to representatives, who participate in the child's acclimations to the world of traditions, meanings, and responsibilities that precede the child's birth. Alone on the island, Prospero has performed the tasks of both tutor and curator for Miranda without help from surrogates or helpmeets, once again embodying the self-sufficiency of royal fatherhood. Yet his reference to the fundamental alienability of education brings into play one of the elements that qualifies paternal power for Locke and for the Western legal tradition. Enunciating his paternal supremacy (the play's Jacobean major key), Prospero exposes the legal limits of fatherhood (the play in liberal minor key).

And the motif recurs in major and minor throughout *The Tempest*. In the romantic epilogue to the distended expositions of act 1, scene 2, Prospero, in a moment of sovereign pseudo-pique, chastises the love-struck Miranda for defending Ferdinand: "What, I say— / My foot my tutor?" (1.2.469–70). According to Prospero, Miranda's mild intervention threatens to turn the

---

15. Arendt, *Between Past and Future*, 185.

Jacobean body politic upside down. The daughter, the "foot," or lowliest appendage of the household-state, has behaved as a "tutor," or official delegate of paternal authority, to her own father. Orgel's note to the line (which never fails to perplex undergraduates) cites the proverb, "Do not make the foot the head." The difference brought into view by the Lockean frame is Shakespeare's substitution of "tutor" for "head," bringing substitution as such into the scene of paternal authority via the forensic vocabulary of guardianship even while snatching an old tune from pop patriarchalism.

More immediately pertinent to the dynamics of paternal sovereignty in the play, however, is Locke's second qualification of the educational duties of the father, namely, its built-in date stamp, "terminat[ing] . . . when the business of Education is over" (§68). Prospero's lengthy lecture to Miranda in act 1, scene 2 is one of several scenes of explicit education in the drama. Although his monologue flows from father to daughter in a mode that could hardly be called Socratic, it is, in contemporary educational parlance, "developmental," aimed at Miranda's particular moment of intellectual, moral, and even biological readiness. Miranda describes the conditions of her ignorance:

> You have often
> Begun to tell me what I am, but stopped,
> And left me with a bootless inquisition,
> Concluding, "Stay, not yet."

And Prospero explains,

> The hour's now come;
> The very minute bids thee ope thine ear.
> Obey, and be attentive. (1.2.33–38)

The "time" or "*tempus*" of The Tempest is kept according to several clocks. One is the service contract binding Ariel to Prospero and resulting in the emancipation anticipated at the end of the play ("Then to the elements / Be free, and fare thou well" [5.1.317–18]). Another, noted in this interchange, is the period of minority binding Miranda to Prospero, terminating in her equally anticipated marriage at the horizon of the play. Prospero chooses this "hour" and "minute" to tell Miranda the story of her life not only because objective conditions ("the accident most strange" of the shipwreck) invite their return to Milan, but also because her subjective capacities have reached the point where he judges her ready to understand and absorb this story, to make it her own. In education, as Locke, Hamlet, and Montessori knew, "Readiness is all."[16] Moreover, the telling of the story, directed at a moment of ripeness in Miranda's own development, aims ultimately to emancipate Miranda from her father's governance ("Obey, and be attentive") if only be delivering her into the "true contract" of her marriage with Ferdinand, passing her from one form of minority to another. In Locke's formulation, the father's command "is but temporary, and reaches not their Life or Property. It is but a help to the weakness and imperfection of their Nonage, a Discipline necessary to their Education" (§65). In "The Crisis of Education," Hannah Arendt makes a similar argument about the qualified inequality that characterizes the scene of education, which deploys "a concept of authority and an attitude toward the past which are appropriate to it but have no general validity and must not claim a general validity in the world of grown-ups."[17] The education of Miranda announces the approaching termination of Prospero's sovereignty over her, a familiar Shakespearean theme brought into greater political focus by the Lockean lens.

Although the forceful intimacy of Prospero's single parenting and home-schooling primarily serves to demonstrate the exclusivity of paternal rule on this unsceptred isle, the Lockean framework points up the limits of paternity in the fact of maternity, the pathos of obligation, and the alienable and self-terminating character of education. Though Locke gives these topoi a markedly liberal expression in the *Second Treatise* that substantially distinguishes his writing from that of Shakespeare, his formulations on childhood are largely drawn from older educational, philosophical, and legal traditions that both men shared. What Gillian Brown says concerning the state of the child in Locke could equally be said of the family in Shakespeare: "Once the parental function becomes an obligation, a moral response to and respect for a potentially rational creature, all relations and conditions, familial and political statuses, appear as provisional states."[18] If such provisionality

---

16. Shakespeare, *Hamlet*, 5.2.220. Locke's educational theories emphasize active engagement of the senses in relation to children's "inadvertency, forgetfulness, unsteadiness, and wandering of Thought" (*Some Thoughts Concerning Education*, §167). He describes his in-house observations of a mother using a globe to teach her son geography: "Being only an exercise of the Eyes and Memory, a child with pleasure will learn and retain [facts]. . . . It is a good step and preparation to [further study], and will make the remainder much easier, when his Judgment is grown ripe for it" (§178). The mother in question was Lady Masham, Locke's hostess in 1693 (Locke, *Some Thoughts Concerning Education*, §79n.). The Yoltons evaluate Locke's relationship to developmentalism (Locke, *Some Thoughts Concerning Education*, 38–43).

17. Hannah Arendt, "The Crisis of Education," in *Between Past and Future*, 191.

18. Brown, *Consent of the Governed*, 18.

characterizes the play's most regular parent-child relationship, it has even deeper implications for the odder couple formed by Prospero and Caliban.

The Minority of Shakespeare's Creature

To speak of Caliban as a minor uncomfortably recalls the Victorian project of narrating the lost childhoods of Shakespeare's heroines. The risk here is not only engagement in a form of imaginative speculation foreign to the rigors of formalism and historicism alike, but also the false imposition of a modern conception of childhood onto Shakespeare's play.[19] Carolyn Steedman writes of the Victorian period that "child-figures, and more generally the idea of childhood, came to be commonly used to express the depths of historicity within individuals. . . . 'Childhood', 'the child', as this kind of configuring of the past, emerged at the same time as did the modern idea of history."[20] Childhood in this modern sense is not the same as legal minority, whose distinctive shaping of social relations tends to be exterior rather than interior, related to a set of domestic and civil instances, and charted by formal more than affective markers of development.[21] Yet legal minority remains part of the deep structure of childhood conceived psychologically; debates about child labor laws, for example, were fueled by emotional identification with the child, taken as a universal stage of human experience. The child-minor fuses sense and sensibility, making both legal and emotional claims on our attention. Moreover, legal minority only becomes a literary element when it resonates with broader cognitive and emotional patterns of recollection, consciousness, and conscience (as it does, I argue, in both Shakespeare and Locke). Gillian Brown identifies citizenship with thinking as such: "The key point in Locke's liberalism [is] the citizen's continuous labor of crediting and discrediting ideas. The citizen of the liberal state emerges in the processes of thought, which, in Locke's view, distinguish humans from other animals."[22] Education in citizenship is education in thinking, and vice versa. Attending to the debts and promises, memories and missions that bind the minor to the child through the politics and poetics of education represents one strand of the project initiated here.

---

19. See the classic text by Clarke, *Girlhood of Shakespeare's Heroines.*

20. Carolyn Steedman, *Strange Dislocations,* 12.

21. Historians of childhood distinguish between "childhood" (understood as the concept) and "children" (taken empirically). See Cunningham, *Children and Childhood,* 1, 13. The classic social history of childhood remains Ariès, *Centuries of Childhood.*

22. Brown, *Consent of the Governed,* 8.

Minority and childhood intersect in the idea of the "person," a legal category that developed in increasingly psychological directions, in part the impact of Locke's philosophy. In the Western legal and philosophical traditions, "personhood" implies the protected and responsible exercise of individual freedom in civil society.[23] Locke defines *person* in the *Essay Concerning Human Understanding* as

> a Forensick Term appropriating Actions and their Merit; and so belongs only to intelligent Agents capable of a Law, and Happiness and Misery. This personality extends it *self* beyond present Existence to what is past, only by consciousness, whereby it becomes concerned and accountable, owns and imputes to it *self* past Actions, just upon the same ground, and for the same reason, that it does the present. (2.27.26)

Locke specifies the "Forensick" origins of the concept of "person," which he identifies here with the moral and legal accountability of a free agent, a concept with its roots in Roman law. Locke's definition bears comparison with that of the jurist Samuel von Pufendorf, on whom Locke often drew: "Among the lawyers mainly, a person is said to be someone who has civil standing, that is, personal freedom—by which token slaves are classified as things."[24] Pufendorf then specifies a series of distinct status-types that define a person in Roman law, including gender, "moral status in time" (age-appropriate behavior), "moral position in the civil state," (as citizen, resident alien or foreigner), "moral position in the family," and "lineage." In Pufendorf's socially calibrated definition, persons are *free* but not *equal*, distinguished from each other by their location in a status-scape variegated by age, sex, and class, and by filial and civic relations. In Roman civil law, the highest form of personhood would belong to an adult male citizen of noble birth, while a slave would not be a legal person at all.[25]

Like Pufendorf's, Locke's definition takes its bearings from the legal tradition; and like Pufendorf, Locke assumes a social dimension to achieved

23. John Rawls summarizes the tradition, explicitly linking personhood with the capacity for citizenship: "Since Greek times, in both philosophy and law, the concept of the person has been understood as the concept of someone who can take part in, or who can play a role in, social life, and hence exercise and respect its various rights and duties. Thus, we say that a person is someone who can be a citizen, that is, a fully cooperating member of society over a complete life" ("Justice as Fairness," 59).

24. Pufendorf, *Political Writings*, 39.

25. On personhood and its disabilities in Roman law, see Gardner, *Being a Roman Citizen*. Status distinctions also continue to differentiate men and women, as well as adults and children, in Locke's scheme.

personhood, involving "Actions and their Merit" in relation to a recognized law. This "law" might be natural, revealed, or civil—the last implied by the "Forensick" reference, the first by the emphasis on reason, and the middle by the concern with conscience. Locke's definition differs, however, by not explicitly linking personhood to status and by elaborating the psychological dimension of what he calls *"personal identity"* within the legal vocabulary inherited from the jurists.[26] Locke's person "extends it *self* beyond present Existence to what is past" through acts of conscientious recollection. Not yet carrying the layered emotional historicity of the Victorian inner child, Lockean personhood does enfold the meaningful accretion of memories over time, and is thus already something more than Pufendorf's purely juridical description. It is perhaps worth noting as well how far this vision of personhood is from *possessive individualism*, a term that has become synonymous with the Lockean legacy. The "ownership" involved in "own[ing] and imput[ing] to it *self* past Actions" resembles not the owning of a piece of land or a car, or even the possession of rights, but *owning up to* or acknowledging an action as one's responsibility.[27]

Such a person is not born but made. John and Jean Yolton place Locke's "novel account of 'person' as a forensic term, in other words as a term for identifying the locus of responsibility," at the dynamic interface of his political and educational programs: "If civil society has the task of *protecting* the person, education has the task of *producing* persons."[28] They link the passage in the *Essay* to Locke's discussion of the exposed or abandoned child in the *Second Treatise:*

> To turn the child loose to an unrestrain'd Liberty, before he has Reason to guide him, is not the allowing him the priviledge of his Nature, to be free; but to thrust him out amongst Brutes, and abandon him to a state so wretched, and as much beneath that of a Man, as theirs. This is what puts the *Authority* into the *Parents* hands to govern the *Minority* of their Children. (§63)

---

26. Locke, *Essay Concerning Human Understanding*, 2.27.9. Status nonetheless returns in Locke's text in various guises, as Macpherson demonstrated in 1962. See Macpherson's demonstration of "differential rights and rationality" among laborers and land-holders, *Political Theory of Possessive Individualism*, 229–38.

27. Brown, also qualifying the Locke of possessive individualism, writes on Lockean personhood: "Locke imagines no fixed locus, private or public, for the mental operations of persons because he regards individual deliberations as dynamic, always interactive, even though issuing from a person's particular place in the world" (*Consent of the Governed*, 9).

28. See their introduction in Locke, *Some Thoughts Concerning Education*, 18.

The liberty of the homeless orphan is not the reserved and protected free-dom of the minor living within family and civil society, but a state of un-guarded license, pre- and antisocial in character, and hence akin to the life of beasts.[29] Such a creature, even if reaching the biological age of adult-hood, would likely not have had the opportunity to make the transition from human being to person that Locke counts as the work of education, since such a child would not yet be "concerned and accountable" for his actions to himself and to others. Gillian Brown argues that the child holds a special place in Locke's conceptions of consent (in its ambiguity, fragility, and urgency) and personhood (as a formal envelope of rights and duties whose fruition in freedom is by no means assured): "In authorizing the ongoing agency of individuals within and against society, Locke's consent theory credits and demands the mental faculties of individuals, who must be educated from childhood for their consensual office."[30]

Using Locke's definition, Caliban before the arrival of Prospero would have been a person only imperfectly, a person in process. This does not mean that he was a child in years. Orgel makes the following calculations:

> Miranda is not yet fifteen—she and Prospero have been on the island for twelve years, and at the time of their expulsion from Milan she was 'not out three years old.' Since Sycorax was pregnant when she came to the island, and died before Prospero arrived, and imprisoned Ariel in the cloven pine a dozen years before that, Caliban is more than ten years older than Miranda, or at least twenty-four.[31]

Orgel posits a Caliban born on the island to his refugee mother and or-phaned soon after, at least twelve years old when the Italians arrive. Caliban does not describe a childhood under his mother's care, but a period spent alone, as "mine own king" (1.2.342). The phrase implies self-governance and self-sufficiency, supported by his intimate knowledge of the resources and habitats of the island to which he was born, with its "fresh springs, brine pits, barren places and fertile" (1.2.338)—vital elements in colonial readings of the play. Yet without a social arena in which to test his interests and capacities, Caliban might have been judged by Locke to have achieved a

29. On children as creatures in Renaissance literature, see Witmore, *Pretty Creatures.* I discuss the "creaturely" estate of Caliban in *Citizen-Saints*, 161–80.
30. Brown, *Consent of the Governed*, 28.
31. Shakespeare, *Tempest*, ed. Orgel, 28n.

practical but not a moral autonomy, demonstrating the remarkable self-reliance of the survivalist but not the deliberative rationality of an adult person interacting with others in a social scene organized by several forms of law.

Caliban's use of language is one indicator of this personhood in process. Miranda describes his speech when they first met him:

> When thou didst not, savage,
> Know thine own meaning, but wouldst gabble like
> A thing most brutish, I endowed thy purposes
> With words that made them known. (1.2.354–57)

Her account may simply reflect a European's disdainful misapprehension of a foreign tongue, an approach developed by Stephen Greenblatt in his landmark essay "Learning to Curse."[32] Caliban's precontact "gabbling" might also, however, indicate an arrested linguistic development, the rudimentary beginnings of a language learned from Sycorax (perhaps Arabic mixed with bits of an indigenous tongue?), but left to turn upon itself in isolation. Caliban recalls Prospero teaching him "how / To name the bigger light and how the less / That burn by day and night" (1.2.334–36), a formulation that implies a fundamental lack of the terms *sun* and *moon* prior to the arrival of the Italians on his shore. Caliban's early education is all *garten*, no *kinder*, lacking the socializing dimension of formal or informal schooling.[33]

Understood this way, Caliban combines features of the medieval romance figure of the "Wild Man"—an adult trapped in speechlessness due to exposure as an infant—with those of the "Wild Child" of the Enlightenment, tended and documented out of a post-Lockean concern with the rhythms and hazards of childhood development.[34] Although he lacks the ethereal

---

32. Greenblatt, *Learning to Curse*, 31–2. For similar accounts of Caliban's language as a mis-recognized native tongue replaced by a colonial tongue, see Hall, *Things of Darkness*, 44–45; and Goldberg, *Tempest in the Caribbean*, 132.

33. On the kindergarten movement in the history of progressive education, see Shapiro, *Child's Garden*. He notes that the "infant-schools" of the early nineteenth century combined Lockean psychology, object theory, and social reform (12).

34. On the medieval Wild Man, see Greenblatt, *Learning to Curse*, 21; Bernheimer, *Wild Men in the Middle Ages*; Cheney, *Spenser's Image of Nature*. Doctor Jean–Marc Itard took over the care and tutelage of Victor, "the Wild Boy of Averyon," in 1800, when Victor was about eleven or twelve years old, perhaps a little younger than Caliban when first encountered by Prospero. Itard applied principles from Locke's *Essay Concerning Human Understanding* in his treatment of Victor, who responded only minimally to the educational program of sensory, social, and linguistic stimulation (Itard, *Wild Boy of Aveyron*, 55).

purity of Ariel and might seem therefore to be a lesser creature, many critics have argued that his being is more closely and clearly tied than Ariel's to the human condition as such.[35] Caliban's association with the earth links him to Adam, the felt heaviness of his being figuring forth what Locke calls "the Clay Cottage" of human embodiment, of liberty limited by flesh.[36] Caliban is a *creature* in the play, a term whose theological provenance still resonates in Locke's treatment of childhood. The special creatures we call children may be the responsibility of their parents, but they are "created" by God, as Locke reminds us: "But to supply the Defects of this imperfect State, till the Improvement of Growth and Age hath removed them, *Adam* and *Eve,* and after them all *Parents* were, by the Law of Nature, *under an obligation to preserve, nourish, and educate the Children,* they had begotten, not as their own Workmanship, but the Workmanship of their own Maker, the Almighty, to whom they were to be held accountable" (§56; Locke's emphases). By reminding us that children are creatures of God, not of their progenitors, Locke uses political theology to limit rather than expand the sovereignty of fathers by emphasizing human responsibility to steward God's creation. In our secular version of this creaturely triangle, the state represents the third party to whom parents are, in situations of abuse and abandonment, "held accountable."

If the creature whom Prospero and Miranda first encountered on the island was still in the "imperfect state of childhood" (*Second Treatise,* S. 58), he had not yet been granted the protections of a minor, which, like the moral and legal personhood they are meant to promote, exist only in civil society and in relation to family life—even or especially when family services must be supplied by other means. In the first phase of their life together, Prospero institutes something like a guardianship over this young man, neither fully adult nor fully child in his development and essentially abandoned to nature by the circumstance of his mother's exile and death. In Locke's phrase, Prospero becomes "the *Foster-Father* of an exposed Child," a parenting arrangement that he includes in the list of alternative domestic scenarios, placing Prospero's guardianship along with Sycorax's maternal parenting in a set of possible exceptions to classical patriarchy (§65).

In this first phase of their relationship, Caliban has indeed been afforded some of the benefits of a minor. Prospero claims that he "used" Caliban "with humane care, and lodged [him] in his own cell" (1.2.344–46). "Humane"

35. Harry Berger Jr. cites David Williams on this point: Ariel is "'an airy spirit,' once imprisoned in a pine, and aspiring towards total liberty.' Caliban, on the other hand, 'is capable of not a few human conditions . . . so that his appearance, however brutal, must indicate an aspiration towards human nature, whereas Ariel's is away from it'" ("Miraculous Harp," 12).

36. Locke, *Some Thoughts Concerning Education,* 2.

characterizes both Prospero's moral bearing toward Caliban (he acted *humanely*) and his expectations for Caliban's moral aptitude (he treated Caliban *as a human*, capable of personhood). "Care" and "curator" share the same Latin root, *cura*; in the terms of Roman law, Prospero exercised the duties of a "curator," while he largely delegated to Miranda the duties of a "tutor," since it is she, we learn, who "took pains to make [him] speak."[37] By housing Caliban and Miranda in the same cell, moreover, Prospero granted at least provisional equality to his adopted and his natural child during this period of guardianship. In contemporary parlance, we might say that Caliban was an "au pair" rather than a servant, invited to sit at the table with his new-created family while nonetheless contributing rather more than his share to the household economy, as foster children often did.

Caliban's education, such that it was, however, has already ended when the play begins, brought to a halt not (as in Miranda's case) by the natural termination of a curriculum that has run its course and done its person-producing work, but arrested by Caliban's act and Prospero's response to it. Caliban, we learn, had made some sort of advance on Miranda: the three had lived together in one cell, family-style, until Caliban "didst seek to violate / the honour" of Miranda (1.2.347–48). If this charge is true (and Caliban does not deny it, though the temper and mood of the advance remain deeply ambiguous), Caliban's education into moral personhood, defined as being "accountable . . . for Actions," appears to have been incomplete, while Caliban's present response to the charge reveals a continued failure of accountability:

> O ho, O ho! Would't had been done!
> Thou didst prevent me—I had peopled else
> This isle with Calibans. (I.2.348–50)

The "major key" Jacobean reading would put the emphasis on Caliban's unregenerate incorrigibility; not only his action in the past but his total lack of compunction in the present justify that he be "deservedly confined into this rock" (1.2.360), reduced from adopted son and brother in a scene of provisional equality to a prisoner and slave without hope of emancipation. Miranda's rejection of Caliban as an "Abhorrèd slave, / Which any print of goodness will not take" repels any Lockean pedagogy based on the inscription of sensory experience on the blank slate of the mind in favor of a psychology configured by the indelible marks of original sin (1.2.350–51).[38] A postcolonial defense might emphasize to the contrary the politics of Caliban's act: to "people the island with Calibans" is to reclaim it from the usurpers, repopulating it in his own image and for his own offspring.

The problem with this defense of Caliban from both a Lockean and a feminist perspective is Caliban's initial and continued lack of regard for Miranda's person, a personhood to be represented and communicated in some form of consent, whether verbal or gestural. The current postcolonial framing of the debate has difficulty defending Caliban without implicitly or explicitly blaming Miranda, or at the very least diminishing any injury to her person, taken here in the moral as well as physical sense. Thus Jonathan Goldberg cites Fanon: "'Whoever says *rape*, says *Negro*,'" effectively shifting the focus from Miranda's injury to her motives and prejudices.[39] I would like to propose that understanding Caliban as a minor protects the capacity for personhood on the parts of both Caliban and Miranda, sacrificing neither's dignity to salvage the other's. Such a defense would run like this: If Caliban was a "minor" at the time of the attempt, he should have been tried as a juvenile, not an adult. Caliban had received some of the benefits of education under Prospero's guardianship, including a movement into fuller language and sociality, but he did not yet understand his own impulses or how to express them civilly when he approached Miranda; he was not yet, in Locke's phrase, "concerned and accountable." After the attempted rape, however, Prospero handed him a permanent sentence of imprisonment and enforced servitude, further stunting his capacities for moral growth. Prospero's ruling brutally replaced personhood as social process with the imputation and enforcement of slavery and sinfulness as "natural" conditions, substituting the intimate cell of the foster family for the biopolitical deprivations of solitary confinement. Denied "humane care" in its objective and subjective senses—treatment *as a person* by a *fellow person*—Caliban has started to become the animal-thing that Prospero, at this terrible juncture in their relationship, has judged him to be. Prospero's ruling diminishes

---

38. Goldberg links the line to traditions of humanistic pedagogy that form the background to both Shakespeare's and Locke's texts (*Tempest in the Caribbean*, 124–26). Enforcing the Jacobean reading from a postcolonial point of view, Goldberg argues that "Miranda's humanist pedagogy underwrites the program of colonialist education. It also anticipates Enlightenment distinctions between those who have and those who lack reason" (126).

39. Goldberg, *Tempest in the Caribbean*, 139. See also Kim Hall, *Things of Darkness*, 143.

the humanity of both parties. Not unlike Bertram's wardship, but in a far heavier key, Caliban has suffered a minority for too long and with too many restrictions, a minority that reneges on the *potentia* implicit in the category, with devastating effects on all parties to the process.

Would such a defense have held water in a court presided over by either Shakespeare or Locke, and if so, in what sense? The answer in strictly historical terms is no, if we follow Holly Brewer's study of children, consent, and the law in the early modern period. Brewer argues that minors were tried as adults until the nineteenth century, but that major conceptual shifts concerning the age of consent and reason began to occur in the later seventeenth and eighteenth centuries, partly under Locke's influence.[40] It is in this virtual space of conceptual change and possibility (rather than in the real space of Jacobean courts) that I suggest we appeal Caliban's case. Blackstone's *Commentaries,* written in the eighteenth century partly in response to Locke, but synthesizing centuries of English law, addresses the culpability of minors in the chapter entitled "Of the Persons Capable of Committing Crimes."[41] Children rank first among those who lack the understanding to be held legally responsible: "FIRST we will consider the case of infancy, or nonage: which is a defect of the understanding. Infants, under the age of discretion, ought not to be punished by any criminal prosecution whatsoever. What the age of discretion is, in various nations is matter of some variety" (4.2). Calculated in absolute terms, the age of discretion appears to reach back into puberty: "During the other half stage of childhood, approaching to puberty, from ten and an half to fourteen, they were indeed punishable . . . but with many mitigations, and not with the utmost rigor of the law. During the last stage (at the age of puberty, and afterwards [fourteen and upward, according to Blackstone]), minors were liable to be punished, as well capitally, as otherwise" (4.2). In number of years, Caliban would have fallen in this last category, or even have been classified as an adult, depending on his age and the severity of the attempted rape. (It is worth repeating that we do not know how violent, if violent at all, Caliban's advances may have been.[42]) The act itself, as the expression of an "adult" urge, seems

40. Brewer, *By Birth or Consent,* especially chapter 6, "Understanding Intent," 181–229.

41. Robert Willman insists that Blackstone rejected key aspects of Locke's political philosophy, including his theory of property. Willman is writing in response to other scholars who have suggested stronger ties between Blackstone and Locke. In either case, it seems fair to say that Blackstone's comments on the rights of minors are not in conflict with Locke's and reflect the legal traditions that they both shared ("Blackstone and the 'Theoretical Perfection' of English Law").

42. Hulme cites Mark Taylor on the question of violence: "Mark Taylor questions whether 'violation' may not be Prospero's interpretation of 'a perfectly honourable action,' on the grounds

to place Caliban in the "age of consent"—which, we might aver, involves his capacity not only to express his own consent, but to listen for consent in others.[43] Yet Blackstone acknowledges that biological years and moral development do not always correspond: "But by the law, as it now stands, and has stood at least ever since the time of Edward the third, the capacity of doing ill, or contracting guilt, is not so much measured by years and days, as by the strength of the delinquent's understanding and judgment" (4.2). A Caliban who has spent half his life living in the wild, then reaches sexual maturity in the proximity of Miranda, was old enough in years, but might not have been mature enough in "understanding and judgment," to gauge the force and meaning of his response to her, while Miranda's own awkward age may also have heightened the tenor of her reaction. In such a situation of dual minority, a sentence "with many mitigations, and not with the utmost rigor of the law" might have led Caliban into the age of consent, whereas the treatment he has received has had the opposite effect. Indeed, his brutely instrumentalizing attitude toward Miranda's child-bearing capacities has hardened precisely to the degree that his own laboring being has been harnessed by Prospero.

Prospero and Miranda judge Caliban to be incorrigible and hence deserving of permanent enslavement. One train of thought in Locke supports this position. Jonathan Goldberg has aptly applied Locke's chapter "On Slavery" to Prospero's terrible reduction of Caliban from person *in potentia* to slave in perpetuity. Glossing Miranda's horrified address to Caliban as an "abhorrèd slave," Goldberg uses Locke's justification of slavery in wartime to explain Caliban's treatment:

> Those who emerge from the just war provoked by an attempted infringement on 'my' liberty remain, according to Locke, forever barred from civil society, forever in the state of war that marked their condition when they assaulted 'me.' . . . The slave—the person who does not recognize my liberty—is abhorrent, deserving to be put to death. Because he is not a person, he cannot be harmed by slavery.[44]

This is the Locke of possessive individualism, who is also the Locke with economic interests in the slaveholding colony of Carolina and hence

---

that 'Caliban's pursuance of the normal forms of courtship, with or without Miranda's responding positively to them, would be seen by him, Prospero, as an effort to violate her" (Hulme, *Colonial Encounters*, 126).

43. I owe this particular point to my student Brian Oglesby.

44. Goldberg, *Tempest in the Caribbean*, 134.

concerned to justify both the enslavement of Africans and the expropriation of the Indians.[45] This is a major Locke indeed, and Goldberg's book
is important, among other reasons, for establishing with such clarity and
urgency Locke's relevance to the colonial legacy of *The Tempest*. A "minor"
Locke, however—the Locke of minority—can also be brought to bear on
Caliban's predicament, even within the confines of Prospero's severe judgment regarding Caliban's capacities for virtue.

In Locke and the legal tradition he develops, not all minors reach majority:

> But if through defects that may happen out of the ordinary course of Nature,
> any one comes not to such a degree of Reason, wherein he might be supposed
> capable of knowing the Law, and so living within the Rules of it, he is *never*
> *capable of being a Free Man*, he is never let loose to the disposure of his own
> Will . . . but is continued under the Tuition and Government of others, all the
> time his own Understanding is uncapable of that Charge. And so *Lunaticks*
> and *Ideots* are never set free from the Government of their Parents. (§60)

Blackstone makes a similar point in his commentary on English law, and
Locke himself cites Richard Hooker's *Of the Laws of Ecclesiastical Polity*.[46]
Locke's aim here is not to defend the rights of the mentally disabled but
to suggest that their situation of continuous dependence is a special case
that cannot be used to prove the permanent and inviolable sovereignty of
fathers (and of monarchs who would derive their claims from patriarchal
arguments). Nonetheless, the case of the permanent minor in chapter 6 is
rather different from that of the slave who *"puts himself into a State of War"*
in chapter 3 (§17). Madmen, for example, "which for the present cannot
possibly have the use of right Reason to guide themselves, have for their
Guide, the Reason that guideth other Men which are *Tutors over them, to*
seek and prepare their good for them" (§60; emphasis added). The language of
guardianship is here explicitly applied to the mentally incompetent. Note
that Locke's guardian acts not simply as a "curator" (attending, in Arendt's
terminology, to the minor's life-functions), but also as a "tutor" (respon-

45. Locke was actually used on both sides of the slavery debate in America, but seems to
have been associated more clearly with the abolitionist argument (Loewenberg, "John Locke
and the Antebellum Defense of Slavery").

46. Locke cites Hooker almost verbatim: "Children which are not as yet come unto those
years whereat they may have [reason]; again innocents which are excluded by natural defect
from ever having; thirdly mad men which for the present cannot possibly have the use of right
reason to guide themselves, have for their guide the reason that guideth other men, which are
tutors over them to seek and to procure their good for them" (*Ecclesiastical Polity*, 1.7.4).

sible, Arendt tells us, for orienting minors within a world while protecting that world from their carelessness). As Locke puts it, tutor-guardians are enjoined to seek and prepare "their good for them," the word *good* implying a shared world of values and responsibilities. The permanent minor, unlike the slave captured in a just war, retains a quotient of personhood; it is a creaturely personhood that remains *in potentia*, perhaps forever unrealized, yet still reserving a dignity and harboring a virtue that even in its dormancy requires care and protection—in some cases including legal protection from the neglect or exploitation of the guardian himself. The presumption of personhood on the part of the disabled, including critical work on the normative elasticity of personhood as concept and content, is a foundational tenet of the modern disability movement, which offers still another "minor" framework for addressing the perceived deformity and monstrosity of Caliban's moral and physical person.[47]

Of course there is no evidence that Shakespeare represents Caliban as an "Ideot" or a "Lunatick," as a creature deprived of reason in the long or the short term. My point is rather that the paradigm of guardianship that governs the first phase of the Caliban-Prospero relationship, *even if put under almost intolerable pressure by Caliban's advances to Miranda*, need not have been abandoned in favor of an argument for slavery in just war. In other words, Prospero's judgment that Caliban's action has proved him incapable of reason need not have led him to neglect his obligation to "seek and prepare [Caliban's] good for [him]." The special circumstances of Caliban's extraordinary childhood, coupled with the unusual pressures of his cohabitation with Miranda, the only female on the island, might have issued instead in a change in living arrangements, conceived in tutorial and curatorial rather than punitive terms. The enslavement argument negates personhood up front, while the minor argument preserves personhood in deferred or suspended form. The extent of that deferral, however, as well as the process by which "the good" is determined, can result in further violence, more insidious because less honest, to those caught in the legal cache of minority.

47. The sense of "the disabled" as a specific group with certain rights and immunities is modern (draft addition to the *OED*, 2002; first use attributed to 1922). *Disability* carries a specifically legal sense from Roman law, meaning "incapacity in the eye of the law, or created by the law; a restriction framed to prevent any person or class of persons from sharing in duties or privileges which would otherwise be open to them; legal disqualification" (*OED* 3; see Jane Gardner, *Being a Roman Citizen*, on disability in Roman law). Legal disability in this sense would apply to such persons as felons, women, minors, madmen, and so forth. *Disability* is a classic case of emancipation operating by transferring the future status of the temporary minor (the propertied white male child) to a class of "permanent" minors (the physically or mentally disabled).

The language of guardianship returns in the final scene of the play, when Prospero "acknowledges" Caliban:

> These two fellows [Stephano and Trinculo] you
> Must know and own; this thing of darkness I
> Acknowledge mine. (5.1.274–76)

The Lockean framework of minority allows us to give special weight to the parental meanings of the word *acknowledge*. To "acknowledge" Caliban as "mine" is to reassume the duties of guardianship after their dereliction. The lines can thus be read to record not only Prospero's quasi-legal acknowledgement of Caliban (as a father would "acknowledge" his bastard, according him certain rights and dignities previously withheld), but also an acknowledgment on Prospero's part that he has not fulfilled his responsibilities vis-á-vis Caliban. He "owns" Caliban not in the major key of possessive individualism but in the minor key of the person who "owns and imputes to it *self* past Actions" (*Essay*, 2.27.26). It is a recognition, moreover, that occurs *in public*, before witnesses, rendering what Kottman calls a politics of the scene and delivering personhood as a dramatic event, by virtue not only of the mask of the *persona* but the assembly of others as guarantors and conservators of the personality so summoned. The acknowledgment remains painfully partial; Caliban is still, in Prospero's vocabulary and perhaps in the play's as well, a "thing of darkness," a daemon or creature not fully included in the realm of persons. Yet the political and ethical momentum of acknowledgment as a public act, working toward both commonality and responsibility in relation to felt differences, and witnessed by others, might ultimately perform some work on "personhood" as such, stretching the range of its norms to reinclude Caliban within it. In any case, the "fatherhood" delivered at the end of such a process of tested and delayed acknowledgment is a chastened and limited one, not the natural paternity of absolutist apologetics but the short-term, artificial, and fundamentally obligated guardianship of the tutor and the curator.

As an imperfect person, a subject on the way to citizenship, the figure of the minor is a conduit of multiple identifications in the literary imagination of liberalism.[48] Nonetheless, an impasse remains, marking the tensions

---

48. Examples from later British and American literature include the heroine of Richardson's *Clarissa*, the monster in Mary Shelley's *Frankenstein*, Nell in *The Old Curiosity Shop*, and the hero of Richard Wright's *Black Boy*. My thanks to Debra Ligorsky for helping generate this list.

within the Lockean legacy between emancipatory and colonial impulses, as well as risks and limitations afflicting the category of the minor itself. Anthony Pagden has argued that comparative ethnology in the seventeenth century shifted from conceptualizing indigenous peoples as "nature's slaves" to "nature's children," requiring civilizing education by their European betters.[49] The danger in construing a "minor" Caliban lies in repeating this same move: yes, a minor has more dignity than a slave, but the relationship remains fundamentally paternalistic and ideologically suspect, and the paternalism has proved at least as destructive as enslavement. Caliban's real condition as a minor—an orphan subsisting alone on the island since his early years, carrying the arrested rudiments of a mother tongue, perhaps suffering from physical impairments or irregularities, exhibiting distinctive behavior and limited speech, and first encountered by other human beings in his puberty or early adulthood—too easily disappears into the mass transfer of minority as a means of managing indigenous peoples in colonial campaigns. A careful reading of Locke, I submit, might indeed help us distinguish between nonage as part of a legal tradition that aims for definitions of personhood distinct from, though always grounded in, cultural particulars, and the translation of those features onto specific ethnic or demographic groups.

The "major key" reading of the play treats Caliban allegorically, as a representative of the indigenous peoples of the New World; in such a scene, the theme of childhood, extended to a race or people, can only reinforce paternalistic and exploitative patterns of colonization. My "minor key" reading, however, stages Caliban in relation to real rather than allegorical childhood, encountering him as a young person who has minimally survived orphaning, foster care, and juvenile incarceration. This frame calls a different set of concerns into view, involving parental responsibilities and children's rights rather than colonial power and indigenous subjection. Nonetheless, it is slippery territory—not in the least because of Locke's own complicities and investments in the colonial enterprise—and these ambiguities keep the project of reading Caliban as a minor in check as itself a minor reading of the play.[50]

---

49. Pagden, *Fall of Natural Man*, 57–108.

50. Another layer in the slave-minor crux concerns the complex relation between abolitionism and children's rights movements in modernity. See Hugh Cunningham, *Children of the Poor*.

"Madmen, Children and Cities": Minority Elsewhere

There is, however, another "place"—namely, the place of the island itself—where we might read *The Tempest* for minority. Linda Charnes has argued in recent work that we reconsider the relationship of character and place in *The Tempest*: rather than viewing the island simply as a backdrop for character-ological growth, experiment, and development, she suggests that Shakespeare represents the island "as a *Thing* in Bill Brown's definition of the term, an *entity* in its own right, a place with a singular agency all its own." The island, she suggests, "is *the* major source of agency in the play, if by agency we mean the origin of whatever power equips intention with the ability to realize itself."[51] If corporations are people, too, why can't places partake in some of the same protections? I would like to link Charnes' account of the island as an active entity to some suggestive comments made by Kantorowicz in *The King's Two Bodies*. There he notes a curious legal fiction that construed the Crown as a *perpetual minor*, a corporate entity requiring guardianship by the king and his advisors, custodial obligations that, far from magnifying the privileges of the king, held him responsible for the alienation of property as well as offenses against the dignity of his office. Kantorowicz cites the Roman jurist Labeo, who declared

> a certain edict to be pertinent to "madmen, children, and cities." The *tertium comparationis* of this seemingly weird scramble was that all three were unable to manage their own affairs except through a curator who had to be a sane, adult, and natural person. When, in the course of the thirteenth century, the corporational doctrines were developed, the notion of "city," *civitas*, was logically transferred to any *universitas* or any body corporate, and it became a stock-in-trade expression to say that the *universitas* was ever an infant and under age because it needed a curator.[52]

The Crown, writes Kantorowicz, is woven from "a tangle of intersecting, overlapping, and contradictory strands of thought," from which emerge the idea that "the Crown was the owner of inalienable fiscal property" and "the embodiment of all sovereign rights."[53] The Crown, of course, is not the

---

51. Charnes, "Extraordinary Renditions."

52. Kantorowicz, *King's Two Bodies*, 374.

53. Ibid., 381. In "The Rape of Lucrece," Shakespeare refers to "the world's minority" (67), indicating the epochal infancy of the Golden Age but also suggesting the transposition of minority from persons to worlds.

same as either the lands possessed or the territory governed by the king, but their verges certainly touch, since "disherison of the Crown"—deprivation in the specific sense of disinheritance, as a guardian might squander the estate of a minor in his care—was one of the charges brought against kings on the grounds of mismanaged minority. Richard II is once again Kantorowicz's test case.[54] Although the "scepter'd isle" speech does not explicitly evoke the Crown as a minor, the dying Gaunt draws on natal imagery ("This nurse, this teeming womb of future kings" [*Richard II*, 2.1.51]), and the speech as a whole holds Richard accountable for crimes of unlawful entailment and alienation. In the concept of the minority of the Crown, Kantorowicz discloses a liberal moment issuing from the strange fictions of political theology, insofar as the doctrine holds the king legally responsible to the common good rather than granting him exception to the law. Here and elsewhere in the book, Kantorowicz derives from sacral kingship alternate figures of collectivity—the *corpus mysticum*, the body politic, the Crown—that exist beyond the king as a natural person and serve to limit his sovereignty.[55]

Today, the environmentalist movement has recast the land not as passive property but as a rights-bearing entity linked to the health and well-being of all, and has done so through recourse to theological as well as political languages of stewardship.[56] Prospero's dereliction of duties in Milan certainly manifests poor stewardship; if he was "like a good parent" to his brother (1.2.94), he was a poor guardian to the Crown, and Antonio's subsequent usurpation leads to Milan's subjection to Naples, arguably a form of disherison. But the island more than Milan is the site of a primal minority that might bear on collective well-being. If we think of the island in *The Tempest* as itself as a kind of perpetual minor, due the protections and privileges of responsible guardianship in relation to forms of agency and dignity that it harbors both in reality and *in potentia*, the minority of Caliban begins to materialize in a temporality distinct from both juridical calculation and ethnographic historicism.

A key passage is Caliban's ode to the island:

54. Ibid., 372. In this instance, he cites the person, not the play.
55. See Victoria Kahn, who argues that Kantorowicz discovers liberal constitutionalism in conservative political theology ("Political Theology and Fiction").
56. See Ken Hiltner's provocative reading of environmental themes and political theology in Milton. Hiltner rereads dominion in terms of an expanded notion of *domus* as dwelling, not property, and he links the raising of children to the care of place: in the Edenic bower imagined by Milton, "The house would grow *with* the child, *around* the child, and *through* the child's hands as the two literally grow together" (*Milton and Ecology*, 28).

Be not afeard, the isle is full of noises,
Sounds, and sweet airs, that give delight and hurt not.
Sometimes a thousand twangling instruments
Will hum about mine ears; and sometime voices,
That if I then had waked after long sleep,
Will make me sleep again, and then in dreaming
The clouds methought would open and show riches
Ready to drop upon me, that when I waked
I cried to dream again. (3.2.133–41)

Generating its own music, the island here affirms Charnes's picture of the place as "neither a normal biosphere nor an ordinary geosphere." The island is doubly *a place that babbles*. It nurtures Caliban in a magical lullaby, an environmental substitute for the dead Sycorax, a "nurse" and "teeming womb" that continues to sustain Caliban even in his abjection by Prospero. And the island is itself a kind of infant, its music Aeolian rather than melodic, presemantic rather than signifying. At once child, madman, and city, the island localizes the pulsing, precious resources of pure place that both nourish its inhabitants and elicit their stewardship without submitting to possession. In the speech, we listen to Caliban recalling the music of his childhood. The rhythmic lullabies of a mother, tutor, or curator meld in memory with the ambient sounds made by the island itself, remixed through Caliban's linguistic and imaginative capacities into music we too can begin to hear. A childlike mood saturates the speech, signed above all by the poignantly infantile image of crying in order to dream again. Yet the speech also unfolds as a series of temporal cuts, including the painful break of the cry itself, that distinguish the chaotic mix of early memory from the ego recollecting the past in the present. In Caliban's speech, we glimpse the phenomenology of an awakening consciousness yearning for sleep, but reconstructed with great labor in the layered tenses of a painfully achieved personhood. In *The Tempest*, to awaken is to *rouse oneself from minority into majority*, through the risk and challenge of political experiment, deliberative dialogue, and linguistic expression as well as through forms of dwelling and curation that invite nonpossessive relationships to both person and place.

The humming island becomes both cradle and mirror for Caliban's own emerging majority, not in order to exercise a pathetic fallacy that ultimately supports the autonomy of the ego, but, in Charnes's analysis, by remaining "irreducible and inappropriable," "an environment that is not merely background for one's will."[57] Insofar as minority is shared by Caliban and the island, the concept may begin to deposit another temporality, distinct from both the colonial ethnographic historicism that would classify indigenous peoples as childish races and a purely juridical time that quantifies minority on an actuarial chart of developmental markers. Here again Arendt may offer illumination: *minority* in this less calculated, more contingent, and less bounded sense recalls *natality*, "the birth of new men and the new beginning, the action they are capable of by virtue of being born."[58] Laws governing minors, like educational regimens, attempt to manage the risks of natality while also protecting the possibilities for new action that natality inserts into the world. The curator is steward of both world and child. Caliban has been born on, and to, the island, and the incalculable futures of both person and place are bound to each other as the Italian ships prepare to exit. Caliban's collaborations with Trinculo and Stephano constitute the experimental period of the play—which is also the time or *tempus* of the play proper—in which Caliban's personhood has become unfrozen, going into process once again. Caliban's confinement is by no means complete, and he manages to act freely in relation to Trinculo and Stephano, seizing on their presence as an opportunity to exercise his own agency. What Gillian Brown argues for Locke is also, I suggest, true for Shakespeare: "By recognizing and protecting an embryonic form of agency in the child, Locke establishes a basis for the principle of self-determination."[59]

When Prospero leaves the island, Caliban will in effect have no master. Like Ariel, he has been emancipated, not so much "by" Prospero as through his own powers of expression and deliberation exercised in concert with others.[60] If Caliban will live free on the island, he may nonetheless live alone—perhaps cooperating with Ariel, but likely without a helpmeet or a political community. In *The Origins of Totalitarianism*, Arendt distinguishes solitude from isolation and loneliness. Solitude characterizes the leisure of the philosopher, who enjoys being alone with himself because he can return to the *sensus communis* of like-minded others, their communal interaction providing the basis of political action. Isolation describes the *homo faber*, the artisan who finds himself *alone with his work*, excluded by choice or necessity from politics but still in possession of a private life, a social world,

57. Charnes, "Extraordinary Renditions."
58. Arendt, *Human Condition*, 247.
59. Brown, *Consent of the Governed*, 20.
60. Brown, "Thinking in the Future Perfect," 116.

and his own creative activity. Loneliness is produced by totalitarianism, whose subjects are reduced to pure labor devoid of a creative dimension (the condition of the slave and the camp inmate) and who no longer even have access to a private or domestic sphere.[61] In his childhood on the island, Caliban, I would suggest, existed in isolation: his own king, he had no community in which to develop patterns of cooperation and compromise, but he performed his survivalist labor according to the rhythm that he set himself in intimate response to the exigencies and gifts of the island. This isolation was relieved during his minority in the cell of Prospero, but the tentative community built there was shattered when Prospero reduced the minor to the slave. During this next phase, Caliban underwent the radical loneliness of encampment, no longer accorded the rights and immunities of a minor and forced to labor without the minimal dignity of self-possession— suspended, as Charnes suggests, "between biological and political life."[62] When the sailors arrive, Caliban breaks out of his loneliness and enters into political relationship; the project fails, but he has nonetheless exercised his virtues and begun to enter into a new majority. When the Italians finally leave Caliban to himself, we might imagine that he has gained the capacity for [...] at-oneness of the philosopher, whose higher *sapientia* echoes [...] pledge to "be wise hereafter" (5.1.294). Perhaps he will write [...] sophy.

In [...] Touchstone says of the shepherd's life, "In respect that it is *so* [...] very well; but in respect that it is *private*, it is a very vile life" ([...] emphasis added). The joke touches an Arendtian insight. Privac[...] s us, was originally derived from privation, the stripping away [...] for public life that we saw dramatized in the Book of Job.[63] [...] ro's imprisonment, Caliban has experienced the radical privat[...] lls loneliness, a "very vile life" indeed, but he may, like Touch[...] ery well" the solitary life he is about to enter. Charnes's reading adds the further possibility that Caliban's solitude will be qualified and countered by the strange agency of the island itself, an acknowledged Thing that is more than a world and other than a subject. In any case, thanks to his own efforts and those of Ferdinand, a great deal of wood has been cut—the land cleared, perhaps for new kinds of labor, new forms of property, and new styles of poetry, personhood, and place-making.

61. Arendt, *Origins of Totalitarianism*, 474–79.
62. Charnes, "Extraordinary Renditions."
63. "In ancient feeling the privative trait of privacy, indicated in the word itself, was all-important; it meant literally a state of being deprived of something, and even of the highest and most human of man's capacities" (Arendt, *Human Condition*, 38).

Minority, I've suggested, gathers up an exemplary conjunction of politics and life, mounting a juridical category eminently capable of emancipatory transfers to new groups competing for civil and political rights, but also prone to species translations that end up infantilizing whole populations in order to secure domination. Like the regimen of taming, minority is thus bound up with both a negative and a positive biopolitics, and the curator, like the host, is kin to the gaoler as well as the custodian. An Arendtian reading of Locke, I've suggested, can help us disclose a *cura* that proceeds not from the paternalistic self-interest of the guardian but from the enigmatic *potentia* of the minor and the improvisational scripts of acknowledgment and conservation that such uncertain virtue solicits. *The Tempest* rises at best imperfectly to this challenge and thus itself remains minor with respect to the politics of personhood it begins to broach.

Ernesto Laclau writes of the importance of universal markers in catalyzing the forms of recognition that make political action across groups possible:

> If social struggles of new social actors show that the concrete practices of our society restrict the universalism of our political ideals to limited sectors of the population, it becomes possible to retain the universal dimension while widening the spheres of its application—which in turn will define the concrete elements of such universality. Through this process, universalism as a horizon is expanded at the same time as its necessary attachment to any particular content is broken. The opposite policy—that of rejecting universalism *in toto* as the particular content of the ethnia of the West—can only lead to a political blind alley.[64]

In these pages, I have suggested that the minor represents a particularly potent case of the universal moment that galvanizes progressive and emancipatory movements within plural polities and across global interests. There is a strong sentimental element here, of course: the face of an African child dying of hunger may be a more palatable icon for foreign aid than the spectral visage of the same child's mother dying of AIDS. But the sentimental face of the *child* floats atop the more muscular structure outlined by the legal claims of the *minor*, giving the composite figure of the child-minor an integrative political potency whose effects are considerably more than imaginary. The minor's protected reservation of rights in relation to a citizenship to come stakes out a powerful model of emancipatory transformation

64. Laclau, *Emancipation(s)*, 34.

218 / Chapter Six

through education that has been extended repeatedly from the "model minor" (a white male child of property) to other groups, such as slaves, working children, women, noncitizens, racial minorities, prisoners, and the disabled, and even to the environment and its nonhuman inhabitants. The figure of the minor as a cipher of potential freedom requiring the discipline and the protection of the law as well as public acknowledgment and engagement in the daily scenes of politics lies at the heart of the liberal project. It has been put to the worst of uses when the social education of minors is conducted in a paternalistic mode cynically designed to constrain rather than promote liberty, a strategy some critics have discerned in Shakespeare's play. Yet the minor's special capacity to focus and synthesize the affective identifications of diverse subjectivities around the common denominator of a stage of life taken to be universal has made discourses of and around the rights of minors an ongoing resource in progressive political programs around the world, especially when those programs require the rallying of distinct parties around a common cause.

The minor Caliban is a homeless child surviving the best he can in the wilderness of modernity; a survivor of foster care; a juvenile tried as an adult; a prisoner deprived of rights; a disabled "monster"; a stateless person; a child laborer both reduced to and alienated from his work. He is also in pursuit of happiness and on the road to majority through the recollective and self-narrating resources of a language that he has made his own, and through the chances for civic education and curatorial dwelling that he has found despite, more than because of, his court-appointed guardians. In each of these formulations an aspect of childhood in its psychological and developmental dimensions borrows its political urgency from a set of rights associated with legal minority. Perhaps this minor Caliban will reach his majority precisely because he aims for personhood in ways that resonate across authors and interests, continents and centuries, and hence that many can acknowledge as their own—recognizing his passion, taking responsibility for his pain, or assuming his rage, across and in response to the differences made by age, ability, education, and birth.

SEVEN

Paul Shakespeare

Paul Shakespeare? No such man is listed in the parish registries of Stratford on Avon or the Stationers Register of the Company of London. This man without qualities, "all things to all men" (1 Cor: 9:19), is an imaginary character, a creature of thought and discourse who frequents the allusive corners of Will Shakespeare's plays. We might think of him as the product of a strange "Knock, knock" joke (*Knock, knock. Who's there? Paul. Paul who? Paul Shakespeare*) in which the double knocks pound out the passage of Judaism into Christianity, of the Catholic Church into its Protestant reformation, and of Scripture into literature. First knock, Paul. Second knock, modernity. Paul Shakespeare's Epistles include two letters to the Venetians concerning circumcision (*Merchant of Venice* and *Othello*), a very early letter to the Ephesians on marriage (*Comedy of Errors*, set in Ephesus), and a pair of later, deeper, and more Corinthian commentaries on marriage, liberty, and the law (*Measure for Measure* and *All's Well That Ends Well*). The Erasmian discourse of folly takes its bearings from the Paul of 1 Corinthians and pops up in the serio-comic visions of Bottom in *A Midsummer Night's Dream*. Our imaginary correspondent does not fail to post a final envoi, modeled on Paul's Maltese shipwreck in the Acts of the Apostles, namely *The Tempest*, which sends Paul's achingly personal agon with universalism into orbit around the fragile singularity of the creature Caliban.[1]

In this final chapter, Paul appears behind four distinct masks: Catholic, Protestant, Jewish, and philosophical. Why *these* four, and why *only* four?

---

1. On Paul and *The Comedy of Errors*, see Parker, *Shakespeare from the Margins*, and Degenhardt, *Islamic Conversion*. On Paul and *The Winter's Tale*, see Diehl, "'Does Not the Stone Rebuke Me?'" 69–82. On Paul and *A Midsummer Night's Dream*, see for example Michael O'Connell, *Idolatrous Eye*, 132. On the Pauline body in *Measure for Measure*, see Rust, *Imagining the Theopolitical Body*. On Paul in *Othello*, *Merchant of Venice*, and *The Tempest*, see Lupton, *Citizen-Saints*.

What of Luther versus Calvin, or Erasmus and Colet? Where are the Ana-
baptists, the Quakers, and the Erastians? Are there not as many Pauls as
there are readers of the New Testament—or, to reason less subjectively, as
many Pauls as there are sects and confessions that authorize their teachings
through him? My interest, however, lies not in celebrating the infinite plurality of the Epistles in history, but in isolating the minimal set of contests
and complementarities that have shaped the destinies of the Pauline corpus
over time, measure for measure. Together, this minimal set establishes the
key themes and parameters through which we can both encounter and account for the exegetical dimensions of Shakespearean dramaturgy.

The tension between Catholic and Protestant understandings of Paul
must of course provide the most immediate setting for any disclosure of
Paul in Shakespeare. *Hamlet*, for example, with its Catholic Ghost and Calvinist sparrows, is both cemetery and laboratory of competing religious affiliations and their persistent half-lives. We could also return to the world
of *All's Well That Ends Well*, whose Franco-Italian landscapes of pilgrimage
and miracle-working are shot through with an insistence on grace native
to Navarre, all of it projected against *la comédie humaine* of the ascendant
bourgeoisie.[2] In English studies, references to Paul are often taken to guar-
antee the Protestant character of Shakespearean drama, yet Paul, as Phebe
Stanton has recently reminded us in the context of *The Winter's Tale*, also
figured in Counter-Reformation theology.[3] At stake here in part is Paul's relationship to Peter: if Catholics stress their dual role as pillars of the Church,
Protestants tend to emphasize the conflicts between the apostle to the Jews
and the apostle to the Gentiles in order to undermine papal authority. The
Pauline corpus not only fueled the great contest between faith and works
in the Reformation crisis of consensus, but also funded the liberal solutions to dissent (toleration, interiority, and the privatization of religion)
that emerged out of its terrible crucible.[4]

Alongside the Catholic and Protestant Pauls lie two *other Pauls*—two
Pauls, that is, *other than Christianity*. These figures emerge late on the scene
of New Testament criticism and thought, though the first—Paul the Jew—is
notionally prior to his Catholic and Protestant avatars, while the second—
the Paul of the philosophers—grows out of the secular answers to religious

---

2. On *All's Well* and the Reformation, see Lisa Hopkins, "Paris Is Worth a Mass"; on *Hamlet*
and Catholicism, see Greenblatt, *Hamlet in Purgatory*; on *Hamlet* and Protestantism, see Curran,
Hamlet.

3. Stanton, *Religion and Revelry*, 226–27.

4. On Paul and liberalism, see for example Steven Dworetz on John Locke's commentaries
on Paul (*Unvarnished Doctrine*, 135–84).

conflict that liberalism discovered in Paul in the seventeenth and eighteenth centuries.[5] Although locked in a death grip with each other, Catholic and Protestant readings were unified by their canonization of Paul as a founder of the Christian church and the main engineer of typological hermeneutics. The two remaining Pauls—Paul the Jew and the Paul of the philosophers— share with each other if nothing else the sheer fact of repelling this pre- sumption of orthodoxy. In the twentieth century, postwar theologians, New Testament scholars, and, increasingly, Jewish readers of the Epistles have ap- proached Paul not as the architect of Western anti-Judaism but as a Pharisee who understood his Messianic convictions as fulfilling the prophetic history and vocation of the Jewish people. Concurrent but by no means identical with this Judaizing impulse is the renaissance of interest in Paul among philosophers and critical theorists; the key figures here are Giorgio Agam- ben (himself responding to reflections on Paul by the Jewish sociologist of religion Jacob Taubes) and Alain Badiou, who reopens the universalism of Paul in a framework outside that concept's Christian articulations.

This final chapter contributes to my ongoing effort to apprehend the meanings of Paul for Shakespeare, not in order to fix the playwright's Protes- tant pedigree once and for all, but, to the contrary, to illuminate the stratified and conflicted texture of Shakespeare's engagement with religious traditions and the humanist, secular, and profane openings that have issued from the scenes of their contest. Throughout this book, the other Pauls of Judaism, Catholicism, and philosophy have helped birth the Messianic moments in *Hamlet* and *All's Well That Ends Well*, and the existential framing of religion disclosed in *Timon of Athens*.[6] Because I touch on a number of plays in this final chapter, my readings are more schematic than elsewhere in this book; the resulting enterprise may seem less an act of "thinking with Shakespeare" than a straightforward "thinking about" Shakespeare and Paul. Yet what I aim to enunciate is the chance for *potential* readings of Shakespeare, in response to *potential* Pauls.[7] Glossing Aristotle, Agamben writes that poten- tiality (*dynamis*) includes "the potential *not to be*," which Agamben takes to

---

5. Brayton Polka calls Paul "a favorite authority of Spinoza" and cites many passages in which Spinoza turns to Paul in order to limit the speculative dimensions of Scripture (*Between Philosophy and Religion*, 253).

6. On the Messianic interim in *Hamlet*, see Pye, *Vanishing*; on the Abrahamic in *Timon of Athens*, see Jackson, "'One Wish.'"

7. "Potential" in the sense perhaps touched upon by Paul himself when he proclaims that Jesus Christ was "established [*horistenthos*, from *horizein*, 'to set a boundary, to limit, delimit']" as the Son of God "with power," *en dynamei*—dynamically, as a fluid set of life-giving possibilities and relationships (Romans 1:3). See Fitzmyer, *Romans*, 235.

be a fecund or creative quiescence, like Hermione's dormant virtue, and not simply a negative state of privation, inertia, or lack.[8] To claim the Catholic, Jewish, and philosophical Pauls as potentialities in and for Shakespearean drama is to delimit a region of dynamic interpretation that sounds the echo chambers of exegesis in order to keep faith with both the dramatist and the evangelist while releasing texts constrained by the history of their actualizations to new hermeneutic horizons. My aim is to expose Shakespeare to forms of thinking about forms of life that did not in any direct sense belong to him or to his age, but to do so through trains of thought that nonetheless remain within the exegetical universe scanned by Shakespearean drama. My hope is to model a reading for potentiality that might bear fruit in response to very different couplings, such as Shakespeare and science, Shakespeare and psychoanalysis, or Shakespeare and design.[9]

Paul, Christianity, and the Temptation of Marcion

*Look there, in front of you. At the center of the stage, which is also a city street, a band of rude mechanicals, ragged refugees from the mystery plays, are dressed up as Papists and Puritans. Pummeling each other with leeks and sausages, they battle over an effigy of St. Paul, his clownish body stitched together from a patchwork of pilled velvet and Jewish gabardine. Finally, they dance a mad moresca around the fallen figure, which slowly begins to rise. (When performed in midsummer: an ass's head is optional.) The dancers part, and the figure stumbles toward us, hands outstretched (is he welcoming us, or just trying to regain his balance?). On his frock coat he wears a large heart built from the kiss of two question marks, with the word "*SECULAR?*" emblazoned in their field.*

For Catholicism, Paul was the architect alongside Peter of a Church that combines faith and works in a fluid relationship that accommodated and absorbed local cults and calendars into the "catholic," or universal, body of the faithful. The key epistle in this regard is Romans, addressed to a mixed congregation of Jewish and Gentile Christians and organized to acknowl-

8. Agamben, *Potentialities*, 182. Although Agamben has surprisingly little to say about Shakespeare, he appears to couch his discussion of potentiality with *Hamlet* in the background: "But what is the relation between impotentiality and potentiality, between the potentiality to not-be and the potentiality to be? And how can there be potentiality, if all potentiality is always already impotentiality? *How is it possible to consider the actuality of the potentiality to not-be?*" (183; emphasis in orig.).

9. For a "potential" rather than historical account of Shakespeare and science, see especially Scott Maisano, *Shakespeare's Science Fictions*. In my next book, I aim to conjoin Shakespeare and design.

edge the claims of both groups to inclusion among God's people. Such a reconciliation also calls Paul to calibrate with great care the status of the Law (associated with Israel, but also, later, with certain practices of the Church) in relationship to Faith.[10] The most comprehensive Catholic reading of Paul has been produced by none other than Pope Benedict XVI, who delivered a series of "general audiences" on Paul in honor of the Year of St. Paul, conducted between the Feasts of Sts. Peter and Paul, 2008–2009. According to Ratzinger, Paul was no inventor of Christianity; rather, he was "confirmed and guaranteed" by the pillars of the Church in Jerusalem, and he teaches further that "faith is not a thought, not an opinion, an idea . . . faith, if it is true, if it is real, becomes love, becomes charity, is expressed in charity."[11] Arguing against faith as an interior state, Ratzinger insists on the embodiment and manifestation of faith in intersubjective acts of charity.

The Protestant reading of Paul, of course, adamantly places faith against works, arguing that salvation is "by faith alone." In the Epistle to the Galatians, which Luther called "my epistle, to which I am betrothed," Paul takes a stronger stance than he does in Romans against the Judaizing factions of the early Church.[12] Most New Testament scholars agree that Galatians was addressed to a Gentile congregation that had been pressured into full ritual observance by a group of Jewish-Christian missionaries, perhaps of Peter's party, a speech situation that explains Paul's more polemical attitude toward the "works" of Jewish law, observances that the Reformers would identify with Catholic practice. Paul's confrontation with Peter at Antioch, narrated in the letter to the Galatians (Gal 2), places these two leaders in conflict with each other over the status of works of the law; whereas Catholics seek to reconcile Peter and Paul, the keys and the book, works and faith, as two pillars of the same institution, for Protestants Peter and Paul increasingly came to represent distinct and opposing legacies of and for Christianity. Thus Luther writes unequivocally of Peter, "Peter, the prince of the apostles, lived and taught contrary to the Word of God," and he goes on to cite the

10. Peter Williamson cites Vanhoye on the same point: "For St. Paul, the faith that counts is the faith that works through love." *Catholic Principles for Interpreting Scripture*, 123.

11. Pope Benedict XVI, *St. Paul*, 36, 84. The Anchor Bible commentator on Romans, Joseph Fitzmyer, S.J., reframes the Catholic position from a text-critical point of view: "For Paul there cannot be any faith without accompanying love, that is to say, deeds that manifest that faith in the concern for God or for other human beings" (*Romans*, 138).

12. Luther, *Lectures on Galatians*, cited in Meeks and Fitzgerald, eds., *Writings of St. Paul*, 2nd ed., 379n. Luther's commentary on Galatians was published in English between 1575 and 1578 by a Protestant printer working with John Foxe. Patrick Collinson calls this work, along with a collection of sermons and commentary on selected Psalms "the little library of Luther" available to the predominately Calvinist English Reformation ("William Tyndale").

incident at Antioch, as recounted in Galatians, as the proof-text for his rejection of papal authority.[13]

In his classic study, *The Pauline Renaissance in England: Puritanism in the Bible*, John S. Coolidge argues that English Puritanism is a *"commentaire vécu* on the Bible."[14] The Puritans, he argued, translated the antinomies of Paul's thought into their own fractured situation. No historian of inwardness, Coolidge is especially interested in how Paul's thinking helped Puritans develop "federal," or composite, accounts of the Church as a fundamentally mixed body that incorporated within its ranks both the elect and recipients of a merely "common grace," those who are "called but not chosen."[15] In *Rethinking the Turn to Religion in Early Modern English Literature*, Gregory Kneidel takes up Coolidge in order to recover a Protestant Paul engaged in the rhetorical work of founding and managing the diverse and divided churches of early Christianity. Similarly, Randall Martin uses the New Testament hermeneutics of the Renaissance humanists in order to connect modern textual criticism (including feminist approaches to the Bible) to the Pauline tenor of Shakespeare's plays. Like Kneidel's Paul, the Paul that Martin discovers in Erasmus, More, Colet, and Shakespeare employs the "witty 'language of accommodation' and 'often and sodden chaunge of persones'" in order to edify his audiences.[16]

Erasmus, More, and Colet were of course Catholics, though in a humanist, pre-Tridentine vein. As the Reformation intensified in England, the language of accommodation associated by Martin with Christian humanism reappears in casuist statements by militant English Catholics. In his treason trial, the English Jesuit Edmund Campion used Paul to defend his recourse to pseudonyms and disguises:

13. See Meeks and Fitzgerald, *Writings of St. Paul*, 2nd ed., 238. Michael Goulder tracks the conflict between Peter and Paul as formative of the Gospels themselves, with Mark representing a more Pauline position and Matthew a more Petrine one (*St. Paul Versus St. Peter*). On Peter considered from both Catholic and Protestant perspectives, see Brown, *Peter in the New Testament*.

14. Coolidge, *Pauline Renaissance*, 141. Coolidge also published a typological reading of *The Merchant of Venice* ("Law and Love").

15. Coolidge, *Pauline Renaissance*, 88.

16. See Kneidel, *Rethinking the Turn to Religion*. Martin, "Shakespearean Biography"; cited from manuscript with permission of the author. Steven Mailloux is also working on the rhetorical dimensions of Paul, with an emphasis on receptions in nineteenth-century America, but with a sense of the long *durée* (and Catholic dimensions) of this story ("Political Theology in Douglass and Melville"). James A. Knapp is taking an existential approach to Paul's appearance in *A Midsummer Night's Dream*, where he seeks the conditions of Shakespeare's "phenomenology of ethical experience" (*Image Ethics*).

We read of sundry shifts whereto he betook him, to increase God's number and to shun persecution; but especially the changing of his name was very oft and familiar, whereby as opportunity and occasion was ministered, he termed himself now Paul now Saul; neither was he of opinion always to be known, but sometime thought it expedient to be hidden, least being discovered persecution should ensue. . . . I wished earnestly the planting of the gospel. I knew a contrary religion professed. I saw if I were known I should be apprehended. I changed my name; I kept secretly. I imitated Paul.[17]

The Tridentine Paul, like the Paul of the Christian humanists, is a rhetorical Paul, but his rhetoric has merged with casuistry within a mentality shaped by surveillance and inquisition. Campion compares his mission to the English Catholics with the world missions launched by the Society of Jesus to "the Indians or uttermost regions in the world"; his colleague Sherwin compares their band to "the apostles and fathers in the primitive church [who] have taught and preached in the dominions and empires of ethnical and heathen rulers."[18] In Campion's *imitatio Pauli*, the English Protestants have become the new gentile nations, while the pockets of Catholics, holding onto the old religion but often superstitious or backward in their practices, resemble the early churches of Paul, with their Corinthian mix of faith, tongues, infighting, and revelry.

In Shakespeare, the outlines of a Catholic Paul are perhaps most distinct in *The Winter's Tale*. Huston Diehl has recently asserted the Protestant character of Paulina. Arguing that Paul's "preaching emphasizes the imperfection of every human being and celebrates the 'grafting' of the new man onto the old," Diehl aims to "examine the way Shakespeare draws on Protestant constructions of the historical Paul for his conception of Paulina."[19] Far from presenting a purely spiritualized Paul, Diehl has a brilliant eye for the mixed and bodily character of Paul for Shakespeare, yet she ultimately assumes that Paulinism in Shakespeare is necessarily Protestant. Responding to Diehl, Phebe Stanton reminds us that "St. Paul was important to

17. Campion, quoted in T. B. Howell, ed., "Arraignment of Edmund Campion," 1059. My thanks to Timothy Turner for providing me with this reference. On Campion's entrapment in the no man's land between discourses of Catholic martyrdom and Elizabethan treason, see Dailey, "Making Edmund Campion." Dailey notes Campion's use of Paul (71). On Campion and Shakespeare, see Wilson, *Secret Shakespeare*, 16–19.

18. Campion, quoted in Howell, "Arraignment of Edmund Campion," 1064, 1058.

19. Diehl, "Does Not the Stone Rebuke Me?" 70, 72.

Counter-Reformation as well as Reformation devotion and theology."[20] Paulina's management of a chapel dedicated to the statue of a saintly mother, presented in a liturgical sensorium that includes both music and curtains, associate her with the curation of Catholic image regimes.[21] Camillo, steward to Leontes, consistently appears as a gatekeeper or *janitor*, like St. Peter both a "clerklike" (1.2.387) keeper of the keys and the unhappy cupbearer in a scene of fractured table fellowship.[22] At the end of the play, Paulina marries the janitor, unifying in the incorporated body of marriage (Eph 5:22) the Pauline and Petrine impulses of the drama. In the English context, however, the second marriage of Paulina and Camillo, imperfectly repairing the twin traumas of exile and widowhood, can achieve only a fractured synthesis of religious impulses. As Richard Wilson argues, Shakespeare's indexing of the Church includes a memorial or nostalgic Catholicism, the pacific ecumenicalism of James, and the militant, even terrorist, ministry of the Jesuits.[23]

The wars of religion were of course fought over the interpretation of Paul, and the great struggle between Catholics and Protestants led to important changes in the definition and exercise of religion as such in the modern West, including both the *Westphalian solution* (the dictum that a people's religion should accord with that of their prince) and the *subjective solution* (the rezoning of religion as a matter of private conscience whose individual practice should be tolerated by the liberal state). Yet despite the violence of the contest between Catholic and Protestant articulations of Paul's message, both Catholics and Protestants took their institutional, theological, and pastoral orientations from their readings of Paul as a foundational figure for Christian worship and community, in opposition to the Judaism from which Paul had, in their view, forever separated himself on the road to Damascus. Moreover, both Catholic and Protestant hermeneutics accept some version of Biblical typology—the figural reading of the Old Testament as an anticipation of the New—as an interpretive principle and a philosophy of history.[24] Typology provided much of the oppositional and even anti-Jewish rhetoric

20. Stanton, *Religion and Revelry*, 226–27.

21. On the Catholic multimedia sensorium, see Ong, S.J., *Presence of the Word*.

22. "How came the posterns so easily open?" Leontes asks. "By his great authority, / Which often hath no less prevailed than so / On your command," responds the lord (2.1.52–54). On Peter as *janitor* of the gates of Heaven, see Shearman, *Raphael's Cartoons*, 80.

23. Wilson, *Secret Shakespeare*, 258–66.

24. There is a vast literature here. See Auerbach, "Figura," 11–76, for the classic modern statement; Miner, ed., *Literary Uses of Typology*, for a sampling of traditional approaches to the problem; Lewalski, "Biblical Allusion and Allegory," for a classical application to Shakespeare. For contemporary critiques, see Biddick, *The Typological Imaginary*, and Harris, *Untimely Matters*.

of Christian hermeneutics and historiography, while also effectively knitting the Hebrew Bible into the literary and scriptural canons and consciousness of the West by retaining and sustaining the historical significance of Israel and her covenants. Much writing on Paul and Renaissance literature, whether philological or more cultural-critical, takes typology as the central dynamic through which Shakespeare uses Paul to interact with the Old Testament.[25]

Paul's creative reliance on the Hebrew Bible distinguishes him from his most radical reader, Marcion, the second-century follower of Paul who intensified the division between faith and works, love and justice, into two distinct gods, the evil Creator God of the Old Testament and the loving Christ of the one and only true revelation.[26] In a series of antitheses collected by his orthodox detractors, Marcion contrasts the two orders: "The Creator establishes the Sabbath; Christ abolishes it"; "Cursing characterizes the Law; blessing, the faith." In what may have been the first attempt to assemble a "New" Testament, Marcion collected Paul's letters but expurgated all references to the Creator and to Hebrew texts. "The inexorable result," writes Marcion's most famous biographer, Adolf von Harnack, "was the abandonment of the Old Testament."[27] Harnack dubs Marcion "a second-century Luther," and we can see Marcionite tendencies at work in Luther's love affair with Galatians as well as the anti-Judaism he derives from that and other Pauline texts.[28] Although Harnack praises the Old Testament as "a book of edification, of consolation, of counsel," he also sees the Hebrew Bible as a foreign body posing a continual threat to Christianity: "There was

25. The philological approach would include the pioneering studies of Protestant poetics, including their typological dimensions, mounted by Lewalski, *Protestant Poetics*. More cultural-critical works would include Lampert, *Gender and Jewish Difference*, my own *Afterlives of the Saints*, and Adelman, *Blood Relations: Christian and Jew*. G. K. Hunter's *Dramatic Identities* is an important transitional work between philology and cultural criticism. See also Adrian Streete, *Protestantism and Drama in Early Modern England*.

26. So, too, docetic Christianity—the early sect that denied Jesus's appearance in the flesh—promised "a Christianity without Judaism," that is, a theology more easily reconciled with Platonism and disencumbered of the Septuagint; see Fredriksen, *Augustine and the Jews*, 57. On Marcionism in modern thought, see Taubes, *From Cult to Culture*, 137–46.

27. Citations from Marcion and Harnack are from Meeks and Fitzgerald, *Writings of St. Paul*, 286–87.

28. The Church Fathers used Romans 7:12, "Wherefore the Law is holy, and that commandment is holy and just and good," to assert the unity of the one God of the two testaments, over against Gnostic and Marcionite dualisms. Thus Pelagius writes, "God is regularly called 'good' in the Old Testament and 'just' in the New. This contradicts the Marcionites" (cited in Bray, ed., *Romans*, 6:181). Compare Origen: "It is plain from this that Paul has not learned the doctrines of those [Gnostics] who separate the just from the good" (6:180).

always a danger of an inferior and obsolete principle forcing its way into Christianity through the Old Testament." Such Judaizing tendencies are also Catholic tendencies: urges to elaborate what Harnack calls "*forms* for a common life and common public worship."[29] Although Harnack does not himself decide in favor of Marcion, he lays out the stakes of the challenge to which Marcion responded.

The Marcionite temptation, itself born out of Paul's self-divided thought, continues to plague contemporary readings of Paul. Liberal secularization strategies reduce Pauline theology to a faith understood not as the active alignment (or "justification") of the embodied person with God's will in symphony with a mixed collective body, but as a purely interior subjective state for whom every "external" ritual has been rendered indifferent under the calculus of bourgeois rationality. To tempt is to touch—to brush against something real in the text. When Paul reduces all of the Law to the love of neighbor (Gal 5:14)—the unifying motive of the second, ethical tablet of the Decalogue, eclipsing the laws of the Sabbath, the debt of Exodus, the memory of Creation, and the sublime singularity of the God of the Jews—he begins to provide the terms of the secular script that would seek to resolve the tensions in Paul's thought by moving outside religion altogether.[30]

Paula Fredriksen writes of the Marcionite solution: "The contrasting pairs that structured Pauline rhetoric—Law and gospel, works and grace, flesh and spirit, Jew and Gentile—Marcion read as antagonistic opposites."[31] It remains seductive to reduce Paul to one half of a set of oppositions, an operation that risks flattening the dimensionality of his thought, excising Judaism from his writing, discounting his accommodation of pluralism, and needlessly setting on edge relations between Catholics and Protestants as well as between Christians and Jews. Marcionism remains a permanent temptation within Christian theology, including aspects of contemporary fundamentalism.[32] Yet it is also a temptation within secular Shakespeare criticism. In recent readings of *The Merchant of Venice*, I detect a Marcionite tendency to identify Paul with an absolutism of faith, a reduction that presumes the triumph of Protestantism even while purportedly critiquing the anti-Judaism of its terms. In simplifying Paul into a kind of Marcionite parody of himself, such criticism itself promotes a kind of interpretive Marcionism. In

29. Adolph Harnack, quoted in Meeks and Fitzgerald, *Writings of St. Paul*, 432, 421.

30. See Žižek, Santner, and Reinhard, *Ethics of the Neighbor*.

31. Fredriksen, *Augustine and the Jews*, 67.

32. Roger Lundin, for example, associates contemporary Christian fundamentalism with an incipient Marcionism (*Culture of Interpretation*, 80).

her 2004 study *Gender and Jewish Difference from Paul to Shakespeare*, Lisa Lampert writes, "Shylock is tied explicitly to the language of Pauline hermeneutics through references to his hardened 'Jewish heart' (4.1.80) and his own vigorous insistence on the word *law*, which continually resonates with the traditional opposition between law and grace."[33] In more recent work on *Merchant*, Janet Adelman describes Paul as "Christianity's most famous convert, who . . . displaced his own fleshly fathers in order to become a child of the promise."[34] Along similar lines are my own early essays, where I attribute to Paul the semioticization of circumcision into mere metaphor, "the external sign of internal faith."[35] Missing in these accounts is the complexity and anguish of Paul's attempt to recalibrate, not simply abandon, the relationship between faith and works in the Messianic era. Such readings foreclose both Catholic readings of Paul and more dialectically tempered Protestant ones in their neo-Marcionite zeal to expose the ideological limits of both Paul and Shakespeare.

For all its shortcomings, typological interpretation is designed to ward off the Marcionite temptation by binding the Hebrew Bible to the history of salvation, in the process assuring a place for Jews and Judaism in the future as well as the past of Christianity, a point masterfully made by Eric Auerbach in his foundational study of typology, "Figura." Typology incurred its own violences, formal inclusion being the grounds for various forms of real exclusion as well as symbolic disfiguring; we have no way of knowing whether the triumph of Marcion, anti-Jewish to the core, might not have been better in the long run for the Jews than the typological interfiling of Old Testament and New. It is safe to say, however, that a Western literature founded on a Paul deprived of his layers and his library would not have delivered either a Shakespeare or a Milton. Typology may be bad reading, but bad reading is better than no reading at all. Although critics such as Adelman, Lampert, and the earlier Lupton hold Paul responsible for the supercessionist hermeneutics derived from his Epistles, a key movement in New Testament studies—the recovery of Paul as a Jew—just might help us render a more generous picture not only of Paul but of Shakespeare as well, in part by yielding a hermeneutics besides typology.

33. Lampert, *Gender and Jewish Difference*, 149.
34. Adelman, *Blood Relations*, 44.
35. Lupton, "*Ethnos* and Circumcision," 201, and "Exegesis, Mimesis, and the Future of Humanism," 126.

Is Paul Good for the Jews?

The patchwork figure has regained his balance. Bewildered, he glances around at his tormentors, and then discovers the heart emblazoned on his coat. He yanks it off the gabardine, but blood begins to flow from the broken stitching. "If you prick us," he cries out, "do we not bleed?"

A major strain of New Testament scholarship, especially after World War II, has taken issue with the self-evident truth—shared by Luther and Adelman alike—that Paul rejected Judaism and that he saw himself as the architect of a fundamentally new and different religion called Christianity. A key figure in this revisionary account is E. P. Sanders, whose monumental study *Paul and Palestinian Judaism*, published in 1977, was followed by *Paul, the Law, and the Jewish People* in 1983.[36] This new scholarship emphasizes the continuities between Paul's rabbinic training and his writings; the coincidence between early Christianity and Jewish Messianism; the universalist elements in the Jewish tradition, from the idea of a single Creation to the injunction to neighbor-love; a general softening of the picture of Paul's "conversion"; and more nuanced views of Jewish law and covenantal theology. Paula Fredriksen summarizes the features of the Jewish Paul: "In his own view, Paul was always a Jew, in both phases of his life . . . Our analytic distinction between Paul the Jew and Paul the Christian simply does not carry over into his own life. He was both, and he saw the message of Christ as absolutely synonymous with his native religion and with God's promises to Israel."[37] Although this work began within New Testament studies, Jewish scholars, most notably Daniel Boyarin, have taken up this interest in Paul's Judaism in order to create more labile, inclusive, and pre-institutional visions of Jews and Christians in late antiquity.[38]

Take, for example, Paul's statement in Romans, "Christ [*Christos*] is the end of the Law [*telos nomou*]" (Romans 10:4). *Christos* means the anointed one, or the Messiah; although we are accustomed to reading "Christ" as the name of a man named "Jesus," it refers here to the office of the Messiah or

36. Sanders, *Paul and Palestinian Judaism*, and *Paul, the Law, and the Jewish People*. One of Sanders's main precursors in New Testament studies in this regard is Davies, *Paul and Rabbinic Judaism*, 1st ed. (London: SPCK, 1948). Endorsements for the republication of Davies's book by Fortress Press in 1980 included those by Susanna Heschel and Daniel Boyarin, major figures in the new, culturally oriented approach to Jewish Studies. N. T. Wright develops Sanders's emphasis on covenant in a narratalogical direction that is also distinctively Christian (Anglican); see *Paul: In Fresh Perspective*.

37. Fredriksen, *Augustine and the Jews*, 63.

38. Boyarin, *A Radical Jew*. See also Taubes, *Political Theology of Paul*; Segal, *Paul the Convert*; and Lieu, *Neither Jew Nor Greek?*

Moshiach, an office filled in Paul's conviction by Jesus, but still emanating from a Jewish, and not yet a specifically "Christian," frame of reference.[39] To say that the Messiah is the end of the law is not in itself heterodox with respect to Judaism—first, because *end* means fulfillment, goal, or purpose, not simply termination; and second, because Messianic thinking included ideas about both Gentile inclusion in Israel and a modification or even suspension of ritual observance during the Messianic reign. Some commentators, especially those working in Catholic traditions, intuit a metaphor of the race, with a sense of active movement toward a finish line, an exertion powered by "faith which worketh by love" (Gal 5:6).[40] Fixing *telos* as "end" or "terminus" seals off Jewish law as something over and accomplished, while also neutralizing the sense of human striving carried by the athletic metaphor. If the telos is a goal, on the other hand, neither the time of the law nor its function has been fully exhausted: we remain, as it were, in the running, and the law orients us toward the Messiah, whose ingathering of the nations remains to be accomplished. Telos as *end or terminus* presents typology as a closed system of meaning; telos as *goal* keeps the door open to new associations.

The 1621 conversion narrative of Daniel Ben Alexander, "heretofore a Jew by Religion, but now a Disciple of Jesus Christ," demonstrates some of the confessional and transconfessional issues that make Paul's Epistles both a battleground of religious conflict and a source of thinking about religious pluralism.[41] Alexander's narrative was translated from Syriac to Dutch to French and finally into English. The speaker, a converted Jew, models his own story on that of St. Paul. Identifying himself as "I *Daniell* Sonne of *Alexander*, borne a iew, and made a Partaker of the Circumcision in the Flesh according to the same," he addresses himself to the "dispierced [dispersed] Jews,"[42] using language that recalls the mixed congregation of Romans: "First, I would entreate you vnderstand, that though I haue vtterly abandoned the Iewish Religion, yet am not become enemie to their persons, nor to the name of *Israel*, which is now so much the more auaileable into mee,

39. On this point, see for example Fredriksen, *From Jesus to Christ*, xxiv and 133–48; and Wright, *Paul: In Fresh Perspective*, 42–50.

40. On the metaphor of the race and the sense of active pursuit and zeal that it implies, see Fitzmyer, *Romans*: "Christ is the goal of the law because through him humanity can reach what was the goal of the law, viz., uprightness in the sight of God" (584). Although Fitzmyer's discussion is compressed, one senses just how much is at stake in how telos is interpreted—at stake, I would add, for Jews as well as for Catholics.

41. Alexander, *The converted Jew of Prague*, B r.

42. Ibid., B r.

in regard I can call my selfe of the house of *Israel*, not onely according to the flesh, but principally according to the Spirit."[43] Yet this testament to his continued participation in Israel is accompanied by his disavowal of the law: "I cast beneath my feete, and doe vtterly renounce and disobey all Iniunctions which shall be contrary to his seruice, that hath made me of a *Saul* a *Paul*."[44] A central section of his confession catalogs major prophetic passages from the Old Testament, reauthorizing the tenets of typology by delivering them from the pen of a Jew.[45]

Alexander's testimony ends with the question most pressing to English readers, namely the error of the Catholic Church. Here, Alexander turns from the Paul of Romans to the Paul of Galatians; the Papists must be rejected, he writes, "because they take from the Merites of our Sauiour in his Death and Passion, and teach that men are iustified by their owne workes. *Gal. 2, 21. For if righteousnes bee by the Law, then Christ dyed without cause. And in the 16. Knowe that a man is not Iustified by the workes of the Law, but by the Faith of Iesus Christ*."[46] If Alexander's confession contracts to the polemical world of Galatians in order to take up arms against the Catholic Church, his essay ends by returning to the more capacious world of Romans. Following a final *Amen* (Hebrew for "So be it") comes an italicized citation from Romans 11:26–28, where Paul's promise that *"all Israel shall be saved"* and his assertion that the Jews *"as touching the Election . . . are beloved for the Fathers sake"* redraws the common stakes of Jews and Christians in a shared covenant and a promised future, albeit defined in Alexander's day from the hegemony of Christendom.[47]

Similar retracings of Pauline autobiography structure other Jewish conversion narratives, as Adelman demonstrates in her careful reading of John Foxe's *Sermon preached at the Christening of a Certaine Iew* (1578).[48] While it makes sense, following Adelman, to view these published confessions of converted Jews as examples of the brute cooption of Judaism by Christianity, we can also choose to hear—we can be open to hearing—an insistent vocalizing of Paul's own situation as an observant Jew who came to believe that Jesus was the Messiah. Such Pauline performances, though certainly

43. Ibid., B v.
44. Ibid., B2 r.
45. Ibid., B4 v–C4 r.
46. Ibid., D2 v.
47. Ibid., D4 v.
48. Adelman, *Blood Relations*, 43–46. See also Kathy Chiles on the sermons of the Native American preacher Samson Occam, who used the template of Romans for his own "cross-cultural ministry" ("Becoming Colored").

designed to confirm Christian orthodoxy, also harbor the chance to reorient the Epistles to the potentialities of their original historical moment, including Paul's mixed congregations, his passionate sense of both temporal urgency and historical debt, and a fluid hermeneutics mobilized but not yet fixed by typology.

Shylock's "Hath not a Jew eyes?" speech (3.1.55–69) radicalizes the kind of Pauline iteration performed in Alexander's confessions. Shakespeare's Venice in many ways resembles the Rome addressed in Paul's longest epistle: a cosmopolitan milieu harboring both a citizenship tradition and an imperial synergy.[49] Like Paul, Shylock makes a case for the universality of human experience, and like Daniel Ben Alexander, he does so from within a situation defined by Judaism ("I am a Jew," he says, leaving no doubt about his affiliations). Shylock's Paul, unlike Daniel Ben Alexander's, however, has not (yet) been converted, and he is certainly no Marcionite. His depiction of humanity is insistently creaturely, focusing on blood, hunger, laughter, and anger, and if he identifies with any god, it is the god of rough justice. When he criticizes Antonio for his country-club Christianity, saying, "He hath disgrac'd me, and hind'red me half a million, laugh'd at my losses, mock'd at my gains, thwarted my bargains, cooled my friends, heated mine enemies—and what's his reason? I am a Jew" (3.1.55–59), we might hear him to be accusing Antonio of those Petrine tendencies against which Paul mobilized his mission. Like Paul at Antioch, Shylock accuses Antonio of hypocrisy, exercising hate not love, exclusivity not generosity, disgrace rather than grace or graciousness, on the basis of the lines between groups that Antonio unreflectively enforces through the sheer fact of enjoying inherited privilege. A long-standing tradition in Shakespeare criticism, stretching from Auden and Barber to Girard, has accused the Christians in the play of being "more Jewish than the Jews." The problem with such accounts, as Richard Halpern first pointed out and as Janet Adelman has recently reiterated, is that a critique of the Venetians mounted in these terms simply reaffirms the anti-Judaism that such critics might want to combat.[50]

If, however, Shakespeare, in the line of Paul, is accusing the Venetians of being *Jewish Christians* and not simply Jews tout court, then the play's Venetian critique becomes more interesting. New Testament scholars agree that when Paul speaks against Jews, he is almost always targeting not that vast majority of Jews who rejected the identification of Jesus as the Moshiach,

49. On the importance of Greek, Roman, and Jewish contexts to Paul's thought, see Wright, *Paul: In Fresh Perspective*, 3–5.

50. Halpern, *Shakespeare Among the Moderns*, 184–210; Adelman, *Blood Relations*, 137.

but Peter's party, who wanted to enforce the full observance of the law for both Jewish and Gentile members of the new movement. Shaul Maggid, following Jacob Taubes, writes, "The Jew in Paul is really the Christian, or at least some Christians. . . . Anyone who believes in the universal and continues to live inside any particularity that effaces the universal, is a 'Jew.'"[51] Is this not the import of Shylock's speech? Antonio, as a Christian, espouses universality, yet he does so from the unexamined point of privilege—the hardened yet unremarked particularism, rendered invisible by his very claims to universality—that sustains him as a Venetian aristocrat, an unassailable pillar of the community. (Peter's calling was never in question; Paul's always was.) Shylock both mimics this doubleness—he, too, speaks for universality from the position of the Jew—and calls attention to the irony of its general distribution among the elite of the city.

Like Paul, Shylock lays claim to a universality of human experience from within the specific location and priority of Jewish history and consciousness. In the Epistles and the play, the universal singularity of the speaker is intensified rather than dissolved in his testament to a common creatureliness. Shylock's question, "If you prick us, do we not bleed?" recollects the "pricke in the flesh," sometimes translated as a "thorn in the flesh" or a "thorn in the side," that Paul confesses at the end of 2 Corinthians (12:7). Whether glossed as desire or disease, the prick indicates Paul's being in the world, his condition in the here and now, and hence the limits of any fully interiorized reading of his situation and his message. The thorn is *in* the flesh, inflaming it with pain, pleasure, or their symptomatic flowering; and *flesh is itself a thorn*, a reminder of createdness that makes the phenomenality of existence appear as such around the stigma of its puncture. If Paul is the exponent of the circumcised heart, it is a heart that can only be reached through the pricking of the flesh itself. Just as his own circumcision forever staples Paul to Judaism, so the thorn in the side makes carnality blossom as a necessary condition for the recognition of grace.[52] Neither flesh, nor Judaism, nor the mixed bodies they produce can simply be discarded or shed; they remain central to the voice and vision of both the Epistles and the play.

Central, but not unchanged: in Maggid's terms, "accepting the universal" means allowing that "the predicate must be transformed. This is not to abandon the particular. But it is not to leave it intact, either."[53] Both Paul

51. Shaul Maggid, "Response to David Nirenberg's 'The Figure of the Jew,'" 3. Unpublished paper; cited with permission of the author.

52. Against any docetism, Paul insists that Jesus was "made of the seede of David according to the flesh" (Romans 1:3).

53. Maggid, "Response to David Nirenberg's 'The Figure of the Jew,'" 3.

and Shylock expose the predicate "Jew" to transformation. When Shylock delivers his speech, he has already appeared to breach Jewish dietary laws by joining the Christians' dinner party; some loosening of the rules of table fellowship, both internally policed by *kashrut* and externally enforced by ghettoization, is already under way in the social experiment called the Republic of Venice. Shylock's forced conversion at the end of the play, however shocking it might be to modern readers, can also be read as Shakespeare's crude and clumsy attempt at beginning to imagine the terms of some form of religious and civic rezoning that would retain an ounce of fidelity to the complexity of Paul's own relationship to Judaism and to the mixed world of Romans.

The case of Paul, "circumcised the eighth day, of the kinred of Israel, of the tribe of Benjamin, an Ebrewe of the Ebrewes, by the law a Pharise" (Philippians 3:5), reminds us that universalism belongs not only to Christianity but also to Judaism, whose accounts of a common Creation and whose Messianic yearnings belie the identification of Judaism with an inveterate particularism, whether in Christian polemic or in Jewish identity politics. In *The Merchant of Venice*, Jessica's uncertain scansion of Judaism—is her father's religion a matter of "blood" or of "manners"?—is not simply a Christian import, but an existential tension resident within Judaism itself, which both accepts converts and jealously guards its borders. The Jewish Paul, unlike the Marcionite Paul, is a deeply embodied and embedded writer who continually expresses the immanent and existential character of his relation to Israel, Torah, and the life of the creature.

Stanley Fish posted a blog entitled, "Is It Good for the Jews?"—the question on his parents' lips when he was coming of age in the 1940s and 1950s. In a similar vein, the question implicit in much of this new work on the Jewish Paul might be phrased, "Is *Paul* good for the Jews?" Most readers would probably respond with a visceral no: after all, wasn't it Paul who cobbled together the whole battery of oppositions upon which Christian anti-Judaism would erect its machinery? If we rephrase the question, "Is a *Jewish* Paul good for the Jews?" then we might offer a provisional yes: Paul's debts to Messianism and midrash moderate Christian claims to originality and force a reconsideration of the supersessionism that has drawn its energies from the polarities of the Epistles. Finally, however, the question "Is Paul good for the Jews?" is designed in its very exorbitance to call attention to the necessarily apologetic and defensive character of the search for the Jewish Paul. The question of Paul's Judaism, whether mounted by Jews or Christians, is meant to do a certain kind of work vis-á-vis Jewish-Christian relations: to neutralize their antagonism by lessening the gap between their worldviews. The result, however, may be to counteract the Marcionism always latent in Christianity with what turns out to be its mirror opposite: a fully embodied and observant "Jewish Paul" called into being Golem-like in order to serve a variety of dubious agendas. If we want to read Paul from a perspective that is not only Jewish, or not Jewish *in a particularized way*, it is worth venturing onto the paths opened by philosophy. This is the way of Giorgio Agamben, most certainly, who takes the Jewish Paul as an invitation to think phenomenologically about Paul's account of temporality. And it is the way of Alain Badiou as well, who aims to restore the universal dimension of Pauline thought in a political and existential framework that is not confined to Christianity.

Paul among the Antiphilosophers

The scene abruptly changes; a small placard reads AEREOPAGUS, ATHENS. *An itinerant rabbi berates a crowd of traveling idol salesmen about some "unknown god." A group of philosophers on their way to the Academy stop by to listen to his harangue. The crowd laughs before dispersing. A wealthy publican and a surly philosopher (Timon and Apemantus) linger bemused and then walk on, silently.*

Agamben's seminar on St. Paul, *The Time That Remains: A Commentary on the Letter to the Romans*, returns to the font of typological thinking in order precisely to find *a time besides typology*. Agamben reads Paul for what he calls "the time that remains." The time of the *kairos,* or occasion, delimits a field of present action, a moment of existential urgency that refuses to be defined by either the inexorable march of tomorrow, and tomorrow, and tomorrow, or by the typological machine that exegetically recaptures the past as nothing more nor less than a prologue to the future. If the looping mechanism of Biblical typology is one of the Christian West's most powerful means of representing time, the *kairos* sought by Messianic time is that "additional time" that exceeds the movement that produces it. "*Kairos,*" writes Agamben, "does not have another time at its disposal; in other words, what we take hold of when we seize *kairos* is not another time, but a contracted and abridged *chronos*."[54] Agamben writes that Paul's image of time contracting evokes "the act of brailing up sails as well as the way in which an animal gathers itself before lunging."[55] It is an image of expectancy, tuned to the beckoning of an action. In Agamben's account of Paul, the telos of the Law is always just ahead of us, summoning us to exert ourselves just a little longer

54. Agamben, *Time That Remains*, 69.
55. Ibid., 68.

as we lunge toward the final goal. For Agamben, Paul makes the Law "inoperative," which by no means entails its abrogation, since the inoperative, for Agamben, names the resources of potentiality: "Only to the extent that the Messiah renders the *nomos* inoperative, that he makes the *nomos* no-longer-at-work and thus restores it to the state of potentiality, only in this way can he represent its *telos* as both end and fulfillment."[56] As we saw in chapter 1, art is a key scene of the inoperative, since the work of art works by not-working, by refusing its ideological instrumentalization. So, too, is the Sabbath, when time is submitted to its most rigorous regulation in order precisely to deregulate it, to allow it to become the holiday in which both Creation and Redemption can be lived in the *kairos* of the present moment.[57]

Although Agamben's account of the Messianic sometimes sounds like Scholem's vision of Judaism as an interminable waiting period for an infinitely deferred end, Agamben emphasizes the Pauline necessity to *seize* the moment, to participate in time's contraction by responding to occasion, finding "the pearl embedded in the ring of chance."[58] For Scholem, the end is always to come. For Agamben, the end is now—not, however, as an eschatological catastrophe, but as an appointment for action, the chance to make something happen here and now, in the present moment. Whereas typology is above all a hermeneutics, Messianism in Agamben's account is a way of being and acting in the world, of encountering time as what he calls, following Paul, "the time that we have" or "the time that remains." To seize the pearl on the ring of chance links the emergency ethics in Paul to the *kairos* of the rhetoricians and the cultivation of occasion and event in Machiavelli.[59]

Agamben accuses both the priests and the rabbis of defusing the Messianic impulses for which they found themselves responsible. Agamben's central concern is not the relation among faiths, sects, or dispensations, but a philosophy and ethics of temporality in and for the present time. Agamben is interested in a universal Messianism—a Messianism derived from a reading of Paul but supported by ventures in philosophy and linguistics, and ultimately disengaged from theology. We could also call it a *profane* Messianism, following Agamben's definition of profanation as the reclaiming

56. Ibid., 98, 95–104.

57. On Messianic time as the time of the Sabbath in Agamben and Badiou, see Kaufman, "The Saturday of Messianic Time." On creation and redemption, see Rosenzweig, *Star of Redemption*.

58. Agamben, *Time That Remains*, 69.

59. On Machiavelli and rhetoric, see Kahn, *Machiavellian Rhetoric*. On Machiavelli and the event, see Miguel Vatter, *Between Form and Event*.

ɔr common use of sacred times and spaces. Agamben distinguishes profanation from secularization: "Whereas [secularization] concerns the exercise of the power that it guarantees in referring it to a sacred model, [profanation] deactivates the apparatuses of power and restores to common usage the spaces that it has seized."[60] Secularization legitimates new state institutions by siphoning the authority due to religious ones; profanation, on the other hand, concerns individual and communal actions exercised on the ground in a mode more performative than procedural. To profane a sacred object (chalice, cope, host, psalm) is to touch it in such a way that it falls out of holiness and into everyday practice, expanding the repertoire of daily life in relation to a sacrality that nonetheless maintains its charisma.[61] Whereas secularization reconsecrates and reinvests, transferring sacred things from one jurisdiction to another, profanation *de-consecrates* and *disinvests*, loosening or "absolving" sacred things from priestly and secular building codes alike, for new, inoperative, rehearsals (as art, festival or theater).

When Hamlet declares that "The interim is mine" in the final lurch of his tragedy toward its promised end, he is laying claim to that Messianic *kairos*, that precious time that remains for action in relation to both a debilitating commandment he has inherited from a petrified Ghost and the freedom to execute that commandment in terms other than the deadly script of a legalistic revenge. The first half of the play is bemired in the opening chapters of Genesis, with their stories of unweeded gardens, soured marriages, and originary fratricide. As we saw in chapter 2, there is also something Moses-like in the "Jewish Oedipus's" inscription of the Ghost's "command" on the "tables" of his mind. The sublimity of the Ghost's revelation to his son increases Hamlet's terrible sense of burden, adding the weight of the law to the heaviness of fallen flesh. For most of the play, Hamlet feels himself cursed by rather than in charge of the mission delivered by the Ghost.

Yet Hamlet's revolted materialism and his subjection to his father's command are the preconditions for his transformation in act 5. Hamlet tells Horatio, "There is special providence in the fall of a sparrow. If it be now, 'tis not to come; if it be not to come, it will be now; if it be not now, yet it will come. The readiness is all. Since no man, of aught he leaves, knows aught, what is't to leave betimes? Let be" (5.2.215–20). The sparrow falls into Shakespeare's text from Matthew: "Are not two sparrowes sold for a

---

60. Agamben, *Profanations*, 96–97.
61. William West comments, "Profanation is the restoring of what has been set aside for the gods to the common, but it is not an undoing of the division of religion so much as a support and continuation of it" ("Humanism and the Resistance to Theology").

farthing, and one of them shal not fall on the ground without your Father?"
(Matt 10:29). In this phase of the drama, Hamlet stills the restless anxiety of
"To be or not to be" by entrusting himself to the simpler "Let be" (translating the Hebrew *Amen*) of God's plan, reshaping his own passive tendencies
into a form of *dynamis*. The "Let be" of providential time invites Hamlet to
live more fully in this world, which he suddenly apprehends as providing
an "interim" for action: "It will be short. The interim is mine" (5.2.73). Although one could chart the play's movement as typological—from Old Testament captivity to New Testament freedom—the interim can also be read
in terms of Messianic time, a temporality within, not beyond, Judaism and
its tablets. Hamlet runs his last race, hurtling towards the telos of the law
in order both to end and to fulfill it: he *will* revenge his father's death, yet
as part of a different script made possible by the choreography of the duel,
an action that unfolds in the creative urgency and ripeness of the time that
remains. In *Hamlet*, Shakespeare activates what Paul calls "the fervent desire
of the creature" (Rom 8:19) in order to express a conception of life whose
very mortal constraints provide occasions for human action in the here and
now. And to say that there is something Pauline in the play's final disposition is not, for me, to determine once and for all either the playwright's
Catholic or Protestant allegiance, but to choreograph the play in a broader,
more mobile, and more layered Scriptural tradition whose coordinates are
existential rather than confessional, and profane rather than either secular
or religious.

If Agamben takes his starting point from the Jewish Paul of Taubes,
Alain Badiou insists on Paul's radical break from Jewish law in the name
of a "universal singularity" founded on neither the abstractions of law and
capital nor the particularism of specific ethnic identifiers, be they Greek or
Jewish.[62] Badiou is not interested in Paul's uses for Christianity per se, but
in Paul as "a poet-thinker of the event" whose Epistles demonstrate the
subjective enunciation of a truth that separates from every local determina-
tion in order to address everyone everywhere. Badiou's Paul is "subjective"
in the sense that he is a human speaker who acts by speaking out loud,
declaring fidelity to an event (Christ's resurrection) that cannot be verified
or substantiated apart from the drama of this testimony.[63] Such subjectivity,
however, is not interiorized or private; instead, Badiou emphasizes the militant and interventionist character of Paul, whose cell-like churches were at

62. Badiou, *St. Paul*, 13.
63. "It is of the essence of faith to declare itself publicly. Truth is either militant or is not"
(ibid., 88).

work fighting the forces of institutionalization represented by Peter, James, and the Jerusalem church. For Badiou the "telos" of Romans 10:4 most definitively means end, not goal: whereas in the dialectical thinking of the Jewish-Christian faction, "The Christ-event accomplishes the Law; it does not terminate it," for Badiou's Paul there can be no such conservation: "In his eyes, the event renders prior markings obsolete, and the new universality bears no privileged relation to the Jewish community."[64] Although Badiou is careful to distinguish Paul from Marcion,[65] he nonetheless argues that Marcion's radical reading of the Epistles eventually forced the Catholic Church to canonize an "official" and "moderate" Paul, more priest than saint, more middle manager than consummate antiphilosopher, in order to blunt the purpose of Paul's break from the law.

Both Agamben and Badiou aim to think the implications of Paul beyond any confessional framework; as such, they are key to any exploration of "Paul Shakespeare" that would take up the affiliation of these two figures in a scene other than sectarian. Both Agamben and Badiou are as concerned about Paul's rejection of Greek "wisdom" or philosophy as they are with the Jewish question; "neither Jew nor Greek" means neither rabbi nor philosopher. The primal scene for Paul and philosophy is the address to the Athenians in the Areopagus (Acts 17), as well as the rejection of Greek "wisdom" in 1 Corinthians.[66] Throughout this chapter, I have used the word *existential* as shorthand for the element of antiphilosophy dogging Paul Shakespeare. If Agamben and Badiou give us a "philosophical Paul," it is philosophy that bears on the conditions of human experience, including the phenomenology of embodiment and temporality, as well as the situations of speech, consciousness, and action. This existential Paul is not, that is, the Paul of a secularized rationality, as one might find in Kant.[67]

---

64. Ibid., 23. In addition to his book on Paul, Badiou has also written a play based on Paul's life, entitled *Incident at Antioch* (unpublished; 1982 first performed in 1984). The play was the subject of a symposium held in 2009 at the University of Glasgow entitled "Paul, Political Fidelity and the Philosophy of Alain Badiou: A Discussion of the Incident at Antioch." Badiou has also published an intentionally controversial set of writings on "the word Jew" and the state of Israel, collected in *Polemics*, trans. Steve Corcoran (London: Verso, 2006).

65. "There is no text of Paul's from which one could draw anything resembling Marcion's doctrine" (Badiou, *St. Paul*, 35).

66. For an encounter with Paul as antiphilosopher developed from within Catholic theology, see Marion, *Idol and the Distance*. Marion presents his book as a reproducing or rediscovering of "the theological situation, the tactical disposition, and the crucial reversal of the discourse that the apostle Paul held on the areopagus before the Athenians" (23).

67. On Kant and Paul, see Cassirer, *Grace and Law*.

Again, I would turn to *Hamlet* to find my bearings in this zone; what Hamlet discovers in the Messianic "interim" that he enters at the end of the play is a time that exists precisely between "to be" and "not to be," as the Sabbatarian "let be" of inoperative virtue. The play begins with the scandal of a wartime economy that fails to "divide the Sunday from the week" (1.1.89); in the play's final endgame with the law of the father, Hamlet *fils* divides the week anew by holding open the time that remains with his very being. Or, to shift to Badiou's terms, "a son is he whom an event relieves of the law and everything related to it for the benefit of a shared egalitarian endeavor."[68] In *Hamlet*, this would mean taking seriously the play's harried groping toward a constitutionalism to come, as I tried to map the play's politics of election in chapter 2.

Agamben and Badiou share, then, a commitment to an existential and profane Paul whose thinking exceeds his institutionalization in what Kierkegaard calls Christendom. Agamben, however, writing from out of the resources of the Jewish Paul reclaimed by Taubes, stands closer to the more Petrine—Catholic and Hebrew—elements of the Pauline legacy, while Badiou expresses more affinity with the truths about Paul borne in the Lutheran and Marcionite readings. Whereas Agamben is more likely to work through traditional exegesis (Origen, John Chrysostom, Ticonius), Badiou refers Paul to Lenin, Pasolini, and Mao.[69] Agamben shares with Davies, Sanders, Fredriksen, Boyarin, and Taubes a sense of the volatility of Paul's context as well as Paul's ascription to Jewish Messianism. Agamben presents Paul as the philosopher of self-difference, in which every kind and category (Jew, Greek, the nations, *nomos*) are relentlessly subjected to a division that produces a dynamic remnant. For Agamben, Paul discloses "the impossibility of the Jews and *goyim* [nations] to coincide with themselves; they are something like a remnant between every people and itself, between every identity and itself."[70] In this analysis, there is neither Greek nor Jew because these categories are different from themselves, no longer the repositories of stable identifiers but constantly mobilized movements toward a beckoning telos. Yet *difference* remains the key term, the bedrock of the existential moment for Agamben, paralleling his sequestering of "bare life" as the

68. Badiou, *St. Paul*, 60.

69. For a similar exposition of the differences between Badiou and Agamben on Paul, see Jonathan Goldberg's extraordinary reading of paintings of Paul's conversion by Tintoretto and Caravaggio (*Seeds of Things*, 7–30).

70. Agamben, *Time That Remains*, 52.

creaturely quotient included by its radical exclusion in the political formations of the West.

For Badiou, on the other hand, there is neither Jew nor Greek, neither Torah nor metaphysics for Paul because there can be no continuities or carryovers when the truth of an event is at stake: "A truth procedure does not comprise degrees. Either one participates in it, declaring the founding event and drawing its consequences, or one remains foreign to it."[71] For Agamben, Romans is the key epistle; for Badiou, it is Galatians. Whereas Agamben speaks from the dynamic of self-difference, Badiou orients his discourse insistently toward the universal. Badiou does not deny that cultural differences exist: *"There are differences,"* he writes; "One can even maintain that there is nothing else."[72] Yet those differences are not the end of thought but its beginning, what thought must pass through and beyond if it is to become universal. When the Paul of 1 Corinthians 9:22 declares that he has become "all things to all men," Badiou discovers a Paul who, like the Chinese "mass line," is "capable of traversing and transcending those opinions and customs without having to give up the differences that allow them to recognize themselves in the world."[73] The Pauline principle of *adiaphora* (things indifferent) becomes for Badiou a way of designing collective agendas for politics, social life, and philosophy. In this regard, Gregory Kneidel attributes a "struggling universality" to the Protestant poetics of the sixteenth and seventeenth centuries: not a totalized, closed set of homogenized persons, but an anticipated universe toward which Paul's congregations find themselves working to embody—working by not-working, by suspending the virulence of their differences in the "as though" of 1 Corinthians 7:29–31.[74]

Badiou writes of the Jerusalem Conference, where Peter and Paul reached a deal on their two missions, that it was "genuinely foundational, because it endows Christianity with a twofold principle of opening and historicity. It thereby holds tight to the thread of the event as the initiation of a truth procedure. That the event is new should never let us forget that it is such only with respect to a determinate situation, wherein it mobilizes the elements of its site."[75] If the Resurrection is the event that requires a break with the past, Judaism continues to delimit the situation from which Paul enunciates that break, providing the "historicity" that prevents Christianity from dissolving into Marcionism. A moderate by temperament and calling,

---

71. Badiou, *St. Paul*, 21.
72. Ibid., 98; emphasis in orig.
73. Ibid., 99.
74. Kneidel, *Poetics of All Believers*, 16.
75. Badiou, *St. Paul*, 25.

I would like to institute my own Jerusalem Conference between Agamben and Badiou. Agamben's appropriation of the Jewish Paul for a profane reflection on Messianic temporality allows us to greet Jewish elements in Renaissance thought in a manner other than sociological or identitarian, and in a time other than that of typology. But if Paul was so Jewish, why is the world he helped build so markedly Christian? Here, Badiou's insistence on Paul's break from the Law reminds us that Paul's teachings were heterodox with respect to the larger Jewish communities of the ancient world. Badiou also invites us to extend Paul's rejection of the "rites and external markings" of particularized cultural identities to scenes of struggle today. Whereas Agamben splits differences in order at once to disperse and reassemble them, Badiou seeks what he calls "the conditions of a *universal singularity*": *universal* because addressed to all people, but *singular* because irreducible to the "available generalities," whether they concern Roman law, late capital, or group culture. Truth, he writes, "is offered to all, or addressed to everyone, without a condition of belonging being able to limit this offer, or this address."[76] The figure of the minor probed in the last chapter is an example of such singular universality, insofar as minority attributes a set of rights and risks to a human condition discernable everywhere, providing the terms for intergroup solidarity and struggle.

Othello, a black convert to Christianity, represents the promise but also the challenges of Pauline universalism. Desdemona's father Brabantio is a type of the Jewish Christian: a pillar of his community whose restriction of civic and confessional "brotherhood" to the native Venetian nobility makes him an easy dupe of Iago, who adroitly juggles racist topoi in order to turn Brabantio against his black son-in-law. Desdemona's name (from *desdaimonia*, unhappiness), on the other hand, says "Greek" all over it, and her ability to discern "Othello's visage in his mind" (1.3.253) implies a Pauline indifference to outer marks and signs. Her affirmation that "black is beautiful," moreover, draws on typological readings of the Song of Songs as a scene of Gentile conversion.[77] One of Job's symptoms was the blackening of his skin: "I am a brother to the dragons, and a companion to the ostriches. *My skinne is blacke upon me*, and my bones are burnt with heat" (Geneva Bible 30:30; emphasis added). Othello is Shakespeare's black Job,

---

76. Ibid., 14.

77. See for example Goldenberg, *Curse of Ham*: Origen "identified various biblical references to Ethiopia or Ethiopian(s), as well as the black maiden in Song 1:5–6, as symbols ('types') for the church of the gentiles, who, not having known God, were born and lived in sin" (48). For a different reading of the "black is beautiful" motif in the play, see Hopkins, "'Black but Beautiful.'"

a figure who hails from the Abrahamic crossroads of the three monotheisms as the failed symbol of their universal promise.[78] As Catherine Winiarski has argued, Othello resembles not only the barbarian of Romans 1:14,[79] but also the Scythians, who appear just once in the Epistles, in the sublime catalogue of Colossians, where Paul proclaims that there is "neither Grecian nor Iew, circumcision nor uncircumcision, Barbarian, Scythian, bond, free; But Christ is all, and in all things" (Col 3:11). Yet Othello's mastery of typological language also indicates a certain affinity between Othello and the circumcised monotheism of the People of the Book; like Alexander Ben David, he knows his Scriptures inside and out, whether it's the story of Exodus, the pattern of Job, or the rules of sacrifice. At once Gentile outlier and base Judean, Othello is, in Jane Hwang Degenhardt's evaluation, the "essential Pauline subject," representing the multicolored promise of the conversion of the nations while also remaining deeply grounded in the Hebrew tradition. Through the august sublimity of his person, Othello holds once and future audiences accountable for the vastness of Paul's vision.[80]

Paul's vision may be coupled, however, with Peter's ministry to the Jews. In 1595, the English Catholic poet-martyr Robert Southwell published a poetic monologue called "St. Peter's Complaint"; taking up Peter's despair at his denial of Christ, Southwell proffers Peter as a model of spiritual exercise for English Catholics.[81] In his final speech, when Othello speaks at the end of the play of his "melting mood, / Drop[ping] tears as fast as the Arabian trees / Their medicinal gum" (5.2.359–61), his language veers close to that of Southwell in *Saint Peters Complaint*: "Weep Balme and mirrhe you sweet Arabian trees, / With purest gummes perfume and pearlye your ryne."[82]

For both Southwell's Peter and Shakespeare's Othello, the exotic gums of the myrrh offer an image of the exorbitant grief that stems from their having cast away a pearl richer than all their tribe (*Othello* 5.2.357–58). The Petrine stoniness of the high priest who wants to turn murder into sacrifice melts

---

78. Lupton, "Job in Venice."

79. Romans 1:14: "I am detter bothe to the Grecians, and to the Barbarians, bothe to the wise men and unto the unwise." See Winiarski, *Adulterers, Idolaters, and Emperors*.

80. Jane Hwang Degenhardt, *Islamic Conversion*, 39.

81. Southwell, *Saint Peters Complaint*. Southwell plays on Peter's name ("My sonty name much better sutes my fall, / My othes were stones; my cruell tongue the sling"), in an implicit comparison with St. Paul's later involvement in the stoning of St. Stephen. In the following stanza, Southwell compares Peter's denial of Jesus to "Jewish tiranies" (6). Later he compares Moses striking the rock (Ex 1:6) to Jesus looking at Peter in his moment of denial (19).

82. Ibid., 21. On Shakespeare and Southwell, see Klause, *Shakespeare, the Earl, and the Jesuit*. On *Othello* and the Catholic question, see Wilson, *Secret Shakespeare*, 155–85, and Watson, "*Othello* as Protestant Propaganda."

into the liquid gifts of the African King Balthazar bringing the balms of his culture to the manger, or the myrrh of a repentant Mary Magdalene, who loved not wisely but too well.[83] If Shakespeare is indeed recalling Southwell here, Othello's mood may be melting in the alembic provided by a certain lyric-dramatic reading of St. Peter, taken as a figure of betrayal and despair within a portable scene of autobiographical complaint.[84] In any case, the speech as a whole swims in a veritable syrup of resonant resin, mixing Balthazar and Magdalene, Judas and Herod, Peter and Paul, circumcision and uncircumcision in an ambient medium that refuses to nail Othello (or Shakespeare) to any one dispensation.[85] We might speak here, following Victoria Silver on St. Paul, of a "figural adiaphorism," in which the same image reflects different religious realities.[86] Shakespeare's extreme unction jar does not secularize the diverse religious paths that lead to and beyond Othello so much as profane them, in Agamben's sense. In William West's gloss, "to profane something . . . recalls and supports the realm of religion even as it draws back from and suspends it."[87] Profanation performs its rites on the open threshold of the temple porch, which continues to offer provisional shelter for these newly released and intermixing resonances.

At the end of the play, Othello commits suicide by (re)circumcising himself in the heart, literalizing the topos that Paul had used against Peter. Othello wants to end the law by fulfilling it to the bloody letter of the book, dying to the law by circumcising himself in the heart. The fate of Othello shows Shakespeare marking the limits of a purely interiorized reading of the Pauline problematic; as in *The Merchant of Venice*, circumcision of the heart

83. Mary Magdalene was the subject of Southwell's other great experiments in spiritual complaints. Anne Sweeney writes of Southwell's two models of repentance for English Catholics that "Peter's dilemma could express the technical problems of oaths and processes, but it was through Magdalen that the problems of the self or soul were exposed." Sweeney also notes the exchange of properties between Southwell's Peter and Southwell's Mary; see Sweeney, *Robert Southwell*, 154. On the myrrh as a sign of repentance linking Mary Magdalene and the Ovidian Myrrha, see Holmer, "Othello's Threnos." Gary Kuchar emphasizes the Catholic character of Peter as a choice for lyric-dramatic representation in *Poetry of Religious Sorrow*, 36.

84. Ameilia Lanyer also links Peter to both "rich pearles of India" and the gummy gifts of Balthazar in her Southwell-infused dedication to the Countess of Cumberland: "'Right Honorable and Excellent Lady, I may say with Saint *Peter*, *Silver nor gold have I none*, *but such as I have*, *I give to you:* for having neither rich pearles of India, nor fine gold of Arabia, nor diamonds of inestimable value: neither these rich treasures, Arramaticall Gums, incense and sweet odrous, which were presented by those Kingly Philosophers to the babe Jesus . . . And as Saint *Peter* gave health to the body, so I deliver health of the soule'" (cited in Woods, "Lanyer and Southwell," 85).

85. In new work, Daniel Boyarin insists on Othello's membership in "the circumcision," understood as a Judeo-Islamic pact marked by *brit milah* ("Double Mark of the Male Muslim").

86. Silver, *Imperfect Sense*, 224.

87. William West, "Humanism and the Resistance to Theology," n.p.

proceeds by way of the pricking of the flesh, a search for grace in response to the creaturely conditions of embodiment, desire, and pain. In both plays, I would argue that Shakespeare calls us to the deeper claims of Pauline universalism, in which physical badges and conditions do persist, but within a horizon that includes within it plural stigmata. Such signs are indifferent with respect to salvation, but not without significance for specific communities and epochs, and remain subject to redivision and redefinition.

To mount a "Pauline Renaissance" today means considering the significance of the new body—a fundamentally mixed body—of work about Paul for problems of plurality and pluralism in Renaissance writing, whether it concerns the vicissitudes of Jews and Judaism, the status of Islam as a third revelation, the contest between Catholics and Protestants, or debates within Protestantism about the true nature of covenant, community, and election. Such a Pauline Renaissance should found itself on the hard historical work of John Coolidge and other historians of Renaissance hermeneutics; it should derive some of its animus from the cultural-critical work of Greenblatt, Lampert, Shapiro, Adelman, and others; and it should also allow itself to be reoriented by the bracing transconfessional and postconfessional perspectives promoted by Agamben and Badiou. The apostle from Tarsus was a tentmaker by trade. Let's use his Epistles to fashion shelters adaptable to harsh climates and states of emergency, but also to communal assembly and seasonal celebration. Build quickly, travel light, and keep moving: the follies and fallout shelters of the new Pauline Renaissance, suited to portable, nomadic, and disestablished forms of congregation, aim to *make use of*—to seize and activate, profane and enjoy—the several legacies of Paul, at once jewgreek, greekjew, and barbarian and Scythian, too. Such work requires that we reread both Paul and Shakespeare outside the familiar polarities of faith/works, flesh/spirit, and free/slave that have regulated pro- and anti-Pauline lines of thought for two millenia—not because such tabulations are wrong, but because their always-incipient Marcionism fails to grasp what remains original and urgent in Paul's thinking—what remains in Paul *besides typology*, but also *because of typology*, because of the resolute if often hostile knitting of Hebrew law, narrative, and prophesy into the consciousness and indeed the unconscious of Western Christendom.

Defrosting the Refrigerator
with Hannah Arendt

In a late essay entitled "Thinking and Moral Considerations," Hannah
Arendt lingers on the word *house*:

> We can use the word "house" for a great number of objects—for the mud-hut
> of a tribe, for the palace of a king, the country home of a city dweller, the
> apartment house in the town—but we can hardly use it for the tents of some
> nomads. . . . The point here is that ["house"] implies something considerably
> less tangible than the structure perceived by our eyes. It implies "housing
> somebody" and being "dwelt in" as no tent could house or serve as a dwelling
> place which is put up today and taken down tomorrow. The word "house,"
> Solon's "unseen measure," "holds the limits of all things" pertaining to dwell-
> ing; it is a word that could not exist unless one presupposes thinking about
> being housed, dwelling, having a home . . . *The word "house" is something like
> a frozen thought which thinking must unfreeze*, defrost as it were, whenever it
> wants to find out its original meaning. . . . This kind of pondering reflection
> does not produce definitions and in this sense is entirely without results;
> it might, however, be that those who, for whatever reason, have pondered
> the meaning of the word "house" will make their apartments look a little
> better—though not necessarily so and certainly without being conscious of
> anything so verifiable as cause and effect.[1]

In Arendt's phenomenological revisitation of Plato's theory of forms, she
finds in the word *house* the idea of dwelling as such, with its attendant sense
of place and boundary, of fragile security and provisional endurance. Although hardly autobiographical, Arendt's disparagement of tents surely

---

1. Arendt, *Responsibility and Judgment*, 172 (her emphasis).

echoes at a distance her years of statelessness and even her temporary internment during the summer of 1940 at Gurs, a detention camp in south-
western France.[2] The apartment rather than the single-family house comes
into focus as the passage moves forward, reflecting Arendt's own gradual
settlement into urban life as a New Yorker after her escape from Europe in
May of 1941.

In *The Human Condition*, Arendt writes that public speech and action
always disclose the "who" of the actor, a manifestation of the self that "can
almost never be achieved as a willful purpose, as though one possessed
and could dispose of this 'who' in the same manner he has and can dispose
of his qualities."[3] A similar disclosure occurs in the passage quoted above
from the chapter entitled "Thinking and Moral Considerations," in which
we observe the word *house* as it softens and ripens on the kitchen counter
of Arendt's thought, gradually yielding a multiplicity of references that
exfoliate into an instance of mental intimacy without ever becoming personal. As the word *house* thaws before us, it slides past a range of concepts,
images, and memories without attaching itself to any of them, reflecting
Arendt's description of thinking as a ruminative mental process not driven
by instrumental concerns.[4] To say that such thinking has no end or goal beyond itself, however, does not mean that it cannot issue forth in a renewed
conduct of living. Although "defrosting" the word house, unlike defrosting
the refrigerator, accomplishes no task, the act of cleaning up one's mental
furniture might well flow into a renewed attention to one's living space, or
become notes toward an essay on the phenomenology of thinking.

There is something Arendtian, then, about the observation made by another New Yorker, Adam Gopnik, concerning the difference between cooking and thinking:

> The act of cooking is an escape from consciousness. . . . Its effect is to reduce
> us to a state of absolute awareness, where we are here now of necessity. You
> can't cook with the news on and still listen to it, any more than you can write
> with the news on and still listen to it. You can cook with music, or talk radio,

2. Young-Bruehl, *Hannah Arendt*, 150–63.
3. Arendt, *Human Condition*, 179.
4. See Arendt, *Life of the Mind*, 62, 129, which attempts to do for the *vita contemplativa* what
Arendt has achieved for the *vita activa* in *The Human Condition*. What continues to rustle and
glisten in this rambling, often dated book is Arendt's glorious poetic rummaging through the
back rooms of philosophy in pursuit of aphorisms that capture the peculiar character of thinking in its purposeless withdrawal from the means and ends of ordinary life.

on, and drift in and out. What you can't do is think and cook, because cooking takes the place of thought.[5]

Cooking roots me in the world of labor and work, since it is both a repetitive activity keyed to meeting the necessities of life and a form of provisional craftsmanship that composes natural goods into a new order and image that I offer to others. When I cook, I might drift, dream, or mutter, but the task at hand always calls errant trains of thought back to the cutting board or the sauté pan. When such regathering fails to occur, the butter burns, or the finger bleeds. For both Arendt and Gopnik, *there is no multitasking*: I cook, and then I think, but I don't do both at once, because these activities engage my capacities in completely different ways.[6] Nonetheless, thinking, precisely in its withdrawal from the world of objects and appearances, can deliver me anew to what Arendt calls "moral considerations," the exercise of judgment in the human world of work and action.

There are several houses in the sprawling precincts of Arendt's thought. In *The Human Condition*, the classical *oikos* is the busy seat of production and consumption, where slaves and women labored to create the conditions that freed their masters and husbands to be philosopher-citizens. The *oikos* is the natural home of *making*, divided in Arendt's typology between *labor* (the repetitive toil exacted by the needs of life) and *work* (the crafting of art and artifacts that build worlds by virtue of their relative endurance). The courtyards, chambers, and porticos of the ancient *oikos* map out what will become the private sphere but encompass more people and more processes, while affording less intimacy, than the family homes of bourgeois modernity. Arendt diagnoses the disaster that has befallen classical politics as the absorption of the polis into the *oikos*, insofar as the modern state casts its lot with the life-processes associated with society: "We see the body of peoples and political communities in the image of a family whose everyday affairs have to be taken care of by a gigantic, nation-wide administration of housekeeping."[7] In Arendt's writing, "society" is the *oikos* externalized, metastasized, and rendered into system, its deregulated appetite for goods and services under capitalism sucking up the properly political functions of action as the disclosure of self in concert with others without respect to ends.

5. Gopnik, "Cooked Books," 85.

6. Arendt, *Life of the Mind*, 43. Arendt quotes Valéry: "*Tantôt je pense et tantôt je suis*' ('At times I think, and at times I am')" (79). On the myth of multitasking, see Raskin, *Humane Interface*. For a popular account of Raskin's arguments, see Ellen and Julia Lupton, *Design Your Life*, 88–91.

7. Arendt, *Human Condition*, 28.

To the *oikos* as microeconomy and society as megahousehold, we should add the actuality of the modern house. Private in relation to the social world that surrounds it, the house of bourgeois modernity is itself zoned into more and less public spaces: the boudoir stands above the parlor (from *parler*, to talk) as its sequestered counterimage, while the bathroom shares its secret plumbing with the more open kitchen below. Although the household under capital continues to sustain those labors in service of life that remain at the core of the *oikos*, the home has become increasingly defined as a scene of consumption rather than production. The homes of modernity are places where families seek sanctuary from the getting and spending of social life by finding new ways to get and spend some more. In the modern marketplace, I "consume" cars or appliances with the same world-destroying voracity with which I once ate a meal or wore a fresh washing of clothes. Consumerism, which Arendt had already begun to analyze in *The Human Condition*, attaches itself to the life functions in order to shelter us from too much knowledge of their limit points. On the frontier of death, the multiplication of products promising to protect us from the perils of accident, aging, or just plain boredom ultimately increase our terrified sense of exposure to biological risk. On the frontier of birth, every minute and mode of conception, pregnancy, infancy, and childhood is anticipated by a product or service, inviting us in effect to buy back our natality—to shop our way out of our condition of being born into a world we have not engineered ourselves.

Finally, the mind itself is a kind of kitchen in Arendt's writing. Although I cannot think and cook at the same time, thinking nonetheless is a form of cooking, since thinking removes the objects of sense from their settings, peeling off their ordinary markers of reality and rendering them into "food for thought" that can be remixed and reorganized: "There is nothing in the ordinary life of man that cannot become food for thought, that is, be subjected to the twofold transformation that readies a sense-object to become a suitable thought-object."[8] Imagination plays sous-chef in the great banquet of thought: "Not sense perception, in which we experience things directly and close at hand, but imagination, coming after it, prepares the objects of our thought."[9] Both bordering on the senses and freed from their constraints, imagination harvests appearances from their worlds in preparation for thinking, while art gives a home to the effervescent flights of thought by conserving them in the form of works: "Art therefore, which transforms

8. Arendt, *Life of the Mind*, 78.
9. Ibid., 86.

sense-objects into thought-things, tears them first of all out of their context in order to de-realize and thus prepare them for their new and different function."[10] Thinking can then return to such frozen feasts of the imagination in order to shake them up again for new creation and enjoyment. The ultimate objects of thinking, however, are not "things that are absent"—the representations generated by imagination and memory—but "things that are always absent," such as the thought-things of immortality, God, or freedom.[11] Although Arendt herself remained deeply secular with respect to such final things, she nonetheless understood their phenomenological emergence in the speculative wandering of the mind, and thus (not unlike Shakespeare) preserved a sanctuary for them in the urban mansion of her insistently profane thinking.

When Arendt speaks of the women and slaves whose labor freed men for citizenship, I am tempted to hear a reference to her second husband, Heinrich Blücher, whose devoted husbandry and intellectual companionship freed her to write, teach, and think, but whose employment problems also required that she earn most of the money needed to keep them afloat. During their first seven years in New York, Heinrich and Hannah also cared for Hannah's mother, Martha Cohn Arendt, until Martha's death in 1948; Heinrich, largely housebound, was thrown into constant contact with a woman who appreciated neither his working-class Gentile origins nor his lack of a steady income. Heinrich wrote to Hannah that Martha "was the one who, more than any other timid blockhead in our circle, simply and thoughtlessly took you for a man."[12] Heinrich's comment reveals not only the hardship of life with Mother, but also the disapproval emanating from the "timid blockheads" who were their peers. Arendt, economically speaking the man of the house, headed what modern critics might call a queer family: theirs was a childless but passionate second marriage, mixed with respect to religion and piloted by a woman who was both the main wage earner and the intellectual powerhouse. In this relationship, Arendt was more often than not the citizen-actor, with Heinrich in the supporting role if not of "woman and slave," at least of secretary and research assistant, a scenario that could not have been purchased without a great deal of psychic work and plain good will on both their parts.

Arendt's insistence on the distinctiveness of thinking, making, and doing by no means precludes epochal shifts in the nature of their relationship.

10. Ibid., 49.
11. "Imagination, coming after [perception], prepares the objects of our thought" (ibid., 86).
12. Young-Bruehl, *Hannah Arendt*, 236.

These human capacities have a history—we could say that history *is* the story of their shifting arrangements—but that does not destroy their status as faculties, as potentialities that lay out without predetermining the possible spheres and shapes of human being. When she writes, echoing topoi from Pericles and Aristotle, that the polis "is not the city-state in its physical location; it is the organization of the people as it arises out of acting and speaking together," she invites us to reinstitute the space of the polis—a virtual space, a "space of appearance"—wherever and whenever we can.[13] Arendt's project is not to restore the Greek polis but to clear spaces where the political can and does separate out from its social absorption, and forms of making can still create worlds. The polis is not a physical location so much as a clustering of activity and affiliation that might emerge, be exercised, and disappear again in any number of settings, whether school or living room, marketplace or kitchen, corporate café or urban farm.

As we saw in chapter 1, the Italian post-Marxist philosopher Paolo Virno argues that the classical ratio among thinking, making, and doing, already reorganized in the first phase of industrialization, has undergone still another sea change under "post-Fordism," the information-, knowledge-, and service-economy characterized by the global deployment of media-driven products and processes. In these transformations, the culture industry represents both an example of post-Fordism and a key provider of the new technologies of communication required by all businesses on the contemporary scene. Arendt had mapped an epochal shift in which the liberal state identified its interests and procedures with those of the economy, choosing the instrumentalizing concerns of the *oikos* over the deliberative arena of the polis as its proper sphere of operations. Following and in part reversing Arendt, Virno charts a second epochal shift. Whereas in Arendt's schema of modernity the state had become a huge household administering the social welfare of its residents, in Virno's take on the current turn, the workplace has incorporated the classically political functions of speech, cooperation, and deliberation into its daily operations and global strategies. The workplaces that our students and our children hope to enter require that every knowledge worker be a publicist, a designer, a curator, and a risk manager.[14] (A background in catering is also helpful.) The manifesto has become the calling card of the software engineer, not the revolutionary. Contemporary office spaces have relinquished the Fordist paradigm of

13. Arendt, *Human Condition*, 198.
14. Virno, *Grammar of the Multitude*, 51.

the factory floor for the post-Fordist image of the museum and the college campus, which in turn increasingly mimic the mall and the food court.[15]

Virno's evaluation of this state of affairs is mixed. On the one hand, he seems to celebrate a genuine advance in human possibilities for thinking, making, and doing. In the place of "the people" produced as the One out of the Many in accounts of sovereignty after Hobbes, Virno envisions "the multitude" as a many that *remains many*, no longer fully captured by national identifications, yet connected to each other by the One of the "general intellect," of thinking made public through communication networks. At the same time, Virno sees capital co-opting the energies of this multitude to the detriment not only of labor but also of thought. Here Virno veers back into agreement with Arendt: a collective order driven by economy, even if that economy takes on features of political action, will ultimately drain the public sphere of its political character, transforming every chance for action into new forms of labor and consumption.

Under these new conditions, I still cannot think and cook at the same time. But the cooking I pursue has a strange new public dimension, participating in a General Intellect of the kitchen created by the cable cooking networks, social media sites, and electronic cookbooks that allow me to blog my menus and shop while I chop. Little of this is political in Arendt's sense; largely fueled by advertising, this newly networked cooking feeds the overgrown *oikos* of modern biopolitics. From my kitchen to yours, and yours, and yours, the insatiable rhythms of consumption, cut-and-pasted from the digestive functions but long freed from digestion's natural thriftiness, steadily eat away at the world-building capacity of human making.

And yet a politics is possible here as well, via the same networking that siphons the energies of the kitchen into the larger economy. Media philosopher Pierre Lévy was one of the first Internet observers to theorize the democratic potential of digital forms of communication. Rather than decreasing or devaluing human sociability (replacing something "real" with something merely "virtual"), cyberspace at its best, Lévy argues, provides new means of actualizing relationships cooperatively, creating "an open system for the dynamic self-mapping of the real, the expression of singularities, the articulation of problems, the weaving of a social bond through reciprocal apprenticeship and the unfettered navigation of knowledge spaces."[16] Such a description borders on action in Arendt's sense: "Action, moreover, no matter what its specific content, always establishes relationships and therefore

15. On the post-Fordist paradigms of post-Fordist office space, see Fabbrizzi, *Office Design*.
16. Lévy, *Cyberculture*, 177.

has an inherent tendency to force open all limitations and cut across all boundaries."[17] For both Lévy and Arendt, action multiplies relationships across divisions, addressing the plurality of people via communicative projects that insert something new, unpredictable, and potentially deter-ritorializing into the current disposition of things. "The development of cy-berspace," writes Lévy, "is a particular form of urbanism or architecture. . . . However, the supreme architecture is really political. It involves the articu-lation of different spaces and their respective roles."[18] Here Lévy works the same topos exercised by Arendt, namely, the identification of the polis not with a physical location but with forms of collective action that actualize relationships precisely because they themselves remain virtual, not tied to a physical territory.

The kitchen is one locale in which such virtual spaces can appear, when, for example, they become the site of communicative decisions to partic-ipate differently in the global food economy. The slow food movement, championing the cultivation of local farms and biodiversity, might seem to be deeply anti-technological and highly privatized, a back-to-nature move-ment for urbanites with restaurant ranges. Yet the development of a global network of chapters, both aided and manifested by a strong Internet pres-ence, points to the power of digital media to enable and enhance local ac-tion. Slow food has flowered in what Lévy calls the "open universal" cleared by cyberspace, "which tends to maintain its indeterminacy because each node in the expanding network can become a producer or transmitter of new and unpredictable information and can reorganize segments of the network for its own use."[19] By using the tools of the information economy to readjust the ratio of consumption and production in the direction of the classical *oikos*, the slow food movement increases the opportunities of sev-eral constituencies to think, make, and do, whether it is the sophisticated foodie who might be reading this book or the entrepreneurial grower who has learned to cut out the middleman by supplying local farmers' markets. Each meal becomes potentially thoughtful, recording its passage among dif-ferent stations of its production on the road to a surplus enjoyment, above and beyond the call of hunger, and thus partaking in virtue.[20]

The rehabilitation of consumers as producers is the other side of post-Fordism. "Prosumerism" reconnects labor to work by using consumer choices

---

17. Arendt, *Human Condition*, 191.
18. Lévy, *Cyberculture*, 177.
19. Ibid., 91.
20. On the virtues of the slow food movement, see Bennett, *Vibrant Matter*, 50–51, and Honig, *Emergency Politics*, 57–64.

to build rather than destroy worlds, and it reconnects society to politics by opening situations of speech and action that address people in their plurality, as makers, thinkers, and doers.[21] The new crafting movement revels in a back-to-basics know-how that, like the slow food crowd, rebuilds features of the preconsumerist *oikos*, yet flourishes in the economic, stylistic, and networking opportunities bred by cyberculture. The coinage *craftivism* brands the politics knitted from the start into these new forms of making, a politics enacted in the reuse-recycle mentality, the gift-giving virtues, and the labor-consciousness manifested by many crafting groups and their ambitious Web sites, which double as marketplaces, social spaces, D.I.Y. education centers, and political forums.

There is something uniquely American about these new countercultures: the United States has always tolerated and indeed nurtured pockets of quirky dissidence and conscientious objection in order better to neutralize them. In "The Jewish Question," Marx comments, following de Tocqueville, on the bewildering diversity of religious forms of life in the very nation that most resolutely styles itself "a stranger to all forms of worship."[22] It is no accident that members of the D.I.Y. movement sometimes congregate as "The Church of Craft," placing the new knitting cells and sewing circles in the long tradition of Presbyterian, Unitarian, and vegetarian experiments that weaves its *e pluribus unum* out of a seemingly endless fringe. Although the privatized, domestic, and often indulgent character of craftivism, as well as its ripeness for economic exploitation and instant mainstreaming, may greatly limit the genuinely political potential of D.I.Y., these new forms of *oikonomics* share genuine links with the larger and more "serious" fair trade and environmental movements. Meanwhile, the new-crafters' reliance on digital forums stitches a political dimension directly into apparently personal acts of making, magnifying the public impact of private acts and growing a new breed of organic intellectual.[23]

21. The term *prosumerism*, in which production and consumption are recombined in the information economy, was coined by Alvin Toffler in *The Third Wave* in 1980 and has become current in both critiques and celebrations of Web 2.0, those internet venues in which users provide content, including social media and file sharing sites, building on the "relational and networking capacities" of the Internet. See David Goldberg, "Socializing Cyberinfrastructure."

22. Marx, *Portable Marx*, 99.

23. In a somewhat different domain, writers such as Richard Sennet (*The Craftsman*), Alain de Botton (*Pleasures and Sorrows of Work*), and Matthew Biberman (*Big Sid's Vincati*) have been sharpening the more masculine edges of work; their phenomenologies of labor form a contemporary counterpoint to the husbandry manuals of Gervase Markham in the seventeenth century.

Much of the work of these movements involves a remapping of temporality. Eric Santner describes the historic zoning of time wrought by biopolitical sovereignty: "In its efforts to overcome the meaningless, homogeneous, succession of time, of one moment after the other, the state introduces 'standstills, stations, epochs.'"[24] Consumerism manages time differently. Its "year" is cyclical rather than monumental; dealing in seasons rather than epochs, marketers release trends and fashions that come and go like the leaves on the trees. Holidays in particular are there for the taking; inherited from older religious and agrarian calendars, the great feasts and fasts have always elicited sumptuary shifts in cuisine and décor. Unfortunately, such temporal variations, scripted into our deepest memories, offer ideal vehicles for market manipulation, with the resources of global capital ready at hand to create a permanent holiday where once there was ebb and flow. Slow food recalls us to the actuality of seasons and regions in a world made flat by strawberries in September and Christmas in July. Meanwhile, the craftistas are stealing holidays back from the Grinch of mass culture by populating a strange vast underworld with mutant Easter eggs, sick Santas, and snowballs in Hell. A craftista still cannot cook and think at the same time, but before she creates her Christmas angel out of the forced blossoms of virgin tampons, she must ponder the icons of Yuletide with a certain slow and icy tenderness, and when she uploads a photo of her new creation to her favorite Web site, she decisively goes public.

For most of the people reading this book, the classroom is the scene of public appearing that we visit most often. We might reconceive teaching in the humanities not as the transmission of specific national traditions or the advocacy of particular politics, but as the chance to address our students as thinkers, makers, and doers in a world in which these forms of human effort are increasingly conjoined. In Foucault's analysis, neoliberal biopower consists in the "multiplication of the 'enterprise' form within the social body."[25] The household is an enterprise, an organ of calculation, competition, and self-branding, and so too is the entrepreneurial self. The brutal mobility of this brave new environment requires that every worker be a lifelong learner, prepared not only to retrain, reinvent, or relocate, but also to brook periods of unemployment and underemployment. The new knowledge workers must be both brand-managers and self-publishers, able to harness the applied semiotics of corporate identity on behalf of the organizations they

24. Santner, *Psychotheology*, 63.
25. Foucault, *Birth of Biopolitics*, 148.

join and for their own advancement and social projects.[26] What is true for our undergraduates is increasingly true for our graduate students as well; as the guild breaks down, and new forms of rogue education driven by market demands and technological advances splinter the academic landscape, Ph.D. students would benefit from a broader and more flexible modeling of the intellectual life as well as a more varied skill set than the academy has been wont to offer.[27] A general education, aimed at the general intellect, and executed at all levels, might help prepare young people for a marketplace that demands virtuosity, while also giving them a suite of conceptual and historical tools to help rezone that landscape through their own thoughtful activity in a shifting ensemble of settings.

Thinking, making, and doing belong to no disciplines, and if their study gravitates toward the humanities, their exercise does not. General education means the chance to engage with *what is general,* an invitation that we can define developmentally (in relation to freshmen beginning a new epoch of life and learning), institutionally (as members of a *universitas*), civically (as citizens of communities and nations), and from the perspective of the species (as *homo sapiens* in a global economy and ecology). The drive toward specialization that has characterized university life in recent decades has increasingly narrowed the "general" in general education into mere thresholds to the particular ("gateways to the major") rather than genuine explorations of common capacities.[28] What is general can no longer be a canon of works, conceived however purely or promiscuously, although such works will always form an important means of convening a common conversation, since they are themselves signifying acts that aim at instituting relationships and acknowledging plurality. (Think: Shakespeare.) Perhaps we should consider instead the *faculties,* which Virno defines as "potential as such, not its countless particular realizations."[29] Students enter the university as thinkers, makers, and doers. Humanistic study can make them more conscious of their

---

26. See Ellen Lupton, ed., *D.I.Y. Design It Yourself,* for a primer in such techniques. For a more critical view of the changing role of branding in contemporary labor and life, see Arvidsson, *Brands,* and Metahaven, *Uncorporate Identity.*

27. For a rosy view of these changes, written from the viewpoint of an "enterprise society," see Kamenetz, *DIY U.* We can decry these changes, or we can help students prepare for them. We'd probably best do both.

28. This particularizing drive takes diverse forms. Students, for example, come to the university in search of the expertise and credentialing that will suit them for the escalating technical demands of employment. In the humanistic disciplines, we see the turn away from theory back to the study of specific identities, cultures, and periods, with decreased communication among scholars working on different objects, languages, and epochs.

29. Virno, *Grammar of the Multitude,* 66.

capacities, more fluent in their abilities, and more responsive to their world through their engagement with some of the frameworks in which thinking, making, and doing have unfolded in time, across the globe, and in the vibrant niches of their own happening worlds. What we need, in effect, is something like an Arendtian pedagogy, one that, following Arendt, grounds itself in the enabling categories of Greek thought before and beyond our many disciplines, yet thinks these categories in response to changing forms of life, labor, and politics in the twenty-first century.

In such a triad, literature belongs fundamentally to the order of *poesis*, or making, but its works can help us mediate the regimes of thinking (philosophy) and doing (history). Take, for example, the case of St. Paul in the last chapter. At a 2005 conference on the new Pauline renaissance, philologists and theorists are reported to have had little to say to each other.[30] Similar impasses plague meetings of theater scholars, students of new media, and historians of the book. It may well be that highly refined historical study remains immune to speculative thought, while most critical theorists resist immersion in the more technical bibliography of their subject matter. It is in literary studies, however, where we see the two kinds of discourse being knit together with some success. And it is not just a question of our flexible training, attuned to both imaginative and empirical realities, that puts literary critics in this special role; literature, our object of study, weaves its narrative nests at the places where the speculative realms of thought, imagination, dream, desire, and anticipation meet the urgencies, impulses, and resistances of real time. "Theory versus history" poses a false choice; their coimplication lends works of literature their dimensionality, persistence, and appeal. Unfolding the entanglements of thought and action in works of literary making, and pursuing this task in as rich, generous, and enabling a way as possible, so as to encourage new efforts at living well, might help literary studies recover its direction in a period when rapidly disappearing resources and the propagation of new models of educational delivery threaten a profession dangerously lacking in confidence about its mission and methods. Literary study has much to contribute to both the desired "outcomes" of a twenty-first-century education, including verbal, visual, digital, and historical competence exercised in several public spheres, and to the ongoing evaluation of such capacities in relation to global labor practices, the futures

30. Clayton Crockett reviews the conference, "Saint Paul among the Philosophers: Subjectivity, Universality and the Event," held at Syracuse University, April 14–16, 2005. Crockett notes a certain level of impasse between the historians and the philosophers; see "St. Paul and the Event."

of citizenship, and environmental change. Judgment is itself a "learning outcome," and not something superadded to other, more instrumental objectives. Judgment, moreover, which occurs between intellection and action, might be a more powerful paradigm for what it is that humanists cultivate in students than the phrase of the day, "critical thinking."

Advances in technology have the capacity both to industrialize teaching on the model of agribusiness (paper-grading is the latest frontier for outsourced labor)[31] and to design settings for writing and exchange that deepen contact and collaboration among teachers and learners. If *distance learning* has come to name the first tendency, I propose *proximity learning* as the name for second: how can we use technology to establish and sustain the spacing appropriate to different kinds of study in an environment marked by rapidly mutating constraints and affordances? Proxemics, invented by anthropologist Edward Hall, studies human distances in the disposition of everything from city streets and public plazas to elevators, café seating, and office cubicles.[32] If we have a proxemics of the bar stool and the park bench, surely we also need a proxemics of education: what intimacies and reserves support successful learning, and how can technology help us better script such encounters? Needless to say, technology has recalibrated distances in post-Fordist workplaces and post-Facebook social life. Taking up these new platforms as both objects of analysis and stages for public writing, speaking, and exchange will be an increasingly important part of literary study and pedagogy. TMI ("too much information") describes both the loquacious narcissism of social media and the great data swarm delivered by the Internet. If the Friend names the too-intimate face of the new sociality, perhaps what we need is to restore the Neighbor, bearer of microdistances, as the proper addressee of our love, both in the ways that we read and the ways that we teach.[33] Meanwhile, tools from design discourses, including proxemics and affordances, might help us move with more fluency and purpose within the many forms of *Öffentlichkeit* that organize our work and play.[34]

Curation is a recurrent theme in this book. In the post-Fordist economy, everyone is a curator, from the fashion retailer to the cupcake merchant and the proud owner of a California closet. Yet the curatorial vocation retains the capacity to remind us of the recalcitrance of trash, the impermanence of

31. June, "Some Papers Are Uploaded to Bangalore to be Graded."

32. Hall, *Hidden Dimension*.

33. See Žižek, Santner, and Reinhard, *Ethics of the Neighbor*.

34. This work of course is being done. See for example Burt, *Shakespeare after Mass Media*; Yates, *Error, Misuse, Failure*; Murray, *Digital Baroque*; and Bryant et al., *Geoffrey Chaucer Hath a Blog*.

worlds, and the virtues of things as well as persons. In literary studies, we are curators as well as tutors. Curation places the emphasis on the fragility of the world itself, built out of the *res publicae*, the public things, of human art and action. *Res publicae* lay claim to our acknowledgment and stewardship rather than our mastery or possession. We curate not only things, but the virtues or capacities associated with them, even when we do not know whither those virtues tend. A syllabus is an act of curation, and so is a meal. Curation involves custodial care and attention, but also taste and judgment, an editor's sense of what should be saved. And curation depends on *Öffentlichkeit*, spaces for public appearing, and thus extends to the conditions as well as the objects of our attention. University service might be understood as our curation of the public spaces peculiar to our calling.

Curation has always housed a dark side. In Roman law, the curator was the guardian responsible for the physical well-being of the minors in his charge. In Shakespeare, the curator is cousin to the gaoler and the janitor; in both Prospero's cell and Paulina's chapel, the curator has the power to lock up life, lock down meaning, and limit access. The enterprising curator can also become a forger, a smuggler, or a robber, whether she is raiding ancient tombs or cool-hunting in the 'hood. James Porter paraphrases Plato: "Whoever is good at keeping things is also a clever thief."[35] The contemporary commodification of the curatorial function, as the aesthetic education proper to enterprise society, inflates and broadcasts the ancient link between politics and life transmitted in Roman law, which communicates both an ethics of care and a paternalism of control. Activating synapses like these—between ancient law and modern retail, between life and lifestyle, between positive and negative destinies of biopower—is one task of thinking with Shakespeare, broadly conceived. Thinking with Shakespeare is not presentist so much as curatorial, which means taking the past seriously, as a resource for unknown futures, unfolding now.

Most of this book was written in my kitchen. On good days, my children were at school or camp ("Camp is the *nomos* of the summer," to reframe Agamben's motto for household use). But on other days I made my way through Shakespeare surrounded by the chatter of pre-algebra anxiety and after-school euphoria. This book really is a document of *living with Shakespeare*, since I found myself writing about the plays under conditions where the self-withdrawing processes of thought made their efforts at exo-

---

35. Porter, "Reflections on Forgery." The classic account of cool hunting is Gladwell's "Cool Hunt," which recounts the relation between retail and hip-hop culture through the case of Converse.

dus amidst the clamor of the *oikos*. During this period, I was also directing the Humanities Core Course at the University of California, Irvine, an ambitious collaborative enterprise that combines breadth requirements in the humanities with freshman writing. I chose the Arendtian and Aristotelian triad "Thinking, Making, Doing" as the theme for my three-year stint, and learned much from both my colleagues and our students in this truly foundational course of general education. Also during this period, I began collaborating with my sister Ellen Lupton on a series of projects on the everyday life of design, which drew me directly into some of the issues raised in this book, including housekeeping and hospitality.[36] At no point did I cook or think at the same time, but I did learn how to alternate between the word processor and the food processor in a manner that not only allowed me to bring this book to a close, but also, I hope, contributed to the crust and the crumb of its readings.

36. Ellen and Julia Lupton, *Design Your Life* and *D. I. Y. Kids.*

BIBLIOGRAPHY

Adelman, Janet. *Blood Relations: Christian and Jew in "The Merchant of Venice."* Chicago: University of Chicago Press, 2008.

———. "'Her Father's Blood': Race, Conversion, and Nation in *The Merchant of Venice.*" *Representations* 81 (Winter 2003): 4–30.

———. *Suffocating Mothers: Fantasies of Maternal Origin in Shakespeare's Plays, "Hamlet" to "The Tempest."* New York: Routledge, 1992.

Agamben, Giorgio. "Form-of-Life." In *Radical Thought in Italy: A Potential Politics,* ed. Paolo Virno and Michael Hardt, 151–58. Minneapolis: University of Minnesota Press, 1996.

———. *The Time That Remains: A Commentary on the Letter to the Romans.* Stanford, CA: Stanford University Press, 2005.

———. "The Work of Man." In *Giorgio Agamben: Sovereignty and Life,* ed. Matthew Calarco and Steven DeCaroli, 1–10. Stanford, CA: Stanford University Press, 2007.

———. *The Open: Man and Animal.* Trans. Kevin Attell. Stanford, CA: Stanford University Press, 2004.

———. *Homo Sacer: Sovereign Power and Bare Life.* Trans. Daniel Heller-Roazen. Stanford, CA: Stanford University Press, 1998.

———. *Potentialities: Collected Essays in Philosophy.* Ed. and trans. Daniel Heller-Roazen. Stanford, CA: Stanford University Press, 1999.

———. *Profanations.* Trans. Jeff Fort. Cambridge, MA: Zone Books/MIT Press, 2007.

Alberti, Leon Battista. *Of Painting.* Trans. and ed. John R. Spencer. New Haven, CT: Yale University Press, 1966.

Alexander, Christopher. *A Pattern Language: Towns, Buildings, Construction.* New York: Oxford University Press, 1977.

Alexander, Daniel Ben. *The converted Jew of Prague in Bohemia, baptized in the Reformed Church of Rouen, the 12. of Aprill. 1621.* [London?]: Tho. Drewe, 1621.

Almquist, Julka, and Julia Reinhard Lupton. "Affording Meaning: Design-Oriented Research from the Humanities and Social Sciences." *Design Issues* 26, no. 1 (2010): 3–14.

Anderson, Chris. *The Long Tail: Why the Future of Business Is Selling Less of More.* New York: Hyperion, 2006.

Anderson, Douglas. "The Old Testament Presence in *The Merchant of Venice.*" *English Literary History* 52 (Spring 1985): 119–32.

Anton, John Peter, George L. Kustas, Anthony Preus, and Society for Ancient Greek Philosophy (U.S.). *Essays in Ancient Greek Philosophy: Aristotle's Ethics*. Albany: State University of New York Press, 1971.

Archard, David. *Children: Rights and Childhood*. London: Routledge, 1993.

———. *Sexual Consent*. Boulder, CO: Westview Press, 1998.

Arendt, Hannah. *Between Past and Future: Eight Exercises in Political Thought*. New York: Penguin, 1961.

———. *The Human Condition*. 1958; repr., with new intro. by Margaret Canovan, Chicago: University of Chicago Press, 1998.

———. "Introduction." In *Illuminations*, by Walter Benjamin. Ed. Hannah Arendt, 1–51. New York: Schocken, 1969.

———. *The Jewish Writings*. Ed. Jerome Kohn and Ron H. Feldman. New York: Schocken Books, 2007.

———. *The Life of the Mind*. San Diego, CA: Harcourt Brace, 1978.

———. *Love and St. Augustine*. Ed. Joanna Vecciarelli Scott and Judith Chelius Stark. Chicago: University of Chicago Press, 1996.

———. *Men in Dark Times*. New York: Harcourt Brace Jovanovich, 1970.

———. *The Origins of Totalitarianism*. 3rd ed. New York: Harcourt, Brace, and World, 1973.

———. "We Refugees." In *Hitler's Exiles: Personal Stories of the Flight from Nazi Germany to America*, ed. Mark M. Anderson, 253–62. New York: New Press, 1998.

———. *Responsibility and Judgment*. Ed. Jerome Kohn. New York: Schocken Books, 2003.

———. *On Violence*. New York: Harcourt, Brace & World, 1970.

Ariès, Philippe. *Centuries of Childhood*. Trans. Robert Baldick. New York: Vintage Books, 1962.

Aristotle. *Complete Works*. 2 Vols. Ed. Jonathan Barnes. Revised Oxford translation. Princeton, NJ: Princeton University Press, 1984.

———. *Nicomachean Ethics*. Trans. David Ross. Ed. J. L. Ackrill and J. O. Urmson. Oxford: Oxford University Press, 1998.

———. *Politics*. Trans. T. A. Sinclair. Ed. T. J. Saunders. New York: Penguin Classics, 1981.

Arvidsson, Adam. *Brands: Meaning and Value in Media Culture*. Oxon: Routledge, 2006.

Aspinall, Dana, ed. *The Taming of the Shrew: Critical Essays*. New York: Routledge, 2002.

Auden, W. H. *The Dyer's Hand and Other Essays*. New York: Random House, 1962.

Auerbach, Eric. "Figura." In *Scenes from the Drama of European Literature*, 11–76. Minneapolis: University of Minnesota Press, 1984.

———. *Mimesis*. Princeton, NJ: Princeton University Press, 1953.

Augustine, St. *Augustine on Romans: Propositions from the Epistle to the Romans, Unfinished Commentary on the Epistle to the Romans*. Ed. and trans. Paula Fredriksen. Chico, CA: Scholars Press, 1982.

Axton, Marie. *The Queen's Two Bodies: Drama and the Elizabethan Succession*. London: Royal Historical Society, 1977.

Badiou, Alain. *Incident at Antioch*. Unpublished play, 1982; first performed in 1984. Currently being translated by Susan Spitzer with an introduction by Kenneth Reinhard for Columbia University Press. Forthcoming.

———. *Manifesto for Philosophy*. Trans. Norman Madarasz. Albany, NY: State University of New York Press, 1999.

———. *Polemics*. Trans. Steve Corcoran. London: Verso, 2006.

―――. "Rhapsody for the Theater." *Theater Survey* 49, no. 2 (2008): 187–238.

―――. *Saint Paul: The Foundation of Universalism.* Trans. Ray Brassier. Stanford , CA: Stanford University Press, 2003.

Balibar, Etienne. "Citizen-Subject." In *Who Comes After the Subject?* Ed. Eduardo Cadava, Peter Connor, and Jean-Luc Nancy, 33–57. New York: Routledge, 1991.

―――. *We the People of Europe: Reflections on Transnational Citizenship.* Trans James Swenson. Princeton, NJ: Princeton University Press, 2004.

Barber, C. L., and Richard Wheeler. *The Whole Journey: Shakespeare's Power of Development.* Berkeley and Los Angeles: University of California Press, 1986.

Baltzer, Klaus. *The Covenant Formulary in Old Testament, Jewish, and Early Christian Writings.* Trans. David E. Green. Philadelphia, PA: Fortress Press, 1971.

Barolsky, Paul. "Florentine Metamorphoses of Ovid." *Arion* 6, no. 1 (1998): 9–31.

Barry, Michael. "Renaissance Venice and Her Moors." In *Venice and the Islamic World.* Ed. Stephano Carboni, 146–73. New Haven, CT: Yale University Press, 2007.

Baskins, Cristelle. *The Triumph of Marriage: Painted Cassoni of the Renaissance.* Boston, MA: Isabella Stewart Gardner Museum and Gutenberg Periscope Publishing, 2008.

Battenhouse, Roy. "The 'Ghost' in *Hamlet*: A Catholic 'Linchpin.'" *Studies in Theology* 48, no. 2 (1951): 161–92.

Belsey, Catherine. "Tarquin Dispossessed: Expropriation and Consent in *The Rape of Lucrece*." *Shakespeare Quarterly* 52, no. 3 (2001): 315–35.

Bendersky, Joseph W. *Carl Schmitt: Theorist for the Reich.* Princeton, NJ: Princeton University Press, 1983.

Benedict XVI. *St. Paul.* San Francisco: Ignatius Press, 2009.

Benhabib, Seyla. *The Reluctant Modernism of Hannah Arendt.* Thousand Oaks, CA: Sage, 1996.

―――, ed. *Democracy and Difference: Contesting the Boundaries of the Political.* Princeton, NJ: Princeton University Press, 1996.

―――. *The Rights of Others: Aliens, Residents and Citizens.* Cambridge, MA: Cambridge University Press, 2004.

Benjamin, Andrew. "Particularity and Exceptions: On Jews and Animals." *South Atlantic Quarterly* 107, no. 1 (2008): 71–86. Reprinted in Ross, *Agamben Effect*, 71–77.

Benjamin, Walter. *The Origin of the German Tragic Drama.* Trans. John Osborne. London: Verso, 1977.

Bennett, Jane. *Vibrant Matter: A Political Ecology of Things.* Durham, NC: Duke University Press, 2010.

Bennett, Josephine Waters. *"Measure for Measure" as Royal Entertainment.* New York: Columbia University Press, 1966.

Benson, Sean. "'If I do prove her haggard': Shakespeare's Application of Hawking Tropes to Marriage." *Studies in Philology* 103, no. 2 (2006): 186–207.

Berger, Harry, Jr. "Marriage and Mercifixion in *The Merchant of Venice*: The Casket Scene Revisited." *Shakespeare Quarterly* 32, no. 2 (1981): 155–262.

―――. "The Miraculous Harp: A Reading of Shakespeare's *Tempest*." In *William Shakespeare's "The Tempest,"* ed. Harold Bloom, 9–41. New York: Chelsea House, 1988.

Bernheimer, Richard. *Wild Men in the Middle Ages: A Study in Art, Sentiment, and Demonology.* Cambridge, MA: Harvard University Press, 1952.

Berry, Edward. *Shakespeare and the Hunt: A Cultural and Social Study.* Cambridge: Cambridge University Press, 2001.

Berry, Philippa. "Incising Venice: The Violence of Cultural Incorporation in *The Merchant* of Venice." In *Center or Margin: Revisions of the English Renaissance in Honor of Leeds Barroll*, ed. Lena Cowen Orlin, 40–53. Selinsgrove, PA: Susquehanna University Press, 2006.

Besserman, Lawrence L. *The Legend of Job in the Middle Ages*. Cambridge, MA: Harvard University Press, 1979.

Beza, Theodore. *Job Expounded*. Cambridge: John Leggatt, 1589.

Biberman, Matthew. *Big Sid's Vincati: The Story of a Father, a Son, and the Motorcycle of a Lifetime*. New York: Hudson Street Press/Penguin Books, 2009.

———. *Masculinity, Anti-Semitism and Early Modern English Literature: From the Satanic to the Effeminate Jew*. Hampshire, England: Ashgate, 2004.

Biddick, Kathleen. *The Typological Imaginary: Circumcision, Technology, History*. Philadelphia: University of Pennsylvania Press, 2003.

Blackstone, William. *Commentaries on the Laws of England*. 4 Vols. Chicago: University of Chicago Press, 1979. (Orig. pub. in London, 1765–69.)

Bloch, Marc. *The Royal Touch: Sacred Monarchy and Scrofula in England and France*. Trans. J. E. Anderson. London: Routledge and Kegan Paul, 1973.

Bodin, Jean. *The Six Bookes of a Commonweale*. London: Impensis G. Bishop, 1606.

Boehrer, Bruce. "Shylock and the Rise of the Household Pet: Thinking Social Exclusion in *The Merchant of Venice*." *Shakespeare Quarterly* 50, no. 2 (1999): 152–70.

Boose, Lynda. "Scolding Brides and Bridling Scolds: Taming the Woman's Unruly Member." *Shakespeare Quarterly* 42, no. 2 (1991): 179–213.

Botero, Giovanni. *Reason of State*. Trans. P. J. and D. P. Waley. London: Routledge, 1956.

Boyarin, Daniel. "The Double Mark of the Male Muslim: Eraceing Othello." In *The Political Theology of Race*, ed. Geoffrey Kaplan and Vincent Lloyd. Stanford, CA: Stanford University Press, forthcoming.

———. *A Radical Jew: Paul and the Politics of Identity*. Berkeley and Los Angeles: University of California Press, 1994.

Bradbrook, Muriel C. *The Tragic Pageant of "Timon of Athens."* Cambridge: Cambridge University Press, 1966.

———. "'Virtue Is the True Nobility': A Study of the Structure of *All's Well That Ends Well*." *Review of English Studies* 1, no. 4 (1950): 289–301.

Bray, Gerald. *Romans*. Vol. 6 of *Ancient Christian Commentary on Scripture*. Downers Grove, IL: InterVarsity Press, 1998.

Brennen, Troyen. *Just Doctoring: Medical Ethics in the Liberal State*. Berkeley and Los Angeles: University of California, Press, 1991.

Brewer, Holly. *By Birth or Consent: Children, Law, and the Anglo-American Revolution in Authority*. Chapel Hill: University of North Carolina Press, 2005.

Bristol, Michael. "In Search of the Bear: Spatiotemporal Form and the Heterogeneity of Economies in *The Winter's Tale*." *Shakespeare Quarterly* 42, no. 3 (1991): 146–67.

Brown, Carolyn E. "Juliet's Taming of Romeo." *Studies in English Literature, 1500–1900* 36, no. 2 (1996): 333–55.

Brown, Gillian. *The Consent of the Governed: The Lockean Legacy in Early American Culture*. Cambridge, MA: Harvard University Press, 2001.

———. "Thinking in the Future Perfect: Consent, Childhood, and Minority Rights." *REAL: Yearbook of Research in English and American Literature*, 2003, vol. 19:113–28.

Brown, Paul. "'This thing of darkness I acknowledge mine': *The Tempest* and the Discourse of Colonialism." In *Political Shakespeares*. Ed. Jonathan Dollimore and Alan Sinfield, 48–71. Ithaca: Cornell University Press, 1985.

Brown, Raymond. *Peter in the New Testament: A Collaborative Assessment by Protestant and Roman Catholic Scholars.* Minneapolis, MN: Augsburg Publishing House, 1973.

Bryant, Brantley L., Bonnie Wheeler, Jeffrey Jerome Cohen, and Robert W. Hanning. *Geoffrey Chaucer Hath a Blog: Medieval Studies and New Media.* New York: Palgrave Macmillan, 2010.

Buccola, Regina, and Lisa Hopkins, eds. *Marian Moments in Early Modern British Drama.* Aldershot: Ashgate, 2007.

Bull, Malcolm. *The Mirror of the Gods: Classical Mythology in Renaissance Art.* London: Allen Lane/Penguin Books, 2005.

Bullough, Vincent, ed. *Encyclopedia of Birth Control.* Santa Barbara: ABC-CLIO, 2001.

Bullen, A. H., ed. *Lyrics from the Dramatists of the Elizabethan Age.* London: John C. Nimmo, 1889.

Burkert, Walter, and John Raffan. *Greek Religion: Archaic and Classical.* Oxford: Blackwell, 1990.

Burr, David. *The Spiritual Franciscans: From Protest to Persecution in the Century after Saint Francis.* University Park: Pennsylvania State University Press, 2003.

Burt, Richard. *Shakespeare after Mass Media.* New York: Palgrave Macmillan, 2002.

Butler, Judith. "'I merely belong to them'" (Review of Hannah Arendt, *The Jewish Writings*). *London Review of Books,* May 10, 2007, 26–28.

Caius, John. *Of Englishe Dogges, the Diuersities, the Names, the Natures, and the Properties.* London: A. Bradley, 1880.

Calarco, Matthew, and Steven DeCaroli. *Giorgio Agamben: Sovereignty and Life.* Stanford, CA: Stanford University Press, 2007.

Calhoun, Craig. "Plurality, Promises, and Public Spaces," In Calhoun and McGowan, *Hannah Arendt and the Meaning of Politics,* 232–61.

———, and John McGowan, eds. *Hannah Arendt and the Meaning of Politics.* Minneapolis: University of Minnesota Press, 1997.

Callimani, Ricardo. *Ghetto of Venice.* Trans. Katherine Silberblatt Wolfthal. New York: M. Evans, 1987.

Callmann, Ellen. "William Blundell Spence and the Transformation of Renaissance Cassoni." *Burlington Magazine* 141, no. 1155 (June 1999): 338–48.

Campbell, Timothy. "Translator's Introduction." In Esposito, *Bíos,* vii–xlii.

———, ed. "Bios, Immunity, Life: The Thought of Roberto Esposito." *Diacritics* 36, no. 2 (2006): 2–22.

Campbell, Thomas. *Henry VIII and the Art of Majesty: Tapestries at the Tudor Court.* New Haven, CT: Yale University Press, 2007.

Cardozo, Nathan Lopes. *Crisis, Covenant and Creativity: Jewish Thoughts for a Complex World.* Jerusalem: Uri Publications, 2005.

Carrig, Joseph. "Liberal Impediments to Liberal Education: The Assent to Locke." *Review of Politics* 63, no. 1 (2001): 41–76.

Cassirer, H. *Grace and Law: St. Paul, Kant, and the Hebrew Prophets.* Grand Rapids, MI: W. B. Eerdmans, 1988.

Cavell, Stanley. *Disowning Knowledge in Six Plays by Shakespeare.* Cambridge: Cambridge University Press, 1984.

Cavarero, Adriana. *For More Than One Voice: Toward a Philosophy of Vocal Expression.* Trans. Paul Kottman. Stanford, CA: Stanford University Press, 2005.

———. *Relating Narratives: Storytelling and Selfhood.* Trans. Paul Kottman. London: Routledge, 2000.

———. *Stately Bodies: Literature, Philosophy, and the Question of Gender*. Trans. Robert de Lucca and Deanna Shemek. Ann Arbor: University of Michigan Press, 2002.

Cefalu, Paul. *English Renaissance Literature and Contemporary Theory: The Sublime Object of Theology*. New York: Palgrave Macmillan, 2007.

———, and Bryan Reynolds, eds. *The Return of Theory in Early Modern Studies*. London: Palgrave Macmillan, forthcoming.

Charnes, Linda. "Extraordinary Renditions: Character and Place Reconsidered." In "Shakespeare After 9-11," ed. Matthew Biberman and Julia Reinhard Lupton. Special issue, *Shakespeare Yearbook*, forthcoming (2011).

———. *Hamlet's Heirs: Shakespeare and the Politics of a New Millennium*. New York: Routledge, 2006.

Cheney, Donald. *Spenser's Image of Nature: Wild Man and Shepherd in "The Faerie Queene."* New Haven, CT: Yale University Press, 1966.

Cherry, Deborah. "Statues in the Square: Hauntings at the Heart of Empire." *Art History* 29, no. 4 (2006): 660–97.

Chiles, Kathy L. "Becoming Colored in Occam and Wheatley's America." *PMLA* 123, no. 5 (2009): 1398–1417.

Clarke, Mary Cowden. *The Girlhood of Shakespeare's Heroines*. 3 vols. London: W. H. Smith, 1850–55.

Colet, John. *An Exposition of St. Paul's Epistle to the Romans*. Ridgewood NJ: Gregg Press, 1965.

———. *An Exposition of St. Paul's First Corinthians*. Ridgewood, NJ: Gregg Press, 1965.

Colie, Rosalie. "The Essayist in His *Essay*." In Yolton, *John Locke*, 234–62.

Collinson, Patrick. "William Tyndale and the Course of the English Reformation." *Reformation*, 1996, vol. 1:72–97.

Connolly, William. *Why I Am Not a Secularist*. Minneapolis: University of Minnesota Press, 1999.

Coolidge, John S. "Law and Love in *The Merchant of Venice*." *Shakespeare Quarterly* 27, no. 3 (1976): 243–64.

———. *The Pauline Renaissance in England*. Oxford: Clarendon Press, 1970.

Copjec, Joan. *Imagine There's No Woman: Ethics and Sublimation*. Cambridge, MA: MIT Press, 2002.

Cox, Samuel. *A Commentary on the Book of Job*. London: C. Kegan and Paul, 1880.

Crockett, Clayton. "St. Paul and the Event." *Journal of Religious and Cultural Theory* 6, no. 2 (2005): 84–89.

Crouter, Richard, and Julie Klassen, eds. *A Debate on Jewish Emancipation and Christian Theology in Old Berlin*. Indianapolis, IN: Hackett, 2004.

Cunningham, Hugh. *Children and Childhood in Western Society since 1500*. Harlow, England: Pearson Longman, 2005.

———. *Children of the Poor: Representations of Childhood since the Seventeenth Century*. Oxford: Blackwell, 1991.

Curran, John. *Hamlet, Protestantism, and the Mourning of Contingency: Not to Be*. Aldershot: Ashgate, 2006.

Da Costa, Beatriz, and Kavita Philip, eds. *Tactical Biopolitics: Art, Activism, and Technoscience*. Cambridge, MA: MIT Press, 2008.

Dailey, Alice. "Making Edmund Campion: Treason, Martyrdom, and the Structure of Transcendence." *Religion and Literature* 38, no. 3 (2006): 65–83.

Daniel, Drew. "'Neither Simple Allusions nor True Mirrorings': Seeing Double with Carl Schmitt." *Telos* 153 (Winter 2010): 51–69.

Davies, W. D. *Paul and Rabbinic Judaism: Some Rabbinic Elements in Pauline Theology.* 1st ed. London: Society for Promoting Christian Knowledge, 1948.

Davis, Philip. *Shakespeare Thinking.* London: Continuum, 2007.

Davis, Robert C., and Benjamin Ravid, eds. *The Jews of Early Modern Venice.* Baltimore, MD: Johns Hopkins University Press, 2001.

de Botton, Alain. *The Pleasures and Sorrows of Work.* London: Hamish Hamilton, 2009.

de Dampierre, Florence. *Chairs: A History.* New York: Abrams, 2006.

Degenhardt, Jane Hwang. *Islamic Conversion and Christian Resistance on the Early Modern Stage.* Edinburgh: University of Edinburgh Press, 2010.

De Grazia, Margreta. *"Hamlet" without Hamlet.* Cambridge: Cambridge University Press, 2007.

Dempsey, Charles. *The Portrayal of Love: Botticelli's Primavera and Humanist Culture at the Court of the Medicis.* Princeton, NJ: Princeton University Press, 1997.

Dent, R. W. "Imagination in *A Midsummer Night's Dream.*" *Shakespeare Quarterly* 15, no. 2 (1964): 115–29.

Derrida, Jacques. *Of Hospitality: Cultural Memory in the Present.* Stanford, CA: Stanford University Press, 2000.

———. *Spectres of Marx.* Trans. Peggy Kamuf. London: Routledge, 1994.

———. *The Animal That Therefore I Am.* Ed. Marie-Louise Mallet. Trans. David Wills. New York: Fordham University Press, 2009.

Detmer, Emily. "Civilizing Subordination: Domestic Violence and *The Taming of the Shrew.*" *Shakespeare Quarterly* 48, no. 3 (1997): 273–94.

Dickey, Stephen. "Shakespeare's Mastiff Comedy." *Shakespeare Quarterly* 42, no. 3 (1991): 255–75.

Diehl, Huston. "'Does Not the Stone Rebuke Me?': The Pauline Rebuke and Paulina's Lawful Magic in *The Winter's Tale.*" In *Shakespeare and the Cultures of Performance*, ed. Yachnin and Patricia Badir, 69–82. Aldershot: Ashgate, 2008.

DiGani, Mario, ed. *"The Winter's Tale": Texts and Contexts.* New York: Bedford/St. Martin's, 2008.

Dobson, Michael, and Stanley Wells, eds. *The Oxford Companion to Shakespeare.* Oxford: Oxford University Press, 2001.

Dodson, Michael. "Prophetic Politics and Political Theory in Latin America." *Polity* 12, no. 3 (1980): 388–408.

Dollerup, Cay. *Denmark, "Hamlet," and Shakespeare.* 2 vols. Salzburg, Austria: Salzburg Studies in English Literature, 1975.

Donlan, Walter. *The Aristocratic Ideal in Ancient Greece.* Lawrence, KS: Coronado Press, 1980.

Dorf, Elliott. "The Meaning of Covenant: A Contemporary Understanding." In *Issues in the Jewish-Christian Dialogue: Jewish Perspectives on Covenant, Mission and Witness*, ed. Helga Croner and Leon Klenicki, 38–61. New York: Paulist Press, 1979.

Draper, John. *The Humors and Shakespeare's Characters.* New York: AMS Press, 1965.

Dubrow, Heather. *Echoes of Desire: English Petrarchism and Its Counterdiscourses.* Ithaca, NY: Cornell University Press, 1995.

Duffy, Eamon. "Bare Ruined Choirs: Remembering Catholicism in Shakespeare's England." In Dutton, *Theatre and Religion*, 40–55.

———. *The Stripping of the Altars: Traditional Religion in England, c. 1400–1580.* 2nd ed. New Haven, CT: Yale University Press, 2005.

Dunn, John. "The Politics of Locke in England and in America in the Eighteenth Century." In Yolton, *John Locke*, 45–80.

Dutton, Richard, Alison Findlay, and Richard Wilson, eds. *Theatre and Religion: Lancastrian Shakespeare*. Manchester: Manchester University Press, 2003.

———, and Jean Howard, eds. *A Companion to Shakespeare's Works*. London: Blackwell, 2003.

Dworetz, Steven M. *The Unvarnished Doctrine: Locke, Liberalism, and the American Revolution*. Durham, NC: Duke University Press, 1990.

Eisen, Robert. *The Book of Job in Medieval Jewish Philosophy*. Oxford: Oxford University Press, 2004.

Elazar, Daniel. *Covenant and Polity in Biblical Israel: Biblical Foundations and Jewish Expressions*. New Brunswick, NJ: Transaction, 1998.

Empson, William. *Some Versions of Pastoral*. New York: New Directions, 1974.

Engle, Lars. "Shakespearean Normativity in *All's Well That Ends Well*." *Shakespearean International Yearbook*, 2004, vol. 4: 264–79.

———. "'Thrift Is Blessing': Exchange and Explanation in *The Merchant of Venice*." *Shakespeare Quarterly* 37, no. 1 (1986): 20–37.

Esposito, Roberto. *Bíos: Biopolitics and Philosophy*. Trans. Timothy Campbell. Minneapolis: University of Minnesota Press, 2008.

———. *Communitas*. Trans. Timothy Campbell. Stanford, CA: Stanford University Press, 2010.

Evett, David. *Discourses of Service in Shakespeare's England*. New York: Palgrave Macmillan, 2005.

Ezell, Margaret J. M. "John Locke's Images of Childhood: Early Eighteenth-Century Response to *Some Thoughts Concerning Education*." *Eighteenth Century Studies* 17, no. 2 (1983–84): 139–55.

Fabbrizzi, Fabio. *Office Design*. Kempen, Germany: teNeues Verlag, 2002.

Fackenheim, Emil. *To Mend the World: Foundations of Future Jewish Thought*. New York: Schocken Books, 1982.

Feldman, Karen. "On Vitality, Figurality and Orality in Hannah Arendt." In *Thinking Allegory Otherwise*, ed. Brenda Machosky, 237–48. Stanford, CA: Stanford University Press, 2010.

Fermor, Sharon. *Piero di Cosimo: Fiction, Invention, and Fantasìa*. London: Reaktion Books, 1993.

Fernie, Ewan, ed. *Spiritual Shakespeares*. London: Routledge, 2005.

Fielitz, Sonja, "Learned Pate and Golden Fool: A Jesuit Source for *Timon of Athens*." In Dutton et al., *Theater and Religion*, 179–76.

Filmer, Sir Robert. *Patriarcha and Other Writings*. Ed. Peter Laslett. New York: Garland Press, 1984.

Fish, Stanley. "Is It Good for the Jews?" *New York Times*. Available online at http://fish.blogs.nytimes.com/2007/03/04/is-it-good-for-the-jews/ (accessed June 7, 2010).

Fitzmyer, Joseph. *Romans: A New Translation with Introduction and Commentary*. 1st ed. Anchor Bible. New York: Doubleday, 1993.

Floyd-Wilson, Mary, and Garrett A. Sullivan Jr., eds. *Environment and Embodiment in Early Modern England*. Houndsmills, UK: Palgrave, 2007.

Foucault, Michel. *The Birth of Biopolitics*. Ed. Michel Sellenart. Trans. Graham Burchell. Basingstoke, England: Palgrave Macmillan, 2008.

Franco, Paul. *The Political Philosophy of Michael Oakeshott*. New Haven, CT: Yale University Press, 1990.

Frank, Stephanie. "Between Idol and Icon: Schmitt's Representation Problematic—and His Escape from It." *Telos* 153 (Winter 2010): 70–93.

Fredriksen, Paula. *Augustine and the Jews: A Christian Defense of Jews and Judaism*. New York: Doubleday, 2008.

———, ed. and trans. *Augustine on Romans: Propositions from the Epistle to the Romans, Unfinished Commentary on the Epistle to the Romans*. Chico, CA: Scholars Press, 1982.

———. *From Jesus to Christ: The Origins of the New Testament Images of Jesus*. New Haven, CT: Yale University Press, 1988.

Freinkel, Lisa. *Shakespeare's Will: The Theology of Figure from Augustine to the Sonnets*. New York: Columbia University Press, 2001.

Freud, Sigmund. *Standard Edition of the Complete Psychological Works*. 24 volumes. Ed. James Strachey. London: Hogarth Press, 1955.

Fried, Michael. *Absorption and Theatricality*. Berkeley and Los Angeles: University of California Press, 1980.

Fudge, Erica. *Renaissance Beasts: Of Animals, Humans, and Other Wonderful Creatures*. Urbana: University of Illinois Press, 2004.

Fyall, Robert S. *Now My Eyes Have Seen You: Images of Creation and Evil in the Book of Job*. Downers Grove, IL: InterVarsity Press, 2002.

Gallagher, Lowell. "Ambivalent Nostalgia in *The Winter's Tale*." *Exemplaria* 7, no. 2 (1995): 465–98.

———. "Waiting for Gobbo." In Fernie, *Spiritual Shakespeares*, 72–93.

Galli, Carlo. "Presentazione dell'edizione italiana" (introduction to Carl Schmitt). In Carl Schmitt, *Amleto o Ecuba*, trans. Simona Forti, 7–35. Bologna: Il mulino, 1983.

Garber, Marjorie. *Shakespeare's Ghost Writers*. New York: Methuen, 1987.

Gardner, Jane. *Being a Roman Citizen*. London: Routledge, 1993.

Gascoigne, George, and George Turberville. *The Noble Art of Venerie or Hunting*. London: Thomas Purfoot, 1611.

Gebhardt, Nicholas. *Going for Jazz*. Chicago: University of Chicago Press, 2001.

The Geneva Bible: A Facsimile of the 1560 Edition. Introduction by Lloyd E. Berry. Madison: University of Wisconsin Press, 1969.

The Geneva Bible: The Annotated New Testament, 1602 Edition. Ed. Gerald Sheppard. New York: Pilgrim Press, 1989.

Gerstein, Alexandra. *Display and Displacement: Sculpture and the Pedestal from Renaissance to Post-Modern*. London: Courtauld Institute Art Research Forum, 2007.

Ghirardo, Diane Yvonne. "The Topography of Prostitution in Renaissance Ferrara." *Journal of the Society of Architectural Historians* 60, no. 4 (2001): 402–31.

Gibson, James J. *The Ecological Approach to Visual Perception*. New York: Taylor and Francis, 1986.

Gillies, John. "Shakespeare's Virginian Masque." *English Literary History* 53, no. 4 (1986): 673–707.

Gittings, Robert. *Shakespeare's Rival: A Study in Three Parts*. London: Heinemann, 1960.

Gladwell, Malcolm. "The Cool Hunt." *New Yorker*, March 17, 1997, 79.

Goldberg, David. "Socializing Cyberinfrastructure." *CTWatch Quarterly* 3, no. 2 (2007): 1–2.

Goldberg, Jonathan. *The Seeds of Things: Theorizing Sexuality and Materiality in Renaissance Representations*. New York: Fordham University Press, 2009.

———. *Tempest in the Caribbean*. Minneapolis: University of Minnesota Press, 2004.

Goldenberg, David. *The Curse of Ham: Race and Slavery in Early Judaism, Christianity, and Islam*. Princeton, NJ: Princeton University Press, 2003.

Gombrich, E. H. "Botticelli's Mythologies: A Study in the Neoplatonic Symbolism of His Circle." *Journal of the Warburg and Courtauld Institutes*, 1954, vol. 8:7–60.

272 / Bibliography

Gopnik, Adam. "Cooked Books: Real Food from Fictional Recipes." *New Yorker*, April 9, 2007, 80–85.

Gordon, Peter. "The Concept of the Apolitical: German Jewish Thought and Weimar Political Theology." *Social Research* 74, no. 3 (2007): 855–78.

Gottlieb, Susannah Young-Ah. *Regions of Sorrow: Anxiety and Messianism in Hannah Arendt and W. H. Auden.* Stanford, CA: Stanford University Press, 2003.

Goulder, Michael. *St. Paul Versus St. Peter: A Tale of Two Missions.* Louisville, KY: Westminster/John Knox Press, 1995.

Grady, Hugh. "Shakespeare's Links to Machiavelli and Montaigne: Constructing Intellectual Modernity in Early Modern Europe." *Comparative Literature* 52, no. 2 (2000): 119–42.

———. *Shakespeare, Machiavelli, and Montaigne: Power and Subjectivity from "Richard II" to "Hamlet."* Oxford: Oxford University Press, 2002.

Gramsci, Antonio. *Prison Notebooks.* Trans. Joseph A. Buttigieg. New York: Columbia University Press, 1996.

Gray, Bradford H. "Complexities of Informed Consent." *Annals, American Academy of Political and Social Science* 437 (May 1978): 37–48.

Green, Jeffrey Edward. *The Eyes of the People: Democracy in the Age of Spectatorship.* Oxford: Oxford University Press, 2010.

Greenblatt, Stephen. *Hamlet in Purgatory.* Princeton, NJ: Princeton University Press, 2001.

———. *Learning to Curse: Essays in Early Modern Culture.* New York: Routledge, 1990.

———. "Marlowe, Marx, and Anti-Semitism." *Critical Inquiry* 5 (Winter 1978): 40–58.

Greene, Thomas. "Pitiful Thrivers: Failed Husbandry in the Sonnets." In Parker and Hartman, *Shakespeare and the Question of Theory*, 230–44.

Gregory the Great. *Morals: On the Book of Job.* Oxford: J. H. Parker, 1845.

Gross, Kenneth. *Shylock Is Shakespeare.* Chicago: University of Chicago Press, 2006.

Guilfoyle, Cherrell. *Shakespeare's Play within Play: Medieval Imagery and Scenic Form in "Hamlet," "Othello," and "King Lear."* Kalamazoo, MI: Medieval Institute Publications, 1990.

Guillory, John. "'To please the wiser sort': Violence and Philosophy in *Hamlet.*" In *Historicism, Psychoanalysis, and Early Modern Culture,* ed. Carla Mazzio and Trevor Douglas, 82–109. New York: Routledge, 2000.

Gurr, Andrew. "The Bear, the Statue, and Hysteria in *The Winter's Tale,*" *Shakespeare Quarterly* 34, no. 4 (1983): 420–25.

Hadfield, Andrew. "The Power and Rights of the Crown in *Hamlet* and *King Lear.*" *Review of English Studies* 54, no. 217 (2003): 566–86.

Hailey, Charlie. *Camps: A Guide to Twenty-First-Century Space.* Cambridge, MA: MIT Press, 2009.

Hall, Edward. *The Hidden Dimension.* New York: Doubleday, 1966.

———. "Proxemics and Design."*Design and Environment* 2, no. 4 (1972): 24–25.

Hall, Kim. *Things of Darkness: Economies of Race and Gender in Early Modern England.* Ithaca, NY: Cornell University Press, 1995.

Halpern, Richard. "The Eclipse of Action: *Hamlet* and the Political Economy of Playing." *Shakespeare Quarterly* 59, no. 4 (2008): 450–482.

———. "The King's Two Buckets: Kantorowicz, *Richard II*, and *Fiscal Trauerspiel.*" *Representations* 106, no. 1 (2009): 67–76.

———. *Shakespeare among the Moderns.* Ithaca, NY: Cornell University Press, 1997.

———. "Theater and Democratic Thought: Arendt to Rancière." Unpublished essay.

Hamlin, Hannibal. "The Patience of Lear." In *Shakespeare and Religion: Early Modern and*

Postmodern Perspectives, ed. Arthur Marotti and Ken Jackson. South Bend, IN: University of Notre Dame Press, forthcoming.

Hammill, Graham. *The Mosaic Constitution from Machiavelli to Milton.* Manuscript in progress.

———. "Time for Marlowe." *English Literary History* 75 (Summer 2008): 291–314.

———, and Julia Reinhard Lupton, eds. *Points of Departure: Political Theology on the Scenes of Early Modernity.* Under contract.

———, and Julia Reinhard Lupton, eds. "Sovereigns, Citizens, and Saints: Political Theology and Renaissance Literature." Special issue, *Religion and Literature* 38, no. 4 (2006): 1–11.

Haraway, Donna. "Training in the Contact Zone: Power, Play, and Invention in the Sport of Agility." In Da Costa and Philip, *Tactical Biopolitics*, 445–64.

Hardin, Richard. *Civil Idolatry: Desacralizing and Monarchy in Spenser, Shakespeare, and Milton.* Newark: University of Delaware, 1992.

Harnack, Adolf. *History of Dogma.* New York: Russell & Russell, 1958.

———. *New Testament Studies.* Vol. 6. *The Origin of the New Testament and the Most Important Consequences of the New Creation,* London: Williams & Norgate, 1925.

Harris, Jonathan Gil. *Untimely Matters in the Time of Shakespeare.* Philadelphia: University of Pennsylvania Press, 2009.

Hartwig, Joan. "Horses and Women in *The Taming of the Shrew.*" *Huntington Library Quarterly* 45, no. 4 (1982): 285–94.

Haverkamp, Anselm. "Eine Allegorie der Latenz: The Pun of a Pound." In *Essays on Latency,* ed. Hans Ulrich Gumbrecht and Florian Klinger. Bonn: Vandenhoeck and Ruprecht, 2010.

———. "Richard II, Bracton, and the End of Political Theology." *Law and Literature* 16, no. 3 (2004): 313–26.

———. *Shakespearean Genealogies of Power: A Whispering of Nothing.* London: Routledge, 2010.

Hawthorne, Gerald, ed. *The Dictionary of Paul and His Letters.* Downers Grove, IL: InterVarsity Press, 1993.

Heal, Felicity. *Hospitality in Early Modern England.* Oxford: Clarendon Press, 1990.

Heffernan, Thomas J., and Thomas E. Burman. *Scripture and Pluralism: Reading the Bible in the Religiously Plural Worlds of the Middle Ages and Renaissance.* Leiden: Brill, 2005.

Heidegger, Martin. "The Thing." In *Poetry, Language, Thought,* trans. Albert Hoftstadter. New York: Harper Colophon, 1971.

———. *What Is Called Thinking?* Trans. J. Glenn Gray. New York: Harper and Row, 1968.

Heller, Agnes. *The Time Is Out of Joint: Shakespeare as Philosopher of History.* Lanham, MD: Rowman and Littlefield, 2002.

———, and Ferenc Fehér. *The Grandeur and Twilight of Radical Universalism.* New Brunswick, NJ: Transaction, 1991.

Herbert, George. *The Complete English Poems.* Ed. John Tobin. New York: Penguin, 1991.

Herman, Edward S., and Noam Chomsky, eds. *Manufacturing Consent: The Political Economy of the Mass Media.* New York: Pantheon Books, 1988.

Hiltner, Ken. *Milton and Ecology.* Cambridge: Cambridge University Press, 2003.

Hirsch, Brett. "'A Gentle and No Jew': The Difference Marriage Makes in *The Merchant of Venice.*" *Parergon* 23, no. 1 (2006): 119–31.

Hobbes, Thomas. *On the Citizen.* Ed. and trans. Richard Tuck. Cambridge: Cambridge University Press, 1998.

———. *Leviathan.* Ed. A. P. Martinich. Peterborough, Ontario: Broadview Press, 2002.

Hobgood-Oster, Lisa. *Holy Dogs and Asses: Animals in the Christian Tradition*. Champaign-Urbana: University of Illinois Press, 2008.

Hodgdon, Barbara. "Katherina Bound; or, Play(K)ating the Strictures of Everyday Life." *PMLA* 107, no. 3 (1992): 538–53.

Höfele, Andreas. "Humanity at Stake: Man and Animal in Shakespeare's Theatre." *Shakespeare Survey*, 2007, vol. 60:118–29.

Holder, R. Ward., ed. *A Companion to Paul in the Reformation*. Leiden: Brill, 2009.

Holmén, Tom. *Jesus and Jewish Covenant Thinking*. Leiden: Brill, 2001.

Holmer, Joan Ozark. "Othello's Threnos: 'Arabian Trees' and 'Indian' versus 'Judean.'" *Shakespeare Studies*, 1980:145–68.

Holsinger, Bruce, ed. "The Religious Turn in Literary Criticism." Special issue, *English Language Notes* 44, no. 1 (2006).

Homer. *The Odyssey*. In *Homer's Odyssey*, trans. Richard Lattimore. New York: Harper Colophon, 1975.

Honig, Bonnie. *Democracy and the Foreigner*. Princeton, NJ: Princeton University Press, 2001.

———. *Emergency Politics: Paradox Law, Democracy*. Princeton: Princeton University Press, 2009.

———, ed. *Feminist Interpretations of Hannah Arendt*. University Park, PA: Pennsylvania State University Press, 1995.

———. "Introduction." In Honig, *Feminist Interpretations of Hannah Arendt*, 1–16.

———. "Toward an Agonistic Feminism." In Honig, *Feminist Interpretations of Hannah Arendt*, 135–66.

Hooker, Richard. *Of the Laws of Ecclesiastical Polity*. Cambridge: Cambridge University Press, 1989.

Hopkins, Lisa. "Paris Is Worth a Mass: *All's Well That Ends Well* and the Wars of Religion." In Taylor and Beauregard, *Shakespeare and the Culture of Christianity*, 369–81. New York: Fordham University Press, 2003.

———. "'Black but Beautiful': *Othello* and the Cult of the Black Madonna." In Buccola and Hopkins, *Marian Moments*, 75–86.

Howell, T. B., ed. "The Arraignment of Edmund Campion, Sherwin, Bosgrave, Cottam, Johnson, Bristow, Kirbie, and Orton, for High Treason." In *A Complete Collection of State Trials and Proceedings for High Treason and Other Crimes and Misdemeanors, from the Earliest Period to the Year 1783*, ed. T. B. Howell, William Cobbett, and David Jardine, 1:1059–80. London: Longman, 1816.

Hulme, Peter. *Colonial Encounters: Europe and the Native Caribbean, 1492–1797*. London: Methuen, 1986.

Hunt, Maurice. "'Bearing Hence': Shakespeare's *The Winter's Tale*." *Studies in English Literature* 44, no. 2 (2004): 333–46.

———. "Helena and the Reformation Problem of Merit in *All's Well That Ends Well*." In Taylor and Beauregard, *Shakespeare and the Culture of Christianity*, 336–67.

Hunter, G. K. *Dramatic Identities and Cultural Tradition: Studies in Shakespeare and His Contemporaries*. New York: Barnes & Noble Books, 1978.

Huntsman, Jeffrey F. *Pepys Ms 2002, Medulla Grammatice: An Edition*. Vols. 1–2. Magdalene College, Cambridge, Pepys Library MS 2002. Available online from http://leme.library.utoronto.ca/ (accessed August 4, 2009).

Hurd, Heidi. "The Moral Magic of Consent." *Legal Theory* 2, no. 2 (1996): 121–46.

Hurstfield, Joel. *The Queen's Wards*. London: Frank Cass, 1973.

Husain, Adrian A. *Politics and Genre in "Hamlet."* Oxford: Oxford University Press, 2004.

Hutson, Lorna. "Imagining Justice: Kantorowicz and Shakespeare." *Representations* 106 (Spring 2009): 118–42.

———. "Not the King's Two Bodies: Reading the Body Politic in Shakespeare's *Henry IV*." In *Rhetoric and Law in Early Modern Europe*, ed. Lorna Hutson and Victoria Kahn, 166–98. New Haven, CT: Yale University Press, 2001.

Ibn Kathir. *Stories of the Prophets*. Trans. Muhammad Mustapha Geme'ah, Al-Azhar. Riyadh, Saudi Arabia: Darussalam, n.d.

Itard, Jean-Marc. *The Wild Boy of Aveyron*. Trans. G. Humphrey and M. Humphrey. New York: Appleton-Century-Crofts, 1962.

Jackson, Ken. " 'One Wish'; or, the Possibility of the Impossible: Derrida, the Gift, and God in *Timon of Athens*." *Shakespeare Quarterly* 52, no. 1 (2002): 34–66.

Jacobs, Kathryn. *Marriage Contracts from Chaucer to the Renaissance Stage*. Gainesville: University of Florida Press, 2001.

Jaquette, James. *Discerning What Counts: The Function of the Adiaphora Topos in Paul's Letters*. Atlanta, GA: Scholars Press, 1995.

Johnson, Adriana. "Everydayness and Subalternity." *South Atlantic Quarterly* 106, no. 1 (2007): 21–38.

Jones, Wendy S. *Consensual Fictions: Women, Liberalism, and the Novel*. Toronto: University of Toronto Press, 2005.

Jordan, Constance. "The Household and the State: Transformations in the Representation of an Analogy from Aristotle to James I." *Modern Language Quarterly* 54, no. 3 (1993): 307–26.

June, Audrey Williams. "Some Papers Are Uploaded to Bangalore to Be Graded." *Chronicle of Higher Education*, April 4, 2010. Available online at http://chronicle.com/article/Outsourced-Grading-With/64954/ (accessed May 22, 2010).

Kahn, Coppélia. "'Magic of Bounty': *Timon of Athens*, Jacobean Patronage, and Maternal Power." *Shakespeare Quarterly* 38, no. 1 (1987): 34–57.

———. "*The Taming of the Shrew*: Shakespeare's Mirror of Marriage." *Modern Language Studies* 5, no. 1 (1975): 88–102.

Kahn, Victoria. "Hamlet or Hecuba: Carl Schmitt's Decision." *Representations* 83 (Summer 2003): 67–96.

———. "Job's Complaint in *Paradise Regained*." *English Literary History* 76, no. 3 (2009): 625–60.

———. *Machiavellian Rhetoric*. Princeton, NJ: Princeton University Press, 2001.

———. "Political Theology and Fiction in *The King's Two Bodies*." *Representations* 106, no. 1 (2009): 77–101.

———. "Political Theology and Liberal Culture: Strauss, Schmitt, Spinoza, and Arendt." Unpublished paper delivered at the West Coast Symposium on Law and Literature, University of Southern California, January 2010.

———. "Political Theology and Reason of State in *Samson Agonistes*." *South Atlantic Quarterly* 99, no. 4 (1996): 1065–97.

———. *Wayward Contracts: Literature, Political Theory, and the Crisis of Political Obligation in England, 1640–1674*. Princeton, NJ: Princeton University Press, 2004.

Kalyvas, Andreas. *Democracy and the Politics of the Extraordinary: Max Weber, Carl Schmitt, and Hannah Arendt*. Cambridge: Cambridge University Press, 2008.

———. "From the Act to the Decision: Hannah Arendt and the Question of Decisionism." *Political Theory* 32, no. 3 (2004): 320–46.

———. "Hegemonic Sovereignty: Carl Schmitt, Antonio Gramsci, and the Constituent Prince." *Journal of Political Ideologies* 5, no. 3 (2000): 343–76.

Kamenetz, Anya. *DIY U: Edupunks, Edupreneurs, and the Coming Transformation of Higher Education*. New York: Chelsea Green, 2010.

Kantorowicz, Ernst. *The King's Two Bodies: A Study in Medieval Political Theology*. Princeton, NJ: Princeton University Press, 1985. (Orig. pub. 1957.)

Kaplan, M. Lindsay. "Jessica's Mother: Medieval Constructions of Jewish Race and Gender in *The Merchant of Venice*." *Shakespeare Quarterly* 58, no. 1 (2007): 1–30.

———, ed. *The Merchant of Venice: Texts and Contexts*. Boston: Bedford, 2002.

Kaufman, Eleanor. "The Saturday of Messianic Time (Agamben and Badiou on the Apostle Paul)." *South Atlantic Quarterly* 107, no. 1 (2008): 37–54.

Kearney, James. *The Incarnate Text: Imagining the Book in Reformation England*. Philadelphia: University of Pennsylvania Press, 2009.

———. "Unaccountable Losses, Impossible Gifts: Strange Fortune in *The Winter's Tale*." Unpublished.

Kendrick, Christopher. *Utopia, Carnival, and Commonwealth in Renaissance England*. Toronto: University of Toronto Press, 2004.

Kernan, Alvin. *Shakespeare, the King's Playwright: Theater in the Stuart Court, 1603–1613*. New Haven, CT: Yale University Press, 1995.

Klause, John. *Shakespeare, the Earl, and the Jesuit*. Madison and Teaneck, NJ: Fairleigh Dickinson University Press, 2008.

Klusmeyer, Douglas B. *Between Consent and Descent: Conceptions of Democratic Citizenship*. Washington, DC: Carnegie Endowment for International Peace, 1996.

Knapp, James. "Image Ethics: Responding to the Visual in Shakespeare and Spenser." London: Palgrave Macmillan, forthcoming.

———. "Visual and Ethical Truth in *The Winter's Tale*." *Shakespeare Quarterly* 55, no. 3 (2004): 253–78.

Knapp, Jeffrey. *Shakespeare's Tribe: Church, Nation, and Theater in Renaissance England*. Chicago: University of Chicago Press, 2002.

Kneidel, Gregory. *Rethinking the Turn to Religion in Early Modern Literature: The Poetics of All Believers*. London: Palgrave Macmillan, 2008.

Knight, G. Wilson. *The Wheel of Fire: Interpretations of Shakespearean Tragedy, with Three New Essays*. London: Methuen, 1954.

Konstan, David. "Reciprocity and Friendship." In *Reciprocity in Ancient Greece*, ed. Christopher Gill, Norman Posthelwaite, and Richard Seaford, 279–301. Oxford: Oxford University Press, 1998.

Korda, Natasha. "Household Kates: Domesticating Commodities in *The Taming of the Shrew*." *Shakespeare Quarterly* 47, no. 2 (1996): 109–31.

———. *Shakespeare's Domestic Economies*. Philadelphia: University of Pennsylvania Press, 2002.

Kott, Jan. *Shakespeare Our Contemporary*. Trans. Boleslaw Taborski. Garden City, NY: Doubleday, 1964.

———, and Boleslaw Taborski. "Hamlet and Orestes." *PMLA* 82, no. 5 (1967): 303–13.

Kottman, Paul. "*Novus Ordo Saecularum*: Hannah Arendt on Revolution." In Hammill and Lupton, *Points of Departure*.

———, ed. *Philosophers on Shakespeare*. Stanford, CA: Stanford University Press, 2009.

———. *A Politics of the Scene*. Stanford, CA: Stanford University Press, 2008.

———. *Tragic Conditions in Shakespeare: Disinheriting the Globe*. Baltimore, MD: Johns Hopkins University Press, 2009.

———. "Translator's Introduction." In Cavarero, *For More Than One Voice*, vi–xxv.

Kramnick, Jonathan Brody. "Locke, Haywood, and Consent." *English Literary History* 72, no. 2 (2005): 453–70.

Kravitz, Leonard. "The Covenant in Jewish Tradition: Historical Considerations." In *Issues in Jewish-Christian Dialogue: Jewish Perspectives on Covenant, Mission and Witness*, eds. Helga Croner and Leon Klenicki, 13–37. New York: Paulist Press, 1979.

Kristeva, Julia. *Hannah Arendt: Life Is a Narrative*. Trans. Frank Collins. Toronto: University of Toronto Press, 2001.

Kuchar, Gary. *The Poetry of Religious Sorrow in Early Modern England*. Cambridge: Cambridge University Press, 2008.

Kunin, Aaron. "Character Lounge." *Modern Language Quarterly* 70, no. 3 (2009): 291–317.

———. "Banish the World." *Contra Mundum* 1–4 (2010): 93–128.

———. "Shakespeare's Preservation Fantasy." *PMLA* 124, no. 1 (2009): 92–126.

Kuspit, Donald. "Fiction and Phenomenology." *Philosophy and Phenomenological Research* 29, no. 1 (1968): 16–33.

Kuzner, James. "Unbuilding the City: *Coriolanus* and the Birth of Republican Rome." *Shakespeare Quarterly* 58, no. 2 (2007): 174–99.

Lacan, Jacques. "Desire and the Interpretation of Desire." In Lacan, *Literature and Psychoanalysis*, 11–52.

———. *Literature and Psychoanalysis: The Question of Reading: Otherwise*. Ed. Shoshana Felman. Baltimore, MD: Johns Hopkins University Press, 1982.

———. *Seminar 8: The Ethics of Psychoanalysis*. London: Routledge, 2008.

Laclau, Ernesto. *Emancipation(s)*. London: Verso, 1996.

Lamb, Jonathan. *The Rhetoric of Suffering: Reading the Book of Job in the Eighteenth Century*. Oxford: Clarendon Press, 1995.

Lampert, Lisa. *Gender and Jewish Difference from Paul to Shakespeare*. Philadelphia: University of Pennsylvania Press, 2004.

Lander, Jesse M. "'Crack'd Crowns' and Counterfeit Sovereigns: The Crisis of Value in *1 Henry IV*." *Shakespeare Studies*, 2002, vol. 30:137–61.

Lane, Christopher, ed. *The Psychoanalysis of Race*. New York: Columbia University Press, 1998.

Lash, Scott. "Forms of Life." *Theory, Culture and Society* 18, no. 1 (2001): 105–20.

Lawson, Charles. *The Country House-wives Garden*. Ferrin, IL: Trovillion Private Press, 1948.

Lebovics, Herman. "The Uses of America in Locke's *Second Treatise of Government*." *Journal of the History of Ideas* 47, no. 4 (1986): 567–81.

Leggatt, Alexander. *The Cambridge Companion to Shakespearean Comedy*. Cambridge: Cambridge University Press, 2002.

Lenker, Lagretta Tallent. *Fathers and Daughters in Shakespeare and Shaw*. New York: Greenwood Press, 2001.

Levey, Santina M. *An Elizabethan Inheritance: The Hardwick Hall Textiles*. London: The National Trust, 1998.

Lévy, Pierre. *Cyberculture*. Trans. Robert Bononno. Minneapolis: University of Minnesota Press, 2001.

Lewalski, Barbara. "Biblical Allusion and Allegory in *The Merchant of Venice*." *Shakespeare Quarterly* 13, no. 3 (1962): 327–43.

———. *Protestant Poetics and the Seventeenth-Century Religious Lyric*. Princeton, NJ: Princeton University Press, 1979.

Lewis, Jayne. *Mary Queen of Scots: Romance and Nation*. London: Routledge, 1998.

———. *The Trial of Mary Queen of Scots: A Brief History with Documents.* Boston: Bedford/St. Martin's, 1999.

Lewkanor, Lewis, trans. *The Commonwealth and Gouernment of Venice,* by Gasper Cantareno [Gasparo Contarini]. Amsterdam: Da Capo Press, 1969. (Orig. pub. 1599.)

Lezra, Jacques. "The Instance of the Sovereign in the Unconscious: The Primal Scenes of Political Theology." In Hammill and Lupton, *Points of Departure.*

Liebler, Naomi Conn. *Shakespeare's Festive Tragedy.* New York: Routledge, 1995.

Lieu, Judith. *Neither Jew nor Greek? Constructing Early Christianity.* Edinburgh: T & T Clark, 2002.

Lilla, Mark. "New, Political Saint Paul?"*New York Review of Books,* October 23, 2008, 69–73.

Locke, John. *An Essay Concerning Human Understanding.* Ed. Peter N. Niddrich. Oxford: Clarendon Press, 1975.

———. *A Paraphrase and Notes on the Epistles of Paul.* In *The Works of John Locke,* Vol. 10. London: Thomas Thegg, 1833.

———. *Some Thoughts Concerning Education.* Ed. John W. Yolton and Jean S. Yolton. Oxford: Oxford University Press, 1989.

———. *Two Treatises of Government.* Ed. Peter Laslett. Cambridge: Cambridge University Press, 1988. (Orig. pub. 1960.)

Loewenberg, Robert J. "John Locke and the Antebellum Defense of Slavery." *Political Theory* 13, no. 2 (1985): 266–91.

Logan, Oliver. *Culture and Society in Venice, 1470–1790.* New York: Charles Scribner's Sons, 1972.

Lukacher, Ned. *Daemonic Figures: Shakespeare and the Question of Conscience.* Ithaca, NY: Cornell University Press, 1994.

Lundin, Roger. *The Culture of Interpretation: Christian Faith and the Postmodern World.* Grand Rapids, MI: W. B. Eerdmans, 1993.

Lupton, Ellen, ed. *D.I.Y. Design It Yourself.* New York: Princeton Architectural Press, 2005.

———, and Julia Lupton. *Design Your Life: The Pleasures and Perils of Everyday Things.* New York: St. Martin's Press, 2009.

———, and Julia Lupton. *D.I.Y. Kids.* New York: Princeton Architectural Press, 2006.

Lupton, Julia Reinhard. *Afterlives of the Saints: Hagiography, Typology, and Renaissance Literature.* Stanford, CA: Stanford University Press, 1996.

———. *Citizen-Saints: Shakespeare and Political Theology.* Chicago: University of Chicago Press, 2005.

———. "Creature Caliban." *Shakespeare Quarterly* 51, no. 1 (2000): 1–23.

———. "*Ethnos* and Circumcision in the Pauline Tradition: A Psychoanalytic Exegesis." In *Psychoanalysis and Race,* ed. Christopher Lane, 193–210. New York: Columbia University Press, 1998.

———. "Exegesis, Mimesis, and the Future of Humanism in *The Merchant of Venice.*" *Religion and Literature* 32, no. 2 (2000): 123–39.

———. "Hamlet, Prince: Tragedy, Citizenship, Political Theology." In *Alternative Shakespeares 3,* ed. Diana Henderson, 181–201. New York: Routledge, 2007.

———, ed. "Hannah Arendt's Renaissance." Special issue, *Journal for Cultural and Religious Theory* 7, no. 2 (2006).

———. "Invitation to a Totem Meal: Kelsen, Schmitt, Freud." In Cefalu and Reynolds, *Return of Theory.*

———. "Job in Venice: Shakespeare and the Travails of Universalism." In *Visions of Venice,* ed. Laura Tossi and Shaul Bassi. London: Ashgate, forthcoming.

—. "The Minority of Caliban: Thinking with Locke and Shakespeare." *REAL: Yearbook of Research in English and American Literature*, 2006, vol. 22:1–34.

—. "Paul Shakespeare: Exegetical Exercises." In *Religion and Drama in Early Modern England: The Performance of Religion on the Renaissance Stage*, ed. Elizabeth Williamson and Jane Degenhardt . London: Ashgate, forthcoming.

—. "Renaissance Edifications: Pauline Designs from Raphael to Shakespeare." In Hammill and Lupton, *Points of Departure*.

—. "Rights, Commandments, and the Literature of Citizenship." *Modern Language Quarterly* 66 , no. 1 (2005): 21–54.

—. "Shylock between Exception and Election: Thinking with Shakespeare, Arendt, and Schmitt." *Journal of Cultural and Religious Theory* 8, no. 3 (2007).

—. "The Taming of the Shrew; or, Arendt in Italy." Forthcoming in special issue of *Law, Culture and the Humanities*, ed. Adam Sitze.

—. "The Wizards of Uz: Shakespeare and the Book of Job." In *Shakespeare and Religion: Early Modern and Postmodern Perspectives*, ed. Arthur Marotti and Ken Jackson. South Bend, IN: University of Notre Dame Press, forthcoming.

—, and Kenneth Reinhard. *After Oedipus: Shakespeare in Psychoanalysis*. Ithaca, NY: Cornell University Press, 1992; repr., Aurora, CO: Davies Publishing Group, 2009.

Luxon, Thomas H. "A Second Daniel: The Jew and the 'True Jew' in *The Merchant of Venice*." *Early Modern Literary Studies* 4, no. 3 (1999): 31–37.

Lyotard, Jean-François. "Jewish Oedipus." *Genre* 10, no. 3 (1977): 395–411.

Mace, Rodney. *Trafalgar Square: Emblem of Empire*. London: Lawrence and Wishart, 1976.

Machiavelli, Niccolò. *The Discourses*. Ed. Bernard Crick. Trans. Leslie J. Walker. London: Penguin, 1983.

—. *The Essential Writings of Machiavelli*. Trans. Peter Constanine. New York: Modern Library, 2007.

—. *Il Principe e altre opere politiche*. Ed. Stefano Andretta. 9th ed. Milano: Garzanti, 1989.

Macpherson, C. B. *The Political Theory of Possessive Individualism*. Oxford: Oxford University Press, 1962.

Maggid, Shaul. "Response to David Nirenberg's 'The Figure of the Jew from Ancient Egypt to the Present.'" Paper presented at the annual convention of the American Academy of Religion (2008). Unpublished.

Mailloux, Steven. "Political Theology in Douglass and Melville." In *Frederick Douglass and Herman Melville: Essays in Relation*, ed. Robert Levine and Samuel Otter, 159–80. Chapel Hill: University of North Carolina Press, 2008.

Maisano, Scott. *Shakespeare's Science Fictions: The Future History of the Late Romances*. PhD diss., Indiana University, 2004.

Makiel, David. "The Ghetto Republic." In Davis and Ravid, *Jews of Early Modern Venice*, 117–42.

Maley, Willy, and Andrew Murphy. *Shakespeare and Scotland*. Manchester: Manchester University Press, 2004.

Malin, Eric. *Godless Shakespeare*. London: Continuum, 2007.

Manoussakis, John, ed. *St. Paul: Between Athens and Jerusalem. Third International Philosophical Conference Proceedings, Athens 10–11 of June, 2004*. Athens: American College of Greece, 2006.

Marion, Jean-Luc. *The Idol and Distance: Five Studies*. New York: Fordham University Press, 2001.

Markham, Gervase. *Cheape and Good Husbandry for the Well-Ordering of All Beasts, and*

Fowles, and for the Generall Cure of Their Diseases. London: T. S. for Roger Jackson, 1614; repr., Amsterdam: Da Capo Press, 1969.

———. *Countrey Contentments; or, The English Huswife*. London: R. Jackson, 1615; repr., Amsterdam: Theatrum Orbis Terrarum and Da Capo Press, 1973.

———. *The English Housewife*. Ed. Michael R. Best. Kingston: McGill-Queen's University Press, 1986.

———. *A Health to the Gentlemanly Profession of Servingmen, 1598*, [London]: Pub. for the Shakespeare Association by H. Milford; repr., Oxford: Oxford University Press, 1931.

Marotti, Arthur. *Religious Ideology and Cultural Fantasy: Catholic and Anti-Catholic Discourses in Early Modern England*. South Bend, IN: University of Notre Dame Press, 2005.

———, and Ken Jackson. "The Religious Turn in Renaissance and Early Modern Studies." *Criticism* 46, no. 1 (2004): 167–90.

Marshall, David. "Exchanging Visions: Reading *A Midsummer Night's Dream*," *English Literary History* 49, no. 3 (1982): 543–47.

Martin, Randall. "Shakespearian Biography, Biblical Allusion, and Early Modern Practices of Reading Scripture." *Shakespeare Survey*, forthcoming.

Marx, Karl. *The Portable Marx*. Ed. Eugene Kamenka. Middlesex, England: Penguin Books, 1983.

Marx, Steven. *Shakespeare and the Bible*. Oxford: Oxford University Press, 2000.

Mauss, Marcel. *The Gift: Forms and Functions of Exchange in Archaic Societies*. London: Cohen and West, 1970.

McCandless, David. "Helena's Bed-Trick: Gender and Performance in *All's Well That Ends Well*." *Shakespeare Quarterly* 45, no. 4 (1994): 449–69.

McConnell, Terrence. *Inalienable Rights: The Limits of Consent in Medicine and Law*. Oxford: Oxford University Press, 2000.

McNulty, Tracy. *The Hostess: Hospitality, Femininity and the Expropriation of Identity*. Minneapolis: University of Minnesota Press, 2007.

McPherson, David. *Shakespeare, Jonson, and the Myth of Venice*. Newark: University of Delaware Press, 2001.

Meeks, Wayne, ed. *The Writings of St. Paul*. New York: Norton, 1972.

———, and John T. Fitzgerald, eds. *The Writings of St. Paul*. 2nd ed. New York: Norton, 2007.

Merleau-Ponty, Maurice. *Phenomenology of Perception*. Trans. Colin Smith. London: Routledge, 2002.

Metahaven (Daniel van der Velden and Vinca Kruk), with Marina Vishmidt. *Uncorporate Identity*. Utrecht: Lars Müller Publishers, 2010.

Metropolitan Museum of Art. *Venice and the Islamic World, 828–1797*. New Haven, CT: Yale University Press, 2007.

Metzger, Mary Janell. "'Now by My Hood, a Gentle and No Jew': Jessica, *The Merchant of Venice*, and the Discourse of Early Modern English Identity." *PMLA* 113, no. 1 (1998): 52–63.

Miller, Adam. *Badiou, Marion and St. Paul: Immanent Grace*. London: Continuum, 2008.

Miller, Nichole E. "The Sexual Politics of Pain: Hannah Arendt Meets Shakespeare's Shrew." *Journal for Cultural and Religious Theory* 7, no. 2 (2006): 18–32.

Milton, John. *The Complete Poems of John Milton*. Vol. 4. Ed. Charles W. Eliot. New York: P. F. Collier & Son, 1909.

Milward, Peter, S.J. *Biblical Influences in Shakespeare's Great Tragedies*. Bloomington, IN: University of Indiana Press, 1987.

Miner, Earl, ed. *Literary Uses of Typology from the Late Middle Ages to the Present.* Princeton, NJ: Princeton University Press, 1977.

Miola, Robert S. "Timon in Shakespeare's Athens." *Shakespeare Quarterly* 31, no. 1 (1980): 21–30.

Monahan, Arthur P. *Consent, Coercion and Limit: The Medieval Origins of Parliamentary Democracy.* Kingston and Montreal: McGill-Queen's University Press, 1987

Montgomery, Jonathan. "Power/Knowledge/Consent: Medical Decisionmaking." *Modern Law Review* 51, no. 2 (1988): 245–51.

Moran, Dermot. *Introduction to Phenomenology.* London: Routledge, 2000.

Morrissey, Lee. *The Constitution of Literature: Literacy, Democracy, and Early English Literary Criticism.* Stanford, CA: Stanford University Press, 2008.

Muir, Edwin. *Civic Ritual in Renaissance Venice.* Princeton, NJ: Princeton University Press, 1981.

Murray, Gilbert. *Hamlet and Orestes: A Study in Traditional Types.* New York: Oxford University Press, 1914.

Murray, Timothy. *Digital Baroque: New Media and Cinematic Folds.* Minneapolis: University of Minnesota Press, 2008.

Musacchio, Jacqueline. *The Art and Ritual of Childbirth in Renaissance Italy.* New Haven, CT: Yale University Press, 1999.

Nancy, Jean-Luc. *The Experience of Freedom.* Trans. Bridget McDonald. Stanford, CA: Stanford University Press, 1988.

Nardi, Bonnie, and Vicki L. O'Day. *Information Ecologies: Using Technology with Heart.* Cambridge, MA: MIT Press, 1999.

Negri, Antonio. *Il Lavoro di Giobbe: Il famoso testo biblico come parabola del lavoro umano.* Milano, Italia: Sugar Co., 1990.

Nevo, Ruth. *Shakespeare's Other Language.* London: Methuen, 1987.

———. "Tragic Form in *Romeo and Juliet.*" *Studies in English Literature* 9, no. 2 (1969): 241–58.

Nicholl, Charles. *The Lodger: Shakespeare on Silver Street.* London: Allen Lane, 2007.

Noble, Richmond. *Shakespeare's Biblical Knowledge and Use of the Book of Common Prayer.* New York: Octagon Books, 1970.

Norbrook, David. "The Emperor's New Body? *Richard II,* Ernst Kantorowicz, and the Politics of Shakespeare Criticism." *Textual Practice* 10, no. 2 (1996): 329–57.

Norman, Donald A. *The Design of Everyday Things.* New York: Basic Books, 1988.

Novak, David. *The Jewish Social Contract.* Princeton, NJ: Princeton University Press, 2005.

Noy, David. *Foreigners at Rome.* London: Duckworth with the Classical Press of Wales, 2000.

Nuremberg Code Directives for Human Experimentation. Available online at the National Institute of Health. http://ohsr.od.nih.gov/guidelines/nuremberg.html.

Nuttall, A. D. *Shakespeare the Thinker.* New Haven, CT: Yale University Press, 2007.

Oakley, Francis. "Natural Law, the Corpus Mysticum, and Consent in Consiliar Thought from John of Paris to Matthias Ugonius." *Speculum* 56, no. 4 (1981): 786–810.

O'Connell, Michael. *The Idolatrous Eye: Iconoclasm and Theater in Early Modern England.* New York: Oxford University Press, 2000.

Oglesby, Brian. "The Locke of the Rape: Caliban and Politics." Unpublished essay. Submitted to Julia Lupton's seminar on Tragedy and Citizenship, University of California, Irvine, 2005.

Ong, Walter, S.J., *The Presence of the Word: Some Prolegomena for Cultural and Religious History.* New Haven, CT: Yale University Press, 1967.

Orgel, Stephen. "Prospero's Wife." *Representations* 8 (Autumn 1984): 1–13.

Orlin, Lena Owen, ed. *Elizabethan Households: An Anthology.* Washington, DC: Folger Shakespeare Library, 1995.

———. "The Performance of Things in *The Taming of the Shrew.*" *Yearbook in English Studies*, 1993, vol. 23:167–88.

———. *Private Matters and Public Culture in Post-Reformation England.* Ithaca, NY: Cornell University Press, 1994.

Osherow, Michele. " 'She is in the right': Biblical Maternity and *All's Well That Ends Well.*" In Waller, *All's Well That Ends Well: New Critical Essays*, 155–68.

Pagden, Anthony. *The Fall of Natural Man.* Cambridge: Cambridge University Press, 1982.

Padel, Ruth. *In and Out of Mind: Greek Images of the Tragic Self.* Princeton, NJ: Princeton University Press, 1992.

Palmer, Daryl W. *Hospitable Performances: Dramatic Genre and Cultural Practices in Early Modern England.* West Lafayette, IN: Purdue University Press, 1992.

Parker, Patricia. "Cutting Both Ways: Bloodletting, Castration/Circumcision, and the 'Lancelet' of *The Merchant of Venice.*" In *Alternative Shakespeares 3*, ed. Diana Henderson, 95–118. London: Routledge, 2008.

———. *Shakespeare from the Margins.* Chicago: University of Chicago Press, 1996.

———, and Geoffrey Hartman, eds. *Shakespeare and the Question of Theory.* New York: Methuen, 1985.

Paster, Gail Kern. "Melancholy Cats, Lugged Bears, and Early Modern Cosmology: Reading Shakespeare's Psychological Materialism Across the Species Barrier." In Paster, Rowe, and Floyd-Wilson, *Reading the Early Modern Passions*, 113–29.

Paster, Gail Kern, Katherine Rowe, and Mary Floyd-Wilson, eds. *Reading the Early Modern Passions: Essays in the Cultural History of Emotion.* Philadelphia: University of Pennsylvania Press, 2004.

Pateman, Carol. *The Problem of Political Obligation: A Critique of Liberal Theory.* Oxford: Basil Blackwell, 1985.

———. *The Sexual Contract.* Stanford, CA: Stanford University Press, 1988.

———. "Women and Consent." *Political Theory* 8, no. 2 (1980): 149–68.

Penuel, Suzanne. "Castrating the Creditor in *The Merchant of Venice.*" *Studies in English* 44, no. 2 (2004): 255–75.

Perdue, Leo G. *The Voice from the Whirlwind: Interpreting the Book of Job.* Nashville, TN: Abingdon Press, 1992.

———. *Wisdom in Revolt: Metaphorical Theology in the Book of Job.* Sheffield, England: Almond Press, 1991.

Perera, Shyama. *Taking Precautions: An Intimate History of Birth Control.* London: New Holland, 2004.

Phillips, D. Z. *Wittgenstein and Religion.* New York: St. Martin's Press, 1993.

Pierce, Robert B. "Shakespeare and the Ten Modes of Scepticism." *Shakespeare Survey*, 2003, vol. 46:145–60.

Pitkin, Hanna. *The Attack of the Blob: Hannah Arendt's Concept of the Social.* Chicago: University of Chicago Press, 1998.

———. *The Concept of Representation.* Berkeley and Los Angeles: University of California Press, 1967.

———. *Fortune Is a Woman: Gender and Politics in the Thought of Niccolo Machiavelli.* Berkeley and Los Angeles: University of California Press, 1984.

———. "Obligation and Consent," pts.1 and 2, *American Political Science Review* 59, no. 4 (1965): 990–99; and 60, no. 1 (1966): 39–52.

———, ed. *Representation*. New York: Atherton Press, 1969.

———. *Wittgenstein and Justice: On the Significance of Ludwig Wittgenstein for Social and Political Thought*. Berkeley and Los Angeles: University of California Press, 1972.

Plantinga, Richard. J., ed. *Christianity and Plurality: Classic and Contemporary Readings*. Oxford: Blackwell, 1999.

Pocock, J. G. A. "The Ideal of Citizenship since Classical Times." In *The Citizenship Debates*, ed. Gershon Shafir, 31–42. Minneapolis: University of Minnesota Press, 1998.

Polka, Brayton. *Between Philosophy and Religion: Spinoza, the Bible, and Modernity*. Lanham, MD: Lexington Books, 2006.

Pope-Hennessy, John, and Keith Christiansen. "Secular Painting in Fifteenth-Century Tuscany: Birth Trays, Cassone Panels, and Portraits." *Metropolitan Museum of Art Bulletin* 38, no. 1 (1980): 2–64.

Population Council. "Locke on Parental Power." *Population and Development Review* 15, no. 4 (1989): 749–57.

Porter, James. "Reflections on Forgery." Unpublished.

Potok, Chaim, and Jewish Publication Society. *The JPS Torah Commentary: The Traditional Hebrew Text with the New JPS Translation*. 5 vols. Philadelphia: Jewish Publication Society, 1989.

Poynter, F. *A Bibliography of Gervase Markham, 1568?–1637*. Oxford: Oxford Bibliographical Society, 1962.

Praz, Mario. *The Flaming Heart: Essays on Crashaw, Machiavelli, and Other Studies in the Relations between Italian and English Literature from Chaucer to T. S. Eliot*. Garden City, NY: Doubleday, 1958.

Pufendorf, Samuel von. *Of the Law of Nature and Nations*. Trans. Basil Kennett. Facsimile of 1729 edition. Clark, NJ: Lawbook Exchange, 2005.

———. *The Political Writings of Samuel Pufendorf*. New York: Oxford University Press, 1994.

Pye, Christopher. *The Vanishing: Shakespeare, the Subject, and Early Modern Culture*. Durham, NC: Duke University Press, 2000.

Raab, Felix. *The English Face of Machiavelli, a Changing Interpretation, 1500–1700*. London: Routledge and Kegan Paul, 1964.

Ranald, Margaret Loftus. "'As Marriage Binds, and Blood Breaks': English Marriage and Shakespeare." *Shakespeare Quarterly* 30, no. 1 (1979): 68–81.

———. *Shakespeare and His Social Context*. New York: AMS Press, 1987.

Randolph, Adrian. *Engaging Symbols: Gender, Politics, and Public Art in Fifteenth-Century Florence*. New Haven, CT: Yale University Press, 2002.

Raskin, Jef. *The Humane Interface: New Directions for Designing Interactive Systems*. Reading, MA: Addison-Wesley, 2000.

Ravid, Benjamin. *Studies on the Jews of Venice, 1382–1797*. Aldershot: Ashgate, 2003.

———. "The Venetian Government and the Jews." In Davis and Ravid, *Jews of Early Modern Venice*, 3–30.

Rawls, John. "Justice as Fairness in the Liberal Polity." In Shafir, *Citizenship Debates*, 53–74.

Rebhorn, Wayne. *Foxes and Lions: Machiavelli's Confidence Men*. Ithaca, NY: Cornell University Press, 1988.

———. "Petruchio's 'Rope Tricks': *The Taming of the Shrew* and the Renaissance Discourse of Rhetoric." *Modern Philology* 92, no. 3 (1995): 294–327.

Reece, Steve. *The Stranger's Welcome: Oral Theory and the Aesthetics of the Homeric Hospitality Scene*. Ann Arbor: University of Michigan Press, 1993.

Richardson, W. C. *Tudor Chamber Administration, 1485–1547*. Baton Rouge: Louisiana State University Press, 1952.

Roberts, Jeanne Addison. "Horses and Hermaphrodites: Metamorphoses in *The Taming of the Shrew.*" *Shakespeare Quarterly* 34, no. 2 (1983): 159–71.

Romano, Dennis. "Gender and the Urban Geography of Renaissance Venice." *Journal of Social History* 23, no. 2 (1989): 339–53.

———. *Patricians and Popolani: The Social Foundations of the Venetian Renaissance State.* Baltimore, MD: Johns Hopkins University Press, 1987.

Rose, Carol M. "Canons of Property Talk; or, Blackstone's Anxiety." *Yale Law Journal* 108, no. 3 (1998): 601–32.

Rosenblatt, Jason. *Renaissance England's Chief Rabbi: John Selden.* Oxford: Oxford University Press, 2006.

Rosenzweig, Franz. *The Star of Redemption.* Trans. William W. Hallo. South Bend, IN: University of Notre Dame Press, 1985.

Ross, Alison, ed. *The Agamben Effect.* Durham, NC: Duke University Press, 2007.

Ross, Lainie Freedman. *Children, Families and Health Care Decision Making.* Oxford: Clarendon Press, 2002.

Rust, Jennifer. "Image of Idolatryes": Iconotropy and the Theo-Political Body in *The Faerie Queene.*" *Religion and Literature* 38, no. 3 (2006): 137–55.

———. *Imagining the Theopolitical Body.* PhD diss., University of California, Irvine, 2007.

———. "Political Theologies of the *Corpus Mysticum*: Schmitt, Kantorowicz and de Lubac." In Hammill and Lupton, *Points of Departure.*

———. "Wittenberg and Melancholic Allegory: The Reformation and Its Discontents in *Hamlet.* In Taylor and Beauregard, *Shakespeare and the Culture of Christianity,* 260–86.

———, and Julia Reinhard Lupton. "Introduction: Schmitt and Shakespeare." In Schmitt, *Hamlet or Hecuba,* xv–li.

Rybczynski, Witold. *Home: A Short History of an Idea.* London: Pocket Books, 1986.

Sanders, E. P. *Paul and Palestinian Judaism: A Comparison of Patterns of Religion.* Philadelphia, PA: Fortress Press, 1977.

———. *Paul, the Law, and the Jewish People.* Philadelphia, PA: Fortress Press, 1983.

Santner, Eric. *On Creaturely Life: Rilke, Benjamin, Sebald.* Chicago: University of Chicago Press, 2006.

———. *My Own Private Germany: Daniel Paul Schreber's Secret History of Modernity.* Princeton, NJ: Princeton University Press, 1996.

———. *The Psychotheology of Everyday Life: Reflections on Freud and Rosenzweig.* Chicago: University of Chicago Press, 2001.

———. *The Royal Remains.* Chicago: University of Chicago Press, forthcoming.

Sarna, Nahum. *Exodus.* In Potok and Jewish Publication Society, *JPS Torah Commentary,* vol. 2.

Schleiner, Louise. "Latinized Greek in Shakespeare's Writing of *Hamlet.*" *Shakespeare Quarterly* 41, no. 1 (1990): 29–48.

Schalkwyk, David. *Shakespeare, Love and Service.* Cambridge: Cambridge University Press, 2008.

Schmitt, Carl. *Der Begriff des Politischen.* 1932; Berlin: Duncker and Humblot 1932; repr., 1963.

———. *The Concept of the Political.* Trans. George Schwab. Chicago: University of Chicago Press, 1996.

———. *Hamlet oder Hekuba: Der Einbruch der Zeit in das Spiel.* Stuttgart: Klett-Kotta, 1985.

———. *Hamlet or Hecuba: The Intrusion of the Time into the Play.* Trans. David Pan and Jennifer Rust; introduction by Jennifer Rust and Julia Reinhard Lupton. New York: Telos Press, 2009.

————. *Hamlet ou Hécube*, trans. Jean-Louis Besson and Jean Jourdheuil. Paris: L'Arche, 1992.

————. *The Nomos of the Earth in the International Law of the Jus Publicum Europaeum*. Trans. G. L. Ulmen. New York: Telos Press, 2003.

————. *Political Theology: Four Chapters on the Concept of Sovereignty*. Trans. George Schwab. Cambridge, MA: MIT Press, 1985.

————. "The Source of the Tragic." Trans. David Pan. *Telos* 72 (Summer 1987): 133–52.

————. "Vorwort." In *Hamlet Sohn der Maria Stuart*, by Lilian Winstanley, trans. Anima Schmitt, 2–25. Pfullingen: Verlag Günther Neske, 1952.

Schneider, Gary. "The Public, the Private, and the Shaming of the Shrew." *Studies in English Literature, 1500–1900* 42, no. 2 (2002): 235–58.

Schochet, Gordon. "The Family and the Origins of the State in Locke's Political Philosophy." In Yolton, *John Locke*, 137–64.

————. "'Guards and Fences': Property and Obligation in Locke's Political Thought." *History of Political Thought* 31, no. 3 (2000): 365–89.

————. "Intending (Political) Obligation: Hobbes and the Voluntary Basis of Society." In *Thomas Hobbes and Political Theory*, ed. Mary Dietz, 55–73. Lawrence: University of Kansas Press, 1990.

————. *Patriarchalism in Political Thought: The Authoritarian Family and Political Speculation and Attitudes, Especially in Seventeenth-Century England*. New York: Basic Books, 1975.

————. "Symposium on David Novak's *The Jewish Social Contract*." *Hebraic Political Studies* 1, no. 5 (2006): 593–96.

Scott, Margaret. "'Our Cities' Institutions': Some Further Reflections on the Marriage Contracts in *Measure for Measure*." *English Literary History* 4 (Winter 1982): 790–804.

Seaford, Richard. *Reciprocity and Ritual: Homer and Tragedy in the Developing City-State*. Oxford: Oxford University Press, 1994.

Segal, Alan. *Paul the Convert: The Apostolate and Apostasy of Saul the Pharisee*. New Haven, CT: Yale University Press, 1990.

Seneca. *De Beneficiis*. Translated by Arthur Golding as *The vvoorke of the excellent philosopher Lucius Annaeus Seneca concerning benefyting*. London: John Day, 1578.

————. *Letters from a Stoic*. Trans. and ed. Robin Campbell. London: Penguin Books, 1969.

Sennett, Richard. *The Craftsman*. New Haven, CT: Yale University Press, 2008.

Shafir, Gershon, ed. *The Citizenship Debates*. Minneapolis: University of Minnesota Press, 1998.

Shaheen, Naseeb. *Biblical References in Shakespeare's Plays*. Cranbury, NJ: Associated University Presses, 1999.

Shakespeare, William. *All's Well That Ends Well*. Ed. G. K. Hunter. Arden/Methuen, 1959; repr., London: Routledge, 1989.

————. *Complete Works*. Ed. David Bevington. New York: Pearson/Longman, 2007.

————. *Hamlet*, ed. Harold Jenkins. London: Methuen, 1982.

————. *The Merchant of Venice*. 7th ed. Cambridge, MA: Harvard University Press, 1959.

————. *Othello*. Ed. David Bevington. New York: Bantam, 1988.

————. *Romeo and Juliet*. Ed. William Gibbons. London: Methuen, 1980.

————. *Sonnets*. Ed. Stephen Booth. New Haven, CT: Yale University Press, 1977.

————. *The Taming of the Shrew*. Ed. Dympna Callaghan. New York: W. W. Norton, 2009.

————. *The Taming of the Shrew*. Ed. J. H. Oliver. Oxford: Clarendon Press, 1982.

————. *The Taming of the Shrew: Texts and Contexts*. Ed. Frances Dolan. Boston: Bedford Books of St. Martin's Press, 1996.

———. *The Tempest.* Ed. Stephen Orgel. Oxford: Oxford University Press, 1987.

———. *Timon of Athens.* Ed. H. J. Oliver. London: Methuen, 1959.

———. *Timon of Athens.* Ed. John Jowett. Oxford: Oxford University Press, 2004.

———. *The Winter's Tale.* Ed. Stephen Orgel. Oxford: Oxford University Press, 1996.

———. *The Winter's Tale.* Ed. Susan Snyder and Deborah T. Curren-Acquino. Cambridge: Cambridge University Press, 2007.

Shannon, Laurie. "The Eight Animals in Shakespeare; or, Before the Human." *PMLA* 124, no. 2 (2009): 472–79.

———. "Poor, Bare, Forked: Animal Sovereignty, Human Negative Exceptionalism, and the Natural History of *King Lear*." *Shakespeare Quarterly* 60, no. 2 (2009): 168–96.

———. *Sovereign Amity: Figures of Friendship in Shakespearean Contexts.* Chicago: University of Chicago Press, 2002.

Shapiro, James. *Shakespeare and the Jews.* New York: Columbia University Press, 1996.

Shapiro, Michael. "Framing the Taming: Metatheatrical Awareness of Female Impersonation in *The Taming of the Shrew*." *Yearbook in English Studies,* (1993), vol. 23:143–66 (special issue on early Shakespeare).

Shapiro, Michael Steven. *The Child's Garden: The Kindergarten Movement from Froebel to Dewey.* University Park: Pennsylvania University Press, 1983.

Shearman, John. *Raphael's Cartoons in the Collection of Her Majesty the Queen.* Cambridge: Cambridge University Press, 1983.

Shell, Marc. "The Wether and the Ewe: Verbal Usury in *The Merchant of Venice*." *Kenyon Review* 1, no. 4 (1979): 65–92.

Shuger, Deborah Kuller. *The Renaissance Bible: Scholarship, Sacrifice, and Subjectivity.* Berkeley and Los Angeles: University of California Press, 1994.

Silver, Victoria. *Imperfect Sense: The Predicament of Milton's Irony.* Princeton, NJ: Princeton University Press, 2001.

Simonds, Peggy Munoz. "Sacred and Sexual Motifs in *All's Well That Ends Well*." *Renaissance Quarterly* 42, no. 1 (1989): 33–59.

Sjögren, Gunnar. *Hamlet the Dane.* Lund, Sweden: New Society of Letters, 1983.

Sloan, LaRue Love. "'Caparisoned like the Horse': Tongue and Tail in Shakespeare's *The Taming of the Shrew*." *Early Modern Literary Studies* 10, no. 2 (2004): 1–24. Available online at http://extra.shu.ac.uk/emls/10-2/sloacapa.htm.

Slocum, Rob. *Capons and Caponizing.* Washington, DC: U.S. Department of Agriculture, 1905.

Smith, Bruce R. *Phenomenol Shakespeare.* London: Blackwell, 2010.

Sollors, Werner. *Beyond Ethnicity: Consent and Descent in American Culture.* New York: Oxford University Press, 1986.

Soncino Book of Job. Ed. Rev. Dr. A. Cohen. London and Jerusalem: Soncino Press, 1985.

Southwell, Robert. *Saint Peters Complaint.* London: Printed by I[ames] R[oberts] for G[abriel] C[awood], 1595.

Sourvinou-Inwood, Christiane. "Greek Tragedy and Ritual." In *A Companion to Tragedy*, ed. Rebecca Bushnell, 8–24. Malden, MA: Blackwell, 2005.

Spinoza, Baruch. *Theological-Political Treatise.* Trans. Samuel Shirley. Ed. Seymour Fenton. Indianapolis: Hackett, 1998.

Spolsky, Ellen, ed. *Summoning: Ideas of the Covenant and Interpretive Theory.* Albany: State University of New York Press, 1993.

Stanton, Phebe. *Religion and Revelry in Shakespeare's Festive World.* Cambridge: Cambridge University Press, 2008.

Steedman, Carolyn. *Childhood, Culture and Class in Britain: Margaret McMillan, 1860–1931.* London: Virago, 1990.

———. *Strange Dislocations: Childhood and the Idea of Interiority, 1780–1930.* London: Virago Press, 1995.

Stoltze, Ted. "Marxist Wisdom: Antonio Negri on The Book of Job." In *The Philosophy of Antonio Negri,* ed. Timothy S. Murphy and Abdul-Karim Mustapha, 129–40. London: Pluto Press, 2005.

Strathausen, Carsten. "Myth or Knowledge? Reading Carl Schmitt's *Hamlet or Hecuba.*" *Telos* 153 (Winter 2010): 7–29.

Streete, Adrian. *Protestantism and Drama in Early Modern England.* Cambridge: Cambridge University Press, 2009.

Sullivan, Garrett A., Jr. "'Be this sweet Helen's knell, and now forget her': Forgetting, Memory, and Identity in *All's Well That Ends Well.*" *Shakespeare Quarterly* 50, no. 1 (1999): 51–69.

Sweeney, Anne. *Robert Southwell: Snow in Arcadia: The Redrawing of the English Lyric Landscape, 1586–95.* Manchester: Manchester University Press, 2006.

Targoff, Ramie. *Common Prayer: The Language of Public Devotion in Early Modern England.* Chicago: University of Chicago Press, 2001.

Taubes, Jacob. *From Cult to Culture: Fragments Towards a Critique of Historical Reason.* Ed. Charlotte Elisheva Fonrobert and Amir Engel. Stanford, CA: Stanford University Press, 2010.

———. *The Political Theology of Paul.* Trans. Dana Hollander. Stanford, CA: Stanford University Press, 2004.

Taylor, Dennis, and David Beauregard, eds. *Shakespeare and the Culture of Christianity in Early Modern England.* New York: Fordham University Press, 2003.

Thomas, Brook. *American Literary Realism and the Failed Promise of Contract.* Berkeley and Los Angeles: University of California Press, 1997.

Thornton, Peter. *Seventeenth-Century Interior Decoration in England, France and Holland.* New Haven, CT: Yale University Press, 1978.

Toffler, Alvin. *The Third Wave.* New York: Morrow, 1980.

Trüstedt, Katrin. "Hamlet against Hecuba." *Telos* 153 (Winter 2010): 70–93.

Tully, James. *An Approach to Political Philosophy: Locke in Contexts.* Cambridge: Cambridge University Press, 1993.

Türk, Johannes. "The Intrusion: Carl Schmitt's Non-Mimetic Logic of Art." *Telos* 142 (January 2008): 73–89.

Turner, Henry. "The Problem of the More-Than-One: Friendship, Calculation, and Political Association in *The Merchant of Venice.*" *Shakespeare Quarterly* 57, no. 4 (2007): 413–42.

Turner, Timothy A. *Torture and the Drama of Emergency: Kyd, Marlowe, Shakespeare.* PhD diss., University of Texas at Austin, 2010.

Tyrell, William Blake, and Larry J. Bennett, *Recapturing Sophocles' "Antigone."* Lanham, MD: Rowman and Littlefield, 1998.

Vasari, Giorgio. *Lives of the Artists.* Vol. 2. Trans. George Bull. Harmondsworth: Penguin, 1987.

———. *Stories of the Italian Artists from Vasari.* Trans. and ed. E. L. Seeley. London: Chatto and Windus, 1908.

Vatter, Miguel. *Between Form and Event: Machiavelli's Theory of Political Freedom.* Dordrecht: Kluwer Academic Publishers, 2000.

———. "Natality and Biopolitics in Hannah Arendt." *Revista de Ciencia Política* 26, no. 2 (2006): 137–59.

Vaughan, Alden T., and Virginia Mason Vaughan. *Shakespeare's Caliban: A Cultural History.* Cambridge: Cambridge University Press, 1991.

Vidal-Naquet, Pierre. "The Black Hunter and the Origin of the Athenian *Ephebeia.*" In *Myth, Religion and Society,* ed. R. L. Gordon, 147–62. Cambridge: Cambridge University Press, 1981.

Vernant, Jean-Pierre, and Pierre Vidal-Naquet. *Tragedy and Myth in Ancient Greece.* Trans. Janet Lloyd. Sussex: Harvester Press, 1981.

Virno, Paolo. *A Grammar of the Multitude: For an Analysis of Contemporary Forms of Life.* Trans. Isabella Bertoletti. Cambridge, MA: Semiotext(e), 2003.

———. "Virtuosity and Revolution: The Political Theory of Exodus." In Virno and Hardt, *Radical Thought in Italy,* 189–212.

———, and Michael Hardt, eds. *Radical Thought in Italy: A Potential Politics.* Minneapolis: University of Minnesota Press, 1996.

von Rad, Gerhard. *Wisdom in Israel.* Trans. James D. Martin. London: SCM Press, 1972.

Waites, Matthew. *The Age of Consent: Young People, Sexuality and Citizenship.* London: Palgrave Macmillan, 2005.

Wall, Wendy. "'Household Stuff': The Sexual Politics of Domesticity and the Advent of English Comedy." *English Literary History* 65, no. 1 (1998): 1–45.

———. "Renaissance National Husbandry: Gervase Markham and the Publication of England." *Sixteenth Century Journal* 27, no. 3 (1996): 767–85.

———. *Staging Domesticity: Household Work and English Identity in Early Modern England.* Cambridge: Cambridge University Press, 2006.

Wallace, John M. "*Timon of Athens* and the Three Graces: Shakespeare's Senecan Study." *Modern Philology* 83, no. 4 (1986): 349–63.

Waller, Gary, ed. *All's Well That Ends Well: New Critical Essays.* New York: Routledge, 2007.

Walzer, Michael, Menachem Lorberbaum, and Noam J. Zohar, eds. *The Jewish Political Tradition.* Vol. 1, *Authority.* New Haven, CT: Yale University Press, 2000.

Warley, Christopher. "Specters of Horatio." *English Literary History* 75, no. 3 (2008): 1023–50.

Watson, Robert. "*Othello* as Protestant Propaganda." In *Religion and Culture in Renaissance England,* eds. Claire McEachern and Debra Shuger, 234–57. Cambridge: Cambridge University Press, 1997.

Weindling, Paul Julian. *Nazi Medicine and the Nuremburg Trials: From Medical War Crimes to Informed Consent.* London: Palgrave Macmillan, 2004.

Wertheimer, Alan. *Coercion.* Princeton, NJ: Princeton University Press, 1987.

West, William. "Humanism and the Resistance to Theology." In Cefalu and Reynolds, *Return of Theory.*

Westen, Peter. *The Logic of Consent: The Diversity and Deceptiveness of Consent as a Defense to Criminal Conduct.* Burlington, VT: Ashgate, 2004.

Westerman, Claus. *The Structure of the Book of Job: A Form-Critical Analysis.* Trans. Charles A. Muenchow. Philadelphia, PA: Fortress Press, 1981.

Wheaton, Sara. *George Herbert's Rhetorical Lyrics.* PhD diss., University of California, Irvine, 2008.

Whedbee, William. "The Comedy of Job." *Semeia* 7 (1977): 1–39.

Williamson, Peter. *Catholic Principles for Interpreting Scripture: A Study of the Pontifical Biblical Commission's "The Interpretation of the Bible in the Church."* Roma: Pontificio Istituto, 2001.

Willman, Robert. "Blackstone and the 'Theoretical Perfection' of English Law in the Reign of Charles II." *Historical Journal* 26, no. 1 (1983): 39–70.

Wilson, J. Dover. *What Happens in Hamlet.* Cambridge: Cambridge University Press, 1959. (Orig. pub. 1935.)

Wilson, Richard. "'Blood Will Have Blood': Regime Change in Macbeth." *Shakespeare Jahrbuch*, 2007, vol. 143:11–33.

———. *Secret Shakespeare: Studies in Theatre, Religion and Resistance.* Manchester: Manchester University Press, 2004.

———. *Shakespeare in French Theory: King of Shadows.* London: Routledge, 2007.

Winiarski, Catherine. *Adulterers, Idolaters, and Emperors: The Politics of Iconoclasm in English Renaissance Drama.* PhD diss., University of California–Irvine, 2007.

Winkler, John. "The Ephebes' Song: *Tragoidia* and the Polis." *Representations* 11 (Summer 1985): 26–62.

Winstanley, Lilian. *Hamlet and the Scottish Succession.* New York: Octagon Books, 1970. (Orig. pub. 1921.)

Witmore, Michael. *Pretty Creatures: Children and Fiction in the English Renaissance.* Ithaca, NY: Cornell University Press, 2007.

———. *Shakespearean Metaphysics.* London: Continuum, 2008.

Witthoft, Brucia. "Marriage Rituals and Marriage Chests in Quattrocento Florence." *Artibus et Historiae* 3, no. 5 (1982): 43–59.

Woods, Susanne. "Lanyer and Southwell: A Protestant Woman's Re-Vision of St. Peter." In *Centered on the Word: Literature, Scripture, and the Tudor-Stuart Middle Way,* ed. Daniel W. Doerksen and Christopher Hodgkins, 73–86. Newark: University of Delaware Press, 2004.

Woolley, Hannah. *The Gentlewomans Companion; or, a Guide to the Female Sex.* Totnes, Devon: Prospect Books, 2001.

Wong, Timothy. "Steward of the Dying Voice: The Intrusion of Horatio into Sovereignty and Representation." *Telos* 153 (Winter 2010): 113–31.

Wright, N. T. *Paul: In Fresh Perspective.* Minneapolis: Fortress Press, 2005.

Yates, Julian. "Accidental Shakespeare." *Shakespeare Studies* 34 (2006): 90–122.

———. *Error, Misuse, Failure: Object Lessons from the English Renaissance.* Minneapolis: University of Minnesota Press, 2003.

———. "What Was Pastoral (Again)?" In Cefalu and Reynolds, *Return of Theory.*

Yolton, John W., ed. *John Locke: Problems and Perspectives.* Cambridge: Cambridge University Press, 1969.

———, and Jean S. Yolton. "Introduction." In Locke, *Some Thoughts Concerning Education,* 1–75.

Young-Bruehl, Elisabeth. *Hannah Arendt: For Love of the World.* New Haven, CT: Yale University Press, 1982.

Zeitlin, Froma. "The Dynamics of Misogyny: Myth and Mythmaking in the *Oresteia.*" In *Women in the Ancient World,* ed. John Peradotto and Y. P. Sullivan, 159–94. Albany: State University of New York Press, 1984.

Žižek, Slavoj. *The Sublime Object of Ideology.* London: Verso, 1989.

———. *The Monstrosity of Christ.* Cambridge, MA: MIT Press, 2009.

———, Eric Santner, and Kenneth Reinhard. *Ethics of the Neighbor: Three Inquiries in Political Theology.* Chicago: University of Chicago Press, 2005.

Zornberg, Aviva. *The Beginning of Desire: Reflections on Genesis.* Philadelphia, PA: Jewish Publication Society, 1995.

INDEX

Taylor, Mark, 206n42
Tempest, The, 8, 19, 120, 172–73, 187–218
theatrum mundi, 15
theology, 14, 21–23, 84–86, 107, 112–13, 132–35, 139–40, 158–59, 203, 220, 226–30, 237–38
theory, 7, 22–23; affordance, 13, 54; political, 7, 16, 21, 97, 145, 189, 200
things, 6, 9–15, 19–20, 27, 29, 31, 34, 40, 47, 53–61, 120, 135, 152, 178, 181–83, 199, 205, 212, 216, 260. *See also* objects; slavery
Timon of Athens, 8, 11, 21–22, 82, 102, 131–32, 140–59, 165, 221
Troilus and Cressida, 140
Trüstedt, Katrin, 69n1, 76n17
Türk, Johannes, 69n1, 75
Turner, Timothy, 176n26
tutor, 58, 120, 194–96, 204, 208–10, 214, 260
typology, 132, 221, 224–33, 236–37, 239, 242–43, 246, 249
Tyrrell, William, 94n60

universality, 4, 18, 22, 86, 91, 132–33, 136, 139–40, 142, 144–45, 147–48, 154, 161, 185, 217–19, 222, 230, 234–36, 240, 242–46, 254

Vatter, Miguel, 4, 14n27, 44n43, 237n59
Vaughan, Alden T., 189n4
Vaughan, Virginia Mason, 189n4
Virno, Paolo, 3, 13, 33–34, 63, 252–53, 257
virtue, 6–7, 10, 28–37, 42–46, 57, 60–64, 87–88, 115–18, 127, 131, 134–35, 169–71, 177–82, 216–17, 254–55, 260; animal, 20, 28, 39, 53, 56, 66; animal, vegetable, and mineral, 10, 27, 38, 46, 55, 109; *virtù*, 44, 53, 83, 121; virtues of things, 10, 37–38, 54, 169–70; virtuosity, 33–35, 63–66, 180, 257. *See also* potentiality

vitality, 5, 9–10, 112, 149, 151, 158, 165, 169, 182; and biopolitics, 28, 49, 111
von Pufendorf, Samuel, 100, 192, 199
von Rad, Gerhard, 134

Wall, Wendy, 27n4
Wallace, John, 143–44
Walzer, Michael, 85n45, 106n30
wardship, 58, 97, 120–23, 190, 206
Warley, Christopher, 80n28
weddings, 46–47, 50, 52, 56, 58–60, 64, 67, 123, 252
Weindling, Paul, 111n40, 125n78
Wells, Stanley, 131n2
West, William, 238n61, 245
Westen, Peter, 104
Wheeler, Richard, 148n37, 155
Wilson, J. Dover, 78n22
Wilson, Richard, 7n10, 23n43, 225n17, 226
Winiarski, Catherine, 8n11, 244
Winstanley, Lilian, 75–76
Winter's Tale, The, 8, 14, 22, 161–85, 219–20, 225
Witmore, Michael, 15n32, 23n43, 183, 201n29
Witthoft, Brucia, 58n82, 59n84, 59n87
wives, 26, 37–38, 47–48, 51–55, 122–23, 166–69, 172–75, 190–94; animal housewife, 26, 29, 62–63, 67
women, 37, 47–49, 55, 99–101, 122, 125–27, 190–92, 218, 251
Wong, Timothy, 69n1
worms, 54, 92, 132, 138–39, 154
Wright, N. T., 230n36, 231n39, 233n49

Yates, Julian, 173n24, 183n40
Yolton, John and Jean, 197, 200
Young-Bruehl, Elisabeth, 19n41, 248n2, 251n12

Žižek, Slavoj, 11n19, 128n83, 140n22, 228n30, 259n33
Zornberg, Aviva, 138n18